The Recognition of Nathaniel Hawthorne

Nathaniel Hawthorne
From a Portrait by Charles Osgood
Courtesy Essex Institute, Salem, Mass.

The
Recognition
of
Nathaniel Hawthorne

Selected Criticism Since 1828

Edited by
B. BERNARD COHEN

Ann Arbor
THE UNIVERSITY OF MICHIGAN PRESS

Copyright © by The University of Michigan 1969
All rights reserved
Library of Congress Catalog Card No. 70-83454
Published in the United States of America by
The University of Michigan Press and simultaneously
in Don Mills, Canada, by Longmans Canada Limited

Paperback ISBN : 978-0-472-75023-8

Permissions

Grateful acknowledgment is made to the following individuals and publishers for kind permission to reprint materials:

To Doubleday & Company, Inc. for "Hawthorne and the Limits of Romance," from *The American Novel and Its Tradition* by Richard Chase. Copyright © 1957 by Richard Chase. Reprinted by permission of Doubleday & Company, Inc.

To Oxford University Press for "Hawthorne, Freud, and Literary Values," from *The Sins of the Fathers: Hawthorne's Psychological Themes* by Frederick C. Crews. Copyright © 1966 by Frederick C. Crews. Reprinted by permission of Oxford University Press, Inc.

To Mrs. Valerie Eliot for T. S. Eliot's "The Hawthorne Aspect." Reprinted by permission of Mrs. Valerie Eliot from *The Little Review*, August, 1918.

To the University of Oklahoma Press for Chapter 1 of *Hawthorne's Fiction: The Light and the Dark* by Richard Harter Fogle. Copyright 1952 and 1964 by the University of Oklahoma Press.

To W. W. Norton & Company, Inc. for "The Hawthorne Myth: A Protest," reprinted from *Re-Appraisals: Some Commonsense Readings in American Literature* by Martin Green. By permission of W. W. Norton & Company, Inc. Copyright © 1965, 1963 by Martin Green.

To Duke University Press for Hubert H. Hoeltje's "Hawthorne, Melville, and 'Blackness'," from *American Literature*, Vol. 37 (1965).

To Twayne Publishers, Inc. for "A Significant Legacy," from Terence Martin's *Nathaniel Hawthorne*.

To Oxford University Press for *"Hawthorne's Psychology: The Acceptance of Good and Evil,"* from *American Renaissance* by F. O. Matthiessen. Copyright 1941 by Oxford University Press, Inc.

To Southern Illinois University Press for "Hawthorne and Faulkner: Some Common Ground," from *The Grotesque: An American Genre and Other Essays* by William Van O'Connor. Copyright © 1962 by Southern Illinois University Press. Reprinted by permission of Southern Illinois University Press.

To Harcourt, Brace & World, Inc. for "Nathaniel Hawthorne: Skeptic," from *Main Currents in American Thought*, Volume II, by Vernon Louis Parrington, copyright, 1927, by Harcourt, Brace & World, Inc.; renewed 1955, by Vernon Louis Parrington, Jr., Louise P. Tucker, Elizabeth P. Thomas. Reprinted by permission of the publishers.

To Harper & Row, Publishers, Inc. for material from pp. 107-110 in *The Development of the American Short Story* by Fred Lewis Pattee. Copyright, 1923 by Harper & Brothers; renewed 1951 by Fred Lewis Pattee. Reprinted by permission of Harper & Row, Publishers, Inc.

To Yale University Press for material from "The Collected Works," in *Nathaniel Hawthorne: A Biography* by Randall Stewart. Copyright © 1948 by Yale University Press.

To Harvard University Press for "The Marble Faun." Reprinted by permission of the publishers from Hyatt H. Waggoner, *Hawthorne: A Critical Study*, Revised Edition. Cambridge, Mass. The Belknap Press of Harvard University Press, Copyright 1955, '63, by the President and Fellows of Harvard College.

To the University of Minnesota Press for material from Hyatt H. Waggoner's *Nathaniel Hawthorne*. University of Minnesota Pamphlets on American Writers, Number 23.

To the American Book Company for material from Austin Warren's "Introduction," from *Nathaniel Hawthorne: Representative Selections, with Introduction, Bibliography, and Notes,* edited by Austin Warren.

Preface

I shall try here to delineate some patterns in the criticism of Hawthorne from 1828 to the present. Most of my illustrations are drawn from the anthology. Although each period covered has its own characteristics, many issues and judgments reverberate through a century and a half of Hawthorne criticism. Some are still being debated today.

1828–64

Contrary to self-disparaging comments about his obscurity, Nathaniel Hawthorne was, indeed, appreciated as a writer by a number of discerning and influential readers before the publication of *The Scarlet Letter* in 1850. Obviously, withdrawing *Fanshawe* from circulation and refusing to identify himself as the author of some early tales and sketches impeded wide recognition, but critical notices of his work were neither negligible nor entirely negative. In 1836 Park Benjamin proclaimed Hawthorne as the author of certain admirable contributions to *The Token*, and with the publication of *Twice-Told Tales* during the next year, Hawthorne's work began to attract considerable attention from literary men and professional critics, if not from the general reading public.

Hawthorne was fortunate in winning notices, usually favorable, from literary men whose reputations would outlast, to one degree or another, their lifetimes, and whose names would thus be intertwined with his. Of these, the first was Longfellow, who, after an enthusiastic commentary on *Twice-Told Tales*, published a second essay in the influential *North American Review*, praising Hawthorne's originality and his choice of American subjects. This emphasis on the use of native material undoubtedly struck a responsive note among the many American authors and critics who were at this time eager to encourage an American literary independence. Although less interested in literary nationalism, another eminent literary figure, Poe, in his first major assessment of Hawthorne's short fiction accorded high praise to Hawthorne's originality and to the purity of his style, while admitting the limitation of his range. However, in 1847, Poe retracted his verdict on Hawthorne's originality and tartly scolded the romancer for his allegorizing and his mysticism. This later review dramatically illustrates the subjective nature of some contemporaneous criticism of Hawthorne: personal and religious crochets, provincial bias, and rivalry in a highly competitive journalistic atmosphere frequently resulted in nonliterary judgments. Both Poe reviews, however, contained his famous definition of the short story, which has been a constant referent in later discussions of that genre. By incorporating his important critical theory in these reviews, Poe unwittingly prolonged Hawthorne's recognition far beyond the 1840's, and indeed Poe's own practice of the short story became a persistent basis of comparison to Hawthorne's technique. Another American literary artist, Herman Melville, writing an anonymous review of *Mosses from an Old Manse*, probably had less immediate influence than Poe, but was of perhaps greater long-range importance because his discussion of "the power of blackness" in Hawthorne's imagination introduced an issue of criticism which transcended its time and is still in controversy. Both the personal friendship of Hawthorne and Melville and the revival of Melville's works in the twentieth century have undoubtedly contributed to increased interest in Hawthorne recently. Although such comments by fellow artists did not necessarily make Hawthorne's fiction popular reading fare, they constitute remarkable appreciation from his peers, and they pinpoint some important critical arguments—discussion of Hawthorne's use of allegory and of his pessimistic philosophy, for instance—which resound in modern criticism.

In addition to attention from literary men, Hawthorne's fiction received early and steady approval from professional and influential reviewers on both sides of the Atlantic. A prominent American editor, Evert A. Duyckinck, was a persistent supporter of Hawthorne. His highly favorable 1841 essay "Nathaniel Hawthorne" did refer to the author's passive observation of life and his seeming attraction to easeful death—issues which others were later to pick up and to develop negatively. Another influential contemporary, Edwin P. Whipple, wrote numerous appraisals of Hawthorne's works and became his favorite critic. In England Hawthorne was very early "discovered" and admired by Henry F. Chorley, a highly respected reviewer for the *Athenaeum*, who subsequently surveyed almost everything Hawthorne wrote. During an era suffused by an American inferiority complex in regard to arts and letters, it was vital that any American author, for the sake of reputation in his own country, gain trans-Atlantic approval. Hence Chorley's endorsement must have enhanced Hawthorne's position at home, in addition to making him known in England.

Even with such support from literary men and professional critics, Hawthorne's reputation was not solidly established until the publication of *The Scarlet Letter*. Although that romance became his acknowledged masterpiece, its immediate popularity may have been boosted by controversy for two reasons peculiar to the circumstances and to the temper of the age. The Custom House essay introducing the book elicited cries of outrage from offended Salemites, as shown in a review in the Salem *Register*, March 21, 1850:

> Indeed, while reading this chapter on the Custom House, we almost began to think that Hawthorne had mistaken his vocation—that, instead of indulging in dreamy transcendentalism, and weaving exquisite fancies to please the imagination and improve the heart, he would have been more at home as a despicable lampooner, and in that capacity would have achieved a notoriety which none of his tribe, either of ancient or modern times, has reached. We were almost induced to throw down the book in disgust, without venturing on the Scarlet Letter, so atrocious, so heartless, so undisguised, so utterly inexcusable seemed his calumnious caricatures of inoffensive men, who could not possibly have given occasion for such wanton insults.

Another outcry against *The Scarlet Letter* was occasioned by the subject matter, which offended some concepts of morality, an indignation perhaps involving a back-lash from the shifting theological conflicts which had agitated New England since its founding. In this regard, moral and religious attacks on the book by A. C. Coxe and others should be juxtaposed against George Loring's remarkably modern analysis of the psychology of Hester's and Dimmesdale's guilt and of the differing relationships of society and the self to sin.

Probably the most widespread of the nonliterary attacks occurred after Hawthorne wrote a campaign biography of Franklin Pierce and after he dedicated *Our Old Home* to President Pierce in 1863. His public support of a politician during a time of national, and even international, divisiveness about slavery caused political bias to taint evaluations of literary merit. American periodicals like the *Whig Review* attacked him, and British intellectuals were equally severe. In addition, comments on the English people and their society in *Our Old Home* became nonliterary criteria for assessing Hawthorne's art. The irony of an article in *Punch*, "A Handful of Hawthorn" (October 1863), demonstrates the anger aroused in the English reading public:

> *Mr. Punch* makes you his best compliments on your smartness, and on the gracious elegance of your descriptions of those with whom you are known to have been so intimate, and he hopes that you will soon give the world a sequel to *Transformation*, in the form of an autobiography. For he is very partial to essays on the natural history of half-civilized animals.

For the most part, however, Hawthorne's reception in England during his lifetime was unusually warm. Despite condescension about Americans, the British reviewers, as Professor Ralph Aderman amply demonstrates in his dissertation "Nathaniel Hawthorne's English Reputation to 1904" (University of Wisconsin, 1950), accepted Hawthorne as a major American writer.

The year 1860 may have marked the high tide of the recognition accorded Hawthorne during his lifetime, for in that year significant and comprehensive reviews of his work appeared in three different countries: Lowell's glowing tribute and E. P. Whipple's impressive survey; Richard Holt Hutton's article in Britain; and Émile Montégut's "Un Romancier pessimiste en Amérique." Such attention indicated appreciation of Hawthorne as a major literary figure within his lifetime and, in their differing opinions, implied or sketched critical issues which are still in contention among Hawthorne students today.

1865–1910

In his essay "'The Wizard Hand': Hawthorne, 1864–1900" (*Hawthorne Centenary Essays*, 1964), Professor Edwin Cady stresses that Hawthorne's fiction became a focal point in the expanding and frequently confusing debate between proponents of idealism and advocates of realism in fiction. Often his work was made a touchstone by which the writings of others might be evaluated in terms of this issue. Idealists considered themselves realists in the sense that only ideality is real. Realists stressed descriptions of people and settings as they are, and probability and possibility in characterization—characters who give the sense of living, and, in Henry James's phrase, are presented with "deeper psychology." Part of the debate dwelt upon the romance as distinguished from the novel, a distinction which Hawthorne had made in the Preface to *The House of the Seven Gables* (1851).

Hawthorne's *Blithedale Romance* (1852) was often a central work in this argument between idealists and realists. Despite the trappings of a Gothic villain and mysterious flourishes surrounding the Veiled Lady, this book appealed to some reviewers because of its seemingly realistic basis in Hawthorne's own experience at Brook Farm. Opposing judgments on one dramatic episode foreshadow the major trend in Hawthorne criticism between 1865 and 1910: idealism versus realism. Whereas one reviewer saw the scene depicting the recovery of Zenobia's body as repulsive violation of the beautiful and the ideal, another singled it out for praise because of its realism.

During the far-ranging discussions of realism from 1865 to 1910, Hawthorne's works again attracted important literary figures, such as Henry James, William Dean Howells, and Anthony Trollope. Much of Hawthorne's fiction appealed to James because he saw in it exploration of "deeper psychology." James's negative views in his critical biography (1879) also pertain to his interest in realism: Hawthorne's lack of cultural background, his provinciality, and his excessive use of fancy. Although James praised *The Scarlet Letter* as an American masterpiece and admitted the reality of tone or atmosphere in the romance, he was critical of a lack of reality in characterization, finding the people too symbolic of states of mind. Later, James was to temper some of his opinions of Hawthorne; however, his critical biography remains the most influential of the commentaries on Hawthorne during the period 1865 to 1910.

Another of the chief proponents of realism in fiction, Howells, although he admired Hawthorne, complained about the characterizations of Clifford and Hepzibah as figures who "move dim, forlorn wraiths before the fancy" and "bring such proof of their reality as ghosts seen by others supply." Like critics before him, he preferred *The Blithedale Romance* because of its realism—"almost a piece of naturalism."

Trollope, an English novelist whose books Hawthorne admired even though their hearty roast-beef-and-ale rendering of reality was so dissimilar to his own world of fantasy, joined James and Howells in appreciation of Hawthorne. Oddly, Trollope described Hawthorne's tragic vision in terms which seem alien to the vocabulary of realists: he found the strength of Hawthorne's work in a "weird, mysterious, thrilling charm," and he saw the effect of Hawthorne's melancholy and "black forebodings" as communicating a transcendent sublimity which ennobled readers. Trollope's acceptance of Hawthorne reflects the attitudes of other English critics and suggests, despite some voices of dissent in Great Britain, that Hawthorne's reputation was well established in the mother country by the turn of the century.

While Hawthorne's writings were being discussed in the context of realism, members of his family were instrumental in establishing another surge of critical interest by sponsoring posthumous publication of his works over a period of two decades after his death: the various notebooks by Hawthorne, several versions of his unfinished English romance, and his collected works. On appearance, these invariably elicited numerous specific reviews and some inclusive evaluations of Hawthorne. Although some critics lamented the intrusions into Hawthorne's privacy as a man and an author, the attention given to him both represented and reenforced the signal recognition which he had already acquired in his lifetime.

This attention was increased as a result of the publication of biographies and memoirs by members of his family and by some of his friends. These attempted to correct the impressions about Hawthorne's gloomy personality and his isolation which had accumulated over the years. Best known of the family productions is Julian Hawthorne's *Hawthorne and His Wife* (1884). However, the study (1876) by Hawthorne's son-in-law, George Parsons Lathrop, represents one of the few attempts within the family to offer literary criticism.

The interest in Hawthorne, the writer and the man, demonstrated in the debate about realism and in the publications sponsored by members of his family and friends culminated in July 1904 in numerous centennial celebrations of his birth. Many of the articles and speeches on these occasions are of the same mediocre quality of criticism as the effusions attending Hawthorne's death in 1864. Bliss Perry's tribute in 1904, later printed, was one of the better statements. Paul Elmer More's analysis of the theme of isolation and alienation in Hawthorne was reprinted during the centennial year and touched upon two issues which are still discussed: the nature of Hawthorne's tragic vision and his Puritan background. Whatever the merit of other speeches and publications in 1904, their total result was to make Hawthorne's reputation even more solid despite the fact that fiction had by then turned from romance to realism.

Prior to and after the centennial celebrations two significant studies of Hawthorne appeared: Woodberry's critical biography (1902) and Brownell's essay on Hawthorne in *American Prose Masters* (1909). Both criticized Hawthorne for his indolence, "the low vital tone of his work," and, echoing Henry James, his provincialism. In Woodberry's book there is an attempt to balance criticism and worth; for instance, he argued that if Hawthorne's Puritan background was the basis of provinciality, it also provided him with an escape to cosmopolitanism through the Christian faith "which presents mankind one and indivisible." More concerned with style, Brownell wrote a devastating indictment of Hawthorne. That portion of Brownell's essay reprinted here runs contrary to the consistent praise of Hawthorne's style in pre-1909 criticism. So effective was Brownell's attack that later critics like F. O. Matthiessen had to cope with his arguments, while others like Martin Green were to elaborate on them. That two critics as talented as Woodberry and Brownell would analyze Hawthorne's fiction extensively is further evidence that his was a literary reputation to be reckoned with in the first decade of the twentieth century and even, in the case of Brownell, to be challenged.

1911 to the Present

After 1909 the course of the critical reception of Hawthorne might be divided into three parts. From 1910 to about 1930 Hawthorne's reputation remained static; in fact, it may have declined, despite significant attention given to it by T. S. Eliot and Fred Lewis Pattee. However, in the 1930's scholarly investigations by Austin Warren and Randall Stewart into the mind, art, and life of Hawthorne gave new impetus to the study and criticism of the New Englander. The period from 1940 to the present, however, must be considered the richest and most complex in the development of Hawthorne's literary reputation in our century. Critics influenced by new criticism began to examine Hawthorne's works minutely. In many studies the assessments included application of knowledge from other disciplines such as philosophy and psychology. In fact, some of the best work on Hawthorne after 1940 demonstrated careful scholarship, close reading of the texts, and the interpretation of Hawthorne's fiction in larger intellectual and formalistic contexts. Some of these books have been reviewed not only in scholarly journals but in periodicals available to vast audiences. In addition, Hawthorne's works have been published in numerous inexpensive editions, and they are now being collected in a scholarly edition issued by Ohio State University. A work like *The Scarlet Letter* has been the subject of several collections of criticism. Hawthorne's place in courses in American literature and American studies seems secure. His fiction has even inspired a prominent contemporary poet, Robert Lowell, to write a poem about him and to adapt "My Kinsman, Major Molineux" as a drama.

Yet many of the topics and patterns evident in the tracing of the critical reputation of Hawthorne from 1910 are not new—for example, his addiction to allegory and his poetic style. These and other issues still remain controversial.

The quality of Hawthorne's mind and the nature of his temperament have intrigued his critics at every step in the development of his literary reputation. Without using the term *ambiguity*, both Hutton and "Matthew Browne" had dealt with this major issue in recent criticism. To Matthiessen ambiguity is a technique which might be called "the device of multiple choice," and to Richard Harter Fogle, perhaps the foremost exponent of the artistic and intellectual integrity of ambiguity in Hawthorne's works, it is "a pervasive quality" of his mind. On the other hand, Green claimed that ambiguity for Hawthorne was "usually a device of caution or a carelessness."

Very early in Hawthorne's career reviewers had noticed and at times had complained about his gloominess, morbidity, or pessimism. Especially was this true of those imbued with a mid-nineteenth-century optimism about the progress of man and society. However, Melville had emphasized "the power of blackness" in Hawthorne's vision of man, and yet had seen him as an author capable of love and compassion. In the twentieth century Melville's phrase and comments have reverberated in the criticism of Hawthorne. Randall Stewart explained the darker side of Hawthorne's vision as an attack on the romantic and transcendental individualism current in Hawthorne's time—a point which Vernon Louis Parrington had used to condemn Hawthorne. Like Melville, Stewart was aware of the positive implications of Hawthorne's emphasis upon warped characters, and he described Hawthorne's central moral as "the importance of understanding mankind in whole, and the need of man's sympathy with man based upon the honest recognition of the good and evil in our common nature." In opposition to Melville and Stewart, Hubert Hoeltje insisted that Hawthorne's vision is completely devoid of "the power of blackness." In developing his thesis he pitted another critic of Hawthorne's time—Henry Tuckerman—against Melville.

This debate is allied to the concern of critics from 1850 to the present about the nature of Hawthorne's view of tragedy. Loring's interpretation of *The Scarlet Letter* really underscored tragic collisions with society without emphasis on the word *tragedy*. Trollope and More were fully aware of Hawthorne's tragic vision, although their concept of the tone of tragedy in Hawthorne's fiction is different. In one of the best discussions of Hawthorne's tragic vision Matthiessen elaborated on More's attempt to link Hawthorne with Greek tragedy. Matthiessen also stressed the tragedy in the distortions of the head or the heart, particularly in the sin of pride, and, like Trollope, lauded the beauty and grandeur in Hawthorne's tragic vision. Green, on the other hand, analyzed *The Scarlet Letter* extensively in order to refute the claim that Hawthorne "delivered a profound and tragic meaning."

Such continuing and controversial attention to Hawthorne's mind and temperament reflects a basic problem which has always existed in the criticism of his works—the relevance of the man to his imaginative art. Despite the attempts of members of his family and recent biographers like Stewart and Hoeltje to dispel the image of Hawthorne as an isolated observer of life dwelling morbidly on the effects of loneliness upon his fictional characters, the issue regarding the correlation of Hawthorne's personality to his imaginative fiction is not resolved. The most recent and comprehensive attempt to answer the questions inherent in the issue is that of Frederick Crews (1966). Concentrating on the theme of incest in the fiction and on the impact upon the fiction of Hawthorne's repression of his own feelings, Crews has tried to link the man and his works through a Freudian approach. However, some of the reviews of Crews's book suggest that the debate will continue.

That these controversial issues are not new does not mean that the criticism since 1910 has made no progress. Armed with considerably more information and with better critical skills, recent commentators on Hawthorne have certainly provided new insights into old problems. In addition, their close reading of his works has had profound influence on evaluations of the relative merits of various romances and stories. Despite Martin Green's dismissal of *The Scarlet Letter*, that romance is now fully accepted as Hawthorne's masterpiece, even though the author himself and such a prominent critic as T. S. Eliot preferred *The House of the Seven Gables*. *The Blithedale Romance*, reasonably well received in its time and during the later debate about realism, is today generally considered defective, but studies concentrating on imagery, point of view, or the character of Coverdale have given fresh perspectives to readers of the book. Recent analyses of Hawthorne's use of art and the Roman setting in *The Marble Faun* have provided answers to some of the objections registered against that romance.

In addition, some of Hawthorne's stories, especially "My Kinsman, Major Molineux," have emerged from oblivion. This story is now regarded by many as Hawthorne's masterpiece in the short form. "Rappaccini's Daughter," condemned by Trollope as "unintelligible," is currently seen as one of Hawthorne's most complex and rewarding stories. The importance of tales like "Young Goodman Brown," which did receive some favorable attention earlier, has been confirmed today.

A pattern in the criticism since 1910 which might be called new is reflected in the numerous attempts to put Hawthorne's fiction in the framework of his times, of tradition, or of the development of a form such as the short story or the romance. Early critics, of course, had noticed some of Hawthorne's intellectual and artistic antecedents (for example, Shakespeare, Spenser, Milton, Bunyan, Lamb, Tieck, and Goethe), but they could not have encompassed the large perspectives represented in some of the recent discussions of Hawthorne.

These perspectives deal with considerably more than literary influences. For instance, Matthiessen illuminates the age of Emerson and Whitman by analyzing and comparing the literary theories and practices of writers, including Hawthorne, during the American renaissance of the mid-nineteenth century. Hyatt Waggoner has discussed Hawthorne in the context of Christian humanism and also of the contemporary interest in existentialism. Just as Fogle brought to his discussion of Hawthorne a vast knowledge of romanticism, so Austin Warren and others have fully explored the Puritan and New England context in which Hawthorne must be placed.

T. S. Eliot tried to delineate the place of Hawthorne and James in a New England tradition. According to Eliot, James possessed talents similar to Hawthorne's but made much more of them. On the other hand, William Van O'Connor, interested in the relevance of Hawthorne to our time, examined a tradition encompassing the seemingly disparate fiction and locales of Hawthorne and William Faulkner. To the connections between Hawthorne and James and Faulkner, Terence Martin would add relationships between the fiction of Hawthorne and Robert Penn Warren.

The objectives of critics like Pattee and Richard Chase were different. They attempted to place Hawthorne in the contexts of the development of the two major art forms which he used—the short story and the romance. Although aware of the defects of Hawthorne's short fiction, Pattee stressed the significant contributions of

Hawthorne to the development of the short story—for example, his turning it from "Germanic romantic extravagance and frivolity and horror into sane and moral channels." Chase argued that Hawthorne was a better writer of the tale because he was "unable to master the novel form without imparting to it a preponderance of romance."

All of the vital critical interest in placing Hawthorne in large contexts culminated in a reassessment of his work during the centennial (1964) of his death. The eulogies attendant upon his death in 1864 and the centennial celebrations (1904) of his birth had occasioned many tributes which reenforced his reputation but offered relatively little criticism of worth. On the other hand, the 1964 centennial inspired discussions which stirred controversy and represented a test of the solidity of his reputation. Immediately before and during the celebrations, the reputation of Hawthorne was jolted by criticism from Martin Green and, ironically, from several critics included in *Hawthorne Centenary Essays* (1964). Among the latter Lionel Trilling denied contemporary relevance to Hawthorne and compared his vision and art unfavorably to Kafka's. However, other essays in the same volume, as well as centennial issues of *Nineteenth Century Fiction* and *Essex Institute Historical Collections*, devoted exclusively to Hawthorne, provided support for Hawthorne's recognition as a major American writer.

It is certain that debates will continue about the nature of Hawthorne's mind, temperament, and artistry—and, more important, about his place in the literary hierarchy. But in view of the voluminous and persistent attention paid him for approximately a century and a half, Hawthorne is likely to remain one of the most important authors whom America has produced.

ACKNOWLEDGMENTS

In addition to the studies by Professors Aderman and Cady cited in the Preface, I wish to express my indebtedness to the authors of the following works: William Reid, "A History of Hawthorne Criticism, 1879–1932" (M. A. thesis, University of Colorado, 1932); Bertha Faust, *Hawthorne's Contemporaneous Reputation* (Philadelphia, 1939); Helen-Jean Moore, "The American Criticism of Hawthorne—1938–1948" (doctoral dissertation, University of Pittsburgh, 1952); Walter Blair, "Hawthorne," in *Eight American Authors*, edited by Floyd Stovall (New York, 1956); Seymour L. Gross and Randall Stewart, "The Hawthorne Revival," in *Hawthorne Centenary Essays*, edited by Roy Harvey Pearce (Columbus, Ohio, 1964); and bibliographical essays on Hawthorne by Hyatt Waggoner and Richard Harter Fogle in several volumes of *American Literary Scholarship*, edited by James Woodress and published by the Duke University Press.

I also wish to express my appreciation to the Research Office of the University of Missouri—St. Louis for funds for photoduplication of materials in this book. To the St. Louis Public Library I am grateful for the opportunity to use its excellent collection of nineteenth-century periodicals.

To my wife, Lucian, I owe an incalculable debt. She assisted me in every phase of the development of this volume, and her knowledge of nineteenth-century British and American critics provided me numerous insights.

Contents

1828–64

WILLIAM LEGGETT (?), Review of *Fanshawe* (*Critic*, 22 November 1828) — 3

PARK BENJAMIN (?), Review of *The Token* and *Atlantic Souvenir* (1837) (*American Monthly Magazine*, October 1836) — 4

EVERT AUGUSTUS DUYCKINCK, Nathaniel Hawthorne (*Arcturus*, May 1841) — 5

[HENRY WADSWORTH LONGFELLOW], Review of *Twice-Told Tales* (*North American Review*, April 1842) — 9

[EDGAR ALLAN POE], Review of *Twice-Told Tales* (*Graham's Magazine*, May 1842) — 12

[HENRY FOTHERGILL CHORLEY], Review of *Mosses from an Old Manse* (*Athenaeum*, 8 August 1846) — 18

ANONYMOUS, The American Library (*Blackwood's Magazine*, November 1847) — 20

EDGAR A. POE, Tale Writing—Nathaniel Hawthorne (*Godey's Lady's Book*, November 1847) — 21

[HENRY F. CHORLEY], Review of *The Scarlet Letter* (*Athenaeum*, 15 June 1850) — 27

[HERMAN MELVILLE], Hawthorne and His *Mosses* (*Literary World*, August 1850) — 29

[GEORGE BAILEY LORING], Review of *The Scarlet Letter* (*Massachusetts Quarterly Review*, September 1850) — 41

[ARTHUR CLEVELAND COXE], The Writings of Hawthorne (*Church Review*, January 1851) — 49

HENRY T. TUCKERMAN, Nathaniel Hawthorne (*Southern Literary Messenger*, June 1851) — 55

GEORGE ELIOT (?), Contemporary Literature of America [*The Blithedale Romance*] (*Westminster Review*, October 1852) — 63

ANONYMOUS, *The Blithedale Romance* (*American Whig Review*, November 1852) — 67

ANONYMOUS, Nathaniel Hawthorne (*Dublin University Magazine*, October 1855) — 71

[JAMES RUSSELL LOWELL], Review of *The Marble Faun* (*Atlantic Monthly*, April 1860) — 75

[EDWIN PERCY WHIPPLE], Nathaniel Hawthorne (*Atlantic Monthly*, May 1860) — 78

[RICHARD HOLT HUTTON], Nathaniel Hawthorne (*National Review*, October 1860) — 90

1865–1910

MATTHEW BROWNE, Nathaniel Hawthorne (*St. Paul's Magazine*, May 1871)	119
GEORGE PARSONS LATHROP, From *A Study of Hawthorne* (1876)	121
ANTHONY TROLLOPE, The Genius of Nathaniel Hawthorne (*North American Review*, September 1879)	123
HENRY JAMES, The Three American Novels [*The Scarlet Letter*] (*Hawthorne*, 1879)	126
WILLIAM DEAN HOWELLS, From *Heroines of Fiction* (1901)	133
GEORGE E. WOODBERRY, The Old Manse (*Nathaniel Hawthorne*, 1902)	138
PAUL ELMER MORE, The Solitude of Nathaniel Hawthorne (*Shelburne Essays*, 1904)	142
BLISS PERRY, The Centenary of Hawthorne (*Park-Street Papers*, 1908)	145
W. C. BROWNELL, Nathaniel Hawthorne (*American Prose Masters*, 1909)	148

1911 TO THE PRESENT

T. S. ELIOT, The Hawthorne Aspect (*The Little Review*, August 1918)	157
FRED LEWIS PATTEE, Nathaniel Hawthorne (*The Development of the American Short Story*, 1923)	163
VERNON LOUIS PARRINGTON, Nathaniel Hawthorne: Skeptic (*The Romantic Revolution in America*, 1927)	167
AUSTIN WARREN, Introduction (*Nathaniel Hawthorne*, 1934)	175
F. O. MATTHIESSEN, Hawthorne's Psychology: The Acceptance of Good and Evil (*American Renaissance*, 1941)	185
RANDALL STEWART, The Collected Works (*Nathaniel Hawthorne*, 1948)	199
RICHARD HARTER FOGLE, The Light and the Dark (*Hawthorne's Fiction*, 1952)	211
RICHARD CHASE, Hawthorne and the Limits of Romance—*The Blithedale Romance* (*The American Novel and Its Tradition*, 1957)	219
WILLIAM VAN O'CONNOR, Hawthorne and Faulkner: Some Common Ground (*The Grotesque*, 1962)	224
HYATT H. WAGGONER, From *Nathaniel Hawthorne* (1962)	239
HYATT H. WAGGONER, *The Marble Faun* (*Hawthorne*, 1963)	243
HUBERT H. HOELTJE, Hawthorne, Melville, and "Blackness" (*American Literature*, March 1965)	257
MARTIN GREEN, The Hawthorne Myth: A Protest (*Re-Appraisals*, 1965)	267
TERENCE MARTIN, A Significant Legacy (*Nathaniel Hawthorne*, 1965)	285
FREDERICK C. CREWS, Hawthorne, Freud, and Literary Value (*The Sins of the Fathers*, 1966)	290

1828-64

WILLIAM LEGGETT [1801–39] published poetry, tales, and sketches, but he was primarily a journalist with the New York *Mirror*, Bryant's *Evening Post*, and *The Plaindealer*. In 1828 Leggett established the *Critic*, a weekly for which he did most of the writing; this venture lasted only ten months. The review of *Fanshawe* is notable for its prediction of future greatness for the anonymous author. It also represents the first significant review of Hawthorne—a very charitable estimate in view of Leggett's reputation as a fiery controversialist. However, by removing *Fanshawe* from circulation, Hawthorne himself performed the severest act of criticism.

[Review of] *Fanshawe*

Attributed to WILLIAM LEGGETT

Who wrote this book? Yet what need is there to know the name of the author, in order to pronounce a decision? Be he whom he may, this is not his first attempt, and we hope it will not be his last. The mind that produced this little, interesting volume, is capable of making great and rich additions to our native literature; and it will, or we shall be sadly mistaken. The author is a scholar, though he makes no ostentatious display of scholarship; he is a poet, though there are not two dozen metrical lines in the volume with which to substantiate the assertion; he is a gentleman, though the nearest approach to gentlemen in his pages, are two country college boys; and he possesses a heart alive to the beauties of nature, and the beauties of sentiment, and replete with all those kindly feelings which adorn and dignify human nature. His story is told in language, simple, chaste and appropriate; describing, so that the eye of the reader sees them, all the beautiful and varied traits of the landscape in which he has chosen to locate his narrative. . . .

. . . .

But the book has faults. The plot lacks probability; there is too much villa[i]ny in some of the characters; or rather, there are too many bad characters introduced; their number is disproportioned to that of the good ones. The flight of the heroine is without sufficient motive, especially as her nature was but little spiced with romance; her rescue is effected by improbable means; and finally, the gulli-

Critic, Vol. 1 (22 November 1828) 53–55.

bility and unsophisticatedness of the amiable principal of Harley College, is rather a caricature than a portrait.

. . . .

... Beside those already mentioned, we have no fault to find with the author of Fanshawe; but we shall have, if he does not erelong give us another opportunity of reading one of his productions. Is it not quite possible that Willis wrote this book? We merely *guess*.

PARK BENJAMIN [1809–64] was a journalist noted for his sensationalism. As assistant editor and editor of the *New England Magazine*, Benjamin knew of Hawthorne's contributions to the magazine—for example, fourteen works, including "Young Goodman Brown," in 1835 alone. When Benjamin shifted to *The American Monthly Magazine*, he continued to solicit stories from Hawthorne. Although hostile to Samuel Goodrich, publisher of *The Token*, Benjamin was favorably inclined toward Hawthorne and thus in his review of *The Token* broke the veil of anonymity covering Hawthorne's career. In 1838, Benjamin's associate on *The American Monthly*, Charles Fenno Hoffman, wrote a favorable review of *Twice-Told Tales* for the periodical.

[Review of] The Token and Atlantic Souvenir (1837)

Attributed to PARK BENJAMIN

. . . .

... The author of "Sights from a Steeple," of "The Gentle Boy," and of "The Wedding Knell," we believe to be one and the same individual. The assertion may sound very bold, yet we hesitate not to call the author second to no man in this country, except Washington Irving. We refer simply to romance writing; and trust that no wise man of Gotham will talk of Dewey, and Channing, and Everett,

American Monthly Magazine, n. s. Vol. 2 (October 1836) 405–7.

and Verplanck. Yes, to us the style of NATHANIEL HAW-THORNE is more pleasing, more fascinating, than any one's, except their dear Geoffry Crayon! This mention of the real name of our author may be reprobated by him. His modesty is the best proof of his true excellence. How different does such a man appear to us from one who anxiously writes his name on every public post! We have read a sufficient number of his pieces to make the reputation of a dozen of our Yankee scribblers; and yet, how few have heard the name above written! He does not even cover himself with the same anonymous shield at all times; but liberally gives the praise which, concentrated on one, would be great, to several unknowns. If Mr. Hawthorne would but collect his various tales and essays into one volume, we can assure him that their success would be brilliant—certainly in England, perhaps in this country. His works would, probably, make twice as many volumes as Mr. Willis's. How extended a notoriety has the latter acquired on productions, whose quantity and quality are both far inferior to those of this voluntarily undistinguished man of genius!

"The Token" would be richly worth its price for "Monsieur du Miroir," "Sunday at Home," "The Man of Adamant," and "The Great Carbuncle," if every other piece were as flat as the editor's verses. "David Swan" is, if we mistake not, from the same graphic hand; and so is "Fancy's Show-Box;" we are sure of "The Prophetic Pictures." A little volume, containing these stories alone, would be a treasure.

. . . We commend the Editor for his good taste in the selection of his prose papers, and we can think of only one method by which he can do better than he has done;—this is, next year to employ Hawthorne to write the whole volume, and not to look at it himself till it be for sale by all booksellers in town and country.

. . . .

EVERT AUGUSTUS DUYCKINCK [1816–78] edited with his brother George Long Duyckinck the *Literary World* (1847–53). With Cornelius Mathews he founded *Arcturus* (1841–42), in which four articles on Hawthorne were published. In 1845 Duyckinck contributed two essays on Hawthorne to the *Democratic Review*, which published numerous tales by Hawthorne. The *Literary World* carried Melville's famous review of *Mosses*, as well as many other pieces devoted to Hawthorne, including reviews of three of his major romances. In 1855 Duyckinck and his brother published the *Cyclopaedia of American Literature*, in which the section on Hawthorne is highly complimentary.

Nathaniel Hawthorne

EVERT AUGUSTUS DUYCKINCK

In his own peculiar walk of fiction and sentiment, there is perhaps no author in English literature who could supply to us the few natural beautiful sketches of Nathaniel Hawthorne. Of the American writers destined to live, he is the most original, the one least indebted to foreign models or literary precedents of any kind, and as the reward of his genius he is the least known to the public. . . .

Doubtless Hawthorne has many admirers: his native New England must contain many who love his awe-stricken tales of the old colony times, of the era of the Province House, of the terror of Salem Witchcraft, of the picturesque gathering at the siege of Louisbourg; there are others who may unwittingly owe him thanks for pure descriptions of nature, passages of refined sentiment and graceful thought, that have found their way into the newspapers without any mention of the author. . . .

It need be no cause of regret to the friends of Hawthorne that he is not popular in the common acceptation of the word, for popularity is not essential to his success. He has written, not because others admire, but because he himself feels. His motive was from within. He could not have written better if a publisher had stood by his side feeding the flame of authorship with checks on the banker, or a body of editors been ready with paste and scissors to manufacture his wares in the best possible shape for the public. His merit does not need the verdict of multitudes to be allowed. It is not with him as with a novelist or dramatist who catches at the favor of the moment, and is every thing or nothing according to the issue of his experiment. The writings of Hawthorne can bear the delay of favor, they cannot perish, for they spring from the depths of a true heart. They are part of the genuine recorded experience of humanity, and must live.

It will be seen that we attribute a deeper philosophy, a higher influence to these writings, than the description tales and essays, might seem to warrant. In truth, though written in prose, they are

Arcturus, Vol. 1 (May 1841) 330–37.

poems of a high order. The poetical temperament is beneath every page, moulding, modifying every thought, coloring every topic of commonplace with the hues of fancy and sensibility. The genius of Hawthorne is peculiar as that of Charles Lamb, with fewer external aids from books and conventional literary expressions. He does not, like the popular author, express the reluctant thoughts and images of other people's minds, but calls the rest to look upon, wonder at, admire, and then love, his own. His writings, like those of all strictly original writers, are the solution of a new problem, the exhibition of the human heart and intellect, under a new array of circumstances. From the depths of New England, the culture of her old history, her domestic faithfulness to simple-hearted living, amid the repulsive anti-poetical tendencies of the present day, the soul of a young man speaks to us in fanciful reveries, a passionate sense of life, in words of gloom and sorrow. Sadness deepened into awe and fear, is the constant attendant of his pen, but it is the sadness of youth—it is the young man's melancholy, with nought of the despair of age, or the cold hardness of practical life. His grave images are the visions of a dreamer who dreams of realities; he is weighed down by an ever present consciousness of real life, but wanting courage to grasp the real action, he catches only the shadow. Not irreverently, with the rashness often attributable to critics, would we say he has in his character much of Hamlet. His imagination leads him into all possible conditions of being; he is purely romantic, conscious all the while of the present world about him, which he lingers around without the energy of will to seize upon and possess. He has, with a higher impulse, something of the waywardness of his own character, Mr. Wakefield the London citizen, who one day absented himself from his wife, and lived twenty years in the next street, in the daily habit of seeing her, without even speaking to her or visiting his own door. So Hawthorne lives rather near the present time than actually belonging to it. His literary life is a fascinated dream, an abstraction. The confessions of an imaginary character, one Oberon, in a paper entitled The Journal of a Solitary Man, betray the secret of the sombre half-disappointed spirit that breathes through his pages. It is the maiden Sympathy, sitting on her cold monument, smiling at grief, having never wedded manly Action.

· · · · · · ·

The distinctive mark of Hawthorne's writings, is a fanciful pathos delighting in sepulchral images. Like the ancient Egyptians, he exhibits the skull and insignia of mortality to temper the gaiety of the feast. His style, pure, serene, cheerful, is dashed with fearful shadows of gloom, as on the brightest midsummer day a passing cloud veils the earth in momentary darkness. This quaint love of the tomb, which he employs as an antagonist force to an exceeding sense of the beauty and grace of life, not from an unhealthy morbid temperament, he has in common with several of the master minds of English literature. The dramatist Webster, who was originally a sexton, casts a strange fascinating gloom over his tragedies by his similes from the charnel house; Jeremy Taylor, in his Holy Dying, indulges in this luxury of wo[e]—we read on, impressed by the profusion of the author's fancy covering the cold walls of the tomb with the drapery of grief and sorrow, till the mind, reposing perhaps on the humanity of the scene, is filled and diverted with a comforting sense of pleasure. The Hydriotaphia of Sir Thomas Browne is a joyous comment on the tomb, the intellect speculating on vanity and decay, and triumphant over death: ' 'Tis all one to lie in St. Innocent's church-yard, as in the sands of Egypt. Ready to be anything, in the ecstasy of being ever, and as content with six foot as the moles of Adrianus!'

The Wedding Knell and the Minister's Black Veil, two of our author's 'Twice Told Tales,' exhibit an ingenious refinement of terror wrought up with none of the ordinary machinery of gloom, no death's heads, or goblins or mysterious portraits, gleaming from the wall, no Radcliffean horror, but a metaphysical exposition of the dark places of the human soul, a preacher's exhibition and warning of guilt and death. Fancy's Show Box, the title of another sketch, is a skilful analysis of the deceitful human heart, tented to the quick. . . .

. . . .

Though sketches of this kind abound in his pages, Hawthorne is not a gloomy writer—his melancholy is fanciful, capricious—his spirit of love for all things, his delight in childhood, his reverence for woman, his sympathy with nature, are constant. We are made better by all that he writes. If he shows the skilful touches of the physician in probing the depths of human sorrow, and noting the earliest stains of guilt upon the soul, he has too a fund of cheerfulness and sympathy that can minister to the mind diseased. What winning accents he might use from the pulpit—what lay sermons, full of hope and tranquillity and beauty, he may yet give the world in his writings!

For the July 1837 issue of *North American Review*, HENRY WADSWORTH LONGFELLOW [1807–82] wrote a review of *Twice-Told Tales* in which he welcomed the volume as a "sweet, sweet book," redolent of poetry in its revelation of the "universal mind of man" and in "the exceeding beauty" of its style. He praised the choice of national themes which endow distant traditions of New England with romance, and he singled out "The Great Carbuncle" as his "especial favorite" among the tales. Longfellow's second review of *Twice-Told Tales* (1842) is superior to the first in that it is less effusive and far more concise about Hawthorne's merits.

[Review of] Twice-Told Tales

[HENRY WADSWORTH LONGFELLOW]

The lovers of delicate humor, natural feeling, observation "like a blind man's touch," unerring taste, and magic grace of style, will greet with pleasure this new, improved, and enlarged edition of Hawthorne's "Twice-told Tales." The first volume appeared several years since, and received notice and fit commendation in a former Number of our Journal.* The second volume is made up of tales and sketches, similar in character to those of the first volume, and not inferior in merit. We are disposed, on the strength of these volumes, to accord to Mr. Hawthorne a high rank among the writers of this country, and to predict, that his contributions to its imaginative literature will enjoy a permanent and increasing reputation. Though he has not produced any elaborate and long-sustained work of fiction, yet his writings are most strikingly characterized by that creative originality, which is the essential life-blood of genius. He does not see by the help of other men's minds, and has evidently been more of an observer and thinker, than of a student. He gives us no poor copies of poor originals in English magazines and souvenirs. He has caught nothing of the intensity of the French, or the extravagance of the German, school of writers of fiction. Whether he writes a story or a sketch, or describes a character or a scene, he employs his own materials, and gives us transcripts of images painted on his own mind. Another characteristic merit of his writings is, that he seeks and finds his subjects at home, among his own people, in the characters, the events, and the traditions of

---

*See *North American Review*, Vol. XLV. pp. 59 *et seq.*

North American Review, Vol. 54 (April 1842) 496–99.

his own country. His writings retain the racy flavor of the soil. They have the healthy vigor and free grace of indigenous plants.

Perhaps there is no one thing for which he is more remarkable than his power of finding the elements of the picturesque, the romantic, and even the supernatural, in the every-day, commonplace life, that is constantly going on around us. He detects the essentially poetical in that which is superficially prosaic. In the alembic of his genius, the subtle essence of poetry is extracted from prose. The history, the traditions, the people, and the scenes of New England, have not generally been supposed favorable to the romance-writer or the poet; but, in his hands, they are fruitful and suggestive, and dispose themselves into graceful attitudes and dramatic combinations. In his little sketch called "David Swan," the subject is nothing more or less than an hour's sleep, by the way-side, of a youth, while waiting for the coach that is to carry him to Boston; yet how much of thoughtful and reflective beauty is thrown round it, what strange and airy destinies brush by the youth's unconscious face, how much matter for deep meditation of life and death, the past and future, time and eternity, is called forth by the few incidents in this simple drama. As illustrations of the same power, we would refer to "The Minister's Black Veil," "The Seven Vagabonds," and "Edward Fane's Rosebud," not to speak of many others, in which this peculiarity is more or less perceptible.

One of Mr. Hawthorne's most characteristic traits is the successful manner in which he deals with the supernatural. He blends together, with a skilful hand, the two worlds of the seen and the unseen. He never fairly goes out of the limits of probability, never calls up an actual ghost, or dispenses with the laws of nature; but he passes as near as possible to the dividing line, and his skill and ingenuity are sometimes tasked to explain, by natural laws, that which produced upon the reader all the effect of the supernatural. In this, too, his originality is conspicuously displayed. We know of no writings which resemble his in this respect.

His genius, too, is characterized by a large proportion of feminine elements, depth and tenderness of feeling, exceeding purity of mind, and a certain airy grace and arch vivacity in narrating incidents and delineating characters. The strength and beauty of a mother's love are poured over that exquisite story, which we are tempted to pronounce, as, on the whole, the finest thing he ever wrote,—"The Gentle Boy." What minute delicacy of touch, and womanly knowledge of a child's mind and character, are perceptible in "Little Annie's Ramble." How much of quiet pathos is contained in "The Shaker Bridal," and of tranquil beauty in "The Three-fold

Destiny." His female characters are sketched with a pencil equally fine and delicate; steeped in the finest hues of the imagination, yet not

> "too bright and good
> For human nature's daily food."

Every woman owes him a debt of gratitude for those lovely visions of womanly faith, tenderness, and truth, which glide so gracefully through his pages.

All that Mr. Hawthorne has written is impressed with a strong family likeness. His range is not very extensive, nor has he any great versatility of mind. He is not extravagant or excessive in any thing. His tragedy is tempered with a certain smoothness; it solemnizes and impresses us, but it does not freeze the blood, still less offend the most fastidious taste. He stoops to no vulgar horrors or physical clap-traps. The mind, in its highest and deepest moods of feeling, is the only subject with which he deals. There is, however, a great deal of calm power, as well as artist-like skill, in his writings of this kind, such as "Howe's Masquerade," "The White Old Maid," "Lady Eleanor's Mantle." In his humor, too, there is the same quiet tone. It is never riotous, or exuberant; it never begets a laugh, and seldom a smile, but it is most unquestioned humor, as any one may see, by reading a "A Rill from the Town Pump," or "Chippings with a Chisel." It is a thoughtful humor, of kindred with sighs as well as tears. Indeed, over all that he has written, there hangs, like an atmosphere, a certain soft and calm melancholy, which has nothing diseased or mawkish in it, but is of that kind which seems to flow naturally from delicacy of organization and a meditative spirit. There is no touch of despair in his pathos, and his humor subsides into that minor key, into which his thoughts seem naturally cast.

As a writer of the language merely, Mr. Hawthorne is entitled to great praise, in our judgment. His style strikes us as one of marked and uncommon excellence. It is fresh and vigorous, not formed by studying any particular model, and has none of the stiffness which comes from imitation; but it is eminently correct and careful. His language is very pure, his words are uniformly well chosen, and his periods are moulded with great grace and skill. It is also a very perspicuous style, through which his thoughts shine like natural objects seen through the purest plate-glass. He has no affectations or prettinesses of phrases, and none of those abrupt transitions, or of that studied inversion and uncouth abruptness, by which attention is often attempted to be secured to what is feeble or commonplace. It is characterized by that same unerring good taste, which presides over all the movements of his mind.

We feel that we have hardly done justice to Mr. Hawthorne's claims in this brief notice, and that they deserve an extended analysis and criticism; but we have not done this, partly on account of our former attempt to do justice to his merits, and partly because his writings have now become so well known, and are so justly appreciated, by all discerning minds, that they do not need our commendation. He is not an author to create a sensation, or have a tumultuous popularity. His works are not stimulating or impassioned, and they minister nothing to a feverish love of excitement. Their tranquil beauty and softened tints, which do not win the notice of the restless many, only endear them the more to the thoughtful few. We commend them for their truth and healthiness of feeling, and their moral dignity, no less than for their literary merit. The pulse of genius beats vigorously through them, and the glow of life is in them. It is the voice of a man who has seen and thought for himself, which addresses us; and the treasures which he offers to us are the harvests of much observation and deep reflection on man, and life, and the human heart.

EDGAR ALLAN POE [1809-49] printed in *Graham's Magazine* (April 1842) a brief but enthusiastic notice of *Twice-Told Tales*. Lauding Hawthorne for purity of style, effectiveness of tone, and "originality both of incident and of reflection," he promised a more extensive review and commended Hawthorne "as one of the few men of indisputable genius to whom our country has given birth." In May 1842 he published the essay printed below. However, in 1847 when Poe reviewed both *Twice-Told Tales* and *Mosses* (see pp. 21-27), he reversed his belief in Hawthorne's originality and condemned his tendency to allegory—although allegory had been present in the 1842 volume.

[Review of] Twice-Told Tales

[EDGAR ALLAN POE]

We said a few hurried words about Mr. Hawthorne in our last number, with the design of speaking more fully in the present. We

Graham's Magazine, Vol. 20 (May 1842) 298-300.

are still, however, pressed for room, and must necessarily discuss his volumes more briefly and more at random than their high merits deserve.

The book professes to be a collection of *tales*, yet is, in two respects, misnamed. These pieces are now in their third republication, and, of course, are thrice-told. Moreover, they are by no means *all* tales, either in the ordinary or in the legitimate understanding of the term. Many of them are pure essays, for example, "Sights from a Steeple," "Sunday at Home," "Little Annie's Ramble," "A Rill from the Town-Pump," "The Toll-Gatherer's Day," "The Haunted Mind," "The Sister Years," "Snow-Flakes," "Night Sketches," and "Foot-Prints on the Sea-Shore." We mention these matters chiefly on account of their discrepancy with that marked precision and finish by which the body of the work is distinguished.

Of the Essays just named, we must be content to speak in brief. They are each and all beautiful, without being characterised by the polish and adaptation so visible in the tales proper. A painter would at once note their leading or predominant feature, and style it *repose*. There is no attempt at effect. All is quiet, thoughtful, subdued. Yet this repose may exist simultaneously with high originality of thought; and Mr. Hawthorne has demonstrated the fact. At every turn we meet with novel combinations; yet these combinations never surpass the limits of the quiet. We are soothed as we read; and withal is a calm astonishment that ideas so apparently obvious have never occurred or been presented to us before. Herein our author differs materially from Lamb or Hunt or Hazlitt—who, with vivid originality of manner and expression, have less of the true novelty of thought than is generally supposed, and whose originality, at best, has an uneasy and meretricious quaintness, replete with startling effects unfounded in nature, and inducing trains of reflection which lead to no satisfactory result. The Essays of Hawthorne have much of the character of Irving, with more of originality, and less of finish; while, compared with the Spectator, they have a vast superiority at all points. The Spectator, Mr. Irving, and Mr. Hawthorne have in common that tranquil and subdued manner which we have chosen to denominate *repose;* but, in the case of the two former, this repose is attained rather by the absence of novel combination, or of originality, than otherwise, and consists chiefly in the calm, quiet, unostentatious expression of commonplace thoughts, in an unambitious unadulterated Saxon. In them, by strong effort, we are made to conceive the absence of all. In the essays before us the absence of effort is too obvious to be mistaken, and a strong under-current of *suggestion* runs continuously beneath the upper stream of the tranquil thesis. In short, these effusions of Mr. Hawthorne are the product of a truly imaginative intellect, restrained, and in some measure repressed, by fastidiousness of taste, by constitutional melancholy and by indolence.

But it is of his tales that we desire principally to speak. The tale proper, in our opinion, affords unquestionably the fairest field for the exercise of the loftiest talent, which can be afforded by the wide domains of mere prose. Were we bidden to say how the highest genius could be most advantageously employed for the best display of its own powers, we should answer, without hesitation—in the composition of a rhymed poem, not to exceed in length what might be perused in an hour. Within this limit alone can the highest order of true poetry exist. We need only here say, upon this topic, that, in almost all classes of composition, the unity of effect or impression is a point of the greatest importance. It is clear, moreover, that this unity cannot be thoroughly preserved in productions whose perusal cannot be completed at one sitting. We may continue the reading of a prose composition, from the very nature of prose itself, much longer than we can persevere, to any good purpose, in the perusal of a poem. This latter, if truly fulfilling the demands of the poetic sentiment, induces an exaltation of the soul which cannot be long sustained. All high excitements are necessarily transient. Thus a long poem is a paradox. And, without unity of impression, the deepest effects cannot be brought about. Epics were the offspring of an imperfect sense of Art, and their reign is no more. A poem *too* brief may produce a vivid, but never an intense or enduring impression. Without a certain continuity of effort—without a certain duration or repetition of purpose—the soul is never deeply moved. There must be the dropping of the water upon the rock. De Béranger has wrought brilliant things—pungent and spirit-stirring—but, like all immassive bodies, they lack *momentum*, and thus fail to satisfy the Poetic Sentiment. They sparkle and excite, but, from want of continuity, fail deeply to impress. Extreme brevity will degenerate into epigrammatism; but the sin of extreme length is even more unpardonable. *In medio tutissimus ibis.*

Were we called upon however to designate that class of composition which, next to such a poem as we have suggested, should best fulfil the demands of high genius—should offer it the most advantageous field of exertion—we should unhesitatingly speak of the prose tale, as Mr. Hawthorne has here exemplified it. We allude to the short prose narrative, requiring from a half-hour to one or two hours in its perusal. The ordinary novel is objectionable, from its length, for reasons already stated in substance. As it cannot be read at one sitting, it deprives itself, of course, of the immense force derivable from *totality*. Worldly interests intervening during the pauses of perusal, modify, annul, or counteract, in a greater or less degree, the impressions of the book. But simple cessation in reading would, of itself, be sufficient to destroy the true unity. In the brief tale, however, the author is enabled to carry out the fulness of his intention, be it what it may. During the hour of perusal the soul of the reader is at the writer's control. There are no external or extrinsic influences—resulting from weariness or interruption.

A skilful literary artist has constructed a tale. If wise, he has not fashioned his thoughts to accommodate his incidents; but having conceived, with deliberate care, a certain unique or single *effect* to be wrought out, he then invents such incidents—he then combines such events as may best aid him in establishing this preconceived effect. If his very initial sentence tend not to the outbringing of this effect, then he has failed in his first step. In the whole composition there should be no word written, of which the tendency, direct or indirect, is not to the one pre-established design. And by such means, with such care and skill, a picture is at length painted which leaves in the mind of him who contemplates it with a kindred art, a sense of the fullest satisfaction. The idea of the tale has been presented unblemished, because undisturbed; and this is an end unattainable by the novel. Undue brevity is just as exceptionable here as in the poem; but undue length is yet more to be avoided.

We have said that the tale has a point of superiority even over the poem. In fact, while the *rhythm* of this latter is an essential aid in the development of the poem's highest idea—the idea of the Beautiful—the artificialities of this rhythm are an inseparable bar to the development of all points of thought or expression which have their basis in *Truth*. But Truth is often, and in very great degree, the aim of the tale. Some of the finest tales are tales of ratiocination. Thus the field of this species of composition, if not in so elevated a region on the mountain of Mind, is a table-land of far vaster extent than the domain of the mere poem. Its products are never so rich, but infinitely more numerous, and more appreciable by the mass of mankind. The writer of the prose tale, in short, may bring to his theme a vast variety of modes or inflections of thought and expression—(the ratiocinative, for example, the sarcastic or the humorous) which are not only antagonistical to the nature of the poem, but absolutely forbidden by one of its most peculiar and indispensable adjuncts; we allude of course, to rhythm. It may be added, here, *par parenthèse,* that the author who aims at the purely beautiful in a prose tale is laboring at great disadvantage. For Beauty can be better treated in the poem. Not so with terror, or passion, or horror, or a multitude of such other points. And here it will be seen how full of prejudice are the usual animadversions against those *tales of effect* many fine examples of which were found in the earlier numbers of Blackwood. The impressions produced were wrought in a legitimate sphere of action, and constituted a legitimate although sometimes an exaggerated interest. They were relished by every man of genius: although there were found many men of genius who condemned them without just ground. The true critic will but demand that the design intended be accomplished, to the fullest extent, by the means most advantageously applicable.

We have very few American tales of real merit—we may say, indeed, none, with the exception of "The Tales of a Traveller" of Washington Irving, and these "Twice-Told Tales" of Mr. Hawthorne. Some of the pieces of Mr. John Neal abound in vigor and originality; but in general, his compositions of this class are excessively diffuse, extravagant, and indicative of an imperfect sentiment of Art. Articles at random are, now and then, met with in our periodicals which might be advantageously compared with the best effusions of the British Magazines; but, upon the whole, we are far behind our progenitors in this department of literature.

Of Mr. Hawthorne's Tales we would say, emphatically, that they belong to the highest region of Art—an Art subservient to genius of a very lofty order. We had supposed, with good reason for so supposing, that he had been thrust into his present position by one of the impudent *cliques* which beset our literature, and whose pretensions it is our full purpose to expose at the earliest opportunity; but we have been most agreeably mistaken. We know of few compositions which the critic can more honestly commend than these "Twice-Told Tales." As Americans, we feel proud of the book.

Mr. Hawthorne's distinctive trait is invention, creation, imagination, originality—a trait which, in the literature of fiction, is positively worth all the rest. But the nature of originality, so far as regards its manifestation in letters, is but imperfectly understood. The inventive or original mind as frequently displays itself in novelty of *tone* as in novelty of matter. Mr. Hawthorne is original at *all* points.

It would be a matter of some difficulty to designate the best of these tales; we repeat that, without exception, they are beautiful. "Wakefield" is remarkable for the skill with which an old idea—a well-known incident—is worked up or discussed. A man of whims conceives the purpose of quitting his wife and residing *incognito*, for twenty years, in her immediate neighborhood. Something of this kind actually happened in London. The force of Mr. Hawthorne's tale lies in the analysis of the motives which must or might have impelled the husband to such folly, in the first instance, with the possible causes of his perseverance. Upon this thesis a sketch of singular power has been constructed.

"The Wedding Knell" is full of the boldest imagination—an imagination fully controlled by taste. The most captious critic could find no flaw in this production.

"The Minister's Black Veil" is a masterly composition of which the sole defect is that to the rabble its exquisite skill will be *caviare*. The *obvious* meaning of this article will be found to smother its insinuated one. The *moral* put into the mouth of the dying minister will be supposed to convey the *true* import of the narrative; and that a crime of dark dye, (having reference to the "young lady") has been committed, is a point which only minds congenial with that of the author will perceive.

"Mr. Higginbotham's Catastrophe" is vividly original and managed most dexterously.

"Dr. Heidegger's Experiment" is exceedingly well imagined, and executed with surpassing ability. The artist breathes in every line of it.

"The White Old Maid" is objectionable, even more than the "Minister's Black Veil," on the score of its mysticism. Even with the thoughtful and analytic, there will be much trouble in penetrating its entire import.

"The Hollow of the Three Hills" we would quote in full, had we space;—not as evincing higher talent than any of the other pieces, but as affording an excellent example of the author's peculiar ability. The subject is commonplace. A witch subjects the Distant and the Past to the view of a mourner. It has been the fashion to describe, in such cases, a mirror in which the images of the absent appear; or a cloud of smoke is made to arise, and thence the figures are gradually unfolded. Mr. Hawthorne has wonderfully heightened his effect by making the ear, in place of the eye, the medium by which the fantasy is conveyed. The head of the mourner is enveloped in the cloak of the witch, and within its magic folds there arise sounds which have an all-sufficient intelligence. Throughout this article also, the artist is conspicuous—not more in positive than in negative merits. Not only is all done that should be done, but (what perhaps is an end with more difficulty attained) there is nothing done which should not be. Every word *tells*, and there is not a word which does *not* tell.

. . . .

In the way of objection we have scarcely a word to say of these tales. There is, perhaps, a somewhat too general or prevalent *tone*—a tone of melancholy and mysticism. The subjects are insufficiently varied. There is not so much of *versatility* evinced as we might well be warranted in expecting from the high powers of Mr. Hawthorne. But beyond these trivial exceptions we have really none to make. The style is purity itself. Force abounds. High imagination gleams from every page. Mr. Hawthorne is a man of the truest genius. We only regret that the limits of our Magazine will not permit us to pay him that full tribute of commendation, which, under other circumstances, we should be so eager to pay.

For many years HENRY FOTHERGILL CHORLEY [1808–72] was associated with the *Athenaeum* (London). In a review of *The Token* for 1836, he singled out for praise all three of Hawthorne's contributions without knowing the name of the author. In subsequent years Chorley reviewed *Mosses* (partially reprinted below) and Hawthorne's four major romances (see pp. 27–28 for his evaluation of *The Scarlet Letter*). Although he occasionally criticized Hawthorne (for example, the excessive flights of fancy in *The House of the Seven Gables* and the inconclusive ending of *The Marble Faun*), Chorley maintained the proprietary interest of a discoverer of Hawthorne.

[Review of] Mosses from an Old Manse

[HENRY FOTHERGILL CHORLEY]

. . . .

. . . Few prose writers possess so rich a treasury in the chambers of their imagination; while our author's riches never make him extravagant. He gives us what suffices for our thorough enchantment and

Athenaeum, 8 August 1846, 807–8.

fullest credence—but nothing more. In such a tale, for instance, as that of 'Rappaccini's Daughter,'—the narrative of a Paduan magician, who, by way of endowing his innocent daughter with power and sovereignty, had nourished her on delicious poisons, till she communicated death to everything which she approached,—any less consummate master of the marvellous would have heaped horror on horror, till the monstrosity of the invention became intolerable. Mr. Hawthorne only leads us by imperceptible degrees into the fearful garden, full of its sumptuous blossoms—then insinuates the dark sympathy between the nature of the lady and her sisters, the death-flowers—then gradually fascinates us, even as she fascinated her lover, to feel a love and a sorrow for the Sorceress greater than our terror, and to attend at the catastrophe with those mingled feelings which no spell less powerful than Truth's can command. Thus it is with most of Mr. Hawthorne's stories. We have elsewhere said, that they resemble Tieck's faëry tales, in their power of translating the mysterious harmonies of Nature into articulate meaning. They may claim kindred, too, in their high finish and purity of style, with the Genevese novels of the late Töpffer; which have been kept out of sight by their unobtrusiveness, —only, we apprehend, that they may steadily advance to a permanent European popularity. There is another author, far dearer to all Englishmen than either Tieck or Töpffer, of whom Mr. Hawthorne reminds us;—who but the excellent John Bunyan? The orthodox will be thrown into fits by our saying that the writings of both have a touch of Puritanical quaintness which is anything but ungraceful. In short, we like this writer and his stories well; and are not afraid that any among the "fit audience," whom the more delicate and thoughtful order of creators prefer to assemble, will be disappointed if, attracted by our panegyric, they take up the book.

. . . .

We desire to recommend these 'Mosses'—only objectionable from the pedantry of their designation—to the reading of such as are select in their pleasures; and, to this end, have drawn upon the prologue rather than the play. Yet, better wonder-stories do not exist than 'The Birth-mark,' and 'Young Goodman Brown':—while 'The Celestial Railroad' deserves to be bound up with the Victorian edition of 'The Pilgrim's Progress'; and 'Earth's Holocaust' merits praise, as being in the grandest style of allegory—whether as regards the accumulation of imagery or the largeness of the truth propounded. Other of the tales, too, are excellent. The one other fault, in addition to the title, which we find with these volumes is, their author's intimation that he intends to write no more short tales. "This"—as the *Edinburgh Review* said of Wordsworth, but in a totally different spirit—"will never do!"

Blackwood's Edinburgh Magazine was founded in 1817 as a rival to the *Edinburgh Review*. The comments on *Mosses* appeared in a survey of Wiley and Putnam books. The reviewer uses "The Birthmark" and "The Artist of the Beautiful" as examples of improbability of characterization in Hawthorne's fiction. Not wholly unfavorable, however, the notice does bestow condescending praise on Hawthorne's style which the author regards as reminiscent of Addison and Steele. For special comment the reviewer singles out "The Celestial Railroad," "Roger Malvin's Burial" (the best of the narrative pieces), "The New Adam and Eve," and "Mrs. Bullfrog." In May 1855 *Blackwood's* attacked Hawthorne's romances vigorously (for further information see pp. 71–72).

The American Library

ANONYMOUS

. . . .

... For whereas Mr[.] Poe is indebted to whatever good effect he produces to a close detail and agglomeration of facts, Mr[.] Hawthorne appears to have little skill and little taste for dealing with matter of fact or substantial incident, but relies for his favourable impression on the charm of style, and the play of thought and fancy.

The most serious defect in his stories is the frequent presence of some palpable improbability which mars the effect of the whole —not improbability, like that we have remarked on, which is intended and wilfully perpetrated by the author—not improbability of incident even, which we are not disposed very rigidly to inquire after in a novelist—but improbability in the main motive and state of mind which he has undertaken to describe, and which forms the turning-point of the whole narrative. As long as the human being

Blackwood's Magazine, Vol. 62 (November 1847) 587–92.

appears to act as a human being would, under the circumstances depicted, it is surprising how easily the mind, carried on by its sympathies with the feelings of the actor, forgets to inquire into the probability of these circumstances. Unfortunately, in Mr[.] Hawthorne's stories, it is the human being himself who is not probable, nor possible.

. . . .

Tale Writing—Nathaniel Hawthorne

EDGAR A. POE

. . . .

The reputation of the author of "Twice-Told Tales" has been confined, indeed, until very lately, to literary society; and I have not been wrong, perhaps, in citing him as *the* example, *par excellence*, in this country, of the privately-admired and publicly-unappreciated man of genius. Within the last year or two, it is true, an occasional critic has been urged, by honest indignation, into very warm approval. Mr. Webber, for instance, (than whom no one has a keener relish for that kind of writing which Mr. Hawthorne has best illustrated,) gave us, in a late number of "The American Review," a cordial and certainly a full tribute to his talents; and since the issue of the "Mosses from an Old Manse," criticisms of similar tone have been by no means infrequent in our more authoritative journals. I can call to mind few reviews of Hawthorne published *before* the "Mosses." One I remember in "Arcturus" (edited by Matthews and Duyckinck) for May, 1841; another in the "American Monthly" (edited by Hoffman and Herbert) for March, 1838; a third in the ninety-sixth number of the "North American Review." These criticisms, however, seemed to have little effect on the popular taste—at least, if we are to form any idea of the popular taste by reference to its expression in the newspapers, or by the sale of the author's book. It was never the fashion (until lately) to speak of him in any summary of our best authors. . . .

Godey's Lady's Book, Vol. 35 (November 1847) 252–56.

Beyond doubt, this inappreciation of him on the part of the public arose chiefly from the two causes to which I have referred—from the facts that he is neither a man of wealth nor a quack;—but these are insufficient to account for the whole effect. No small portion of it is attributable to the very marked idiosyncrasy of Mr. Hawthorne himself. In one sense, and in great measure, to be peculiar is to be original, and than the true originality there is no higher literary virtue. This true or commendable originality, however, implies not the uniform, but the continuous peculiarity—a peculiarity springing from ever-active vigor of fancy—better still if from ever-present force of imagination, giving its own hue, its own character to everything it touches, and, especially, *self impelled to touch everything*.

It is often said, inconsiderately, that very original writers always fail in popularity—that such and such persons are too original to be comprehended by the mass. "Too peculiar," should be the phrase, "too idiosyncratic." It is, in fact, the excitable, undisciplined and child-like popular mind which most keenly feels the original. The criticism of the conservatives, of the hackneys, of the cultivated old clergymen of the "North American Review," is precisely the criticism which condemns and alone condemns it. "It becometh not a divine," saith Lord Coke, "to be of a fiery and salamandrine spirit." Their conscience allowing them to move nothing themselves, these dignitaries have a holy horror of being moved. "Give us *quietude*," they say. Opening their mouths with proper caution, they sigh forth the word "*Repose.*" And this is, indeed, the one thing they should be permitted to enjoy, if only upon the Christian principle of give and take.

The fact is, that if Mr. Hawthorne were really original, he could not fail of making himself felt by the public. But the fact is, he is *not* original in any sense. Those who speak of him as original, mean nothing more than that he differs in his manner of tone, and in his choice of subjects, from any author of their acquaintance—their acquaintance not extending to the German Tieck, whose manner, in *some* of his works, is absolutely identical with that *habitual* to Hawthorne. But it is clear that the element of the literary originality is novelty. The element of its appreciation by the reader is the reader's sense of the new. Whatever gives him a new and insomuch a pleasurable emotion, he considers original, and whoever frequently gives him such emotion, he considers an original writer. In a word, it is by the sum total of these emotions that he decides upon the writer's claim to originality. I may observe here, however, that there is clearly a point at which even novelty itself would cease to produce the legitimate originality, if we judge this originality, as we should, by the effect designed: this point is that at which *novelty becomes nothing novel;* and here the artist, *to preserve his originality,* will subside into the commonplace. . . .

These points properly understood, it will be seen that the critic (unacquainted with Tieck) who reads a single tale or essay by Hawthorne, may be justified in thinking him original; but the tone, or manner, or choice of subject, which induces in this critic the sense of the new, will—if not in a second tale, at least in a third and all subsequent ones—not only fail of inducing it, but bring about an exactly antagonistic impression. In concluding a volume, and more especially in concluding all the volumes of the author, the critic will abandon his first design of calling him "original," and content himself with styling him "peculiar."

With the vague opinion that to be original is to be unpopular, I could, indeed, agree, were I to adopt an understanding of originality which, to my surprise, I have known adopted by many who have a right to be called critical. They have limited, in a love for mere words, the literary to the metaphysical originality. They regard as original in letters, only such combinations of thought, of incident, and so forth, as are, in fact, absolutely novel. It is clear, however, not only that it is the novelty of *effect* alone which is worth consideration, but that this effect is *best* wrought, for the end of all fictitious composition, pleasure, by shunning rather than by seeking the absolute novelty of combination. Originality, thus understood, tasks and startles the intellect, and so brings into undue action the faculties to which, in the lighter literature, we least appeal. And thus understood, it cannot fail to prove unpopular with the masses, who, seeking in this literature amusement, are positively offended by instruction. But the true originality—true in respect of its purposes—is that which, in bringing out the half-formed, the reluctant, or the unexpressed fancies of mankind, or in exciting the more delicate pulses of the heart's passion, or in giving birth to some universal sentiment or instinct in embryo, thus combines with the pleasurable effect of *apparent* novelty, a real egoistic delight. The reader, in the case first supposed, (that of the absolute novelty,) is excited, but embarrassed, disturbed, in some degree even pained at his own want of perception, at his own folly in not having himself hit upon the idea. In the second case, his pleasure is doubled. He is filled with an intrinsic and extrinsic delight. He feels and intensely enjoys the seeming novelty of the thought, enjoys it as really novel, as absolutely original with the writer—*and himself.* They two, he fancies, have, alone of all men, thought thus. They two have, together, created this thing. Henceforward there is a bond of sympathy between them, a sympathy which irradiates every subsequent page of the book.

There is a species of writing which, with some difficulty, may be admitted as a lower degree of what I have called the true original. In its perusal, we say to ourselves, not "how original this is!" nor "here is an idea which I and the author have alone entertained," but "here is a charmingly obvious fancy," or sometimes even, "here is a thought which I am not sure has ever occurred to myself, but which, of course, has occurred to all the rest of the world." This kind of composition (which still appertains to a high order) is usually designated as "the natural." It has little external resemblance, but strong internal affinity to the true original, if, indeed, as I have suggested, it is not of this latter an inferior degree. It is best exemplified, among English writers, in Addison, Irving and *Hawthorne*. The "ease" which is so often spoken of as its distinguishing feature, it has been the fashion to regard as ease in appearance alone, as a point of really difficult attainment. This idea, however, must be received with some reservation. The natural style is difficult only to those who should never intermeddle with it—to the unnatural. It is but the result of writing with the understanding, or with the instinct, that the *tone*, in composition, should be that which, at any given point or upon any given topic, would be the tone of the great mass of humanity. The author who, after the manner of the North Americans, is merely at *all* times *quiet*, is, of course, upon *most* occasions, merely silly or stupid, and has no more right to be thought "easy" or "natural" than has a cockney exquisite or the sleeping beauty in the waxworks.

The "peculiarity" or sameness, or monotone of Hawthorne, would, in its mere character of "peculiarity," and without reference to what *is* the peculiarity, suffice to deprive him of all chance of popular appreciation. But at his failure to be appreciated, we can, *of course*, no longer wonder, when we find him monotonous at decidedly the worst of all possible points—at that point which, having the least concern with Nature, is the farthest removed from the popular intellect, from the popular sentiment and from the popular taste. I allude to the strain of allegory which completely overwhelms the greater number of his subjects, and which in some measure interferes with the direct conduct of absolutely all.

In defence of allegory, (however, or for whatever object, employed,) there is scarcely one respectable word to be said. Its best appeals are made to the fancy—that is to say, to our sense of adaptation, not of matters proper, but of matters improper for the purpose, of the real with the unreal; having never more of intelligible connection than has something with nothing, never half so much of effective affinity as has the substance for the shadow. The deepest emotion aroused within us by the happiest allegory, *as* allegory, is a very, very imperfectly satisfied sense of the writer's ingenuity in overcoming a difficulty we should have preferred his not having attempted to overcome. The fallacy of the idea that allegory, in any of its moods, can be made to enforce a truth—that metaphor, for example, may illustrate as well as embellish an argument—could be promptly demonstrated: the converse of the supposed fact might be shown, indeed, with very little trouble—but these are topics foreign to my present purpose. One thing is clear, that if allegory ever establishes a fact, it is by dint of overturning a fiction. Where the suggested meaning runs through the obvious one in a *very* profound under-current, so as never to interfere with the upper one without our own volition, so as never to show itself unless *called* to the surface, there only, for the proper uses of fictitious narrative, is it available at all. Under the best circumstances, it must always interfere with that unity of effect which, to the artist, is worth all the allegory in the world. Its vital injury, however, is rendered to the most vitally important point in fiction—that of earnestness or verisimilitude. That "The Pilgrim's Progress" is a ludicrously over-rated book, owing its seeming popularity to one or two of those accidents in critical literature which by the critical are sufficiently well understood, is a matter upon which no two thinking people disagree; but the pleasure derivable from it, in any sense, will be found in the direct ratio of the reader's capacity to smother its true purpose, in the direct ratio of his ability to keep the allegory out of sight, or of his *in*ability to comprehend it. Of allegory properly handled, judiciously subdued, seen only as a shadow or by suggestive glimpses, and making its nearest approach to truth in a not obtrusive and therefore not unpleasant *appositeness,* the "Undine" of De La Motte Fouqué is the best, and undoubtedly a very remarkable specimen.

 The obvious causes, however, which have prevented Mr. Hawthorne's *popularity,* do not suffice to condemn him in the eyes of the few who belong properly to books, and to whom books, perhaps, do not quite so properly belong. These few estimate an author, not as do the public, altogether by what he does, but in great measure—indeed, even in the greatest measure—by what he evinces a capability of doing. In this view, Hawthorne stands among literary people in America much in the same light as did Coleridge in England. The few, also, through a certain warping of the taste, which long pondering upon books as books merely never fails to induce, are not in condition to view the errors of a scholar as errors altogether. At any time these gentlemen are prone to think the public not right rather than an educated author wrong. But the simple truth is, that the writer who aims at impressing the people, is *always* wrong when he fails in forcing that people to receive the impression. How far Mr. Hawthorne has addressed the people at all, is, of course, not a question for me to decide. His books afford strong internal evidence of having been written to himself and his particular friends alone.

. . . .

Of skillfully-constructed tales—I speak now without reference to other points, some of them more important than construction—there are very few American specimens. I am acquainted with no better one, upon the whole, than the "Murder Will Out" of Mr. Simms, and this has some glaring defects. The "Tales of a Traveler," by Irving, are graceful and impressive narratives—"The Young Italian" is especially good—but there is not one of the series which can be commended as a whole. In many of them the interest is subdivided and frittered away, and their conclusions are insufficiently *climactic*. In the higher requisites of composition, John Neal's magazine stories excel—I mean in vigor of thought, picturesque combination of incident, and so forth—but they ramble too much, and invariably break down just before coming to an end, as if the writer had received a sudden and irresistible summons to dinner, and thought it incumbent upon him to make a finish of his story before going. One of the happiest and best-sustained tales I have seen is "Jack Long; or, The Shot in the Eye," by Charles W. Webber, the assistant editor of Mr. Colton's "American Review." But in general skill of construction, the tales of Willis, I think, surpass those of any American writer—with the exception of Mr. Hawthorne.

. . . .

He is peculiar and *not* original—unless in those detailed fancies and detached thoughts which his want of general originality will deprive of the appreciation due to them, in preventing them forever reaching the *public eye*. He is infinitely too fond of allegory, and can never hope for popularity so long as he persists in it. This he will not do, for allegory is at war with the whole tone of his

nature, which disports itself never so well as when escaping from
the mysticism of his Goodman Browns and White Old Maids into
the hearty, genial, but still Indian-summer sunshine of his Wake-
fields and Little Annie's Rambles. Indeed, *his* spirit of "metaphor
run-mad" is clearly imbibed from the phalanx and phalanstery
atmosphere in which he has been so long struggling for breath.
He has not half the material for the exclusiveness of authorship that
he possesses for its universality. He has the purest style, the finest
taste, the most available scholarship, the most delicate humor, the
most touching pathos, the most radiant imagination, the most consummate ingenuity; and with these varied good qualities he has
done *well* as a mystic. But is there any one of these qualities which
should prevent his doing doubly as well in a career of honest, upright, sensible, prehensible and comprehensible things? Let him
mend his pen, get a bottle of visible ink, come out from the Old
Manse, cut Mr. Alcott, hang (if possible) the editor of "The Dial,"
and throw out of the window to the pigs all his odd numbers of
"The North American Review."

[Review of] The Scarlet Letter

[HENRY F. CHORLEY]

This is a most powerful but painful story. Mr. Hawthorne must be
well known to our readers as a favourite with the *Athenæum*. We
rate him as among the most original and peculiar writers of American fiction. There is in his works a mixture of Puritan reserve and
wild imagination, of passion and description, of the allegorical and
the real, which some will fail to understand, and which others will
positively reject,—but which, to ourselves, is fascinating, and which
entitles him to be placed on a level with Brockden Brown and the
author of 'Rip Van Winkle.' 'The Scarlet Letter' will increase his
reputation with all who do not shrink from the invention of the tale;
but this, as we have said, is more than ordinarily painful. When we
have announced that the three characters are a guilty wife, openly
punished for her guilt,—her tempter, whom she refuses to unmask,
and who during the entire story carries a fair front and an un-

Athenaeum, 15 June 1850, 634.

blemished name among his congregation,—and her husband, who, returning from a long absence at the moment of her sentence, sits himself down betwixt the two in the midst of a small and severe community to work out his slow vengeance on both under the pretext of magnanimous forgiveness,—when we have explained that 'The Scarlet Letter' is the badge of Hester Prynne's shame, we ought to add that we recollect no tale dealing with crime so sad and revenge so subtly diabolical, that is at the same time so clear of fever and of prurient excitement. The misery of the woman is as present in every page as the heading which in the title of the romance symbolizes her punishment. Her terrors concerning her strange elvish child present retribution in a form which is new and natural:—her slow and painful purification through repentance is crowned by no perfect happiness, such as awaits the decline of those who have no dark and bitter past to remember. Then, the gradual corrosion of heart of Dimmesdale, the faithless priest, under the insidious care of the husband, (whose relationship to Hester is a secret known only to themselves,) is appalling; and his final confession and expiation are merely a relief, not a reconciliation.—We are by no means satisfied that passions and tragedies like these are the legitimate subjects for fiction: we are satisfied that novels such as 'Adam Blair' and plays such as 'The Stranger' may be justly charged with attracting more persons than they warn by their excitement. But if Sin and Sorrow in their most fearful forms are to be presented in any work of art, they have rarely been treated with a loftier severity, purity, and sympathy than in Mr. Hawthorne's 'Scarlet Letter.' The touch of the fantastic befitting a period of society in which ignorant and excitable human creatures conceived each other and themselves to be under the direct "rule and governance" of the Wicked One, is most skilfully administered. The supernatural here never becomes grossly palpable:—the thrill is all the deeper for its action being indefinite, and its source vague and distant.

HERMAN MELVILLE [1819–91] discovered the literary art of Hawthorne prior to the composition of *Moby-Dick*, which he dedicated to Hawthorne. Actually the review of *Mosses* had far less influence in 1850 than it has had in recent years. The rediscovery of Melville in the twentieth century resurrected his comments on the "power of blackness" in Hawthorne's fiction; hence the review has had a profound and controversial impact on modern evaluations of both Hawthorne and Melville (see, for example, pp. 257–67).

Hawthorne and His *Mosses*
By a Virginian Spending July in Vermont

[HERMAN MELVILLE]

A papered chamber in a fine old farm-house, a mile from any other dwelling, and dipped to the eaves in foliage—surrounded by mountains, old woods, and Indian ponds,—this, surely, is the place to write of Hawthorne. Some charm is in this northern air, for love and duty seem both impelling to the task. A man of deep and noble nature has seized me in this seclusion. His wild, witch-voice rings through me; or, in softer cadences, I seem to hear it in the songs of the hill-side birds that sing in the larch trees at my window.

Would that all excellent books were foundlings, without father or mother, that so it might be we could glorify them, without including their ostensible authors! Nor would any true man take exception to this; least of all, he who writes, "When the Artist rises high enough to achieve the Beautiful, the symbol by which he makes it perceptible to mortal senses becomes of little value in his eyes, while his spirit possesses itself in the enjoyment of the reality."

But more than this. I know not what would be the right name to put on the title-page of an excellent book; but this I feel, that the names of all fine authors are fictitious ones, far more so than that of Junius; simply standing, as they do, for the mystical, ever-eluding spirit of all beauty, which ubiquitously possesses men of genius. Purely imaginative as this fancy may appear, it nevertheless seems to receive some warranty from the fact, that on a personal interview no great author has ever come up to the idea of his reader. But that dust of which our bodies are composed, how can it fitly express the nobler intelligences among us? With reverence be it spoken, that not even in the case of one deemed more than man, not even in our Saviour, did his visible frame betoken anything of the augustness of the nature within. Else, how could those Jewish eyewitnesses fail to see heaven in his glance!

It is curious how a man may travel along a country road, and yet miss the grandest or sweetest of prospects by reason of an intervening hedge, so like all other hedges, as in no way to hint of the wide landscape beyond. So has it been with me concerning the enchanting landscape in the soul of this Hawthorne, this most excellent Man of Mosses. His "Old Manse" has been written now four years, but I never read it till a day or two since. I had seen it in the bookstores—heard of it often—even had it recommended to me by a tasteful friend, as a rare, quiet book, perhaps too deserving of popularity to be popular. But there are so many books called "excellent," and so much unpopular merit, that amid the thick stir of other things, the hint of my tasteful friend was disregarded; and for four years the Mosses on the Old Manse never refreshed me with their perennial green. It may be, however, that all this while the book, like wine, was only improving in flavor and body. At any rate, it so chanced that this long procrastination eventuated in a happy result. . . .

. . . .

Stretched on that new mown clover, the hill-side breeze blowing over me through the wide barn-door, and soothed by the hum of the bees in the meadows around, how magically stole over me this Mossy Man! and how amply, how bountifully, did he redeem that delicious promise to his guests in the Old Manse, of whom it is written—"Others could give them pleasure, or amusement, or instruction—these could be picked up anywhere—but it was for me to give them rest. Rest, in a life of trouble! What better could be done for weary and world-worn spirits? What better could be done for anybody, who came within our magic circle, than to throw the spell of a magic spirit over him?" So all that day, half-buried in the new clover, I watched this Hawthorne's "Assyrian dawn, and Paphian sunset and moonrise, from the summit of our Eastern Hill."

The soft ravishments of the man spun me round about in a web of dreams, and when the book was closed, when the spell was over, this wizard "dismissed me with but misty reminiscences, as if I had been dreaming of him."

What a wild moonlight of contemplative humor bathes that Old Manse! the rich and rare distilment of a spicy and slowly-oozing heart. No rollicking rudeness, no gross fun fed on fat dinners, and bred in the lees of wine,—but a humor so spiritually gentle, so high, so deep, and yet so richly relishable, that it were hardly inappropriate in an angel. It is the very religion of mirth; for nothing so human but it may be advanced to that. The orchard of the Old

Manse seems the visible type of the fine mind that has described it—those twisted and contorted old trees, "that stretch out their crooked branches, and take such hold of the imagination, that we remember them as humorists and odd-fellows." And then, as surrounded by these grotesque forms, and hushed in the noon-day repose of this Hawthorne's spell, how aptly might the still fall of his ruddy thoughts into your soul be symbolized by "the thump of a great apple, in the stillest afternoon, falling without a breath of wind, from the mere necessity of perfect ripeness!" For no less ripe than ruddy are the apples of the thoughts and fancies in this sweet Man of Mosses—

"Buds and Bird-voices"—

What a delicious thing is that! "Will the world ever be so decayed, that Spring may not renew its greenness?" And the "Fire-Worship." Was ever the hearth so glorified into an altar before? The mere title of that piece is better than any common work in fifty folio volumes. How exquisite is this:—"Nor did it lessen the charm of his soft, familiar courtesy and helpfulness, that the mighty spirit, were opportunity offered him, would run riot through the peaceful house, wrap its inmates in his terrible embrace, and leave nothing of them save their whitened bones. This possibility of mad destruction only made his domestic kindness the more beautiful and touching. It was so sweet of him, being endowed with such power, to dwell, day after day, and one long, lonesome night after another, on the dusky hearth, only now and then betraying his wild nature, by thrusting his red tongue out of the chimney-top! True, he had done much mischief in the world, and was pretty certain to do more, but his warm heart atoned for all; He was kindly to the race of man."

But he has still other apples, not quite so ruddy, though full as ripe;—apples, that have been left to wither on the tree, after the pleasant autumn gathering is past. The sketch of "The Old Apple-Dealer" is conceived in the subtlest spirit of sadness; he whose "subdued and nerveless boyhood prefigured his abortive prime, which, likewise, contained within itself the prophecy and image of his lean and torpid age." Such touches as are in this piece cannot proceed from any common heart. They argue such a depth of tenderness, such a boundless sympathy with all forms of being, such an omnipresent love, that we must needs say that this Hawthorne is here almost alone in his generation,—at least, in the artistic manifestation of these things. Still more. Such touches as these,—and many, very many similar ones, all through his chapters—furnish clues whereby we enter a little way into the intricate, profound heart where they originated. And we see that suffering, some time or other and in some shape or other,—this only can enable any man to depict it in others. All over him, Hawthorne's melancholy rests like an Indian-summer, which, though bathing a whole country in one softness, still reveals the distinctive hue of every towering hill and each far-winding vale.

But it is the least part of genius that attracts admiration. Where Hawthorne is known, he seems to be deemed a pleasant writer, with a pleasant style,—a sequestered, harmless man, from whom any deep and weighty thing would hardly be anticipated—a man who means no meanings. But there is no man, in whom humor and love, like mountain peaks, soar to such a rapt height as to receive the irradiations of the upper skies;—there is no man in whom humor and love are developed in that high form called genius; no such man can exist without also possessing, as the indispensable complement of these, a great, deep intellect, which drops down into the universe like a plummet. Or, love and humor are only the eyes through which such an intellect views this world. The great beauty in such a mind is but the product of its strength. What, to all readers, can be more charming than the piece entitled "Monsieur du Miroir"; and to a reader at all capable of fully fathoming it, what, at the same time, can possess more mystical depth of meaning?—yes, there he sits and looks at me,—this "shape of mystery," this "identical Monsieur du Miroir." "Methinks I should tremble now, were his wizard power of gliding through all impediments in search of me, to place him suddenly before my eyes."

How profound, nay appalling, is the moral evolved by the "Earth's Holocaust"; where—beginning with the hollow follies and affectations of the world,—all vanities and empty theories and forms are, one after another, and by an admirably graduated, growing comprehensiveness, thrown into the allegorical fire, till, at length, nothing is left but the all-engendering heart of man; which remaining still unconsumed, the great conflagration is naught.

Of a piece with this, is the "Intelligence Office," a wondrous symbolizing of the secret workings in men's souls. There are other sketches still more charged with ponderous import.

"The Christmas Banquet," and "The Bosom Serpent," would be fine subjects for a curious and elaborate analysis, touching the conjectural parts of the mind that produced them. For spite of all the Indian-summer sunlight on the hither side of Hawthorne's soul, the other side—like the dark half of the physical sphere—is shrouded in a blackness, ten times black. But this darkness but gives more effect to the ever-moving dawn, that for ever advances through it, and circumnavigates his world. Whether Hawthorne has simply availed himself of this mystical blackness as a means to the wondrous effects he makes it to produce in his lights and shades; or whether there really lurks in him, perhaps unknown to himself, a touch of Puritanic gloom,—this, I cannot altogether tell. Certain it is, however, that this great power of blackness in him derives its force from its appeals to that Calvinistic sense of Innate Depravity and Original Sin, from whose visitations, in some shape or other, no deeply thinking mind is always and wholly free. For, in certain moods, no man can weigh this world without throwing in something, somehow like Original Sin, to strike the uneven balance. At all events, perhaps no writer has ever wielded this terrific thought with greater terror than this same harmless Hawthorne. Still more: this black conceit pervades him through and through. You may be witched by his sunlight,—transported by the bright gildings in the skies he builds over you; but there is the blackness of darkness beyond; and even his bright gildings but fringe and play upon the edges of thunder-clouds. In one word, the world is mistaken in this Nathaniel Hawthorne. He himself must often have smiled at its absurd misconception of him. He is immeasurably deeper than the plummet of the mere critic. For it is not the brain that can test such a man; it is only the heart. You cannot come to know greatness by inspecting it; there is no glimpse to be caught of it, except by intuition; you need not ring it, you but touch it, and you find it is gold.

Now, it is that blackness in Hawthorne, of which I have spoken, that so fixes and fascinates me. It may be, nevertheless, that it is too largely developed in him. Perhaps he does not give us a ray of his light for every shade of his dark. But however this may be, this blackness it is that furnishes the infinite obscure of his back-ground, —that back-ground, against which Shakspeare plays his grandest conceits, the things that have made for Shakspeare his loftiest but most circumscribed renown, as the profoundest of thinkers. For by philosophers Shakspeare is not adored as the great man of tragedy and comedy.—"Off with his head; so much for Buckingham!" This sort of rant, interlined by another hand, brings down the house,— those mistaken souls, who dream of Shakspeare as a mere man of Richard-the-Third humps and Macbeth daggers. But it is those deep far-away things in him; those occasional flashings-forth of the intuitive Truth in him; those short, quick probings at the very axis of reality;—these are the things that make Shakspeare, Shakspeare. Through the mouths of the dark characters of Hamlet, Timon, Lear, and Iago, he craftily says, or sometimes insinuates the things which we feel to be so terrifically true, that it were all but madness for any good man, in his own proper character, to utter, or even hint of them. Tormented into desperation, Lear, the frantic king, tears off the mask, and speaks the same madness of vital truth. But, as I before said, it is the least part of genius that attracts admiration. And so, much of the blind, unbridled admiration that has been heaped upon Shakspeare, has been lavished upon the least part of him. And few of his endless commentators and critics seem to have remembered, or even perceived, that the immediate products of a great mind are not so great as that undeveloped and sometimes undevelopable yet dimly-discernible greatness, to which those immediate products are but the infallible indices. In Shakspeare's tomb lies infinitely more than Shakspeare ever wrote. And if I magnify Shakspeare, it is not so much for what he did do as for what he did not do, or refrained from doing. For in this world of lies, Truth is forced to fly like a scared white doe in the woodlands; and only by cunning glimpses will she reveal herself, as in Shakspeare and other masters of the great Art of Telling the Truth,— even though it be covertly and by snatches.

But if this view of the all-popular Shakspeare be seldom taken by his readers, and if very few who extol him have ever read him deeply, or perhaps, only have seen him on the tricky stage (which alone made, and is still making him his mere mob renown)—if few men have time, or patience, or palate, for the spiritual truth as it is in that great genius;—it is then no matter of surprise, that in a contemporaneous age, Nathaniel Hawthorne is a man as yet almost utterly mistaken among men. Here and there, in some quiet armchair in the noisy town, or some deep nook among the noiseless mountains, he may be appreciated for something of what he is. But unlike Shakspeare, who was forced to the contrary course by circumstances, Hawthorne (either from simple disinclination, or else from inaptitude) refrains from all the popularizing noise and show of broad farce and blood-besmeared tragedy; content with the still, rich utterance of a great intellect in repose, and which sends few thoughts into circulation, except they be arterialized at his large warm lungs, and expanded in his honest heart.

Nor need you fix upon that blackness in him, if it suit you not. Nor, indeed, will all readers discern it; for it is, mostly, insinuated to those who may best understand it, and account for it; it is not obtruded upon every one alike.

Some may start to read of Shakspeare and Hawthorne on the same page. They may say, that if an illustration were needed, a lesser light might have sufficed to elucidate this Hawthorne, this small man of yesterday. But I am not willingly one of those who, as touching Shakspeare at least, exemplify the maxim of Rochefoucauld, that "we exalt the reputation of some, in order to depress that of others";—who, to teach all noble-souled aspirants that there is no hope for them, pronounce Shakspeare absolutely unapproachable. But Shakspeare has been approached. There are minds that have gone as far as Shakspeare into the universe. And hardly a mortal man, who, at some time or other, has not felt as great thoughts in him as any you will find in Hamlet. We must not inferentially malign mankind for the sake of any one man, whoever he may be. This is too cheap a purchase of contentment for conscious mediocrity to make. Besides, this absolute and unconditional adoration of Shakspeare has grown to be a part of our Anglo-Saxon superstitions. . . .

Now I do not say that Nathaniel of Salem is a greater than William of Avon, or as great. But the difference between the two men is by no means immeasurable. Not a very great deal more, and Nathaniel were verily William.

This, too, I mean, that if Shakspeare has not been equalled, give the world time, and he is sure to be surpassed, in one hemisphere or the other. Nor will it at all do to say, that the world is getting grey and grizzled now, and has lost that fresh charm which she wore of old, and by virtue of which the great poets of past times made themselves what we esteem them to be. Not so. The world is as young to-day as when it was created; and this Vermont morning dew is as wet to my feet, as Eden's dew to Adam's. . . .

Let America, then, prize and cherish her writers; yea, let her glorify them. They are not so many in number as to exhaust her good-will. And while she has good kith and kin of her own, to take to her bosom, let her not lavish her embraces upon the household of an alien. For believe it or not, England, after all, is in many things an alien to us. China has more bonds of real love for us than she. But even were there no strong literary individualities among us, as there are some dozens at least, nevertheless, let America first praise mediocrity even, in her own children, before she praises (for everywhere, merit demands acknowledgment from every one) the best excellence in the children of any other land. Let her own authors, I say, have the priority of appreciation. . . .

. . . .

And now, my countrymen, as an excellent author of your own flesh and blood,—an unimitating, and, perhaps, in his way, an inimitable man—whom better can I commend to you, in the first place, than Nathaniel Hawthorne. He is one of the new, and far better generation of your writers. The smell of your beeches and hemlocks is upon him; your own broad prairies are in his soul; and if you travel away inland into his deep and noble nature, you will hear the far roar of his Niagara. Give not over to future generations the glad duty of acknowledging him for what he is. Take that joy to yourself, in your own generation; and so shall he feel those grateful impulses on him, that may possibly prompt him to the full flower of some still greater achievement in your eyes. And by confessing him you thereby confess others; you brace the whole brotherhood. For genius, all over the world, stands hand in hand, and one shock of recognition runs the whole circle round.

In treating of Hawthorne, or rather of Hawthorne in his writings (for I never saw the man; and in the chances of a quiet plantation life, remote from his haunts, perhaps never shall); in treating of his works, I say, I have thus far omitted all mention of his "Twice Told Tales," and "Scarlet Letter." Both are excellent, but full of such manifold, strange, and diffusive beauties, that time would all but fail me to point the half of them out. But there are things in those two books, which, had they been written in England a century ago, Nathaniel Hawthorne had utterly displaced many of the bright names we now revere on authority. But I am content to leave Hawthorne to himself, and to the infallible finding of posterity; and however great may be the praise I have bestowed upon him, I feel that in so doing I have more served and honored myself, than him. For, at bottom, great excellence is praise enough to itself; but the feeling of a sincere and appreciative love and admiration towards it, this is relieved by utterance; and warm, honest praise, ever leaves a pleasant flavor in the mouth; and it is an honorable thing to confess to what is honorable in others.

But I cannot leave my subject yet. No man can ever read a fine author, and relish him to his very bones while he reads, without subsequently fancying to himself some ideal image of the man and his mind. And if you rightly look for it, you will almost always find that the author himself has somewhere furnished you with his own picture. For poets (whether in prose or verse), being painters of nature, are like their brethren of the pencil, the true portrait-painters, who, in the multitude of likenesses to be sketched, do not invariably omit their own; and in all high instances, they paint them without any vanity, though at times with a lurking something, that would take several pages to properly define.

I submit it, then, to those best acquainted with the man personally, whether the following is not Nathaniel Hawthorne;—and to himself, whether something involved in it does not express the temper of his mind,—that lasting temper of all true, candid men—a seeker, not a finder yet:—

"A man now entered, in neglected attire, with the aspect of a thinker, but somewhat too rough-hewn and brawny for a scholar. His face was full of sturdy vigor, with some finer and keener attribute beneath; though harsh at first, it was tempered with the glow of a large, warm heart, which had force enough to heat his powerful intellect through and through. He advanced to the Intelligencer, and looked at him with a glance of such stern sincerity, that perhaps few secrets were beyond its scope.

"'I seek for Truth.' said he."

* * *

Twenty-four hours have elapsed since writing the foregoing. I have just returned from the hay-mow, charged more and more with love and admiration of Hawthorne. For I have just been gleaning through the Mosses, picking up many things here and there that had previously escaped me. And I found that but to glean after this man, is better than to be in at the harvest of others. To be frank (though, perhaps, rather foolish) notwithstanding what I wrote yesterday of these Mosses, I had not then culled them all; but had, nevertheless, been sufficiently sensible of the subtle essence in them, as to write as I did. To what infinite height of loving wonder and admiration I may yet be borne, when by repeatedly banqueting on these Mosses I shall have thoroughly incorporated their whole stuff into my being,—that, I cannot tell. But already I feel that this Hawthorne has dropped germinous seeds into my soul. He expands and deepens down, the more I contemplate him; and further and further, shoots his strong New England roots in the hot soil of my Southern soul.

By careful reference to the "Table of Contents," I now find that I have gone through all the sketches; but that when I yesterday wrote, I had not at all read two particular pieces, to which I now desire to call special attention,—"A Select Party," and "Young Goodman Brown." Here, be it said to all those whom this poor fugitive scrawl of mine may tempt to the perusal of the "Mosses," that they must on no account suffer themselves to be trifled with, disappointed, or deceived by the triviality of many of the titles to these sketches. For in more than one instance, the title utterly belies the piece. It is as if rustic demijohns containing the very best and costliest of Falernian and Tokay, were labelled "Cider," "Perry," and "Elder-berry wine." The truth seems to be, that like many other geniuses, this Man of Mosses takes great delight in hoodwinking the world,—at least, with respect to himself. Personally, I doubt not that he rather prefers to be generally esteemed but a so-so sort of author; being willing to reserve the thorough and acute appreciation of what he is, to that party most qualified to judge—that is, to himself. Besides, at the bottom of their natures, men like Hawthorne, in many things, deem the plaudits of the public such strong presumptive evidence of mediocrity in the object of them, that it would in some degree render them doubtful of their own powers, did they hear much and vociferous braying concerning them in the public pastures. True, I have been braying myself (if you please to be witty enough to have it so), but then I claim to be the first that has so brayed in this particular matter; and therefore, while pleading guilty to the charge, still claim all the merit due to originality.

But with whatever motive, playful or profound, Nathaniel Hawthorne has chosen to entitle his pieces in the manner he has, it is certain that some of them are directly calculated to deceive—egregiously deceive, the superficial skimmer of pages. To be downright and candid once more, let me cheerfully say, that two of these titles did dolefully dupe no less an eagle-eyed reader than myself; and that, too, after I had been impressed with a sense of the great depth and breadth of this American man. "Who in the name of thunder" (as the country-people say in this neighborhood), "who in the name of thunder, would anticipate any marvel in a piece entitled 'Young Goodman Brown'?" You would of course suppose that it was a simple little tale, intended as a supplement to "Goody Two Shoes." Whereas, it is deep as Dante; nor can you finish it, without addressing the author in his own words—"It is yours to penetrate, in every bosom, the deep mystery of sin." And with Young Goodman, too, in allegorical pursuit of his Puritan wife, you cry out in your anguish:

"'Faith!' shouted Goodman Brown, in a voice of agony and desperation; and the echoes of the forest mocked him, crying, —'Faith! Faith!' as if bewildered wretches were seeking her all through the wilderness."

Now this same piece, entitled "Young Goodman Brown," is one of the two that I had not all read yesterday; and I allude to it now, because it is, in itself, such a strong positive illustration of that blackness in Hawthorne, which I had assumed from the mere occasional shadows of it, as revealed in several of the other sketches. But had I previously perused "Young Goodman Brown," I should have been at no pains to draw the conclusion, which I came to at a time when I was ignorant that the book contained one such direct and unqualified manifestation of it.

The other piece of the two referred to, is entitled "A Select Party," which, in my first simplicity upon originally taking hold of the book, I fancied must treat of some pumpkin-pie party in old Salem, or some chowder-party on Cape Cod. Whereas, by all the gods of Peedee, it is the sweetest and sublimest thing that has been written since Spenser wrote. Nay, there is nothing in Spenser that surpasses it, perhaps nothing that equals it. And the test is this: read any canto in "The Faery Queen," and then read "A Select Party" and decide which pleases you the most,—that is, if you are qualified to judge. Do not be frightened at this; for when Spenser was alive, he was thought of very much as Hawthorne is now,—was generally accounted just such a "gentle" harmless man. It may be, that to common eyes, the sublimity of Hawthorne seems lost in his sweetness,—as perhaps in that same "Select Party" of his; for whom he has built so august a dome of sunset clouds, and served them on richer plate than Belshazzar's when he banqueted his lords in Babylon.

But my chief business now, is to point out a particular page in this piece, having reference to an honored guest, who under the name of "The Master Genius," but in the guise "of a young man of poor attire, with no insignia of rank or acknowledged eminence," is introduced to the man of Fancy, who is the giver of the feast. Now, the page having reference to this "Master Genius," so happily expresses much of what I yesterday wrote, touching the coming of the literary Shiloh of America, that I cannot but be charmed by the coincidence; especially, when it shows such a parity of ideas, at least in this one point, between a man like Hawthorne and a man like me.

And here, let me throw out another conceit of mine touching this American Shiloh, or "Master Genius," as Hawthorne calls him. May it not be, that this commanding mind has not been, is not, and never will be, individually developed in any one man? And would it, indeed, appear so unreasonable to suppose, that this great fulness and overflowing may be, or may be destined to be, shared by a plurality of men of genius? Surely, to take the very greatest example on record, Shakspeare cannot be regarded as in himself the concretion of all the genius of his time; nor as so immeasurably beyond Marlow, Webster, Ford, Beaumont, Jonson, that those great men can be said to share none of his power? For one, I conceive that there were dramatists in Elizabeth's day, between whom and Shakspeare the distance was by no means great. Let any one, hitherto little acquainted with those neglected old authors, for the first time read them thoroughly, or even read Charles Lamb's Specimens of them, and he will be amazed at the wondrous ability of those Anaks of men, and shocked at this renewed example of the fact, that Fortune has more to do with fame than merit,—though, without merit, lasting fame there can be none.

Nevertheless, it would argue too ill of my country were this maxim to hold good concerning Nathaniel Hawthorne, a man, who already, in some few minds, has shed "such a light, as never illuminates the earth save when a great heart burns as the household fire of a grand intellect."

The words are his,—in the "Select Party"; and they are a magnificent setting to a coincident sentiment of my own, but ramblingly expressed yesterday, in reference to himself. Gainsay it who will, as I now write, I am Posterity speaking by proxy—and after times will make it more than good, when I declare, that the American, who up to the present day has evinced, in literature, the largest brain with the largest heart, that man is Nathaniel Hawthorne. Moreover, that whatever Nathaniel Hawthorne may hereafter write, "The Mosses from an Old Manse" will be ultimately accounted his masterpiece. For there is a sure, though a secret sign in some works which proves the culmination of the powers (only the developable ones, however) that produced them. But I am by no means desirous of the glory of a prophet. I pray Heaven that Hawthorne may *yet* prove me an impostor in this prediction. Especially, as I somehow cling to the strange fancy, that, in all men, hiddenly reside certain wondrous, occult properties—as in some plants and minerals—which by some happy but very rare accident (as bronze was discovered by the melting of the iron and brass at the burning of Corinth) may chance to be called forth here on earth; not entirely waiting for their better discovery in the more congenial, blessed atmosphere of heaven.

Once more—for it is hard to be finite upon an infinite subject, and all subjects are infinite. By some people this entire scrawl of mine may be esteemed altogether unnecessary, inasmuch "as years ago" (they may say) "we found out the rich and rare stuff in this Hawthorne, whom you now parade forth, as if only *yourself* were the discoverer of this Portuguese diamond in our literature." But even granting all this—and adding to it, the assumption that the books of Hawthorne have sold by the five thousand,—what does that signify? They should be sold by the hundred thousand; and read by the million; and admired by every one who is capable of admiration.

A physician, agriculturalist, and political leader, GEORGE BAILEY LORING [1817–91] was a surgeon at the Marine Hospital in Chelsea, Massachusetts, when Theodore Parker asked him to review *The Scarlet Letter* for the *Massachusetts Quarterly Review*. The essay is strikingly modern in its assessment of the redeeming power of sin; it probably was partially responsible for provoking A. C. Coxe's vitriolic attack on *The Scarlet Letter*. In 1880 Loring's essay "Hawthorne" was published in *Papyrus Leaves*, edited by William F. Gill.

[Review of] The Scarlet Letter

[GEORGE BAILEY LORING]

No author of our own country, and scarcely any author of our times, manages to keep himself clothed in such a cloak of mystery as Nathaniel Hawthorne. From the time when his "Twice-Told Tales" went, in their first telling, floating through the periodicals of the day, up to the appearance of "The Scarlet Letter," he has stood on the confines of society, as we see some sombre figure, in the dim light of the stage scenery, peering through that narrow space, when a slouched hat and a muffling cloak do not meet, upon the tragic events which are made conspicuous by the glare of the footlights. From nowhere in particular, from an old manse, and from the drowsy dilapidation of an old custom-house, he has spoken such oracular words, such searching thoughts, as sounded of old from the mystic God whose face was never seen even by the most worthy. It seems useless now to speak of his humor, subtile and delicate as Charles Lamb's; of his pathos, deep as Richter's; of his penetration into the human heart, clearer than that of Goldsmith or Crabbe; of his apt and telling words, which Pope might have envied; of his description, graphic as Scott's or Dickens's; of the delicious lanes he opens, on either hand, and leaves you alone to explore, masking his work with the fine *"faciebat"* which removes all limit from all high art, and gives every man scope to advance and develop. He seems never to trouble himself, either in writing or living, with the surroundings of life. He is no philosopher for the poor or the rich, for the ignorant or the learned, for the righteous or the wicked, for any special rank or condition in life, but for human nature as given by God into the hands of man. He calls us to be indignant witnesses of no particular social, religious, or political enormity. He asks no admiration for this or that individual or associated virtue. The face of society, with its manifold features, never comes before you, as you study the extraordinary experience of his men and women, except as a necessary setting for the picture. They might shine at tournaments, or grovel in cellars, or love, or fight, or meet with high adventure, or live the deepest and quietest life in unknown corners of the earth,—their actual all vanishes before the strange and shifting picture he gives of the motive heart of man. In no work of his is this characteristic more strikingly visible than in "The Scarlet Letter;" and in no work has he presented so clear and perfect an image of himself, as a speculative philosopher, an ethical thinker, a living man. Perhaps he verges strongly upon the supernatural, in the minds of those who would recognize nothing but the corporeal existence of human life. But man's nature is, by birth, *super*natural; and the deep mystery which lies beneath all his actions is far beyond the reach of any mystical vision that ever lent its airy shape to the creations of the most intense dreamer.

. . . .

. . . It would be hard to conceive of a greater outrage upon the freezing and self-denying doctrines of that day, than the sin for which Hester Prynne was damned by society, and for which Arthur Dimmesdale damned himself. For centuries, the devoted and superstitious Catholic had made it a part of his creed to cast disgrace upon the passions; and the cold and rigid Puritan, with less fervor, and consequently with less beauty, had driven them out of his paradise, as the parents of all sin. . . . The state of society which this grizzly form of humanity created, probably served as little to purify men as any court of voluptuousness; and, while we recognize with compressed lip that heroism which braved seas and unknown shores, for opinion's sake, we remember, with a warm glow, the elegances and intrepid courage and tropical luxuriance of the cavaliers whom they left behind them. Asceticism and voluptuarism on either hand, neither fruitful of the finer and truer virtues, were all that men had arrived at in the great work of sensuous life.

It was the former which fixed the scarlet letter to the breast of Hester Prynne, and which drove Arthur Dimmesdale into a life of cowardly and selfish meanness, that added tenfold disgrace and ignominy to his original crime. . . . It was as heir of these virtues, and impressed with this education, that Arthur Dimmesdale, a clergyman, believing in and applying all the moral remedies of the times, found himself a criminal. We learn nothing of his experience during the seven long years in which his guilt was secretly gnawing at his breast, unless it be the experience of pain and remorse. He speaks no word of wisdom. He lurks and skulks behind the protection of his profession and his social position, neither growing wiser nor stronger, but, day after day, paler and paler, more and more abject. We do not find that, out of his sin, came any revelation of virtue. No doubt exists of his repentance,—of that repentance which is made up of sorrow for sin, and which grows out of fear of consequences; but we learn nowhere that his enlightened conscience, rising above the dogmas and catechistic creeds of the day, by dint of his own deep and solemn spiritual experiences, taught him what obligations had gathered around him, children of his crime, which he was bound to acknowledge before men, as they stood revealed to God. Why had his religious wisdom brought him no more heroism? He loved Hester Prynne—he had bound himself to her by an indissoluble bond, and yet he had neither moral courage nor moral honesty, with all his impressive piety, to come forth and assert their sins and their mutual obligations. He was, evidently, a man of powerful nature. His delicate sensibility, his fervor, his influence upon those about him, and, above all, his sin, committed when the tides of his heart rushed in and swept away all the bulrush barriers he had heaped up against them, through years of studious self-discipline,—show what a spirit, what forces, he had. Against none of these forces had he sinned. And yet he was halting, and wavering, and becoming more and more perplexed and worn down with woe, because he had violated the dignity of his position, and had broken a law which his education had made more prominent than any law in his own soul. In this way, he presented the twofold nature which belongs to us as members of society;—a nature born from ourselves and our associations, and comprehending all the diversity and all the harmony of our individual and social duties. Violation of either destroys our fitness for both. And when we remember that, in this development, no truth comes except from harmony, no beauty except from a fit conjunction of the individual with society, and of society with the individual, can we wonder that the great elements of Arthur Dimmesdale's character should have been overbalanced by a detestable crowd of mean and grovelling qualities, warmed into life by the hot antagonism he felt radiating upon himself and all his fellow-men—from the society in which he moved, and from which he received his engrafted moral nature? He sinned in the arms of society, and fell almost beyond redemption; his companion in guilt became an outcast, and a flood of heroic qualities gathered around her. Was this the work of social influences?

Besides all this, we see in him the powerlessness of belief, alone, to furnish true justification through repentance. . . . The spirit of the young clergyman struggled for this right, which his soul still recognized. He was a dogmatist by education alone, not by nature. His crime, rebuked by his theories, and by those religious rigors which destroyed all his cognizance of his soul's elements and rights, made him selfish and deceitful, while his heart rebelled against such a craven course, and demanded, with an importunity at last fatal to him, that he should become justified before man as he was before God, and longed to be before his own conscience, by the sincerity of his position. After imbibing unwonted strength from an interview with her whom worldly scorn had rendered resolute, he made an open avowal, which disarmed this wary enemy, and gave a calm and peaceful death to himself. In the same way might he have earned a peaceful life—and in no other. Not a human eye could look on him, and recognize the sinner. His secret was well locked and guarded. But all this safety was the poorest shame to him, whose nobility of nature demanded assertion.

In this matter of crime, as soon as he became involved, he appeared before himself no longer a clergyman, but a man—a human being. He answered society in the cowardly way we have seen. He answered himself in that way which every soul adopts, where crime does not penetrate. The physical facts of crime alone, with which society has to do, in reality constitute sin. Crimes are committed under protest of the soul, more or less decided, as the weary soul itself has been more or less besieged and broken. The war in the individual begins, and the result of the fierce struggle is the victory of the sensual over the spiritual, when the criminal act is committed. If there is no such war, there is no crime; let the deed be what it may, and be denominated what it may, by society. The soul never assents to sin, and weeps with the angels when the form in which it dwells violates the sacred obligations it imposes upon it. When this human form, with its passions and tendencies, commits the violation, and, at the same time, abuses society, it is answerable to this latter tribunal, where it receives its judgment; while the soul flees to her God, dismayed and crushed by the conflict, but not deprived of her divine inheritance. . . . The solemn gloom which shuts down over a mighty nature, during the struggle, which it recognizes with vivid sense, between its demon and its divinity, is like that fearful night in which no star appears to relieve the murky darkness. And yet, from such a night as this, and from no other, the grandeur of virtue has risen to beautify and warm and bless the broad universe of human hearts, and to make the whole spiritual creation blossom like the rose. . . .

Thus it stands with the individual and his soul. With himself and society come up other obligations, other influences, other laws. The tribunal before which he stands as a social being cannot be disregarded with impunity. . . .

We doubt if there is a stronger element in our natures than that which forbids our resisting with impunity surrounding social institutions. However much we may gain in the attempt, it is always attended with some loss. The reverence which enhanced so beautifully the purity and innocence of childhood, often receives its death-blow from that very wisdom out of which comes our mature virtue. . . . The institutions in which we were born controlled in a great degree the mental condition of our parents, as surrounding nature did their physical, and we owe to these two classes of internal and external operations the characters we inherit. An attack, therefore, upon these institutions, affects us to a certain degree as if we were warring against ourselves. . . .

This law of our nature, which applies to the well-directed and honest efforts of good progressive intentions, applies also to misguided and sinful actions. The stormy life of the erring mother affords no rest for the healthy development of her embryonic child. It amounts to but little for her to say, with Hester Prynne, "what we did had a consecration of its own," unless that consecration produces a heavenly calm, as if all nature joined in harmony. Pearl, that wild and fiery little elf, born of love, was also born of conflict; and had the accountability of its parents extended no farther than the confines of this world, the prospective debt due this offspring involved fearful responsibilities. How vividly this little child typified all their startled instincts, their convulsive efforts in life and thought, their isolation, and their self-inflicted contest with and distrust of all mankind. Arthur Dimmesdale, shrinking from intimate contact and intercourse with his child, shrunk from a visible and tangible representation of the actual life which his guilty love had created for himself and Hester Prynne;—love, guilty, because, secured as it may have been to them, it drove them violently from the moral centre around which they revolved.

We have seen that this was most especially the case with the man who was bound and labelled the puritan clergyman; that he had raised a storm in his own heavens which he could not quell, and had cast the whirlwind over the life of his own child. How was it with Hester Prynne?

On this beautiful and luxuriant woman, we see the effect of open conviction of sin, and the continued galling punishment. The heroic traits awakened in her character by her position were the great self-sustaining properties of woman, which, in tribulation and perplexity, elevate her so far above man. The sullen defiance in her, was imparted to her by society. Without, she met only ignominy, scorn, banishment, a shameful brand. Within, the deep and sacred love for which she was suffering martyrdom,—for her crime was thus sanctified in her own apprehension,—was turned into a store of perplexity, distrust, and madness, which darkened all her heavens. Little Pearl was a token more scarlet than the scarlet letter of her guilt; for the child, with a birth presided over by the most intense conflict of love and fear in the mother's heart, nourished at a breast swelling with anguish, and surrounded with burning marks of its mother's shame in its daily life, developed day by day into a void little demon perched upon the most sacred horn of the mother's altar. Even this child, whose young, plastic nature caught the impress which surrounding circumstances most naturally gave, bewildered and maddened her. The pledge of love which God had given her, seemed perverted into an emblem of hate. And yet how patiently and courageously she labored on, bearing her burthen the more firmly, because, in its infliction, she recognized no higher hand than that of civil authority! In her earnest appeal to be allowed to retain her child, she swept away all external influences, and seems to have inspired the young clergyman, even now fainting with his own sense of meaner guilt, to speak words of truth, which in those days must have seemed born of heaven.

. . . .

Her social ignominy forced her back upon the true basis of her life. She alone, of all the world, knew the length and breadth of her own secret. Her lawful husband no more pretended to hold a claim, which may always have been a pretence; the father of her child, her own relation to both, and the tragic life which was going on beneath that surface which all men saw, were known to her alone. How poor and miserable must have seemed the punishment which society had inflicted! The scarlet letter was a poor type of the awful truth which she carried within her heart. Without deceit before the world, she stands forth the most heroic person in all that drama. When, from the platform of shame, she bade farewell to that world, she retired to a holier, and sought for such peace as a soul cast out by men may always find. This was her right. No lie hung over her head. Society had heard her story, and had done its worst. And while Arthur Dimmesdale, cherished in the arms of that society which he had outraged, glossing his life with a false coloring which made it beautiful to all beholders, was dying of an inward anguish, Hester stood upon her true ground, denied by this world, and learning that true wisdom which comes through honesty and self-justification. In casting her out, the world had torn from her all the support of its dogmatic teachings, with which it sustains its disciples in their inevitable sufferings, and had compelled her to rely upon that great religious truth which flows instinctively around a life of agony, with its daring freedom. How far behind her in moral and religious excellence was the accredited religious teacher, who was her companion in guilt! . . .

It is no pleasant matter to contemplate what is called the guilt of this woman; but it may be instructive, nevertheless. We naturally shrink from any apparent violation of virtue and chastity, and are very ready to forget, in our eager condemnation, how much that is beautiful and holy may be involved in it. . . .

We would not condemn the vigilance and sensitiveness of society, were it really a tribute paid to the true sanctity of virtue. . . . It may be necessary, perhaps, that the safety of associated man demands all the compromises which the superficiality of social law creates, but the sorrow may be none the less acute because the evil is necessary. We see in the lives of Arthur Dimmesdale and Hester Prynne, that the severity of puritanic law and morals could not keep them from violation; and we see, too, that this very severity drove them both into a state of moral insanity. . . . We doubt not that, to many minds, this severity constitutes the saving virtue of the book. But it is always with a fearful sacrifice of all the gentler feelings of the breast, of all the most comprehensive humanity, of all the most delicate affections and appreciations, that we thus rudely shut out the wanderer from us; especially when the path of error leads through the land whence come our warmest and tenderest influences. We gain nothing by this hardness, except a capability to sin without remorse. The elements of character upon which vice and virtue hang are so nearly allied, that the rude attempts to destroy the one may result in a fatal wounding of the other; the harvest separates the tares from the wheat with the only safety. . . .

. . . .

To those who would gladly learn the confidence, and power, and patient endurance, and depth of hallowed fervor, which love can create in the human heart, we would present the life of this woman, in her long hours of suffering and loneliness, made sweeter than all the world beside, by the cause in which she suffered. We dare not call that a wicked perversity, which brought its possessor into that state of strong and fiery resolution and elevation, which enabled her to raise her lover from his craven sense of guilt, into a solemn devotion to his better nature. She guided him rightly, by her clear vision of what was in accordance with the holiest promptings of her true heart. Aided by this, she learned what all his theology had never taught him—the power of love to sustain and guide and teach the soul. This bore her through her trial; and this, at that glowing hour when both rose above the weight which bowed them down, tore the scarlet letter from her breast, and made her young and pure again.

. . . .

The wisdom and power which came to this woman from the scarlet letter, which society imprinted on her breast, may come to every one who will honestly affix this token to his own. As who of us may not? It is only an open confession of our weakness which brings us strength. . . . But that cowardice which prompts to the denial of error to one's own soul; which refuses to receive the impression that all experience brings, with honesty and intelligence, and, intrenched behind good intentions, feels safe from attacks of sin, is the most hopeless of all mortal defects. There is a false delicacy which avoids the contemplation of evil, and which severe experience may destroy. There is a sweeping belief that vice stands at one pole and virtue at the other, which the deep trials of life may eradicate. There is a want of sympathy for the erring, and an ignorant closing of the heart against those whose entrance would enlarge and beautify and warm our souls, which the knowledge of our own temptations may remove. But no experience, no knowledge, no power, short of miracle, will bring the needed relief to that spirit which will not confess its guilt either to itself, or to its God. The heroic power which comes through avowal, is like the soft and vernal earth, giving life to a sweet and flowery growth of virtues. It gives self-knowledge, and the deepest and most startling wisdom, by which to test our fellow-men. But is it not most sad and most instructive that Love, the great parent of all power and virtue and wisdom and faith, the guardian of the tree of knowledge of good and evil, the effulgence of all that is rich and generous and luxuriant in nature, should rise up in society to be typified by the strange features of "The Scarlet Letter?"

ARTHUR CLEVELAND COXE [1818–96] became an Episcopal bishop and was noted for his conservative theology. In his rambling and lengthy review of *The Scarlet Letter,* Coxe admits that Hawthorne is one of the best of the "Bay School"—essentially transcendentalists of whom Coxe disapproved—and he finds considerable merit in "The Celestial Railroad" as "one of the cleverest, best sustained, and most ingenious specimens of quiet satire to be found in our language." Coxe even defends Hawthorne against some of the criticisms in the review of *Mosses* in *Blackwood's Magazine* (see pp. 20–21). For the most part, however, Coxe's condemnation of *The Scarlet Letter* is savage. His vehemence is matched only by the outcries of Salemites against Hawthorne's comments on Salem and on his fellow workers at the Custom House (see *Salem Register,* 21 March 1850).

The Writings of Hawthorne

[ARTHUR CLEVELAND COXE]

. . . .

... As yet our literature, however humble, is undefiled, and as such is a just cause for national pride, nor, much as we long to see it elevated in style, would we thank the Boccaccio who should give it the classic stamp, at the expense of its purity. Of course we cannot expect to see it realize that splendid ideal which a thoughtful Churchman would sketch for it, as equally chaste in morals, lofty in sentiment, uncorrupt in diction, and in all points conformable to

Church Review, Vol. 3 (January 1851) 489–511.

truth; but surely we may demand that it shall keep itself from becoming an offense to faith, and a scandal to virtue. Not that we expect the literary pimp to cease from his disgusting trade, but that we hope to keep writers of that class out of the pale of Letters, and to effect the forcible expulsion of any one of a higher class, who, gaining upon our confidence by dealing at first in a sterling article, afterwards debases his credit, by issuing with the same stamp a vile, but marketable, alloy. In a word, we protest against any toleration to a popular and gifted writer, when he perpetrates bad morals. Let this brokerage of lust be put down at the very beginning. Already, among the million, we have imitations enough of George Sand and Eugene Sue; and if as yet there be no reputable name, involved in the manufacture of a Brothel Library, we congratulate the country that we are yet in time to save such a reputation as that of Hawthorne. . . .

The success which seems to have attended this bold advance of Hawthorne, and the encouragement which has been dealt out by some professed critics,* to its worst symptoms of malice prepense, may very naturally lead, if unbalanced by a moderate dissent, to his further compromise of his literary character. We are glad, therefore, that "The Scarlet Letter" is, after all, little more than an experiment, and need not be regarded as a step necessarily fatal. It is an attempt to rise from the composition of petty tales, to the historical novel; and we use the expression *an attempt*, with no disparaging significance, for it is confessedly a trial of strength only just beyond some former efforts, and was designed as part of a series. It may properly be called a novel, because it has all the ground-work, and might have been very easily elaborated into the details, usually included in the term; and we call it *historical*, because its scene-painting is in a great degree true to a period of our Colonial history, which ought to be more fully delineated. We wish Mr. Hawthorne would devote the powers which he only partly discloses in this book, to a large and truthful portraiture of that period, with the patriotic purpose of making us better acquainted with the stern old worthies, and all the *dramatis personæ* of those times, with their yet surviving habits, recollections, and yearnings, derived from maternal England. . . .

. . . We like him all the better for his tenderness of the less exceptionable features of the Puritan character; but we are hardly sure that we like his flings at their failings. If it should provoke a smile to find us sensitive in this matter, our consistency may be very

*See a late article in the Massachusetts Quarterly.

briefly demonstrated. True, we have our own fun with the follies of the Puritans; it is our inseparable privilege as Churchmen, thus to compensate ourselves for many a scar which their frolics have left on our comeliness. But when a degenerate Puritan, whose Socinian conscience is but the skimmed-milk of their creamy fanaticism, allows such a conscience to curdle within him, in dyspeptic acidulation, and then belches forth derision at the sour piety of his forefathers—we snuff at him, with an honest scorn, knowing very well that he likes the Puritans for their worst enormities, and hates them only for their redeeming merits.

. . . Now without asserting that it is so, we are not quite so sure, as we would like to be, that our author is not venting something of this spirit against the Puritans, in his rich delineation of "godly Master Dimmesdale," and the sorely abused confidence of his flock. There is a provoking concealment of the author's motive, from the beginning to the end of the story; we wonder what he would be at; whether he is making fun of all religion, or only giving a fair hint of the essential sensualism of enthusiasm. But, in short, we are astonished at the kind of incident which he has selected for romance. It may be such incidents were too common, to be wholly out of the question, in a history of the times, but it seems to us that good taste might be pardoned for not giving them prominence in fiction. . . . We may acknowledge, with reluctance, the historical fidelity of the picture, which retailers of fact and fiction thus concur in framing, but we cannot but wonder that a novelist should select, of all features of the period, that which reflects most discredit upon the cradle of his country, and which is in itself so revolting, and so incapable of receiving decoration from narrative genius.

And this brings inquiry to its point. Why has our author selected such a theme? Why, amid all the suggestive incidents of life in a wilderness; of a retreat from civilization to which, in every individual case, a thousand circumstances must have concurred to reconcile human nature with estrangement from home and country; or amid the historical connections of our history with Jesuit adventure, savage invasion, regicide outlawry, and French aggression, should the taste of Mr. Hawthorne have preferred as the proper material for romance, the nauseous amour of a Puritan pastor, with a frail creature of his charge, whose mind is represented as far more debauched than her body? Is it, in short, because a running undertide of filth has become as requisite to a romance, as death in the fifth act to a tragedy? Is the French era actually begun in our literature? And is the flesh, as well as the world and the devil, to be henceforth dished up in fashionable novels, and discussed at parties, by spinsters and their beaux, with as unconcealed a relish as they give to the vanilla in their ice cream? We would be slow to believe it, and we hope our author would not willingly have it so, yet we honestly believe that "the Scarlet Letter" has already done not a little to degrade our literature, and to encourage social licentiousness: it has started other pens on like enterprises, and has loosed the restraint of many tongues, that have made it an apology for "the evil communications which corrupt good manners." We are painfully tempted to believe that it is a book made for the market, and that the market has made it merchantable, as they do game, by letting everybody understand that the commodity is in high condition, and smells strongly of incipient putrefaction.

We shall entirely mislead our reader if we give him to suppose that "the Scarlet Letter" is coarse in its details, or indecent in its phraseology. This very article of our own, is far less suited to ears polite, than any page of the romance before us; and the reason is, we call things by their right names, while the romance never hints the shocking words that belong to its things, but, like Mephistophiles, insinuates that the arch-fiend himself is a very tolerable sort of person, if nobody would call him Mr. Devil. We have heard of persons who could not bear the reading of some Old Testament Lessons in the service of the Church: such persons would be delighted with our author's story; and damsels who shrink at the reading of the Decalogue, would probably luxuriate in bathing their imagination in the crystal of its delicate sensuality. The language of our author, like patent blacking, "would not soil the whitest linen," and yet the composition itself, would suffice, if well laid on, to Ethiopize the snowiest conscience that ever sat like a swan upon that mirror of heaven, a Christian maiden's imagination. We are not sure we speak quite strong enough, when we say, that we would much rather listen to the coarsest scene of Goldsmith's "Vicar," read aloud by a sister or daughter, than to hear from such lips, the perfectly chaste language of a scene in "the Scarlet Letter," in which a married wife and her reverend paramour, with their unfortunate offspring, are introduced as the actors, and in which the whole tendency of the conversation is to suggest a sympathy for their sin, and an anxiety that they may be able to accomplish a successful escape beyond the seas, to some country where their shameful commerce may be perpetuated. Now, in Goldsmith's story there are very coarse words, but we do not remember anything that saps the foundations of the moral sense, or that goes to create unavoidable sympathy with unrepenting sorrow, and deliberate, premeditated sin. The "Vicar of Wakefield" is sometimes coarsely virtuous, but "the Scarlet Letter" is delicately immoral.

. . . .

... But in Hawthorne's tale, the lady's frailty is philosophized into a natural and necessary result of the Scriptural law of marriage, which, by holding her irrevocably to her vows, as plighted to a dried up old book-worm, in her silly girlhood, is viewed as making her heart an easy victim to the adulterer. The sin of her seducer too, seems to be considered as lying not so much in the deed itself, as in his long concealment of it, and, in fact, the whole moral of the tale is given in the words—"Be true—be true," as if sincerity in sin were virtue, and as if "Be clean—be clean," were not the more fitting conclusion. "The untrue man" is, in short, the hang-dog of the narrative, and the unclean one is made a very interesting sort of a person, and as the two qualities are united in the hero, their composition creates the interest of his character. Shelley himself never imagined a more dissolute conversation than that in which the polluted minister comforts himself with the thought, that the revenge of the injured husband is worse than his own sin in instigating it. "Thou and I never did so, Hester"—he suggests: and she responds—"never, never! What we did had *a consecration of its own*, we felt it so—we said so to each other!" This is a little too much—it carries the Bay-theory a little too far for our stomach! "Hush, Hester!" is the sickish rejoinder; and fie, Mr. Hawthorne! is the weakest token of our disgust that we can utter. The poor bemired hero and heroine of the story should not have been seen wallowing in their filth, at such a rate as this.

We suppose this sort of sentiment must be charged to the doctrines enforced at "Brook-farm," although "Brook-farm" itself could never have been Mr. Hawthorne's home, had not other influences prepared him for such a Bedlam. At all events, this is no mere slip of the pen; it is the essential morality of the work. If types, and letters, and words can convey an author's idea, he has given us the key to the whole, in a very plain intimation that the Gospel has not set the relations of man and woman where they should be, and that a new Gospel is needed to supersede the seventh commandment, and the bond of Matrimony. Here it is, in full: our readers shall see what the world may expect from Hawthorne, if he is not stopped short, in such brothelry. Look at this conclusion:—

"*Women*—in the continually recurring trials of wounded,

wasted, wronged, misplaced, or erring and sinful passion, or with the dreary burden of a heart unyielded, because unvalued and unsought—came to Hester's cottage, demanding why they were so wretched, and what the remedy! Hester comforted and counseled them as best she might. She assured them too *of her firm belief, that, at some brighter period, when the world should have grown ripe for it, in Heaven's own time, a new truth would be revealed, in order to establish the whole relation between man and woman on a surer ground of mutual happiness.*"

This is intelligible English; but are Americans content that such should be the English of their literature? This is the question on which we have endeavored to deliver our own earnest convictions, and on which we hope to unite the suffrages of all virtuous persons, in sympathy with the abhorrence we so unhesitatingly express. To think of making such speculations the amusement of the daughters of America! The late Convention of females at Boston, to assert the "rights of woman," may show us that there are already some, who think the world is even now *ripe for it;* and safe as we may suppose our own fair relatives to be above such a low contagion, we must remember that to a woman, the very suggestion of a mode of life for her, as preferable to that which the Gospel has made the glorious sphere of her duties and her joys, is an insult and a degradation, to which no one that loves her would allow her to be exposed.

We assure Mr. Hawthorne, in conclusion, that nothing less than an earnest wish that his future career may redeem this misstep, and prove a blessing to his country, has tempted us to enter upon a criticism so little suited to our tastes, as that of his late production. . . . We would see him, too, rising to a place among those immortal authors who have "clothed the lessons of religion in the burning words of genius;" and let him be assured, that, however great his momentary success, there is no lasting reputation for such an one as he is, except as it is founded on real worth, and fidelity to the morals of the Gospel. . . .

HENRY T. TUCKERMAN [1813–71] published numerous books of criticism, essays and sketches, biographies, travel books, and poetry. The essay on Hawthorne is probably the first comprehensive survey of Hawthorne's works. The review is predicated on transcendental principles of criticism: his interest lies in "meditative" and not melodramatic fiction. In "meditative" fiction he finds an ineffability—"a secret, indescribable grace, a vital principle, a superhuman element imparting the distinctive and magnetic character to literature, art and society, which gives them individual life." The reader responds to this individuality, not by analysis but by "direct intellectual perception." The kind of fiction which appeals mysteriously has a universal quality and constitutes genius. Hawthorne himself found Tuckerman's evaluation extremely gratifying (see p. 264).

Nathaniel Hawthorne

HENRY T. TUCKERMAN

. . . .

... What the scientific use of lenses—the telescope and the microscope—does for us in relation to the external universe, the psychological writer achieves in regard to our own nature. He reveals its wonder and beauty, unfolds its complex laws and makes us suddenly aware of the mysteries within and around individual life. In the guise of attractive fiction and sometimes of the most airy sketches, Hawthorne thus deals with his reader. His appeal is to consciousness and he must, therefore, be met in a sympathetic relation; he shadows forth,—hints,—makes signs,—whispers,—muses aloud,—gives the keynote of melody—puts us on a track;—in a word, addresses us as nature does—that is unostentatiously, and with a significance not to be realized without reverent silence and gentle feeling—a sequestration from bustle and material care, and somewhat of the meditative insight and latent sensibility in which his themes are conceived and wrought out. Sometimes they are purely descriptive, bits of Flemish painting—so exact and arrayed in such mellow colors, that we unconsciously take them in as objects of sensitive rather than imaginative observation; the "Old Manse" and the "Custom House"—those quaint portals to his fairy-land, as peculiar and rich in contrast in their way, as Boccacio's sombre introduction to his gay stories—are memorable instances of this fidelity in the details of local and personal portraiture; and that chaste yet deep tone of colouring which secure an harmonious whole. Even in allegory, Hawthorne imparts this sympathetic unity to his conception; "Fire Worship," "The Celestial Railroad," "Monsieur du

Miroir," "Earth's Holocaust," and others in the same vein, while they emphatically indicate great moral truth, have none of the abstract and cold grace of allegorical writing; besides the ingenuity they exhibit, and the charm they have for the fancy, a human interest warms and gives them meaning to the heart. On the other hand, the imaginative grace which they chiefly display, lends itself quite as aptly to redeem and glorify homely fact in the plastic hands of the author. "Drowne's Wooden Image," "The Intelligence Office," and other tales derived from common-place material, are thus moulded into artistic beauty and suggestiveness. Hawthorne, therefore, is a prose-poet. He brings together scattered beauties, evokes truth from apparent confusion, and embodies the tragic or humorous element of a tradition or an event in lyric music—not, indeed, to be sung by the lips, but to live, like melodious echoes, in the memory. We are constantly struck with the felicity of his invention. What happy ideas are embodied in "A Virtuoso's Collection," and "The Artist of the Beautiful"—independent of the grace of their execution! There is a certain uniformity in Hawthorne's style and manner, but a remarkable versatility in his subjects; and each as distinctly carries with it the monotone of a special feeling or fancy, as one of Miss Baillie's plays:—and this is the perfection of psychological art. . . .

. . . .

. . . There is a peculiar zest about them which proves a vital origin; and this is the distinction of Hawthorne's tales. They almost invariably possess the reality of tone which perpetuates imaginative literature;—the same that endears to all time De Foe, Bunyan, Goldsmith, and the old dramatists. . . .

It may be regarded as a proof of absolute genius to create a mood; to inform, amuse, or even interest is only the test of superficial powers sagaciously directed; but to infuse a new state of feeling, to change the frame of mind and, as it were, alter the consciousness—this is the triumph of all art. . . . It may safely be asserted that by virtue of his individuality every author and artist of genius creates a peculiar mood, differing somewhat according to the character of the recipient, yet essentially the same. If we were obliged to designate that of Hawthorne in a single word, we should call it metaphysical, or perhaps soulful. He always takes us below the surface and beyond the material; his most inartificial stories are eminently suggestive; he makes us breathe the air of contemplation, and turns our eyes inward. It is as if we went forth, in a dream, into the stillness of an autumnal wood, or stood alone in a vast gallery of old pictures, or moved slowly, with muffled tread, over a wide plain, amid a gentle fall of snow, or mused on a ship's deck, at sea, by moonlight; the appeal is to the retrospective, the introspective to what is thoughtful and profoundly conscious in our nature and whereby it communes with the mysteries of life and the occult intimations of nature. And yet there is no painful extravagance, no transcendental vagaries in Hawthorne; his imagination is as human as his heart; if he touches the horizon of the infinite, it is with reverence; if he deals with the anomalies of sentiment, it is with intelligence and tenderness. His utterance too is singularly clear and simple; his style only rises above the colloquial in the sustained order of its flow; the terms are apt, natural and fitly chosen. Indeed, a careless reader is liable continually to lose sight of his meaning and beauty, from the entire absence of pretension in his style. It is requisite to bear in mind the universal truth, that all great and true things are remarkable for simplicity; the direct method is the pledge of sincerity, avoidance of the conventional, an instinct of richly-endowed minds; and the perfection of art never dazzles or overpowers, but gradually wins and warms us to an enduring and noble love. The style of Hawthorne is wholly inevasive; he resorts to no tricks of rhetoric or verbal ingenuity; language is to him a crystal medium through which to let us see the play of his humor, the glow of his sympathy, and the truth of his observation.

Although he seldom transcends the limited sphere in which he so efficiently concentrates his genius, the variety of tone, like different airs on the same instrument, gives him an imaginative scope rarely obtained in elaborate narrative. Thus he deals with the tragic element, wisely and with vivid originality, in such pieces as "Roger [Malvin's] Burial" and "Young Goodman Brown;" with the comic in "Mr. Higginbotham's Catastrophe," "A Select Party," and "Dr. Heidegger's Experiment," and with the purely fanciful in "David Swan," "The Vision of the Fountain," and "Fancy's Show Box." Nor is he less remarkable for sympathetic observation of nature than for profound interest in humanity; witness such limning as the sketches entitled "Buds and Bird Voices," and "Snow-Flakes"—genuine descriptive poems, though not cast in the mould of verse, as graphic, true and feeling as the happiest scenes of Bryant or Crabbe. With equal tact and tenderness he approaches the dry record of the past, imparting life to its cold details, and reality to its abstract forms.

The early history of New England has found no such genial and vivid illustration as his pages afford. Thus, at all points, his genius touches the interests of human life, now overflowing with a love of external nature, as gentle as that of Thomson, now intent upon the quaint or characteristic in life with a humor as zestful as that of Lamb, now developing the horrible or pathetic with something of Webster's dramatic terror, and again buoyant with a fantasy as aerial as Shelley's conceptions. And, in each instance, the staple of charming invention is adorned with the purest graces of style. This is Hawthorne's distinction. We have writers who possess in an eminent degree, each of these two great requisites of literary success, but no one who more impressively unites them; cheerfulness as if caught from the sea-breeze or the green-fields, solemnity as if imbibed from the twilight, like colors on a palette, seem transferable at his will, to any legend or locality he chooses for a frame-work whereon to rear his artistic creation; and this he does with so dainty a touch and so fine a disposition of light and shade, that the result is like an immortal cabinet picture—the epitome of a phase of art and the miniature reflection of a glorious mind. Boccaccio in Italy, Marmontel in France, Hoffman and others in Germany, and Andersen in Denmark, have made the tale or brief story classical in their several countries; and Hawthorne has achieved the same triumph here. He has performed for New England life and manners, the same high and sweet service which Wilson has for Scotland—caught and permanently embodied their "lights and shadows."

Brevity is as truly the soul of romance as of wit; the light that warms is always concentrated, and expression and finish, in literature as in painting, are not dependent upon space. Accordingly the choicest gems of writing are often the most terse; and as a perfect lyric or sonnet outweighs in value a mediocre epic or tragedy, so a carefully worked and richly conceived sketch, tale or essay is worth scores of diffuse novels and ponderous treatises. . . . We, therefore, deem one of Hawthorne's great merits a sententious habit, a concentrated style. He makes each picture complete and does not waste an inch of canvass. Indeed the unambitious length of his tales is apt to blind careless readers to their artistic unity and suggestiveness; he abjures quantity, while he refines upon quality.

A rare and most attractive quality of Hawthorne, as we have already suggested, is the artistic use of familiar materials. The imagination is a wayward faculty, and writers largely endowed with it, have acknowledged that they could expatiate with confidence only upon themes hallowed by distance. It seems to us less marvellous that Shakespeare peopled a newly discovered and half-traditional island with such new types of character as Ariel and Caliban; we can easily reconcile ourselves to the enchanting impossibilities of Arabian fiction; and the superstitious fantasies of northern romance have a dream-like reality to the natives of the temperate zone. To clothe a familiar scene with ideal interest, and exalt things to which our senses are daily accustomed, into the region of imaginative beauty and genuine sentiment, requires an extraordinary power of abstraction and concentrative thought. Authors in the old world have the benefit of antiquated memorials which give to the modern cities a mysterious though often disregarded charm; and the very names of Notre Dame, the Rialto, London Bridge, and other time-hallowed localities, take the reader's fancy captive and prepare him to accede to any grotesque or thrilling narrative that may be associated with them. It is otherwise in a new and entirely practical country; the immediate encroaches too steadily on our attention; we can scarcely obtain a perspective. . . .

Yet with a calm gaze, a serenity and fixedness of musing that no outward bustle can disturb and no power of custom render hackneyed, Hawthorne takes his stand, like a foreign artist in one of the old Italian cities,—before a relic of the past or a picturesque glimpse of nature, and loses all consciousness of himself and the present, in transferring its features and atmosphere to canvas. In our view the most remarkable trait in his writings is this harmonious blending of the common and familiar in the outward world, with the mellow and vivid tints of his own imagination. It is with difficulty that his maturity of conception and his finish and geniality of style links itself, in our minds, with the streets of Boston and Salem, the Province House and even the White Mountains; and we congratulate every New Englander with a particle of romance, that in his native literature, "a local habitation and a name," has thus been given to historical incidents and localities;—that art has enshrined what of tradition hangs over her brief career—as characteristic and as desirable thus to consecrate, as any legend or spot, German or Scottish genius has redeemed from oblivion. The "Wedding Knell," the "Gentle Boy," the "White Old Maid," the "Ambitious Guest," the "Shaker Bridal," and other New England subjects, as embodied and glorified by the truthful, yet imaginative and graceful art of Hawthorne, adequately represent in literature, native traits, and this will ensure their ultimate appreciation. But the most elaborate effort of this kind, and the only one, in fact, which seems to have introduced Hawthorne to the whole range of American readers, is "the Scarlet Letter." With all the care in point of style and authenticity which mark his lighter sketches, this genuine and unique romance, may be considered as an artistic exposition of Puritanism as modified by New England colonial life. In truth to costume, local manners and scenic features, the Scarlet Letter is as reliable as the best of Scott's novels; in the anatomy of human passion and consciousness it resembles the most effective of Balzac's illustrations of Parisian or provincial life, while in developing bravely and justly the sentiment of the life it depicts, it is as true to humanity as Dickens. Beneath its picturesque details and intense characterization, there lurks a profound satire. The want of soul, the absence of sweet humanity, the predominance of judgment over mercy, the tyranny of public opinion, the look of genuine charity, the asceticism of the Puritan theology,—the absence of all recognition of natural laws, and the fanatic substitution of the letter for the spirit—which darken and harden the spirit of the pilgrims to the soul of a poet—are shadowed forth with a keen, stern and eloquent, yet indirect emphasis, that haunts us like "the cry of the human." Herein is evident and palpable the latent power which we have described as the most remarkable trait of Hawthorne's genius;—the impression grows more significant as we dwell upon the story; the states of mind of the poor clergymen. Hester, Chillingworth and Pearl, being as it were transferred to our bosoms through the intense sympathy their vivid delineation excites;—they seem to conflict, and glow and deepen and blend in our hearts, and finally work out a great moral problem. It is as if we were baptized into the consciousness of Puritan life, of New England character in its elemental state; and knew, by experience, all its frigidity, its gloom, its intellectual enthusiasm and its religious aspiration. "The House of the Seven Gables" is a more elaborate and harmonious realization of these characteristics. The scenery, tone and personages of the story are imbued with a local authenticity which is not, for an instant, impaired by the imaginative charm of romance. We seem to breathe, as we read, the air and be surrounded by the familiar objects of a New England town. The interior of the House, each article described within it, from the quaint table to the miniature by Malbone;—every product of the old garden, the street-scenes that beguile the eyes of poor Clifford, as he looks out of the arched window, the noble elm and the gingerbread figures at the little shop window—all have the significance that belong to reality when seized upon by art. In these details we have the truth, simplicity and exact imitation of the Flemish painters. So life-like in the minutiæ and so picturesque in general effect are these sketches of still-life, that they are daguerreotyped in the reader's mind, and form a distinct and changeless background, the light and shade of which give admirable effect to the action of the story; occasional touches of humor, introduced with exquisite tact, relieve the grave undertone of the narrative and form vivacious and quaint images which might readily be transferred to canvas—so effectively are they drawn in words; take, for instance, the street-musician and the Pyncheon fowls, the judge balked of his kiss over the counter, Phœbe reading to Clifford in the garden, or the old maid, in her lonely chamber, gazing on the sweet lineaments of her unfortunate brother. Nor is Hawthorne less successful in those pictures that are drawn exclusively for the mind's eye and are obvious to sensation rather than the actual vision. Were a New England Sunday, breakfast, old mansion, easterly storm, or the morning after it clears, ever so well described? The skill in atmosphere we have noted in his lighter sketches, is also as apparent: around and within the principal scene of this romance, there hovers an alternating melancholy and brightness which is born of genuine moral life; no contrasts can be imagined of this kind, more eloquent to a sympathetic mind, than that between the inward consciousness and external appearance of Hepzibah or Phœbe and Clifford, or the Judge. They respectively symbolize the poles of human existence; and are fine studies for the psychologist. Yet this attraction is subservient to fidelity to local characteristics. Clifford represents, though in its most tragic imaginable phase, the man of fine organization and true sentiments environed by the material realities of New England life; his plausible uncle is the type of New England selfishness, glorified by respectable conformity and wealth; Phœbe is the ideal of genuine, efficient, yet loving female character in the same latitude; Uncle Venner, we regard as one of the most fresh, yet familiar portraits in the book; all denizens of our eastern provincial towns must have known such a philosopher; and Holgrave embodies Yankee acuteness and hardihood redeemed by integrity and enthusiasm. The contact of these most judiciously selected and highly characteristic elements, brings out not only many beautiful revelations of nature, but elucidates interesting truth; magnetism and socialism are admirably introduced; family tyranny in its most revolting form, is powerfully exemplified; the distinction between a mental and a heartfelt interest in another, clearly unfolded; and the tenacious and hereditary nature of moral evil impressively shadowed forth. The natural-refinements of the human heart, the holiness of a ministry of disinterested affection, the gracefulness of the homeliest services when irradiated by cheerfulness and benevolence, are illustrated with singular beauty. . . .

Thus narrowly, yet with reverence, does Hawthorne analyze the delicate traits of human sentiment and character; and open vistas into that beautiful and unexplored world of love and thought, that exists in every human being, though overshadowed by material circumstance and technical duty. This, as we have before said, is his great service; digressing every now and then, from the main drift of his story, he takes evident delight in expatiating on phases of character and general traits of life, or in bringing into strong relief the more latent facts of consciousness. Perhaps the union of the philosophic tendency with the poetic instinct is the great charm of his genius. It is common for American critics to estimate the interest of all writings by their comparative glow, vivacity and rapidity of action: somewhat of the restless temperament and enterprising life of the nation infects its taste: such terms as 'quiet,' 'gentle' and 'tasteful,' are equivocal when applied in this country, to a book; and yet they may envelope the rarest energy of thought and depth of insight as well as earnestness of feeling; these qualities, in reflective minds, are too real to find melo-dramatic development; they move as calmly as summer waves, or glow as noiselessly as the firmament; but not the less grand and mighty is their essence; to realize it, the spirit of contemplation, and the recipient mood of sympathy, must be evoked, for it is not external but moral excitement that is proposed; and we deem one of Hawthorne's most felicitous merits—that of so patiently educing artistic beauty and moral interest from life and nature, without the least sacrifice of intellectual dignity.

The healthy spring of life is typified in Phœbe so freshly as to magnetize the feelings as well as engage the perceptions of the reader; its intellectual phase finds expression in Holgrave, while the state of Clifford, when relieved of the nightmare that oppressed his sensitive temperament, the author justly compares to an Indian summer of the soul. Across the path of these beings of genuine flesh and blood, who constantly appeal to our most humane sympathies, or rather around their consciousness and history, flits the pale, mystic figure of Alice—whose invisible music and legendary fate overflow with a graceful and attractive superstition—yielding an Ariel-like melody to the more solemn and cheery strains of the whole composition. Among the apt though incidental touches of the picture, the idea of making the music-grinder's monkey an epitome of avarice, the daguerreotype a test of latent character, and the love of the reformer Holgrave for the genially practical Phœbe, win him to conservatism, strike us as remarkably natural yet quite as ingenuous and charming as philosophical. We may add that the same pure, even, unexaggerated and perspicuous style of diction that we have recognized in his previous writing, is maintained in this.

As earth and sky appear to blend at the horizon though we cannot define the point of contact, things seen and unseen, the actual and the spiritual, mind and matter, what is within and what is without our consciousness, have a line of union, and, like the colour of the iris, are lost in each other. About this equator of life the genius of Hawthorne delights to hover as its appropriate sphere; whether indulging a vein of Spenserian allegory, Hogarth sketching, Goldsmith domesticity, or Godwin metaphysics, it is around the boundary of the possible that he most freely expatiates; the realities and the mysteries of life to his vision are scarcely ever apart; they act and re-act as to yield dramatic hints or vistas of sentiment. Time broods with touching solemnity over his imagination; the function of conscience awes while it occupies his mind; the delicate and the profound in love, and the awful beauty of death transfuse his meditation; and these supernal he loves to link with terrestial influences—to hallow a graphic description by a sacred association or to brighten a commonplace occasion with the scintillations of humour—thus vivifying or chastening the "light of common day."

According to James D. Rust (*Boston Public Library Quarterly*, Vol. 7, 207–15), GEORGE ELIOT [1819–80] was the author of the review of *Blithedale Romance* reprinted below. In 1851 she became assistant editor of the *Westminster Review*, a post which she held until 1853; hence she could have written the review. In August 1860, the *North British Review* published an essay on George Eliot and Hawthorne based on the following premise: "The imagination in different men works under different laws. The more powerful intellects keep it in subjection, but it takes the feebler captive. In the one case, it vitalizes and exalts; in the other, it discolours and exaggerates. The author of *Adam Bede* represents the first class; Nathaniel Hawthorne, the second."

Contemporary Literature of America [*The Blithedale Romance*]

Attributed to GEORGE ELIOT

. . . "The Blithedale Romance" will never attain the popularity which is vouchsafed (to borrow a pulpit vocable) to some of its contemporaries, but it is unmistakably the finest production of

Westminster Review, Vol. 58 (October 1852) 592–98.

genius in either hemisphere, for this quarter at least—to keep our enthusiasm within limits so far. Of its literary merits we wish to speak, at the outset, in the highest terms, inasmuch as we intend to take objection to it in other respects.

"Blithedale" is an idealization of Brook Farm, where, about ten years ago, a few young and hearty enthusiasts, tired of moving on so slowly toward the millennium, took Destiny into their own hands, and set up "Paradise Regained," not by writing verses or romances, but by the more prosaic method of planting their own potatoes, baking their own bread, and cobbling their own shoes, as in the days before the Flood, when every man was his own master and his own servant, and political economy had not yet brought social death into the world, "and all our woe." . . .

Of this experience Hawthorne, who was one of them, has availed himself, in writing this romance. With our limited space, we cannot pretend to give even a faint outline of a tale which depends for its interest altogether upon the way of telling it. Hawthorne's *forte* is the analysis of character, and not the dramatic arrangement of events. . . . The adoption of the autobiographical form (now so common in fictions) is, perhaps, the most suitable for the exercise of such peculiar powers. Not more than six or seven characters are introduced, and only four of them are prominent figures. They have, therefore, ample room for displaying their individuality, and establishing each an independent interest in the reader's regards. But this is not without disadvantages, which become more apparent towards the close. The analysis of the characters is so minute, that they are too thoroughly individualized for dramatic co-operation, or for that graduated subordination to each other which tends to give a harmonious swell to the narrative, unity to the plot, and concentrated force to the issue. They are simply contemporaries, obliged, somehow, to be on familiar terms with each other, and, even when coming into the closest relationship, seeming rather driven thereto by destiny, than drawn by sympathy. It is well that the *dramatis personæ* are so few. They are a manageable number, and are always upon the stage; but had there been more of them, they would only have presented themselves there in turns, which, with Hawthorne's slow movement, would have been fatal to their united action and combined effect. Even with a consecutive narrative, and a concentration of interest, the current flows with an eddying motion, which tends to keep them apart, unless, as happens once or twice, it dash over a precipice, and then it both makes up for lost time, and brings matters to a point rather abruptly. But the main tendency is toward isolation—for the ruling faculty is analytic. It is ever hunting out the anomalous; it discovers more points of repulsion than of attraction; and the creatures of its fancy are all morbid beings—all "wandering stars," plunging, orbitless, into the abyss of despair—confluent but not commingling streams, winding along to the ocean of disaster and death: for all have a wretched end—Zenobia and Priscilla, Hollingsworth and Coverdale—the whole go to wreck. The queenly Zenobia drowns herself in a pool; her ghost haunts Hollingsworth through life; and, as for Coverdale, he falls into a moral scepticism more desolating than death. . . .

. . . .

. . . Hawthorne has a rich perception of the beautiful, but he is sadly deficient in moral depth and earnestness. His moral faculty is morbid as well as weak; all his characters partake of the same infirmity. Hollingsworth's project of a penitentiary at Blithedale is here carried out in imagination. Hawthorne walks abroad always at night, and at best it is a moonlight glimmering which you catch of reality. He lives in the region and shadow of death, and never sees the deep glow of moral health anywhere. He looks mechanically (it is a habit) at Nature and at man through a coloured glass, which imparts to the whole view a pallid, monotonous aspect, painful to behold. And it is only because Hawthorne can see beauty in everything, and will look at nothing but beauty in anything, that he can either endure the picture himself, or win for it the admiration of others. The object of art is the development of beauty—not merely sensuous beauty, but moral and spiritual beauty. Its ministry should be one of pleasure, not of pain; but our anatomist, who removes his subjects to Blithedale, that he may cut and hack at them without interference, clears out for himself a new path in art, by developing the beauty of deformity! He would give you the poetry of the hospital, or the poetry of the dissecting-room; but we would rather not have it. Art has a moral purpose to fulfil; its mission is one of mercy, not of misery. Reality should only be so far introduced as to give effect to the bright ideal which Hope pictures in the future. In fact, a poet is nothing unless also a prophet. Hawthorne is the former; but few poets could be less of the latter. He draws his inspiration from Fate, not from Faith. He is not even a Jeremiah, weeping amid the ruins of a fallen temple, and mourning over the miseries of a captive people. He is a Mephistophiles, doubtful whether to weep or laugh; but either way it would be in mockery. "It is genuine tragedy, is it not?" said Zenobia (referring to the fatal blow which laid her hopes prostrate), at the same time coming out "with *a sharp, light laugh.*" Verily, a tragedy!—burlesqued by much of the same maniac levity. That "Blithedale" itself should end in smoke, was, perhaps, fit matter for mirth; that Hollingsworth's huge tower of selfishness should be shattered to pieces was poetically just; but that the imperial Zenobia should be vanquished, was to give the victory to Despair. Zenobia is the only one in the group worthy to be the Trustee of Human Right, and the Representative of Human Destiny; and she, at least, should have come out of all her struggles in regal triumph. But, after the first real trial of her strength with adversity, and when there was resolution yet left for a thousand conflicts, to throw her into that dirty pool, and not even to leave her there, but to send her base-hearted deceiver, and that lout of a fellow, Silas Foster, to haul her out, and to let the one poke up the corpse with a boat-hook, and the other tumble it about in the simplicity of his desire to make it look more decent—these, and many other things in the closing scene, are an outrage upon the decorum of art, as well as a violation of its purpose. That such things do happen, is no reason why they should be idealized; for the Ideal seeks not to imitate Reality, but to perfect it. The use it makes of that which *is* true, is to develope that which *ought* to be true; and it ought *never* to be true that the strong should be conquered by the weak, as Zenobia was by Priscilla; or, that the most buoyant spirit should sink soonest in the struggle of life, as did Zenobia, who was the first that found a grave in "Blithedale;" or, that *all* should be wrecked that sail on troubled waters, as were all who figure in this romance. It is a hard saying to proclaim to a fallen world, that the first false step is a fatal one. There was more truth in the words, and more beauty in the picture, of the man standing by the outcast, telling her to go and sin no more. From thence let Hawthorne draw his inspiration. Let him study that benignant attitude, and endeavour to realize it in himself toward a similar subject, and he might yet write with a prophet's power, and accomplish a saviour's mission.

· · · · · · ·

. . . Everybody will naturally regard this story, whether fact or fiction, as a socialistic drama, and will expect its chief interest as such to be of a moral kind. "Blithedale," whatever may be its relation to Brook Farm, is itself a socialistic settlement, with its corresponding phases of life, and therefore involves points both of moral and material interest, the practical operation of which should have been exhibited so as to bring out the good and evil of the system. But this task Hawthorne declines, and does not "put forward the slightest pretensions to illustrate a theory, or elicit a conclusion favourable or otherwise to Socialism." He confines himself to the delineation of its picturesque phases, as a "thing of beauty," and either has no particular convictions respecting its deeper relations, or hesitates to express them. . . . "Blithedale," then, as a socialistic community, is merely used here as a scaffolding—a very huge one—in the construction of an edifice considerably smaller than itself! And then, the artist leaves the scaffolding standing! Socialism, in this romance, is prominent enough to fill the book, but it has so little business in it, that it does not even grow into an organic part of the story, and contributes nothing whatever toward the final catastrophe. It is a theatre—and, as such, it should have a neutral tint; but it should also be made of neutral stuff; and its erection, moreover, should not be contemporaneous with the performance of the play. But the incongruity becomes more apparent when we consider the kind of play acted in it. Take the moral of Zenobia's history, and you will find that Socialism is apparently made responsible for consequences which it utterly condemned, and tried, at least, to remedy. We say, apparently, for it is really not made responsible for anything, good, bad, or indifferent. It forms a circumference of circumstances, which neither mould the characters, nor influence the destinies, of the individuals so equivocally situated, —forms, in short, not an essential part of the picture, but an enormous fancy border, not very suitable for the purpose for which it was designed. Zenobia's life would have been exhibited with more propriety, and its moral brought home with more effect, in the "theatre" of the world, out of which it really grew, and of which it would have formed a vital and harmonious part. Zenobia and Socialism should have been acted in the ready-made theatre of ordinary humanity, to see how it would fare with them there. Having occupied the ground, Hawthorne owed it to truth, and to a fit opportunity, so to dramatize his experience and observation of Communistic life, as to make them of practical value for the world at large.

The *American Whig Review* was founded in 1845 to champion Henry Clay's presidential campaign, after which it continued as a political and literary review. The portion printed below is the introduction to a long review of *The Blithedale Romance*. The rest of the essay is a severe indictment of the romance based on the assumption that Hawthorne "has no right to blacken and defame humanity, by animating his shadowy people with worse passions and more imperfect souls than we meet with in the world." The reviewer does praise the scene describing the recovery of Zenobia's body. A postscript is added to the essay condemning Hawthorne's biography of Pierce. The reviewer challenges Hawthorne: "Give us such works as the *Scarlet Letter* and the *Blithedale Romance*—works of art and beauty with all their deformities—and let your rare genius soar for ever above the atmosphere of mushroom heroes and penny biographies."

The Blithedale Romance

ANONYMOUS

Every work which proposes to develop a new phase of human character, or philosophize upon an assumption of original responsibilities, derives a species of adventitious interest from the novelty of its subject, independent of any artistic ability by which it may be accompanied. When it was publicly understood that Mr. Hawthorne was engaged in the composition of a romance, having for its origin, if not its subject, a community which once had a brief existence at Brook Farm, speculation was awakened, anticipations grew vivid, and the reading public awaited anxiously the issue of a book which it was hoped would combine in itself the palatable spices of novelty and personality. A portion of these expectations were doomed to disappointment. In the preface to the Blithedale Romance, Mr. Hawthorne distinctly disavowed any intention of painting portraits. To his sojourn at Brook Farm he attributes his inspiration, but that is all. Blithedale is no caligraph of Brook Farm. Zenobia first sprang into actual existence from the printing press of Ticknor, Reed and Fields, and the quiet Priscilla is nothing more than one of those pretty phantoms with which Mr. Hawthorne occasionally adorns his romances.

We believe that if Mr. Hawthorne had intended to give a faithful portrait of Brook Farm and its inmates, he would have signally failed. He has no genius for realities, save in inanimate nature. Between his characters and the reader falls a gauze-like veil of imagination, on which their shadows flit and move, and play

American Whig Review, Vol. 16 (November 1852) 417–24.

strange dramas replete with second-hand life. An air of unreality enshrouds all his creations. They are either dead, or have never lived, and when they pass away they leave behind them an oppressive and unwholesome chill.

This sluggish antiquity of style may suit some subjects admirably. When, as in the Scarlet Letter, the epoch of the story is so far removed from the present day as to invest all the events with little more than a reminiscient interest; when characters and customs were so different to all circumstance that jostles us in the rude, quick life of today, and when we do not expect to meet, in the long corridors of Time down which the author leads us, any company beyond the pale, shadowy ancestry with whose names we are faintly familiar, but with whom we have no common sympathies. Mr. Hawthorne's genius, if we may be permitted to use so extravagant a simile, reminds us forcibly of an old country mansion of the last century. It seems as if it had been built a very long time. It is but half inhabited, and throbs with only a moiety of life. The locks and bolts are rusty, and the doors creak harshly on their hinges. Huge twisted chimneys branch out of every gable, and in every chimney is lodged some capricious, eccentric old rook, who startles us unexpectedly with his presence. Great wings, and odd buttresses, jut out from all the corners, the phrenological bumps of architecture; while here and there, in warm sheltered nooks, sweet climbing flowers, dewy roses, and jessamine prodigal of its perfume, cling lovingly to the old moss-grown walls, and strive, but with ill success, to conceal the quaint deformity of the building.

In the House of the Seven Gables this dreary beauty is eminently prominent. The poetry of desolation, and the leaden vapors of solitude are wreathed around the scene. The doings of the characters awaken only a faint, dream-like interest in our hearts. We seem to hear the hollow echoes of their footsteps in the silence, and follow them with our fingers as if we expected them each moment to melt and mingle with the surrounding air. This sad and unsubstantial painting is no doubt excellently well achieved. Mr. Hawthorne deals artistically with shadows. There is a strange, unearthly fascination about the fair spectres that throng his works, and we know no man who can distort nature, or idealize abortions more cleverly than the author of the Scarlet Letter. But we question much, if we strip Mr. Hawthorne's works of a certain beauty and originality of style which they are always sure to possess, whether the path which he has chosen is a healthy one. To us it does not seem as if the fresh wind of morning blew across his track; we do not feel the strong pulse of nature throbbing beneath the turf he treads upon. When an author sits down to make a book, he should not alone consult the inclinations of his own genius regarding its purpose or its construction. If he should happen to be imbued with strange, saturnine doctrines, or be haunted by a morbid suspicion of human nature, in God's name let him not write one word. Better that all the beautiful, wild thoughts with which his brain is teeming should moulder for ever in neglect and darkness, than that one soul was overshadowed by stern, uncongenial dogmas, which should have died with their Puritan fathers. It is not alone necessary to produce a work of art. The soul of beauty is Truth, and Truth is ever progressive. The true artist therefore endeavors to make the world better. He does not look behind him, and dig out of the graves of past centuries skeletons to serve as models for his pictures; but looks onward for more perfect shapes, and though sometimes obliged to design from the defective forms around him, he infuses, as it were, some of the divine spirit of the future into them, and lo! we love them with all their faults. But Mr. Hawthorne discards all idea of successful human progress. All his characters seem so weighed down with their own evilness of nature, that they can scarcely keep their balance, much less take their places in the universal march. Like the lord mentioned in Scripture, he issues an invitation to the halt, the blind, and the lame of soul, to gather around his board, and then asks us to feast at the same table. It is a pity that Mr. Hawthorne should not have been originally imbued with more universal tenderness. It is a pity that he displays nature to us so shrouded and secluded, and that he should be afflicted with such a melancholy craving for human curiosities. His men are either vicious, crazed, or misanthropical, and his women are either unwomanly, unearthly, or unhappy. His books have no sunny side to them. They are unripe to the very core.

We are more struck with the want of this living tenderness in the Blithedale Romance than in any of Mr. Hawthorne's previous novels. In the Scarlet Letter and the House of the Seven Gables, a certain gloominess of thought suited the antiquity of the subjects; but in his last performance, the date of the events, and the nature of the story, entitle us to expect something brighter and less unhealthy. . . .

. . . .

The *Dublin University Magazine* published in 1855 a survey of Hawthorne's short fiction and three romances. The essay is partially a response to a vitriolic attack on Hawthorne in *Blackwood's* (May 1855)—the "adverse critic" referred to below. The *Blackwood's* reviewer condemns the disease and unwholesomeness in Hawthorne's fiction. For example, he finds Clifford particularly repellent and the death scene of Judge Pyncheon "fairly worn to pieces." Zenobia's drowning herself he describes as "a piece of sham entirely" without "the slightest idea of reality."

Nathaniel Hawthorne

ANONYMOUS

. . . .

With not a few points of resemblance to recent English and American authors, Hawthorne has yet many peculiarities of his own, so nicely characterized that we cannot think of anything like a complete prototype to him in literature. Now, the quaint, still humor of his thoroughly English style, reminds us of Washington Irving; now the delicate, imperceptible touches of Longfellow become apparent; now the calm, genial, effortless flow of Helps. We have often fancied, also, that we could detect a resemblance to John Foster, but we suspect, were we to attempt a comparison of parallel passages, it would turn out to be rather imaginary. There is a tendency, no doubt, in both, to pry into all the odd nooks, and corners, and dark places of the mind; but the firm, strong, practical nature of Foster never suffers him to carry this beyond a certain point, and always shapes his researches to some masterly conclusion, while Hawthorne often runs riot in the pursuit from mere apparent wantonness. Yet, undoubtedly, it is this ruling feature of Hawthorne's mind that invests his writings with much of their peculiar charm;—producing extravagant and overdrawn description in some; in others it is the zest and spirit of the whole. . . .

Like almost every original author, Hawthorne occasionally verifies our great dramatist's remark about vaulting ambition o'er-leaping itself and falling on the other side, giving utterance to the veriest drivel, such as scribblers of the lowest order could hardly be guilty of perpetuating. It would be hard to say how many readers he has lost who have had the misfortune to take up, say the

"Twice-Told Tales," and opened with "Tales of the Province House," or "The Three-fold Destiny." Even in the "Mosses from an Old Manse," which abounds in unmistakable evidences of his genius, abundance of pieces might be cited which would require the utmost stretch of charity to pass by. . . .

Were we particularly anxious to impress a reader favorably with Hawthorne at starting, we do not think we could succeed better than by directing him to take up the "Mosses from an Old Manse," and begin at the beginning, when, if he did not go to the end of the first article, we should certainly pronounce him an incorrigible dullard. . . .

To the merits of the "House of the Seven Gables," the most pleasing and complete of Hawthorne's tales, an adverse critic, in our opinion, unconsciously pays a high compliment, when he complains that the author seizes on the reader by the button, as it were, and, like the Ancient Mariner, compels him to hear the story to an end, which, after all, turns out to be no story at all. . . . An original idea, truly, to censure an author for contriving so to rivet your attention that you must read his book through, even though, as the saying is, there is nothing in it! . . . "The House of the Seven Gables" may be very faulty as a story, and we certainly would not recommend it as a model to apprentice fiction-mongers; but as we have abundance of good story-writers, and, judging from the past, will have till doomsday, we think such an author as Hawthorne may be allowed to let his genius find its own vent, and diverge as often as it pleases from any path it may ostensibly follow. "The House of the Seven Gables," we venture to say, would have wanted the best part of its attractions, had the author rigidly repressed the promptings of his luxuriant fancy, and closely pursued the even tenor of his narrative, even though the plot and winding-up had been exciting enough to please our fastidious censor.

As might be expected from Hawthorne's peculiar idiosyncrasy, he possesses, in a remarkable degree, the faculty of indicating by imperceptible shades the approaching event long ere it is announced, like the hush becoming stiller and stiller as the noiseless battalia of clouds creep denser and denser together before the storm. . . . Only the pen that flung that strange, terrible gloom over the closing scenes of "Bleak House" could rival the incidental touches immediately antecedent to the death of Judge Pyncheon.

"The Scarlet Letter" (Hawthorne's most popular book, by the way) has the same button-seizing power; but as the narrative is made up of more excitable materials, its interest is of a much more intense and even feverish nature. . . . It is, certainly, open to the charge of encouraging a taste for the "morbid and horrible." . . .

"The Blithedale Romance," one of Hawthorne's most recent publications, lies more open than any other to unsparing and well-deserved ridicule—in the characters especially: one being inflated to bursting with about as much success as the frog of old; another insipid; another wofully wishy-washy; and the hero of the tale himself, who tells the story in the first person, an impertinent sort of eavesdropper. Perhaps the very undignified character of the latter, Mr. Miles Coverdale, may be accounted for on the supposition, that as the author evidently intends him to be understood as his mouthpiece, his anxiety to avoid anything like egotism may have led him astray. Yet, with all drawbacks, there is hardly one of his works we could read over with more pleasure than this eccentric production, which professes to be a romance founded on the author's own youthful experience, setting forth how, as one of a band of Socialists, he attempted to commence the work of regenerating the world by laboring with his "brothers and sisters" on a model farm. The mode of life at this new Arcadia is the great charm of the book, for Hawthorne can hardly fail to delight when he catches a glimpse of nature. . . .

The rest of Hawthorne's works consist principally of tales and sketches; and in these, notwithstanding his filial love for the pleasant, tangible realities of earth, and the shafts he occasionally aims at transcendentalism and mysticism, allegory is frequently employed, with masterly effect, to give life to his conceptions. His most brilliant and finished effort of this kind is "The Celestial Railroad," in which the mantle of Bunyan appears to have descended on him with a double portion of his spirit—the quaint, nervous simplicity of the prince of dreamers blending with his own rich vividness of descriptive power, and quiet under-current humor. . . .

Most of Hawthorne's other allegorical compositions sound as incomplete half utterances, hinting but vaguely at the meaning intended to be conveyed, though we are not sure if we should call this indefiniteness a defect—the power of negative suggestion thus displayed being often perfectly magical. Yet we cannot say that allegory is made much more attractive to us by Hawthorne than by his predecessors; and, as with them, the degree of pleasure corresponds in great measure to that in which the sense of allegory is lost. . . . It is pleasant enough now and then to step out of the material world; but we do not like to be incessantly reminded that all is unreal, mist and shadow. The mind craves a firmer foothold, and prefers swallowing downright impossibilities, if presented with an unblushing air of veracity, and imbued with a sufficient tinge of the *vraisemblable*. This has not escaped Hawthorne; and he has very happily embodied ideas in this form in one or two papers, telling his tale as if perfectly prepared to vouch for the authenticity of the whole. "The Artist of the Beautiful" is a fine instance of this; and the moral conveyed loses none of its effect, that the reader is left to find it out for himself. In another narrative on this principle, however, as might be expected from Hawthorne's constant tendency to overleap his object, he goes too much astray, we fear, for the most devoted idealist.

Perhaps, on the whole, the walk in which Hawthorne most excels is in that blending of the essay, sketch, and tale, for which we have no definite term as yet—a style which seems so careless and easy, but which is perhaps the most difficult of all, and one we would defy any of our artificial writers to acquire—Macaulay, for instance, notwithstanding all his brilliance and nerve. One of Hawthorne's dreamy reveries, clothed in the glittering array of Macaulay's rounded, nicely balanced sentences, would be as supremely ridiculous as an idyl of Tennyson's "done into" Popeian heroic measure. A volume of Hawthorne's compositions of this nature, selected from his works, and cleared from all surrounding rubbish, would be a perfect *chef-d'œuvre* of its kind, worthy to take its place beside "Companions of my Solitude." There is one paper in his "Mosses from an Old Manse" which would have made the fortune of any ordinary literary aspirant—original, so far as our memory serves us, in conception, and rivalling the happiest efforts of Goldsmith and Irving in execution. "P.'s Correspondence," as it is styled, purports to be a letter from a friend of the author's, whose intellect being partially disordered, jumbles together past and present, living and dead, and is a great traveller, without stirring from the white-washed, iron-grated room to which he is confined, meeting in his imaginary wanderings a variety of personages who have long ceased to be visible to any eye save his own. . . .

. . . .

There is one other work of Hawthorne's in a totally different vein, which we must not pass by in concluding, though we should not have regretted its non-publication very much—his "Life of General Pierce, the American President." We could not help thinking it a pity, as we perused it, that such parties as Whigs and Democrats existed, or at all events that in his zeal for the latter he should have been led to step so far out of his own sphere, and descant on patriotism, the union, anti-and-pro-slavery, in a style bordering somewhat on that of the stump orator. Occasionally, no doubt, faint reflections of his former self may be detected, but these partake in some measure of the character of features distorted in the bowl of a spoon. . . . It is evident that dealing with the dry, practical doings of life is not his forte, and the field over which his genius can range is so wide and varied that we can well dispense with any excursions beyond it.

In the desultory remarks we have been making, we must not be understood as putting forward any claims for Hawthorne to rank as a model anything. Exceptions of every kind may be taken to his works, which, though perhaps *sans peur*, are certainly not always *sans reproche*. But withal he is a man of genius, and as such without any further "peroration" we leave him to our readers. . . .

JAMES RUSSELL LOWELL [1819–91] edited *The Pioneer*, to which Hawthorne contributed in 1843. In 1848 Lowell included a sketch of Hawthorne in *A Fable for Critics*. He sees in Hawthorne a genius "shrinking and rare" and yet a strength; each poetic image combines delicacy and robustness—a touch of the feminine and yet perfect manliness. In April 1851 Lowell wrote to Hawthorne expressing high praise for *The House of the Seven Gables*, "the most valuable contribution to New England history that has been made." Lowell's comparison of Hawthorne to Shakespeare in the review of *The Marble Faun* was sincere; he considered Hawthorne "the rarest creative imagination of the century, the rarest in some ideal respects since Shakespeare."

[Review of] The Marble Faun

[JAMES RUSSELL LOWELL]

It is, we believe, more than thirty years since Mr. Hawthorne's first appearance as an author; it is twenty-three since he gave his first collection of "Twice-told Tales" to the world. His works have received that surest warranty of genius and originality in the widening of their appreciation downward from a small circle of refined admirers and critics, till it embraced the whole community of

Atlantic Monthly, Vol. 5 (April 1860) 509–10.

readers. With just enough encouragement to confirm his faith in his own powers, those powers had time to ripen and toughen themselves before the gales of popularity could twist them from the balance of a healthy and normal development. Happy the author whose earliest works are read and understood by the lustre thrown back upon them from his latest! for then we receive the impression of continuity and cumulation of power, of peculiarity deepening to individuality, of promise more than justified in the keeping: unhappy, whose autumn shows only the aftermath and rowen of an earlier harvest, whose would-be replenishments are but thin dilutions of his fame!

The nineteenth century has produced no more purely original writer than Mr. Hawthorne. A shallow criticism has sometimes fancied a resemblance between him and Poe. But it seems to us that the difference between them is the immeasurable one between talent carried to its ultimate, and genius,—between a masterly adaptation of the world of sense and appearance to the purposes of Art, and a so thorough conception of the world of moral realities that Art becomes the interpreter of something profounder than herself. In this respect it is not extravagant to say that Hawthorne has something of kindred with Shakspeare. But that breadth of nature which made Shakspeare incapable of alienation from common human nature and actual life is wanting to Hawthorne. He is rather a denizen than a citizen of what men call the world. We are conscious of a certain remoteness in his writings, as in those of Donne, but with such a difference that we should call the one super- and the other subter-sensual. Hawthorne is psychological and metaphysical. Had he been born without the poetic imagination, he would have written treatises on the Origin of Evil. He does not draw characters, but rather conceives them and then shows them acted upon by crime, passion, or circumstance, as if the element of Fate were as present to his imagination as to that of a Greek dramatist. Helen we know, and Antigone, and Benedick, and Falstaff, and Miranda, and Parson Adams, and Major Pendennis,—these people have walked on pavements or looked out of club-room windows; but what are these idiosyncrasies into which Mr. Hawthorne has breathed a necromantic life, and which he has endowed with the forms and attributes of men? And yet, grant him his premises, that is, let him once get his morbid tendency, whether inherited or the result of special experience, either incarnated as a new man or usurping all the faculties of one already in the flesh, and it is marvellous how subtilely and with what truth to as much of human nature as is included in a diseased consciousness he traces all the finest nerves of impulse and motive, how he compels every trivial circumstance into an accomplice of his art, and makes the sky flame with foreboding or the landscape chill and darken with remorse. It is impossible to think of Hawthorne without at the same time thinking of the few great masters of imaginative composition; his works, only not abstract because he has the genius to make them ideal, belong not specially to our clime or generation; it is their moral purpose alone, and perhaps their sadness, that mark him as the son of New England and the Puritans.

It is commonly true of Hawthorne's romances that the interest centres in one strongly defined protagonist, to whom the other characters are accessory and subordinate,—perhaps we should rather say a ruling Idea, of which all the characters are fragmentary embodiments. They remind us of a symphony of Beethoven's, in which, though there be variety of parts, yet all are infused with the dominant motive, and heighten its impression by hints and far-away suggestions at the most unexpected moment. As in Rome the obelisks are placed at points toward which several streets converge, so in Mr. Hawthorne's stories the actors and incidents seem but vistas through which we see the moral from different points of view,—a moral pointing skyward always, but inscribed with hieroglyphs mysteriously suggestive, whose incitement to conjecture, while they baffle it, we prefer to any prosaic solution.

Nothing could be more original or imaginative than the conception of the character of Donatello in Mr. Hawthorne's new romance. His likeness to the lovely statue of Praxiteles, his happy animal temperament, and the dim legend of his pedigree are combined with wonderful art to reconcile us to the notion of a Greek myth embodied in an Italian of the nineteenth century; and when at length a soul is created in this primeval pagan, this child of earth, this creature of mere instinct, awakened through sin to a conception of the necessity of atonement, we feel, that, while we looked to be entertained with the airiest of fictions, we were dealing with the most august truths of psychology, with the most pregnant facts of modern history, and studying a profound parable of the development of the Christian Idea.

Everything suffers a sea-change in the depths of Mr. Hawthorne's mind, gets rimmed with an impalpable fringe of melancholy moss, and there is a tone of sadness in this book as in the rest, but it does not leave us sad. In a series of remarkable and characteristic works, it is perhaps the most remarkable and characteristic. If you had picked up and read a stray leaf of it anywhere, you would have exclaimed, "Hawthorne!"

The book is steeped in Italian atmosphere. There are many landscapes in it full of breadth and power, and criticisms of pictures and statues always delicate, often profound. In the Preface, Mr. Hawthorne pays a well-deserved tribute of admiration to several of our sculptors, especially to Story and Akers. The hearty enthusiasm with which he elsewhere speaks of the former artist's "Cleopatra" is no surprise to Mr. Story's friends at home, though hardly less gratifying to them than it must be to the sculptor himself.

A popular lecturer, EDWIN PERCY WHIPPLE [1819–86] was also a prolific critic. On Hawthorne he wrote numerous reviews and ultimately became Hawthorne's favorite critic. Although Whipple praised *The Scarlet Letter*, he expressed the hope that in his next work Hawthorne would create "a romance equal to the *Scarlet Letter* in pathos and power, but more relieved by touches of that beautiful and peculiar humor, so serene and searching, in which he excells almost all living writers." Hawthorne apparently agreed with this criticism. In fact, Whipple's reaction to the unrelieved gloom of *The Scarlet Letter* may have influenced Hawthorne in shaping the tone of *The House of the Seven Gables*, which Whipple greeted as "Hawthorne's greatest work." Later he claimed that *Blithedale* was "the most perfect in the execution of any of Hawthorne's works, and as a work of art, hardly equalled by anything else which this country produced." The essay printed below covers previous ground and includes *The Marble Faun*. It is the first of two important survey reviews in 1860, the other being by Hutton.

Nathaniel Hawthorne

[EDWIN PERCY WHIPPLE]

The romance of "The Marble Faun" will be widely welcomed, not only for its intrinsic merits, but because it is a sign that its writer, after a silence of seven or eight years, has determined to resume his place in the ranks of authorship. In his preface he tells us, that in each of his previous publications he had unconsciously one person in his eye, whom he styles his "gentle reader." He meant it "for that

Atlantic Monthly, Vol. 5 (May 1860) 614–22.

one congenial friend, more comprehensive of his purposes, more appreciative of his success, more indulgent of his short-comings, and, in all respects, closer and kinder than a brother,—that all-sympathizing critic, in short, whom an author never actually meets, but to whom he implicitly makes his appeal, whenever he is conscious of having done his best." He believes that this reader did once exist for him, and duly received the scrolls he flung "upon whatever wind was blowing, in the faith that they would find him out." "But," he questions, "is he extant now? In these many years since he last heard from me, may he not have deemed his earthly task accomplished, and have withdrawn to the paradise of gentle readers, wherever it may be, to the enjoyments of which his kindly charity on my behalf must surely have entitled him?" As we feel assured that Hawthorne's reputation has been steadily growing with the lapse of time, he has no cause to fear that the longevity of his gentle reader will not equal his own. As long as he writes, there will be readers enough to admire and appreciate.

The publication of this new romance seems to offer us a fitting occasion to attempt some description of the peculiarities of the genius of which it is the latest offspring, and to hazard some judgments on its predecessors. It is more than twenty-five years since Hawthorne began that remarkable series of stories and essays which are now collected in the volumes of "Twice-Told Tales," "The Snow Image and other Tales," and "Mosses from an Old Manse." From the first he was recognized by such readers as he chanced to find as a man of genius, yet for a long time he enjoyed, in his own words, the distinction of being "the obscurest man of letters in America." His readers were "gentle" rather than enthusiastic; their fine delight in his creations was a private perception of subtile excellences of thought and style, too refined and self-satisfying to be contagious; and the public was untouched, whilst the "gentle" reader was full of placid enjoyment. Indeed, we fear that this kind of reader is something of an Epicurean,—receives a new genius as a private blessing, sent by a benign Providence to quicken a new life in his somewhat jaded sense of intellectual pleasure; and after having received a fresh sensation, he is apt to be serenely indifferent whether the creator of it starve bodily or pine mentally from the lack of a cordial human shout of recognition.

There would appear, on a slight view of the matter, no reason for the little notice which Hawthorne's early productions received. The subjects were mostly drawn from the traditions and written records of New England, and gave the "beautiful strangeness" of imagination to objects, incidents, and characters which were familiar facts in the popular mind. The style, while it had a purity, sweetness, and grace which satisfied the most fastidious and exacting taste, had, at the same time, more than the simplicity and clearness of an ordinary school-book. But though the subjects and the style were thus popular, there was something in the shaping and informing spirit which failed to awaken interest, or awakened interest without exciting delight. Misanthropy, when it has its source in passion,—when it is fierce, bitter, fiery, and scornful,—when it vigorously echoes the aggressive discontent of the world, and furiously tramples on the institutions and the men luckily rather than rightfully in the ascendant,—this is always popular; but a misanthropy which springs from insight,—a misanthropy which is lounging, languid, sad, and depressing,—a misanthropy which remorselessly looks through cursing misanthropes and chirping men of the world with the same sure, detecting glance of reason,—a misanthropy which has no fanaticism, and which casts the same ominous doubt on subjectively morbid as on subjectively moral action,—a misanthropy which has no respect for impulses, but has a terrible perception of spiritual laws,—this is a misanthropy which can expect no wide recognition; and it would be vain to deny that traces of this kind of misanthropy are to be found in Hawthorne's earlier, and are not altogether absent from his later works. He had spiritual insight, but it did not penetrate to the sources of spiritual joy; and his deepest glimpses of truth were calculated rather to sadden than to inspire. A blandly cynical distrust of human nature was the result of his most piercing glances into the human soul. He had humor, and sometimes humor of a delicious kind; but this sunshine of the soul was but sunshine breaking through or lighting up a sombre and ominous cloud. There was also observable in his earlier stories a lack of vigor, as if the power of his nature had been impaired by the very process which gave depth and excursiveness to his mental vision. Throughout, the impression is conveyed of a shy recluse, alternately bashful in disposition and bold in thought, gifted with original and various capacities, but capacities which seemed to have developed themselves in the shade, without sufficient energy of will or desire to force them, except fitfully, into the sunlight. Shakspeare calls moonlight the sunlight *sick;* and it is in some such moonlight of the mind that the genius of Hawthorne found its first expression. A mild melancholy, sometimes deepening into gloom, sometimes brightened into a "humorous sadness," characterized his early creations. Like his own Hepzibah Pyncheon, he appeared "to be walking in a dream"; or rather, the life and reality assumed by his emotions "made all outward occurrences unsubstantial, like the teasing phantasms of an unconscious slumber." Though dealing largely in description, and with the most accurate perceptions of outward objects, he still, to use again his own words, gives the impression of a man "chiefly accustomed to look inward, and to whom external matters are of little value or import, unless they bear relation to something within his own mind." But that "something within his own mind" was often an unpleasant something, perhaps a ghastly occult perception of deformity and sin in what appeared outwardly fair and good; so that the reader felt a secret dissatisfaction with the disposition which directed the genius, even in the homage he awarded to the genius itself. As psychological portraits of morbid natures, his delineations of character might have given a purely intellectual satisfaction; but there was audible, to the delicate ear, a faint and muffled growl of personal discontent, which showed they were not mere exercises of penetrating imaginative analysis, but had in them the morbid vitality of a despondent mood.

Yet, after admitting these peculiarities, nobody who is now drawn to the "Twice-Told Tales," from his interest in the later romances of Hawthorne, can fail to wonder a little at the limited number of readers they attracted on their original publication. For many of these stories are at once a representative of early New-England life and a criticism on it. They have much of the deepest truth of history in them. "The Legends of the Province House," "The Gray Champion," "The Gentle Boy," "The Minister's Black Veil," "Endicott and the Red Cross," not to mention others, contain important matter which cannot be found in Bancroft or Grahame. They exhibit the inward struggles of New-England men and women with some of the darkest problems of existence, and have more vital import to thoughtful minds than the records of Indian or Revolutionary warfare. In the "Prophetic Pictures," "Fancy's Show-Box," "The Great Carbuncle," "The Haunted Mind," and "Edward Fane's Rose-Bud," there are flashes of moral insight, which light up, for the moment, the darkest recesses of the individual mind; and few sermons reach to the depth of thought and sentiment from which these seemingly airy sketches draw their sombre life. It is common, for instance, for religious moralists to insist on the great spiritual truth, that wicked thoughts and impulses, which circumstances prevent from passing into wicked acts, are still deeds in the sight of God; but the living truth subsides into a dead truism, as enforced by common-place preachers. In "Fancy's Show-Box," Hawthorne seizes the prolific idea; and the respectable merchant and respected church-member, in the still hour of his own meditation, convicts himself of being a liar, cheat, thief, seducer, and murderer, as he casts his glance over the mental events which form his spiritual biography. Interspersed with serious histories and moralities like these, are others which embody the sweet and playful, though still thoughtful and slightly saturnine action of Hawthorne's mind, —like "The Seven Vagabonds," "Snow-Flakes," "The Lily's Quest," "Mr. Higginbotham's Catastrophe," "Little Annie's Ramble," "Sights from a Steeple," "Sunday at Home," and "A Rill from the Town-Pump."

The "Mosses from an Old Manse" are intellectually and artistically an advance from the "Twice-Told Tales." The twenty-three stories and essays which make up the volumes are almost perfect of their kind. Each is complete in itself, and many might be expanded into long romances by the simple method of developing the possibilities of their shadowy types of character into appropriate incidents. In description, narration, allegory, humor, reason, fancy, subtilty, inventiveness, they exceed the best productions of Addison; but they want Addison's sensuous contentment and sweet and kindly spirit. Though the author denies that he has exhibited his own individual attributes in these "Mosses," though he professes not to be "one of those supremely hospitable people who serve up their own hearts delicately fried, with brain-sauce, as a tidbit for their beloved public,"—yet it is none the less apparent that he has diffused through each tale and sketch the life of the mental mood to which it owed its existence, and that one individuality pervades and colors the whole collection. The defect of the serious stories is, that character is introduced, not as thinking, but as the illustration of thought. The persons are ghostly, with a sad lack of flesh and blood. They are phantasmal symbols of a reflective and imaginative analysis of human passions and aspirations. The dialogue, especially, is bookish, as though the personages knew their speech was to be printed, and were careful of the collocation and rhythm of their words. The author throughout is evidently more interested in his large, wide, deep, indolently serene, and lazily sure and critical view of the conflict of ideas and passions, than he is with the individuals who embody them. He shows moral insight without moral earnestness. He cannot contract his mind to the patient delineation of a moral individual, but attempts to use individuals in order to express the last results of patient moral perception. Young Goodman Brown and Roger Malvin are not persons; they are the mere, loose, personal expression of subtile thinking. "The Celestial Railroad," "The Procession of Life," "Earth's Holocaust," "The Bosom Serpent," indicate thought of a character equally deep, delicate, and comprehensive, but the characters are ghosts of men rather than substantial individualities. In the "Mosses from an Old Manse," we are really studying the phenomena of human nature, while, for the time, we beguile ourselves into the belief that we are following the fortunes of individual natures.

Up to this time the writings of Hawthorne conveyed the impression of a genius in which insight so dominated over impulse, that it was rather mentally and morally curious than mentally and morally impassioned. The quality evidently wanting to its full expression was intensity. In the romance of "The Scarlet Letter" he first made his genius efficient by penetrating it with passion. This book forced itself into attention by its inherent power; and the author's name, previously known only to a limited circle of readers, suddenly became a familiar word in the mouths of the great reading public of America and England. It may be said, that it "captivated" nobody, but took everybody captive. Its power could neither be denied nor resisted. There were growls of disapprobation from novel-readers, that Hester Prynne and the Rev. Mr. Dimmesdale were subjected to cruel punishments unknown to the jurisprudence of fiction,—that the author was an inquisitor who put his victims on the rack,—and that neither amusement nor delight resulted from seeing the contortions and hearing the groans of these martyrs of sin; but the fact was no less plain that Hawthorne had for once compelled the most superficial lovers of romance to submit themselves to the magic of his genius. The readers of Dickens voted him, with three times three, to the presidency of their republic of letters; the readers of Hawthorne were caught by a *coup d'état*, and fretfully submitted to a despot whom they could not depose.

The success of "The Scarlet Letter" is an example of the advantage which an author gains by the simple concentration of his powers on one absorbing subject. In the "Twice-Told Tales" and the "Mosses from an Old Manse" Hawthorne had exhibited a wider range of sight and insight than in "The Scarlet Letter." Indeed, in the little sketch of "Endicott and the Red Cross," written twenty years before, he had included in a few sentences the whole matter which he afterwards treated in his famous story. In describing the various inhabitants of an early New-England town, as far as they were representative, he touches incidentally on a "young woman, with no mean share of beauty, whose doom it was to wear the letter A on the breast of her gown, in the eyes of all the world and her own children. And even her own children knew what that initial signified. Sporting with her infamy, the lost and desperate creature had embroidered the fatal token in scarlet cloth, with golden thread and the nicest art of needle-work; so that the capital A might have been thought to mean Admirable, or anything, rather than Adulteress." Here is the germ of the whole pathos and terror of "The Scarlet Letter"; but it is hardly noted in the throng of symbols, equally pertinent, in the few pages of the little sketch from which we have quoted.

Two characteristics of Hawthorne's genius stand plainly out, in the conduct and characterization of the romance of "The Scarlet Letter," which were less obviously prominent in his previous works. The first relates to his subordination of external incidents to inward events. Mr. James's "solitary horseman" does more in one chapter than Hawthorne's hero in twenty chapters; but then James deals with the arms of men, while Hawthorne deals with their souls. Hawthorne relies almost entirely for the interest of his story on what is felt and done within the minds of his characters. Even his most picturesque descriptions and narratives are only one-tenth matter to nine-tenths spirit. The results that follow from one external act of folly or crime are to him enough for an Iliad of woes. It might be supposed that his whole theory of Romantic Art was based on these tremendous lines of Wordsworth:—

"Action is momentary,—
The motion of a muscle, this way or that:
Suffering is long, obscure, and infinite."

The second characteristic of his genius is connected with the first. With his insight of individual souls he combines a far deeper insight of the spiritual laws which govern the strangest aberrations of individual souls. But it seems to us that his mental eye, keen-sighted and far-sighted as it is, overlooks the merciful modifications of the austere code whose pitiless action it so clearly discerns. In his long and patient brooding over the spiritual phenomena of Puritan life, it is apparent, to the least critical observer, that he has imbibed a deep personal antipathy to the Puritanic ideal of character; but it is no less apparent that his intellect and imagination have been strangely fascinated by the Puritanic idea of justice. His brain has been subtly infected by the Puritanic perception of Law, without being warmed by the Puritanic faith in Grace. Individually, he would much prefer to have been one of his own "Seven Vagabonds" rather than one of the austerest preachers of the primitive church of New England; but the austerest preacher of the primitive church of New England would have been more tender and considerate to a real Mr. Dimmesdale and a real Hester Prynne than this modern romancer has been to their typical representatives in the world of imagination. Throughout "The Scarlet Letter" we seem to be following the guidance of an author who is personally good-natured, but intellectually and morally relentless.

"The House of the Seven Gables," Hawthorne's next work, while it has less concentration of passion and tension of mind than "The Scarlet Letter," includes a wider range of observation, reflection, and character; and the morality, dreadful as fate, which hung like a black cloud over the personages of the previous story, is exhibited in more relief. Although the book has no imaginative creation equal to little Pearl, it still contains numerous examples of characterization at once delicate and deep. Clifford, especially, is a study in psychology, as well as a marvellously subtle delineation of enfeebled manhood. The general idea of the story is this,— "that the wrong-doing of one generation lives into the successive ones, and, divesting itself of every temporary advantage, becomes a pure and uncontrollable mischief"; and the mode in which this idea is carried out shows great force, fertility, and refinement of mind. A weird fancy, sporting with the facts detected by a keen observation, gives to every gable of the Seven Gables, every room in the House, every burdock growing rankly before the door, a symbolic significance. The queer mansion is haunted,—haunted with thoughts which every moment are liable to take ghostly shape. All the Pyncheons who have resided in it appear to have infected the very timbers and walls with the spiritual essence of their lives, and each seems ready to pass from a memory into a presence. The stern theory of the author regarding the hereditary transmission of family qualities, and the visiting of the sins of the fathers on the heads of their children, almost wins our reluctant assent through the pertinacity with which the generations of the Pyncheon race are made not merely to live in the blood and brain of their descendants, but to cling to their old abiding-place on earth, so that to inhabit the house is to breathe the Pyncheon soul and assimilate the Pyncheon individuality. The whole representation, masterly as it is, considered as an effort of intellectual and imaginative power, would still be morally bleak, were it not for the sunshine and warmth radiated from the character of Phœbe. In this delightful creation Hawthorne for once gives himself up to homely human nature, and has succeeded in delineating a New-England girl, cheerful, blooming, practical, affectionate, efficient, full of innocence and happiness, with all the "handiness" and native sagacity of her class, and so true and close to Nature that the process by which she is slightly idealized is completely hidden.

In this romance there is also more humor than in any of his other works. It peeps out, even in the most serious passages, in a kind of demure rebellion against the fanaticism of his remorseless intelligence. In the description of the Pyncheon poultry, which we think unexcelled by anything in Dickens for quaintly fanciful humor, the author seems to indulge in a sort of parody on his own doctrine of the hereditary transmission of family qualities. At any rate, that strutting chanticleer, with his two meagre wives and one wizened chicken, is a sly side fleer at the tragic aspect of the law of descent. Miss Hepzibah Pyncheon, her shop, and her customers, are so delightful, that the reader would willingly spare a good deal of Clifford and Judge Pyncheon and Holgrave, for more details of them and Phœbe. Uncle Venner, also, the old wood-sawyer, who boasts "that he has seen a good deal of the world, not only in people's kitchens and back-yards, but at the street-corners, and on the wharves, and in other places where his business" called him, and who, on the strength of this comprehensive experience, feels qualified to give the final decision in every case which tasks the resources of human wisdom, is a very much more humane and interesting gentleman than the Judge. Indeed, one cannot but regret that Hawthorne should be so economical of his undoubted stores of humor,—and that, in the two romances he has since written, humor, in the form of character, does not appear at all.

Before proceeding to the consideration of "The Blithedale Romance," it is necessary to say a few words on the seeming separation of Hawthorne's genius from his will. He has none of that ability which enabled Scott and enables Dickens to force their powers into action, and to make what was begun in drudgery soon assume the character of inspiration. Hawthorne cannot thus use his genius; his genius always uses him. This is so true, that he often succeeds better in what calls forth his personal antipathies than in what calls forth his personal sympathies. His life of General Pierce, for instance, is altogether destitute of life; yet in writing it he must have exerted himself to the utmost, as his object was to urge the claims of an old and dear friend to the Presidency of the Republic. The style, of course, is excellent, as it is impossible for Hawthorne to write bad English, but the genius of the man has deserted him. General Pierce, whom he loves, he draws so feebly, that one doubts, while reading the biography, if such a man exists; Hollingsworth, whom he hates, is so vividly characterized, that the doubt is, while we read the romance, whether such a man can possibly be fictitious.

Midway between such a work as the "Life of General Pierce" and "The Scarlet Letter" may be placed "The Wonder-Book" and

"Tanglewood Tales." In these Hawthorne's genius distinctly appears, and appears in its most lovable, though not in its deepest form. These delicious stories, founded on the mythology of Greece, were written for children, but they delight men and women as well. Hawthorne never pleases grown people so much as when he writes with an eye to the enjoyment of little people.

Now "The Blithedale Romance" is far from being so pleasing a performance as "Tanglewood Tales," yet it very much better illustrates the operation, indicates the quality, and expresses the power, of the author's genius. His great books appear not so much created by him as through him. They have the character of revelations,—he, the instrument, being often troubled with the burden they impose on his mind. His profoundest glances into individual souls are like the marvels of clairvoyance. It would seem, that, in the production of such a work as "The Blithedale Romance," his mind had hit accidentally, as it were, on an idea or fact mysteriously related to some morbid sentiment in the inmost core of his nature, and connecting itself with numerous scattered observations of human life, lying unrelated in his imagination. In a sort of meditative dream, his intellect drifts in the direction to which the subject points, broods patiently over it, looks at it, looks into it, and at last looks through it to the law by which it is governed. Gradually, individual beings, definite in spiritual quality, but shadowy in substantial form, group themselves around this central conception, and by degrees assume an outward body and expression corresponding to their internal nature. On the depth and intensity of the mental mood, the force of the fascination it exerts over him, and the length of time it holds him captive, depend the solidity and substance of the individual characterizations. In this way Miles Coverdale, Hollingsworth, Westervelt, Zenobia, and Priscilla become real persons to the mind which has called them into being. He knows every secret and watches every motion of their souls, yet is, in a measure, independent of them, and pretends to no authority by which he can alter the destiny which consigns them to misery or happiness. They drift to their doom by the same law by which they drifted across the path of his vision. Individually, he abhors Hollingsworth, and would like to annihilate Westervelt, yet he allows the superb Zenobia to be their victim; and if his readers object that the effect of the whole representation is painful, he would doubtless agree with them, but profess his incapacity honestly to alter a sentence. He professes to tell the story as it was revealed to him; and the license in which a romancer might indulge is denied to a biographer of spirits. Show him a fallacy in his logic of passion and character, point out a false or defective step in his analysis, and he will gladly alter the whole to your satisfaction; but four human souls, such as he has described, being given, their mutual attractions and repulsions will end, he feels assured, in just such a catastrophe as he has stated.

Eight years have passed since "The Blithedale Romance" was written, and during nearly the whole of this period Hawthorne has resided abroad. "The Marble Faun," which must, on the whole, be considered the greatest of his works, proves that his genius has widened and deepened in this interval, without any alteration or modification of its characteristic merits and characteristic defects. The most obvious excellence of the work is the vivid truthfulness of its descriptions of Italian life, manners, and scenery; and, considered merely as a record of a tour in Italy, it is of great interest and attractiveness. The opinions on Art, and the special criticisms on the masterpieces of architecture, sculpture, and painting, also possess a value of their own. The story might have been told, and the characters fully represented, in one-third of the space devoted to them, yet description and narration are so artfully combined that each assists to give interest to the other. Hawthorne is one of those true observers who concentrate in observation every power of their minds. He has accurate sight and piercing insight. When he modifies either the form or the spirit of the objects he describes, he does it either by viewing them through the medium of an imagined mind or by obeying associations which they themselves suggest. We might quote from the descriptive portions of the work a hundred pages, at least, which would demonstrate how closely accurate observation is connected with the highest powers of the intellect and imagination.

The style of the book is perfect of its kind, and, if Hawthorne had written nothing else, would entitle him to rank among the great masters of English composition. Walter Savage Landor is reported to have said of an author whom he knew in his youth, "My friend wrote excellent English, a language now obsolete." Had "The Marble Faun" appeared before he uttered this sarcasm, the wit of the remark would have been pointless. Hawthorne not only writes English, but the sweetest, simplest, and clearest English that ever has been made the vehicle of equal depth, variety, and subtilty of thought and emotion. His mind is reflected in his style as a face is reflected in a mirror; and the latter does not give back its image with less appearance of effort than the former. His excellence consists not so much in using common words as in making common words express uncommon things. Swift, Addison,

Goldsmith, not to mention others, wrote with as much simplicity; but the style of neither embodies an individuality so complex, passions so strange and intense, sentiments so fantastic and preternatural, thoughts so profound and delicate, and imaginations so remote from the recognized limits of the ideal, as find an orderly outlet in the pure English of Hawthorne. He has hardly a word to which Mrs. Trimmer would primly object, hardly a sentence which would call forth the frosty anathema of Blair, Hurd, Kames, or Whately, and yet he contrives to embody in his simple style qualities which would almost excuse the verbal extravagances of Carlyle.

In regard to the characterization and plot of "The Marble Faun," there is room for widely varying opinions. Hilda, Miriam, and Donatello will be generally received as superior in power and depth to any of Hawthorne's previous creations of character; Donatello, especially, must be considered one of the most original and exquisite conceptions in the whole range of romance; but the story in which they appear will seem to many an unsolved puzzle, and even the tolerant and interpretative "gentle reader" will be troubled with the unsatisfactory conclusion. It is justifiable for a romancer to sting the curiosity of his readers with a mystery, only on the implied obligation to explain it at last; but this story begins in mystery only to end in mist. The suggestive faculty is tormented rather than genially excited, and in the end is left a prey to doubts. The central idea of the story, the necessity of sin to convert such a creature as Donatello into a moral being, is also not happily illustrated in the leading event. When Donatello kills the wretch who malignantly dogs the steps of Miriam, all readers think that Donatello committed no sin at all; and the reason is, that Hawthorne has deprived the persecutor of Miriam of all human attributes, made him an allegorical representation of one of the most fiendish forms of unmixed evil, so that we welcome his destruction with something of the same feeling with which, in following the allegory of Spenser or Bunyan, we rejoice in the hero's victory over the Blatant Beast or Giant Despair. Conceding, however, that Donatello's act was murder, and not "justifiable homicide," we are still not sure that the author's conception of his nature and of the change caused in his nature by that act, are carried out with a felicity corresponding to the original conception.

In the first volume, and in the early part of the second, the author's hold on his design is comparatively firm, but it somewhat relaxes as he proceeds, and in the end it seems almost to escape from his grasp. Few can be satisfied with the concluding chapters, for the reason that nothing is really concluded. We are willing to follow the ingenious processes of Calhoun's deductive logic, because we are sure, that, however severely they task the faculty of attention, they will lead to some positive result; but Hawthorne's logic of events leaves us in the end bewildered in a labyrinth of guesses. The book is, on the whole, such a great book, that its defects are felt with all the more force.

In this rapid glance at some of the peculiarities of Hawthorne's genius, we have not, of course, been able to do full justice to the special merits of the works we have passed in review; but we trust that we have said nothing which would convey the impression that we do not place them among the most remarkable romances produced in an age in which romance-writing has called forth some of the highest powers of the human mind. In intellect and imagination, in the faculty of discerning spirits and detecting laws, we doubt if any living novelist is his equal; but his genius, in its creative action, has been heretofore attracted to the dark rather than the bright side of the interior life of humanity, and the geniality which evidently is in him has rarely found adequate expression. In the many works which he may still be expected to write, it is to be hoped that his mind will lose some of its sadness of tone without losing any of its subtilty and depth; but, in any event, it would be unjust to deny that he has already done enough to insure him a commanding position in American literature as long as American literature has an existence.

RICHARD HOLT HUTTON [1826–97] was a theologian, journalist, and man of letters. In 1855 he and Walter Bagehot became editors of *The National Review*. In 1860 he published a survey of Hawthorne's works; without question it is the most mature assessment of Hawthorne during his lifetime. At the conclusion of the essay Hutton, like others, condemned Hawthorne's campaign biography of Pierce and his "political fatalism" regarding reform and slavery. He wrote, "We do say that he prostitutes the noblest speculative faculties when he attempts to perpetuate a fearful national crime, in the dishonest plea that those who strive to resist its extension and to limit its duration are endangering the Union for the sake of a 'misty philanthropic theory.'"

Nathaniel Hawthorne

[RICHARD HOLT HUTTON]

Mr. Hawthorne speaks more than once in his various thoughtful and artistic tales of the "moonlight of romance," and the phrase has a special applicability to the fictions which it is his delight to weave. It is one of his favourite theories that there must be a vague, remote, and shadowy element in the subject-matter of any narrative with which his own imagination can successfully deal. Sometimes he apologises for this idealistic limitation to his artistic aims. "It was a folly," he says in his preface to the *Scarlet Letter*, "with the materiality of this daily life pressing so intrusively upon me, to attempt to fling myself back into another age, or to insist on creating the semblance of a world out of airy matter, when, at every moment, the impalpable beauty of my soap-bubble was broken by the rude contact of some actual circumstance. The wiser effort would have been to diffuse thought and imagination through the opaque substance of to-day, and thus to make it a bright transparency; to spiritualise the burden that began to weigh so heavily; to seek resolutely the true and indestructible value that lay hidden in the petty and wearisome incidents and ordinary characters with which I was now conversant. The fault was mine. The page of life that was spread out before me was so dull and commonplace only because I had not fathomed its deeper import. A better book than I shall ever write was there; leaf after leaf presenting itself to me, just as it was written out by the reality of the flitting hour, and vanishing as fast as written, only because my brain wanted the insight and my hand the cunning to transcribe it. At some future day, it may be, I shall remember a few scattered fragments and broken paragraphs and write them down, and find the letters turn to gold upon the page." But the dissatisfaction with his own idealism which he here expresses has at least not sufficed to divert his efforts into the channel indicated. In the *Blithedale Romance* he tells us that he chose the external scenery of the Socialist community at Brook Farm "merely to establish a theatre, a little removed from the highway of ordinary travel, where the creatures of his brain may play their phantasmagorical antics without exposing them to too close a comparison with the actual events of real lives. In the old countries with which fiction has long been conversant, a certain conventional privilege seems to be awarded to the romancer; his work is not put exactly side by side with nature; and he is allowed a license with regard to every-day probability, in view of the improved effects which he is bound to produce thereby. Among ourselves, on the contrary, there is as yet no such Faëry Land so like the real world that, in a suitable remoteness, one cannot well tell the difference, but with an atmosphere of strange enchantment, beheld through which, the inhabitants have a propriety of their own. This atmosphere is what the American romancer wants. In its absence, the beings of imagination are compelled to show themselves in the same category as actually living mortals,—a necessity that generally renders the paint and pasteboard of their composition but too painfully discernible." And once more, in the preface to his latest work, *Transformation*, he reiterates as his excuse for laying the scene in Italy, that "no author without a trial can conceive of the difficulty of writing a romance about a country where there is no shadow, no antiquity, no mystery, no picturesque and gloomy wrong, nor any thing but a commonplace prosperity in broad and simple daylight, as is happily the case with my dear native land. It will be very long, I trust, before romance-writers may find congenial and easily-handled themes either in the annals of our stalwart republic, or in any characteristic and probable event of our individual lives. Romance and poetry, ivy, lichens, and wall-flowers, need ruin to make them grow." These passages throw much light on the secret affinities of Mr. Hawthorne's genius. But it would be a mistake to conclude from them, as he himself would apparently have us, that he is a mere romantic idealist, in the sense in which these words are commonly used,—that he is one all whose dramatic conceptions are but the unreal kaleidoscopic combinations of fancies in his own brain.

We may perhaps accept Mr. Hawthorne's own phrase,—"the moonlight of romance,"—and compel it to help us to a distinction which will explain something of the secret of his characteristic genius. There are writers—chiefly poets, but also occasionally writers of fanciful romances like Mr. Longfellow's *Hyperion*—whose productions are purely ideal, not only seen by the light of their own imagination but constituted out of it,—made of moonshine, —and rendered vivid and beautiful, if they are vivid and beautiful, merely with the vividness and beauty of the poet's own mind. In these cases there is no distinction at all between the delineating power and the delineated object; the dream is indistinguishable from the mind of the dreamer, and varies wholly with its laws. Again, at the opposite extreme there is a kind of creative imagination which has its origin in a deep sympathy with, and knowledge of, the real world. That which it deals with is actual life as it has existed, or still exists, in forms so innumerable that it is scarcely possible to assert that its range is more limited than life itself. Of course the only adequate example of such an imagination is Shakespeare's; and this kind of imaginative power resembles sunlight, not only in its brilliancy, but especially in this, that it casts a light so full and equable over the universe it reveals, that we never think of its source at all. We forget altogether, as we do by common daylight, that the light by which we see is not part and parcel of the world which it presents to us. The sunlight is so efficient that we forget the sun. We find so rich and various a world before us, dressed in its own proper colours, that no one is reminded that the medium by which those proper colours are seen is uniform and from a single source. We merge the delineative magic by which the scene is illuminated in the details of the scene itself. Between these two kinds of creative imagination there is another, which also shows a real world, but shows it so dimly in comparison with the last as to keep constantly before our minds the unique character of the light by which we see. The ideal light itself becomes a more prominent element in the picture than even the objects on which it shines; and yet is made so, chiefly by the very fact of shining on those objects which we are accustomed to think of as they are seen in their own familiar details in full daylight. If the objects illuminated were not real and familiar, the light would not seem so mysterious; it is the pale uniform tint, the loss of colour and detail, and yet the vivid familiar outline and the strong shadow, which produces what Mr. Hawthorne calls the "moonlight of romance." "Moonlight in a familiar room," he says in his preface to the *Scarlet Letter*, "falling so white upon the carpet, and showing all its figures so distinctly, making every object so minutely visible, yet so unlike a morning or noontide visibility,—is a medium the most suitable for a romance-writer to get acquainted with his illusive guests. There is the little domestic scenery of the well-known apartment; the chairs, with each its separate individuality; the centre table, sustaining a work-basket, a volume or two, and an extinguished lamp; the sofa, the bookcase, the picture on the wall;—all these details, so completely seen, are so spiritualised by the unusual light, that they seem to lose their actual substance, and become things of intellect. Nothing is too small or too trifling to undergo this change, and acquire dignity thereby. A child's shoe, the doll seated in her little wicker carriage, the hobby-horse,—whatever, in a word, has been used or played with during the day, is now invested with a quality of strangeness and remoteness, though still almost as vividly present as by daylight. Thus, therefore, the floor of our familiar room has become a neutral territory, somewhere between the real world and fairyland, where the Actual and the Imaginary may meet, and each imbue itself with the nature of the other." Sir Walter Scott's delineative power partakes of both this moonlight imagination and the other more powerful and brilliant and realistic kind. Often it is a wide genial sunshine, of which we quite forget the source in the vividness of the common life which it irradiates. At other times, again, when he is in his Black Douglas mood, as we may call it, it has all the uniformity of tint and the exciting pallor, of what Mr. Hawthorne terms the moonlight of romance.

At all events, there is no writer to whose creations the phrase applies more closely than to Mr. Hawthorne's own. His characters are by no means such unreal webs of moonshine as the idealists proper constitute into the figures of their romance. They are real and powerfully conceived, but they are all seen in a single light,—the contemplative light of the particular idea which has floated before him in each of his stories,—and they are seen, not fully and in their integrity, as things are seen by daylight, but like things touched by moonlight, *only so far* as they are lighted up by the idea of the story. The thread of unity which connects his tales is always some pervading thought of his own; they are not written mainly to display character, still less for the mere narrative interest, but for the illustration they cast on some idea or conviction of their author's. Amongst English writers of fiction, we have many besides Shakespeare whose stories are merely appropriate instruments for the portraiture of character, and who therefore never conceive themselves bound to confine themselves scrupulously to the one aspect most naturally developed by the tale. Once introduced, their characters are given in full,—both that side of them which is, so to say, turned *towards* the story, and others which are not. Other writers, again, make the characters quite subsidiary to the epical interest of the plot, using them only to heighten the colouring of the action it describes. Mr. Hawthorne's tales belong to neither of these classes. Their unity is ideal. His characters are often real and vivid, but they are illuminated only from one centre of thought. So strictly is this true of them, that he has barely *room* for a novel in the ordinary sense of the word. If he were to take his characters through as many phases of life as are ordinarily comprised in a novel, he could not keep the ideal unity of his tales unbroken; he would be obliged to delineate them from many different points of view. Accordingly his novels are not novels in the ordinary sense; they are ideal situations expanded by minute study and trains of closely-related thought into the dimensions of novels. A very small group of figures is presented to the reader in some marked ideal relation; or if it be in consequence of some critical event, then it must be some event which has struck the author as rich in ideal or moral suggestion. But it is not usually in his way—though his latest novel gives us one remarkable exception to this observation—to seize any glowing crisis of action when the passion is lit or the blow is struck that gives a new mould to life, for his delineation; he prefers to assume the crisis past, and to delineate as fully as he can the ideal situation to which it has given rise, when it is beginning to assume more of a chronic character.

But, however this may be, almost all his tales embody single ideal situations, scarcely ever for a moment varied in their course in any essential respect. For instance, to take his shorter tales, the mockery of the attempt to renew in wasted age the blasted hopes of youth is crystallised into a *tableau vivant* in the *Wedding-Knell*. The absolute spiritual isolation of every man's deepest life, and the awe which any visible assertion of that isolation inspires, even when made by the mildest of our guilty race, is translated into an ideal picture in the *Minister's Black Veil*. So in the *Great Stone Face* we have an embodiment of the conviction that *he* is best fitted to fulfil any great human hope or trust whose heart is constantly fed upon the yearning to find the perfect fulfilment of it in another. So in *Roger Malvin's Burial* we are shown how an innocent man, who is too cowardly to face the mere appearance of guilt, may thereby incur a remorse and guilt as deep as that from the faintest suspicion of which he shrank. And so we may run through almost all the *tales* properly so called. We do not mean that in any of them the author thinks the thought first in its abstract form, and then condenses it into a story. We should suppose, on the contrary, that the artistic form is the one in which the idea of the tale first flashes on him, and that the work of elaboration only gives more substance and greater variety of colour to the parts. But not the less is the essence originally ideal, since every touch and line in his imagined picture is calculated to impress some leading thought on the reader.

But it is only when we look at his longer tales, whose dimensions would lead us to expect more variety of aspect in the characters, more circumstance, and less sameness of leading *thought*, that this characteristic of Mr. Hawthorne's tales becomes striking. The stories of the *Scarlet Letter*, of the *House of the Seven Gables*, and of *Transformation*, might all have been included, in their full ideal integrity, and with all the *incident* they contain, in the *Twice-told Tales* without adding more than a few pages to the book. We do not mean that thus compressed they would produce the same, or any thing like the same, imaginative impression, but only that, as far as either the *aspect* of his characters or the circumstantial interest of the stories is concerned, there need be no compression in thus shortening them. The omissions would be most important, indeed, to the effect, but they would be the omission of minute contemplative touches, imaginative self-repetitions, and so forth, which seldom indeed give us a single glimpse of any other than the one side of his characters, or add a second thread to the one interest of the tale.

In the *Scarlet Letter*, for instance, there is but one conception, which is developed in three—perhaps we should say four—scenes of great power, and that is the analysis of the deranging effect of the sin of adultery on the intrinsically fine characters of those principally affected by it, with a special view to its different influence on the woman, who is openly branded with the shame, and on the man, whose guilt is not published and who has a double remorse to suffer, for the sin, and for the growing burden of insincerity. The effect of the sin on the child who is the offspring of it is made a special study, as are the false relations it introduces between the mother and child. Throughout the tale every one of the group of characters studied is seen in the lurid light of this sin and in no other. The only failure is in the case of the injured and vindictive husband, whose character is subordinated entirely to the artistic development of the other three.

In the same way the predominant idea of the *Blithedale Romance* is to delineate the deranging effect of an absorbing philanthropic idea on a powerful mind,—the unscrupulous sacrifices of personal claims which it induces, and the misery in which it ends. There is scarcely one *incident* in the tale properly so called except the catastrophe, and what there is is so anxiously shrouded in mystery as to have really all the enigmatic character of a *tableau vivant* of clear general meaning but doubtful interpretation as to details. The author seems to say to the reader, 'Here is a group of characters in relations tending to illustrate how much more sacred are personal affections than any abstract *cause* however noble; what these relations exactly are, except as they illustrate my idea, I will not say, as that is quite nonessential; you may imagine them what you please,—I tell you only enough to impress you with my predominant conviction.'

Again, in the *House of the Seven Gables* we have a picture studied to impress on us that both personal character, and the malign influences of evil action, are transmitted, sometimes with accumulating force, even through centuries, blighting every generation through which they pass. This subject would apparently involve a series of sketches; but only two are introduced from the past, and the family characteristics are so anxiously preserved as to make even these seem like slight modifications of some of the living group. But Mr. Hawthorne with rare art pictures the shadow of the past as constantly hanging, like a baneful cloud, over the heads of his figures; and every detail, even the minutest, is made to point backwards to the weary past from which it has derived its constitutional peculiarities. Even the little shop which "old maid Pyncheon" reopens in the dark old house is not new. A miserly ancestor of the family had opened it a century before, who is supposed to haunt it, and the scales are rusty with the rust of generations. The half-effaced picture of the ancestral Pyncheon which hangs on the walls, the garden-mould black with the vegetable decay of centuries, the exhausted breed of aristocratic fowls which inhabit the garden,—every touch is studied to condense the dark past into a cloud hanging over the living present, and make the reader feel its malign influence. The only incident in the tale is the light thrown upon a crime,—which had been committed thirty years before the story opens,—by the sudden death of the principal representative of the family, from the same specific disease, in the same chair, and under the same circumstances, as that of the old ancestor and founder of the family whose picture hangs above the chair.

The same criticism may be made on Mr. Hawthorne's latest work. The sole idea of *Transformation* is to illustrate the intellectually and morally awakening power of a sudden impulsive sin, committed by a simple, joyous, instinctive, "natural" man. The whole group of characters is imagined solely with a view to the development of this idea. Mr. Hawthorne even hints, though rather hesitatingly, that without sin the higher humanity of man could not be taken up at all; that sin may be essential to the first conscious awakening of moral freedom and the possibility of progress. The act of sin itself is the only distinct incident of the tale; all the rest is either extraneous dissertation on Art, or the elaboration and study of the group of characters requisite to embody this leading idea. A tale containing the whole ideal essence of the book, and in this instance, though only in this instance, almost equally powerful, might have been told in a few pages.

And yet we are very far indeed from meaning to say that the microscopic diffuseness with which Mr. Hawthorne enlarges these ideal studies into the length of an ordinary novel is wasted. For the secret of his power lies in the great art with which he reduplicates and reflects and re-reflects the main idea of the tale from the countless faces of his imagination, until the reader's mind is absolutely saturated and haunted by it. There are many among his shorter tales, which now occupy perhaps only five or ten pages, which would have gained infinitely in power by similar treatment, without the addition of a single fresh incident or scene. As they read now they have almost a feeble effect; they give the writer's idea and no more; they do not fill the reader with it; and Mr. Hawthorne's peculiar genius lies in the power he possesses to be haunted, and in his turn to haunt the reader, with his conceptions, far more than in their intrinsic force. Look at the central notion of his various minor tales, and you will be perhaps struck with a certain ideal simplicity, and a strange dash of lurid colour in them that will impress you as promising, but no more. But let him summon this idea before you in the innumerable Protean shapes of his own imagination, with alterations of form just striking enough to make it seem at once the same and something fresh; and before he has done with you you are pursued, you are possessed, you are beset with his notion: it is in your very blood; it stares at you with ghastly force from every word of his narrative; it is in the earth and in the air; and every mouth that opens among his characters, however little they may be involved in the mystery of the tale, only sends it thrilling with greater force through your heart. What a story, for instance, might he not have made out of the very eerie tales called *Roger Malvin's Burial,* or *Rappacini's Daughter,* if he had elaborated them with any thing like the art shown in the *House of the Seven Gables!*

Mr. Hawthorne was quite aware of the slight ideal structure of his earlier and shorter tales. He has himself criticised them with rare candour and subtlety, though not with a fair appreciation of the promise of deeper power which they contained, in his preface to one of the editions of the *Twice-told Tales.*

[Quote from 1851 "Preface"]

. . . .

This passage contains some of the truest and finest touches in the way of literary self-criticism with which we are acquainted;

but it does not, as we said, do justice to the undeveloped germs of power in many of the pieces comprised in this and Mr. Hawthorne's other collections of shorter tales. It is true, indeed, that, throughout almost all he has yet written, sentiment takes the place of passion, and it is not seldom true, though it by no means holds of the majority of his finished studies of character, that, in the place of "pictures of actual life, we have allegory not always so warmly dressed in its habiliments of flesh and blood as to be taken into the reader's mind without a shiver." But there is enough even in the early tales of which Mr. Hawthorne here speaks to prove that the allegorical turn which his tales are apt to take was not with him, as it often is, a sign of meagre or shallow imaginative endowments,—a proof that fancy predominates in him rather than genuine imagination. When a man sits down professing to paint human life and character, and in place thereof succeeds only in representing abstract virtues, vices, passions, and the like, under human names, we may fairly say that with him the allegorical vein proves the general poverty of his spiritual blood. He has peeled off the outer surface where he professed to model the substance. But when, on the other hand, the same truth, which by an ordinary intellect would be expressed in a purely abstract form, naturally takes shape in a man's mind under an imaginative clothing which savours of allegory, no inference of the kind is legitimate. In the one case the allegory is a degenerate romance, in the other it is a thought expressing itself in the language of the imagination. The weakness in the former case is measured by the inability of the imagination to see the broad chasm between the reality and the allegorical shadow. In the latter case there is no such inability, but the thought which would have entered an ordinary mind in a purely abstract form presents itself to this in the form of a vivid shadow-picture.

And it is a sign that Mr. Hawthorne's genius has not the weakness usually belonging to allegorists, that the longer a subject rests in his mind, the more certainly do the allegorical shadows of its first outline gather solidity of form and variety of colour, and gradually substantiate themselves into real living men. In the ideal situation or conception, as it first presents itself to the author's mind, the places of the human actors are perhaps occupied by appropriate symbols of some predominant sentiment or characteristic which each of the group subsequently embodies. If written down in that faint early form, the tale seems allegorical. But if allowed to lie by in the imagination, it deepens into a real dramatic situation; a body of real human life and character gathers round, and clothes, each of the ideal skeletons in the original plan, turning the faint allegory into a chapter of vivid human experience. So clearly did Mr. Edgar Poe perceive this vein of genuine imaginative power in Mr. Hawthorne's writings, even at a time when he had published only his shorter tales, that he boldly asserted,—in this, as we think, overleaping the truth,—that the conspicuously ideal scaffoldings of Mr. Hawthorne's stories were but the monstrous fruits of the bad transcendental atmosphere which he had breathed so long,—the sign of the Emersonian school of thought in which he had studied. "He is infinitely too fond of allegory," said Edgar Poe, "and can never hope for popularity so long as he persists in it. . . ."

The caustic American critic was, we think, confusing two things in this brief summary of Mr. Hawthorne's qualifications and deficiencies. He saw that Mr. Hawthorne could produce the most skilful studies from real life, as, for instance—to take one amongst many—in his sketch of the old Apple Dealer; he saw also that almost all his tales proper embodied an idea or a truth, and he thought the former the natural bent of Mr. Hawthorne's mind, the latter the imported mannerism of a clique. But the truth is, that both are equally natural to him, the ideal framework being quite as essential to him in putting together a tale as an unlimited store of unforeseen coincidences and exciting emergencies is to Fennimore Cooper or G. P. R. James, or a picturesque episode in history to Sir Walter Scott. Mr. Hawthorne could never weave his studies of human nature into a continuous narrative, based on mere circumstantial incident and striking adventure. The constructive talent, probably the special tastes and interests, requisite for that kind of framework of a tale are not a part of his genius. He must have an ideal centre and an ideal bond for his characters, or they would fall asunder into loose unconnected atoms. He has either no power or else no desire to construct what is ordinarily meant by a plot; that is, a chain of circumstantial coincidences in which the interest depends on the unusual and unforeseen character of the contingent events. The purely ideal clue of his stories supersedes entirely the function of the ordinary circumstantial thread.

But notwithstanding the simplicity and ideality which invariably mark the outline of Mr. Hawthorne's stories, the most notable characteristic of his genius distinguishes him widely from the school of allegorists. His imagination only departs from that basis of New England simplicity which is the foundation and staple of its creations, to represent in his figures and excite in the reader those fearfully blended and yet mutually repellent emotions which thrill us with a sense of something at once real and preternatural,—true to a life and a moral state which has in it a dash of sin and of ghastly contradictions, and yet exciting those fitful pulses, those flushings and shiverings of the spirit, which testify to an uncanny or unholy origin. If we want to find Mr. Hawthorne's power at the very highest, we must look to this instinctive knowledge of what we may call the laws, not exactly of *discordant* emotions, but of emotions which *ought* to be mutually exclusive, and which combine with the thrill and the shudder of disease. This is almost the antithesis of Allegory. And he makes his delineation of such "unblest unions" the more striking, because it stands out from a background of healthy life, of genial scenes and simple beauties, which renders the contrast the more thrilling. We have often heard the term "cobweby" applied to his romances; and their most marking passages certainly give the same sense of unwelcome shrinking to the spirit which a line of unexpected cobweb suddenly drawn across the face causes physically when one enters a deserted but familiar room. Edgar Poe, indeed, is much fuller of uncanny terrors; but then there is nothing in his writings of the healthy, simple, and natural background which gives sin and disease all its horror. It is the pure and severe New England simplicity which Mr. Hawthorne paints so delicately that brings out in full relief the adulterous mixture of emotions on which he spends his main strength. We might almost say that he has carried into human affairs the old Calvinistic type of imagination. The same strange combination of clear simplicity, high faith, and reverential reality, with one reluctant, but for that very reason intense and devouring, conviction of the large comprehensiveness of the Divine Damnation which that grim creed taught its most honest believers to consider as the true trust in God's providence, Mr. Hawthorne copies into his pictures of human life. He presents us with a scene of clear severe beauty, full of truthful goodness, and then he uncovers in some one point of it a plague-spot that, half-concealed as he keeps it, yet runs away with the imagination till one is scarcely conscious of any thing else. Just as Calvinism, with all its noble features, can never keep its eyes off that one fact, as it thinks it, of God's calm foreknowledge of a wide-spread damnation; and this gradually encroaches on the attention till the mind is utterly absorbed in the fascinating terror of the problem how to combine the clashing emotions of love and horror which its image of Him inspires;—so Mr. Hawthorne's finest tales, with all the fair simplicity of their general outline, never detain you long from some uneasy mixture of emotions which only deep disease can combine on one object, until at last you ask for nothing but the disentangling of the infected web.

There are many illustrations of this peculiarity of Mr. Hawthorne's genius in his earlier and shorter tales. In one of them he exclaims, and it is the key to his genius, "Blessed are all simple emotions, be they dark or bright! It is the lurid intermixture of the two that produces the illuminating blazes of the infernal regions." The tale in which Mr. Hawthorne makes this remark, *Rappacini's Daughter*, itself exemplifies in a somewhat fanciful but striking form this constant bent of his imagination. Dr. Rappacini is a professor of medical science in the University of Padua. He has devoted himself to the study of deadly poisons, and learnt how to infuse them so subtly into both animal and vegetable natures as to render that which would be fatal in the ordinary way, essential to life and health, and even productive of unusual lustre and bloom. Mr. Hawthorne has evidently based his tale on the physiological fact—which, at least in the case of arsenic, is well attested—that a malignant poison, if gradually administered, may at length become a condition of life and conducive to beauty. Dr. Rappacini has filled his garden with flowers so poisonous that he himself dare not touch them, and can scarcely venture to breathe the air around them. But the life of his daughter Beatrice has been imbued and fed with the same poisons which give so rich a bloom and so sweet but deadly a perfume to these rare plants; and to her they are health and added loveliness. Her breath is instantly fatal to the insect or the butterfly that drinks it in, and even her touch is deadly. But her heart is stainless and noble, and she shudders herself at the malign influences which she involuntarily puts forth as insects fall dead around her. Her great beauty fascinates one of the students, whose lodging looks out above this strange garden; and by Rappacini's skill, exercised without the young man's knowledge, he is gradually imbued with the same poisons which enter so deeply into the life and constitution of Beatrice. The point and art of this eerie tale lie in the conflict of emotions which Beatrice's true spiritual beauty and malignant physical influences raise in the mind of her lover, filling him with a passion blended equally of love and horror; and in the description of the despair with which he discovers that the same malignant influences are already part of himself.

The same tendency of imagination, in perhaps quite as characteristic, but in a far more unpleasant form, is shown in the tale called the *Birth-Mark*, which turns on the morbid horror inspired by a slight birth-mark on the cheek of a beautiful woman in the mind of her husband, who is at the same time passionately attached to her and bent on eradicating it. This tale has no imaginative beauty, and is only remarkable for the diseased mixture of emotions which it depicts. Again, in the tale concerning "The Man with the Snake in his Bosom" and "Young Goodman Brown," with all the most remarkable of Mr. Hawthorne's shorter tales, the same prominent feature, in some form or other, may be discerned.

But it is in the more elaborate tales that Mr. Hawthorne has most scope, at once for the relieving elements which these morbid interests, if they are to be artistically treated at all, especially require, and for the fuller development and *justification,* so to say, of emotions so subtle and unhealthy. In the *Scarlet Letter* he has a subject naturally so painful as exactly to suit his genius. He treats it with perfect delicacy, for his attention is turned to the morbid anatomy of the relations which have originated in the sin of adultery, rather than to the sin itself. There are two points on which Mr. Hawthorne concentrates his power in this remarkable book. The first is the false position of the minister, who gains fresh reverence and popularity as the very fruit of the passionate anguish with which his heart is consumed. Frantic with the stings of unacknowledged guilt, he is yet taught by those very stings to understand the hearts and stir the consciences of others. His character is a pre-Raphaelite picture of the tainted motives which fill a weak but fine and sensitive nature when placed in such a position; of self-hatred quite too passionate to conquer self-love; of a quailing conscience smothered into insane cravings for blasphemy; of the exquisite pain of gratified ambition conscious of its shameful falsehood. The second point on which Mr. Hawthorne concentrates his power is the delineation of anomalous characteristics in the child who is the offspring of this sinful passion. He gives her an inheritance of a lawless, mischievous, and elvish nature, not devoid of strong affections, but delighting to probe the very sorest points of her mother's heart, induced in part by some mysterious fascination to the subject, in part by wanton mischief. The scarlet A, which is the brand of her mother's shame, is the child's delight. She will not approach her mother unless it be on her bosom; and the unnatural complication of emotions thus excited in Hester Prynne's heart present one of the most characteristic features of the book, and are painfully engraved on the reader's mind. The scene of most marvellous power which the book contains contrives to draw to a focus all the many clashing affections portrayed. Mr. Dimmesdale, the unhappy minister, eager to invent vain penances in expiation of the guilt which he dares not avow, creeps out at midnight in his canonical robe to stand for an hour on the scaffold on which Hester and her child had been pilloried years before. It is the night when many are watching by the dying-bed of the governor of Massachusetts, and one of the minister's reverend colleagues, who has been praying with the governor, passes under the scaffold, lantern in hand. In his nervous and excited mood, Dimmesdale almost addresses him aloud, and then, paralysed by dread and his limbs stiffened by cold, it occurs to him that he will never be able to descend the steps of the scaffold, and that morning will break to show him there to all his revering flock.

. . . .

[In the lengthy excerpts from Chapter XII, Dimmesdale summons Hester and Pearl to the scaffold, the meteoric phenomenon occurs, and Dimmesdale recognizes Chillingworth hovering nearby.]

This strange vigil, the grim hysteric humour of the minister, the proud and silent fortitude of Hester, the mocking laughter of the child as she detects her unknown father's cowardice, together make as weird-like a tangle of human elements as ever bubbled together in a witches' caldron. Yet this scene, though probably the most powerful which Mr. Hawthorne has ever painted, scarcely exemplifies his uncanny fashion of awakening the most mutually-repellent feelings at the same moment towards the same person so characteristically as many of his other tales.

In the most striking chapter in the *House of the Seven Gables*, he makes Judge Pyncheon, who has died in his chair from some sudden effusion of blood, holding his still ticking watch in his hand, a subject at once for awe and scorn. He recalls all the judge's engagements for the day,—the bank-meeting at which he was to take the chair,—the business appointment he was to keep,—the private purchases he was to make,—the little act of charity which he had thought of, time and purse permitting,—the half-formal call on his physician concerning some trifling symptoms of indisposition,—the political dinner to discuss the election of the next State Governor; and then he taunts the judge with his forgetfulness. . . . And so Mr. Hawthorne goes on through the list of his engagements, reminding him separately of each as the time comes for it, recalling to the dead man the importance he had attached to them when he made his plans in the morning. . . . Thus Mr. Hawthorne goes on throughout the twenty-four hours during which the judge's body remains undiscovered,—mingling with the most powerful picture of the supernatural side of death, which he never ceases to keep vividly before us, the feelings that cluster round petty business, the sarcasms that might sting the sensitive, the urgency that might hasten the dilatory, the incentives that would spur the ambitious, flinging them all in cold irony at the corpse with an eerie effect that only Mr. Hawthorne could produce.

But the most characteristic instance of Mr. Hawthorne's power in studying combinations of emotions that are as it were at once abhorrent to nature and true to life, is in *Transformation.* The one powerful scene in that distended work is the scene of crime. The young Tuscan Count Donatello,—the "natural man" of the book, who is rumoured to be a descendant of an ancient Faun, and described in the opening of the tale as possessed only of the happy spontaneous life of the natural creatures, but who is afterwards awakened to the higher responsibilities and life of man by his remorse for an impulsive crime,—has fallen in love with Miriam, a lady artist of warm and passionate nature, high powers, and mysterious origin. This young lady is pursued by some half-madman, half-demon, who from some (unexplained) connection with her previous life has power to torment her by his threats to the very verge of unsettling her reason. Walking with Donatello, one moonlight night, at a little distance from their party, on the verge of the Tarpeian rock, this tormenting being is discovered, dogging her footsteps as usual, under the shadow of an archway. Donatello seizes him, holds him over the precipice, catches Miriam's eye, reads in it eager and fierce assent to the act he is meditating, and drops him down; there is a dead thump on the stones below and all is over. Up to this instant Miriam had felt nothing but pity for her young lover. Now for the first time, in this hideous moment, horror and love are born together in her breast, and the monstrous birth, the delirium of love born in blood, is thus powerfully described;— except, by the way, that Miriam certainly never addressed Donatello at such a moment as "Oh, friend!" either "with heavy richness of meaning" or otherwise: this is clearly a sentimental blot on Mr. Hawthorne's picture.

"'Did you not mean that he should die?' sternly asked Donatello, still in the glow of that intelligence which passion had developed in him. 'There was short time to weigh the matter; but he had his trial in that breath or two, while I held him over the cliff, and his sentence in that one glance, when your eyes responded to mine! Say that I have slain him against your will—say that he died without your whole consent —and, in another breath, you shall see me lying beside him.' 'Oh, never!' cried Miriam. 'My one own friend! Never, never, never!' She turned to him—the guilty, blood-stained, lonely woman—she turned to her fellow-criminal, the youth so lately innocent, whom she had drawn into her doom. She pressed him close, close to her bosom, with a clinging embrace that brought their two hearts together, till the horror and agony of each was combined into one emotion, and that a kind of rapture. 'Yes, Donatello, you speak the truth!' said she; 'my heart consented to what you did. We two slew yonder wretch. The deed knots us together for time and eternity, like the coil of a serpent!' They threw one other glance at the heap of death below, to assure themselves that it was there; so like a dream was the whole thing. Then they turned from that fatal precipice, and came out of the courtyard, arm in arm, heart in heart. Instinctively, they were heedful not to sever themselves so much as a pace or two from one another, for fear of the terror and deadly chill that would thenceforth wait for them in solitude. Their deed—the crime which Donatello wrought, and Miriam accepted on the instant—had wreathed itself, as she said, like a serpent, in inextricable links about both their souls, and drew them into one by its terrible contractile power. It was closer than a marriage-bond. So intimate, in those first moments, was the union that it seemed as if their new sympathy annihilated all other ties, and that they were released from the chain of humanity; a new sphere, a special law, had been created for them alone. The world could not come near them; they were safe! . . . . 'Oh, friend,' cried Miriam, so putting her soul into that word that it took a heavy richness of meaning, and seemed never to have been spoken before,—'oh, friend, are you conscious, as I am, of this companionship that knits our heart-strings together?' 'I feel it, Miriam,' said Donatello. 'We draw one breath; we live one life!' 'Only yesterday,' continued Miriam; 'nay, only a short half-hour ago, I shivered in an icy solitude. No friendship, no sisterhood, could come near enough to keep the warmth within my heart. In an instant, all is changed! There can be no more loneliness!' 'None, Miriam!' said Donatello. 'None, my beautiful one!' responded Miriam, gazing in his face, which had taken a higher, almost an heroic aspect from the strength of passion. 'None, my innocent one! Surely, it is no crime that we have committed. One wretched and worthless life has been sacrificed, to cement two other lives for evermore.' 'For evermore, Miriam!' said Donatello; 'cemented with his blood!' The young man started at the word which he had himself spoken; it may be that it brought home, to the simplicity of his imagination, what he had not before dreamed of—the ever-increasing loathsomeness of a union that consists in guilt. Cemented with blood, which would corrupt and grow more noisome for ever and for ever, but bind them none the less strictly for that! 'Forget it! Cast it all behind you!' said Miriam, detecting, by her sympathy, the pang that was in his heart. 'The deed has done its office, and has no existence any more.' They flung the past behind them, as she counselled, or else distilled from it a fiery intoxication, which sufficed to carry them triumphantly through those first moments of their doom. For guilt has its moment of rapture too. The foremost result of a broken law is ever an ecstatic sense of freedom. And thus there exhaled upward (out of their dark sympathy, at the base of which lay a human corpse) a bliss, or an insanity, which the unhappy pair imagined to be well worth the sleepy innocence that was for ever lost to them. As their spirits rose to the solemn madness of the occasion, they went onward—not stealthily, not fearfully—but with a stately gait and aspect. Passion lent them (as it does to meaner shapes) its brief nobility of carriage. They trode through the streets of Rome as if they too were among the majestic and guilty shadows that, from ages long gone by, have haunted the blood-stained city."

This is very finely conceived and yet revolting. Have we not reason for saying, that Mr. Hawthorne's chief power lies in the delineation of unnatural alliances of feeling, which are yet painfully real,—of curdling emotions that may mix for a moment, but shrink apart again quickly, as running water from clotted blood?

But it would be very unjust to Mr. Hawthorne to represent him as in any degree addicted, like Edgar Poe, to the invention of monstrosities and horrors. We only mean that his genius naturally leads him to the analysis and representation of certain outlying moral anomalies, which are not the anomalies of ordinary evil and sin, but have a certain chilling unnaturalness of their own. But under Mr. Hawthorne's treatment these anomalies are only the subtle flaws or passionate taints of natures full of fine elements; they are never superlatives of iniquity and abomination, like Edgar Poe's. They are the dark spots in a fine picture, never the very substance of the whole. There is, for instance, every palliation which a charitable imagination can invent for Hester's sin and Dimmesdale's cowardice in the *Scarlet Letter;* and even the child's elfish wantonness, though in some degree preternatural, is not demoniacal, but the mere lawless taint in an otherwise warm and open heart. So too in *Transformation* there is every excuse that circumstances can give to the crime which Donatello commits and Miriam sanctions;—after the first moment of mad excitement is over, it fills them with unspeakable anguish; it rouses all the tender devotion of the woman in Miriam for the man who had thus stained his conscience under the impulse of love to her; it awakens the sleeping soul of Donatello;—and the book is meant to record their uninterrupted upward progress from that moment. Moreover, in the two other characters we find a peaceful contrast to the turbid hearts of the sinful lovers. Neither in this nor in any other tale does Mr. Hawthorne cast any slur on human nature. He loves to picture it in its highest and tenderest aspects. And when he delineates what is revolting, one of the main elements that makes it so revolting is the Manichean incarceration of some noble and half-angelic affection in a malignant body of evil, from which it vainly seeks to be divorced.

This bent of Mr. Hawthorne's genius is no doubt in great degree determined by the speculative character of his mind. Even his *imagination* is inquisitive and—shall we call it what he calls it himself in the *Blithedale Romance?*—rather *prying* than ardent. It is fertile, but in a cold and restless way. It is used more to help him to explore mysteries than from the glowing creative impulse that cannot choose but paint. He states to himself a problem, and sets his imagination to work to solve it. How was it the woman felt who wore publicly the symbol of her own sin and shame fancifully embroidered on her bosom? What would be the state of mind of one who had unhappily killed another, and could never clearly determine in his own conscience whether his *will* had consented to the deed or not? What would be the result of a wrongful life-imprisonment on a soft æsthetic nature made for the enjoyment of the beautiful? How would a sin of passion work on a healthy, innocent, natural man of unawakened spirit? These are the kind of hypotheses on which Mr. Hawthorne's imagination works; and from the nature of the case, images summoned up in obedience to such questionings cannot always be of a very wholesome kind. The problems that Mr. Hawthorne starts are usually connected with the deepest mysteries of the human mind and conscience; and the imagination which attempts to keep pace with the inquisitive intellect cannot but paint strange and thrilling anomalies in reply to its queries. "That cold tendency," says Mr. Coverdale, the hero of the *Blithedale Romance*, who has many points of intellectual affinity with its author,—"that cold tendency between instinct and intellect, which made me pry with a speculative interest into people's passions and impulses, appeared to have gone far towards unhumanising my heart." We do not mean to say that it has gone far, or any way at all, towards unhumanising Mr. Hawthorne's heart, which is evidently tender. But no doubt, he is led by the speculative bias of his mind to steep his imagination in *arcana* on which it is scarcely good to gaze at all.

It is remarkable, and perhaps a symptom of the same imaginative constitution, that while Mr. Hawthorne has the most eager desire to penetrate the secret attitudes of minds painfully or anomalously situated, he has little or no interest in picturing the exact combination of circumstances which brought them into these attitudes. His imagination is the very converse of De Foe's. De Foe seizes the outer fact with the most vivid force; indirectly only, by the very force and minuteness of his conception of the visible circumstances, actions, and gestures he narrates, do you get at the inward mind of his characters. Mr. Hawthorne, on the contrary, is often positively anxious to *suppress* all distinct account of the actual facts which have given rise to his ideal situations. He wishes to save the mental impression from being swallowed up, so to say, in the interest of the outward facts and events. He sees that people of a matter-of-fact turn of mind attach more value to knowing the exciting causes than to knowing the state of mind which results. If they hear what seems to them an insufficient cause for a heroine's misery, they set her down as feeble-minded, and give up their interest in her fate. If they hear a *too* sufficient cause, they say she deserved all she suffered, and for that reason discard her from their sympathies. Mr. Hawthorne sees the difficulty of inventing facts that will exactly hit the shade of feeling that he desires to excite in his reader's minds, and so he often refuses to detail the facts distinctly at all. He often gives us our choice of several sets of facts which might be adequate to the results, declines to say which he himself prefers, and insists only on the attitude of mind produced. Thus, in the *Blithedale Romance*, he preludes a far from explanatory or lucid conversation with this mystifying sentence, "I hardly could make out an intelligible sentence on either side. What I seem to remember I yet suspect may have been patched together by my fancy in brooding over the matter afterwards." Again, in another part of the same book, "The details of the interview that followed being unknown to me, while notwithstanding it would be a pity quite to lose the picturesqueness of the situation, I shall attempt to sketch it mainly from fancy, although with some general grounds of surmise in regard to the old man's feelings." But he has carried this preference for delineating states of mind, and obscurely suggesting the class of facts which may have given rise to them, to the furthest point in his new work *Transformation*. "Owing, it may be," he tells us, in a chapter justly headed "Fragmentary Sentences," at a critical conjunction in the tale, "to this moral estrangement,—this chill remoteness of their position,—there have come to us but a few vague whisperings of what passed in Miriam's interview that afternoon with the sinister personage who had dogged her footsteps ever since her visit to the catacomb. In weaving these mystic utterances into a continuous scene, we undertake a task resembling in its perplexity that of gathering up and piecing together the fragments of a letter which has been torn and scattered to the winds. Many words of deep significance,—many entire sentences, and these probably the most important ones,—have flown too far on the winged breeze to be recovered. If we insert our own conjectural amendments, we may perhaps give a purport utterly at variance with the true one." And then Mr. Hawthorne continues, "Of so much we are sure, that there seemed to be a sadly mysterious fascination in the influence of this ill-omened person over Miriam; it was such as beasts and reptiles of subtle and evil natures sometimes exercise over their victims. . . . Yet let us trust there may have been no crime in Miriam, but only one of those fatalities which are among the insoluble riddles propounded to mortal comprehension—the fatal doom by which every crime is made to be the agony of many innocent persons, as well as of the single guilty one." In other words, Mr. Hawthorne wishes us to picture a mind perturbed, flushed, on the verge of despair, but does not wish us to know how far the exciting causes had involved her in real guilt, or merely in misery. It is not essential, he thinks, to the purpose of the book, which is rather to trace the effects of the subsequent guilt on the relation between Miriam and Donatello than to develop fully the previous character of the woman who draws the poor young Count into crime. As far as regards Miriam, the problem set himself by the author in this book is only to delineate the influence exerted over her heart by Donatello's plunge into guilt on her behalf. He thinks it enough to indicate that she who led Donatello into guilt was either herself guilty, or at least intimately imbued with all the infectious fever of a guilty atmosphere. More is not essential to the author's purpose, and more he will not tell us. He seems to hint, perhaps truly, that the chasm between guilt and wretchedness in a woman's mind is not always so clear as in a man's; and that, at all events, there is as much power in any deeply roused affection to extricate her from the one as from the other. For like reasons, we suppose, the end of the tale is as shadowy as the beginning. The *transformation* is accomplished; the Faun is no longer a Faun; and all the author contemplated is therefore attained. The wreath of mist which hangs over Miriam's past is allowed also to settle over her own and Donatello's future. The problem has been solved in the dissolving colours of two richly-painted minds. And their earthly destiny is nothing to the reader; to know it might even divert his attention from the artist's true purpose, to concentrate it on the *dénouement* of a commonplace story.

This predominance of moral colouring over the definite forms of actual fact in Mr. Hawthorne's novels is to us, we confess, unsatisfactory. And the degree to which it is absent or prevails in his several works, seems to us a fair measure of their relative artistic worth. The *Scarlet Letter*, in which there is by far the most solid basis of fact, is, we think, also considerably the finest and most powerful of his efforts. The *House of the Seven Gables*, in itself nearly a perfect work of art, is yet composed of altogether thinner materials. Yet the details are worked up with so much care and finish,—the whole external scenery of this, as well as of the *Scarlet Letter*, is so sharply defined, so full of the clear air of New-England life,—that we can bear better the subtle moral colouring and anatomy with which they both abound. In the *Blithedale Romance* we observe the first tendency to shroud certain portions of the narrative in an intentional veil, and to attempt to paint a distinct moral *expression* without giving a distinct outline of fact. The effect is powerful, but vague and not satisfying. The figures wander vagrant-like through the imagination of the reader. They seem to have no distinct place of their own assigned to them. You know what sort of characters you have beheld, but not when and under what circumstances you have beheld them. In *Transformation* these defects are at their maximum; and the evil is exaggerated by the mass of general padding—artistic criticisms, often powerful, and always subtle, upon Italian art;—puffs, not in very good taste, of the works of American sculptors;—silly attacks upon nude figures, and the like,—which distend, alloy, and ungracefully speckle the ideal tenor of the tale.

But we must draw to a conclusion. The most distinguishing deficiency in Mr. Hawthorne's mind, which is also in close connection with its highest power, is his complete want of sympathy not only with the world of voluntary action, but with the next thing to action, namely, the world of impulsive passion. With exceedingly rare exceptions,—the scene of crime and passion which we have quoted from *Transformation* is the only exception we can recall,—the highest power of Mr. Hawthorne is all spent on the delineation of *chronic* suffering or sentiment, in which all desire to act on others is in a measure paralysed. He likes to get past the rapids any way he can;—as we have seen, he not seldom introduces you to his tale with only the distant rush of them still audible behind you, his delight being to trace the more lasting perturbations which they effect for winding miles below. But what he does paint for you, he likes to study thoroughly; he loves to get beneath the surface, to sound the deeper and mysterious pools, measure the power of the fretted waters, and map carefully out the sandy shallows. The result is necessarily a considerable limitation in the field of his genius. The excitement which other writers find in delineating the swaying fortunes of an active career, he is—we will not say *obliged* to find, for of course the positive capacity of his genius, not its incapacity for other fields, leads him in this direction—but he is obliged to find *only* in rare and often painful pictures of unhealthy sentiment. This is what circles so closely the range of his characters. They are necessarily very limited both in number and in moral attitude. We have but two studies, in his tales, of characters with any active bent—Hollingsworth in the *Blithedale Romance*, and Phœbe in the *House of the Seven Gables*. Both are carefully drawn, but both are far slighter sketches, and more evidently taken from observation only, than his other characters. His nearest approach to the delineation of impulsive passion is seen in the sketch of Zenobia in the *Blithedale Romance*, and of Miriam in *Transformation*. But in neither case is it real impulse to act on others which he draws well; it is rather the turbid tossing of a rich mind ill at ease with itself, and casting about for sympathy and help. The characters which he draws most completely,— though they are not always the pleasantest,—are those which, like Mr. Coverdale in the *Blithedale Romance*, and Holgrave in the *House of the Seven Gables*, have "no impulse to help or to hinder," caring only "to look on, to analyse, to explain matters to themselves." Clifford too, in the latter tale,—who evidently represents the sensitive and æsthetic side of the author's own mind, "that squeamish love of the beautiful" (to use his own expressive phrase) which is in him, when stripped of that cold centre of contemplative individuality, which seems to us to be at the centre of Mr. Hawthorne's literary genius and personality,—is a fine study.

But one criticism more. The moral ideal which Mr. Hawthorne keeps before himself and his readers throughout his works is on the whole not only pure but noble. It is defective, however, as we might expect, on the same side on which his genius seems to fail. He is, in political and social conviction, a democratic quietist; one might almost say a fatalist. Is it not a part of this fatalistic disposition, we may ask in passing, to encourage the cultivated and thinking portion of society to resign to the masses the duty of forming the political judgment of his nation, and to permit himself to be quietly sucked in by that fatally fascinating and overmastering tide called the Will of the democracy? However this may be, in political and social life, he is one who deprecates all spasmodic reforms, and attaches little value to reformatory efforts at all, except as the indispensable conditions of generous hopes and youthful aspirations. Speaking of such an experiment of social reform, he says, "After all, let us acknowledge it wise, if not more sagacious, to follow out one's day-dream to its natural consummation, although, if the vision have been worth the having, it is certain never to be consummated otherwise than by a failure." Again he says, in another tale, and with much of true moral insight, though it be the onesided moral insight of the quietist recluse, "the haughty faith with which he [the enthusiastic practical reformer] began life would be well bartered for a far humbler one at its close, in discerning that man's best-directed effort accomplishes a kind of dream, while God is the sole worker of realities." Nor should we find fault with him for his very deeply-rooted conviction that, so far as any real and deep reform is accomplished, it may in a certain sense be said to *accomplish itself*, instead of being forced on society by the enthusiastic patronage of crusading philanthropists, could he but confine this theory within modest limits,—did he not press it into the service of what seems to us the grossest political immorality. We can sympathise with him when he so finely moralises at the end of the *Blithedale Romance* on the dangers of philanthropy:

> "Admitting what is called philanthropy, when adopted as a profession, to be often useful by its energetic impulses to society at large, it is perilous to the individual whose ruling passion, in one exclusive channel, it thus becomes. It ruins, or is fearfully apt to ruin, the heart, the rich juices of which God never meant should be pressed violently out and distilled into alcoholic liquor by an unnatural process; but should render

life sweet, bland, and gently beneficent, and insensibly influence other hearts and other lives to the same blessed end."

Yet more; we can even go with him, quite as far as he wishes his readers to go, when he ironically prescribes a universal slumber as the only cure for the world's overstretched nerves:

'The world should recline its vast head on the first convenient pillow, and take an age-long nap. It has gone distracted through a morbid activity, and while preternaturally wide awake is nevertheless tormented by visions that seem real to it now, but would assume their true aspect and character were all things once set right by an interval of sound repose. This is the only method of getting rid of old delusions and avoiding new ones,—of regenerating our race so that it might in due time awake as an infant out of dewy slumber,—of restoring to us the simple perception of what is right and the single-hearted desire to achieve it, both of which have long been lost in consequence of this weary activity of brain, and torpor or passion of the heart, that now afflict the universe."

For none of these thoughts and sayings, however depreciative of effort, or destructive of the sanguine hopes with which effort spurs itself on, do we reproach Mr. Hawthorne. It is fitting that, after the preacher of one-sided action and overstrained vigilance has spoken, this too restless age should also hear the invitation to distrust its own "earnestness," and renew its highly-strung energies by rest. Nay, we are quite willing to admit that the function of the contemplative man, who keeps clear of the many streams of human energy, and passes his solitary criticisms upon their tendency from some nook of seemingly selfish retirement, is justified in the scheme of Providence by the very existence of the philanthropic class of one-sided workers. But it is when Mr. Hawthorne comes to apply his quietistic creed to the actual political world in which he lives, that we find his moral shortcomings painfully evident, and see that he has permitted a mere theory to confuse "that simple perception of what is right, and the single-hearted desire to achieve it," of which he speaks so well, as grievously as ever did the one dominant idea of a professional philanthropist.

. . . .

We need scarcely apologise for treating Mr. Hawthorne as something more than a mere writer of fiction. His writings have a very wide and justly-deserved influence in America; for as a literary artist, if not in mere rough genius, he may safely be considered almost the first, and quite the highest, fruit of American culture. He has himself recognised the close connection between the political and literary condition of nations in his plea that America is too happy, too prosperous, too free "from any picturesque and gloomy wrong," to be made the scene of a romance. Let us sum up our criticism on his literary deficiencies in a single sentence by expressing our conviction, that if he conceded less to his "squeamish love of the beautiful," if he could cultivate a deeper sympathy with action and its responsibilities, he would not only begin to take some interest in the removal of wrongs that are gloomy enough without being picturesque, but might widen greatly the range of his artistic power, and deepen indefinitely the spell of the fascination which he wields over his countrymen.

1865-1910

MATTHEW BROWNE is a pseudonym of WILLIAM BRIGHTLY RANDS [1823–82], author of numerous books for children and of *Chaucer's England*. His essay on Hawthorne in *St. Paul's Magazine* debates the question of the "Americanism" of authors like Emerson, Poe, Hawthorne, and Whitman and provides a British response to the constant emphasis by American writers on an indigenous literature. Rands comments at length on Hawthorne's tendency to offer several alternative responses to situations or to make unexpected shifts in characters and plot details. Only two qualities, "a very *dogmatic* moral faculty" and "a much stronger sense of humour," both of which Hawthorne lacks, could turn "such awkward corners as his mind is always running against." Rands criticizes Hawthorne's inability to state or develop a problem completely and his emphasis upon "remorse and failure." Although Rands is unhappy with "one essential quality of Hawthorne's genius—namely inconclusiveness," he provides in the passage printed below an unusual discussion of what the modern critic calls Hawthorne's ambiguity. Rands praises Hawthorne's style and comments on the personal qualities exhibited in his notebooks, for example, "the burrowing, or almost inquisitorial, character of Hawthorne's studies of humanities."

Nathaniel Hawthorne

MATTHEW BROWNE

. . . .

We have hinted that Hawthorne is a great artist in parable, and that his characters are almost all of them types created with a capacity for serving the purposes of the parable. This is strictly true, and it is one of the greatest triumphs of the wonderful genius of the man that he has usually continued to make them still human and natural, and to put them in motion in narratives that work artistically to the appointed climax. There are some exceptions to this rule—Clifford, the "abortive lover of the beautiful," as he has been called, is one. It is still more surprising that this naturalness of effect should have been attained in spite of, or rather in most wonderful harmony with, the results of that inconclusiveness which we have mentioned as giving in more than one particular the stamp to his novels. It may, indeed, be called the brand of the Hawthorne genius. The way in which it most powerfully works is this. He never allows you to make up your mind,

St. Paul's Magazine, Vol. 8 (May 1871) 150–61.

and seems never to have made up his own, whether there is a preternatural element at work in the narrative or not. The manner in which he takes up a wild tradition or an awful superstition (*e.g.*, that the body of the wounded will bleed at the approach of the murderer), or some startling unexplained phenomena (*e.g.*, those of mesmerism), and impacts, so to speak, ordinary events and persons into such things, is familiar to all his readers. His scenery and his persons are wrought out with the utmost distinctness, but every now and then he lets down a curtain of lurid haze all round, or sends a shudder over the page, before you well know where you are. This is the characteristic way in which the indeterminateness of his mind works for us. To the last we are not quite sure that we have got to "the rights" of the connection or identity of Priscilla and the Veiled Lady, or the connection between Zenobia and the tropical flower she wore, or the "Maule's blood" of the Pyncheon tradition, or the harpsichord music in the old Pyncheon house, or Donatello's faun-like ears, or the "red letter A". . . . Again, this indeterminateness will be found to be of the essence of the Hawthorne humour. The best example of that is the exquisite account of the Salem custom-house, or, rather, of its people. In Hawthorne's mind, everything seemed capable of meaning something else, and the endless filaments of suggestion sent out in search of symbolic meanings,—you can see them trembling all round at every capture like a spider's web. There is one other source of the extreme fascination of this man's writings. A plain word for it would be concentration, or pertinacity; but in the lurid haze under which his genius so often works it becomes something for which we really want a name. Perhaps we might call it a fatality of method which carries an almost awfully impersonal look with it. When Judge Pyncheon sits dead in his chair in the dark room all night and the genius of the author, through all that most terrible time, walks round and round him in the gloom, gradually closing in upon the solemn fact that you well know all the while, you feel with a shudder, that this bad man is not only dead, he is dead-dead—fatally dead, so to speak. Now, the movement of Hawthorne as a narrator is always of this kind. He gradually *closes in* upon his idea; but as you feel that his imagination is doing this spontaneously, the effect is like that of some preternatural fatality.

. . . .

GEORGE PARSONS LATHROP [1851–98] married Hawthorne's daughter Rose in 1871. He adapted *The Scarlet Letter* for Walter Damrosch's opera (1896) based on the book, and he wrote the introductory notes and biographical sketch for the Riverside edition of Hawthorne's works. Thus he joined the efforts of the family to keep Hawthorne's name before the public either through biography and reminiscences or through posthumous publications of writings (notebooks and unfinished romances such as *Septimius Felton*).

From *A Study of Hawthorne*

GEORGE PARSONS LATHROP

... The subject [pursuit of the elixir of earthly immortality] had been one of the earliest themes of meditation with Hawthorne, and he wrote as with a fountain-pen in which was locked the fluid thought of a lifetime. One of the less obvious aspects of the book is the typification in Septimius's case of that endless struggle which is the lot of every man inspired by an ideal aim. The poet and the painter are, equally with Septimius, seekers after immortality, though of a more ethereal kind; and his morbidness and exaggeration serve to excite in us a tenderness and pity over him, assisting the reception of truth. These relate mainly to the temptation of the artist to effect a severance of ordinary, active human relations. (Sad to think what bitter cause the author had to brood upon this, the fault attributed to himself!) The poet, the creator in whatever art, must maintain his own circle of serene air, shutting out from it the flat reverberations of common life; but if he fail to live generously toward his fellows,—if he cannot make the light of every day supply the nimbus in which he hopes to appear shining to posterity,—then he will fall into the treacherous pit of selfishness where Septimius's soul lies smothered. But this set of meanings runs imperceptibly into others, for the book is much like the cabalistic manuscript described in its pages: now it is blurred over with deceptive sameness, and again it brims with multifarious beauties like those that swim within the golden depth of Tieck's enchanted goblet. The ultimate and most insistent moral is perhaps that which brings it into comparison with Goethe's "Faust"; this, namely, that, in order to defraud Nature of her dues, we must enter into compact with the Devil. Both Faust and Septimius study magic in their separate ways, with the hope of securing

(Boston, 1876) 271–75.

results denied to their kind by a common destiny; but Faust proves infinitely the meaner of the two, since he desires only to restore his youth, that he may engage in the mere mad joy of a lusty existence for a few years, while Septimius seeks some mode, however austere and cheerless, of prolonging his life through centuries of world-wide beneficence. Yet the satanically refined egoism which lays hold of Septimius is the same spirit incarnated in Goethe's Mephistopheles,—*der Geist der stets verneint*. To Faust he denies the existence of good in anything, primarily the good of that universal knowledge to the acquisition of which he has devoted his life, but through this scepticism mining his faith in all besides. To Septimius he denies the worth of so brief a life as ours, and the good of living to whatever end seems for the hour most needful and noble. Septimius might perhaps be described as Faust at an earlier stage of development than that in which Goethe represents him.

As a further point of resemblance between the two cases, it may be noticed that the false dreams of both are dispelled by the exorcising touch of a woman. Both have fallen into error through perceiving only half of the truth which has hovered glimmering before them; these errors originate in the exclusively masculine mood, the asceticism, which has prevailed in their minds. It will be observed that, in the first relation of Rose to Septimius, Hawthorne takes pains to contrast with this mood, delicately but strongly, the woman's gentle conservatism and wisely practical tendency to be satisfied with life, which make her influence so admirable a poising force to man. The subsequent alteration of the situation, by which he makes her the half-sister of his hero, is owing, as Mr. Higginson has pointed out, to the fact "that a heroine must be supplied who corresponds to the idea in the lover's soul; like Helena in the second part of Faust."

But there is a suitable difference between the working of the womanly element in "Faust" and in Hawthorne's romance. In the former instance it is through the gratification of his infernal desire that the hero is awakened from his trance of error and restored to remorse; while Septimius's failure to accomplish his intended destiny appears to be owing to the inability of his aspiring nature to accommodate itself to that code of "moral dietetics" which is to assist his strange project. "Kiss no woman if her lips be red; look not upon her if she be very fair," is the maxim taught him. "If thou love her, all is over, and thy whole past and remaining labor and pains will be in vain." How pathetic a situation this, how much more terrible than that of Faust, when he has reached the turning-point in his career! A nature which could accept an earthly immortality on these terms, for the sake of his fellows, must indeed have been a hard and chilly one. But there is still too much of the heart in it, to admit of being satisfied with so cruel an abstraction. On the verge of success, as he supposes, with the long-sought drink standing ready for his lips, Septimius nevertheless seeks a companion. Half unawares, he has fallen in love with Sybil, and thenceforth, though in a way he had not anticipated, "all is over." Yet, saved from death by the poison in which he had hoped to find the spring of endless life, his fate appears admirably fitting. There is no picture of Mephisto hurrying him off to an apparently irrevocable doom. The wrongs he has committed against himself, his friends, humanity,—these, indeed, remain, and are remembered. He has undoubtedly fallen from his first purity and earnestness, and must hereafter be content to live a life of mere conventional comfort, full of mere conventional goodness, conventional charities, in that substantial English home of his. Could anything be more perfectly compensatory?

Nothing is more noticeable than the way in which, while so many symbolisms spring up out of the story, the hero's half-crazed and bewildered atmosphere is the one which we really accept, until the reading is ended. By this means we are enabled to live through the whole immortal future which he projects for himself, though he never in reality achieves any of it. This forcing of the infinite into the finite, we are again indebted to Mr. Higginson for emphasizing as "one of the very greatest triumphs in all literature." "A hundred separate tragedies," he says, "would be easier to depict than this which combines so many in one."

. . . .

In 1861 ANTHONY TROLLOPE [1815–82] met Hawthorne in America. When consul at Liverpool, Hawthorne had read some of Trollope's novels and described them admiringly as "solid and substantial, written on the strength of beef and through the inspiration of ale." In his article "The Genius of Nathaniel Hawthorne" Trollope reciprocated Hawthorne's appreciation. The mutual respect came from two entirely different kinds of writers of fiction, representing the sharp distinction between romance and realism. In a portion of Trollope's article omitted here, he writes about *The Scarlet Letter*: "But through all this intensity of suffering, through the blackness of narrative, there is ever running a vein of drollery." Trollope considers *The Scarlet Letter* superior to both *The House of the Seven Gables* and *The Marble Faun* in plot-making. In this respect, he, like many others, condemns Hawthorne's refusal to clear up the mysteries in *The Marble Faun*. In all of the tales written after *The Scarlet Letter*, the reader, Trollope claims, "must look rather for a series of pictures than for a novel." Amid these criticisms of the romances Trollope does single out some excellent features: the characterization of Hepzibah and Hawthorne's portrayal of Rome and Italian scenery. He is particularly critical of *Mosses*; "Rappaccini's Daughter" he finds "unintelligible," but he describes "The Procession of Life" as "suggestive and most satisfactory."

The Genius of Nathaniel Hawthorne

ANTHONY TROLLOPE

. . . .

There never surely was a powerful, active, continually effective mind less round, more lop-sided, than that of NATHANIEL HAWTHORNE. If there were aught of dispraise in this, it would not be said by me,—by an Englishman of an American whom I knew, by an Englishman of letters of a brother on the other side of the water, much less by me, an English novelist, of an American novelist. The blacksmith, who is abnormally strong in his arm, gives the world the advantage of his strength. The poor bird, whose wretched life is sacrificed to the unnatural growth of that portion of him which the gourmands love, does produce the desired dainties in all their perfection. We could have hardly had "Childe Harold" except from a soured nature. The seraphic excellence of "Hiawatha" and "Evangeline" could have proceeded only from a mind which the world's roughness had neither toughened nor tainted. So from Hawthorne we could not have obtained that weird, mysterious, thrilling charm with which he has awed and delighted us had he not allowed his mind to revel in one direction, so as to lose its fair proportions.

I have been specially driven to think of this by the strong divergence between Hawthorne and myself. It has always been my object to draw my little pictures as like to life as possible, so that my readers should feel that they were dealing with people whom

North American Review, Vol. 129 (September 1879) 203–22.

they might probably have known, but so to do it that the every-day good to be found among them should allure, and the every-day evil repel; and this I have attempted, believing that such ordinary good and ordinary evil would be more powerful in repelling or alluring than great and glowing incidents which, though they might interest, would not come home to the minds of readers. Hawthorne, on the other hand, has dealt with persons and incidents which were often but barely within the bounds of possibility, —which were sometimes altogether without those bounds,—and has determined that his readers should be carried out of their own little mundane ways, and brought into a world of imagination in which their intelligence might be raised, if only for a time, to something higher than the common needs of common life.

... That some remnant of Puritan asceticism should be found in the writings of a novelist from Concord, in Massachusetts, would seem natural to an English reader,—though I doubt whether there be much of the flavor of the Mayflower left at present to pervade the literary parterres of Boston. But, had that been the Hawthorne flavor, readers both in England and in the States would have accepted it without surprise.

It is, however, altogether different, though ascetic enough. The predominating quality of Puritan life was hard, good sense,—a good sense which could value the realities of life while it rejected the frivolities,—a good sense to which buttered cakes, water-tight boots, and a pretty wife, or a kind husband could endear themselves. Hawthorne is severe, but his severity is never of a nature to form laws for life. His is a mixture of romance and austerity, quite as far removed from the realities of Puritanism as it is from the sentimentalism of poetry. He creates a melancholy which amounts almost to remorse in the minds of his readers. There falls upon them a conviction of some unutterable woe which is not altogether dispelled till other books and other incidents have had their effects. The woe is of course fictitious, and therefore endurable,—and therefore alluring. And woe itself has its charm. It is a fact that the really miserable will pity the comfortable insignificance of those who are not unhappy, and that they are apt even to boast of their own sufferings. There is a sublimity in mental and even in corporal torment which will sometimes make the position of Lucifer almost enviable. "All is not lost" with him! Prometheus chained, with the bird at his liver, had wherewithal to console himself in the magnificence of his thoughts. And so in the world of melancholy romance, of agony more realistic than melancholy, to which Hawthorne brings his readers, there is compensation to the reader in the feeling that, in having submitted himself to such sublime affliction, he has proved himself capable of sublimity. The bird that feeds upon your vitals would not have gorged himself with common flesh. You are beyond measure depressed by the weird tale that is told to you, but you become conscious of a certain grandness of nature in being susceptible of such suffering. When you hear what Hawthorne has done to others, you long to search his volumes. When he has operated upon you, you would not for worlds have foregone it. You have been ennobled by that familiarity with sorrow. You have been, as it were, sent through the fire and purged of so much of your dross. For a time, at least, you have been free from the mundane touch of that beef and ale with which novelists of a meaner school will certainly bring you in contact. No one will feel himself ennobled at once by having read one of my novels. But Hawthorne, when you have studied him, will be very precious to you. He will have plunged you into melancholy, he will have overshadowed you with black forebodings, he will almost have crushed you with imaginary sorrows; but he will have enabled you to feel yourself an inch taller during the process. Something of the sublimity of the transcendent, something of the mystery of the unfathomable, something of the brightness of the celestial, will have attached itself to you, and you will all but think that you too might live to be sublime, and revel in mingled light and mystery.

. . . .

HENRY JAMES [1843–1916] wrote on Hawthorne several times (see Peter Buitenhuis, *New England Quarterly,* Vol. 32, 207–25). James's 1879 study of Hawthorne—the only American author in the English Men of Letters series—is one of the most influential criticisms of Hawthorne ever published. Although James was later to alter some aspects of his attitude toward Hawthorne, the 1879 book has overshadowed his other commentaries (particularly his discussion in *A Library of the World's Best Literature,* Vol. 12) and is constantly referred to and discussed in recent criticism. The influence of Hawthorne on James's fiction has also stimulated some discussion (for example, Marius Bewley, *The Complex Fate,* 1952).

The Three American Novels
[*The Scarlet Letter*]

HENRY JAMES

... In fact, the publication of *The Scarlet Letter* was in the United States a literary event of the first importance. The book was the finest piece of imaginative writing yet put forth in the country. There was a consciousness of this in the welcome that was given it—a satisfaction in the idea of America having produced a novel that belonged to literature, and to the forefront of it. Something might at last be sent to Europe as exquisite in quality as anything that had been received, and the best of it was that the thing was absolutely American; it belonged to the soil, to the air; it came out of the very heart of New England.

It is beautiful, admirable, extraordinary; it has in the highest degree that merit which I have spoken of as the mark of Hawthorne's best things—an indefinable purity and lightness of conception, a quality which in a work of art affects one in the same way as the absence of grossness does in a human being. His fancy, as I just now said, had evidently brooded over the subject for a long time; the situation to be represented had disclosed itself to him in all its phases. When I say in all its phases, the sentence demands modification; for it is to be remembered that if Hawthorne laid his hand upon the well-worn theme, upon the familiar combination of the wife, the lover, and the husband, it was, after all, but to one period of the history of these three persons that he attached himself. The situation is the situation after the woman's fault has been committed, and the current of expiation and repentance has set in. In spite of the relation between Hester Prynne and Arthur Dimmesdale, no story of love was surely ever less of a "love-story." To Hawthorne's imagination the fact that these two persons had loved each other too well was of an interest comparatively vulgar; what appealed to him was the idea of their moral situation in the long years that were to follow. The story, indeed, is in a secondary degree that of Hester Prynne; she becomes, really, after the first scene, an accessory figure; it is not upon her the *dénoûment* depends. It is upon her guilty lover that the author projects most frequently the cold, thin rays of his fitfully-moving lantern, which makes here and there a little luminous circle, on the edge of which

Hawthorne. English Men of Letters. (New York, 1879) 108–18.

hovers the livid and sinister figure of the injured and retributive husband. The story goes on, for the most part, between the lover and the husband—the tormented young Puritan minister, who carries the secret of his own lapse from pastoral purity locked up beneath an exterior that commends itself to the reverence of his flock, while he sees the softer partner of his guilt standing in the full glare of exposure and humbling herself to the misery of atonement—between this more wretched and pitiable culprit, to whom dishonour would come as a comfort and the pillory as a relief, and the older, keener, wiser man, who, to obtain satisfaction for the wrong he has suffered, devises the infernally ingenious plan of conjoining himself with his wronger, living with him, living upon him; and while he pretends to minister to his hidden ailment and to sympathise with his pain, revels in his unsuspected knowledge of these things, and stimulates them by malignant arts. The attitude of Roger Chillingworth, and the means he takes to compensate himself—these are the highly original elements in the situation that Hawthorne so ingeniously treats. None of his works are so impregnated with that after-sense of the old Puritan consciousness of life to which allusion has so often been made. If, as M. Montégut says, the qualities of his ancestors *filtered* down through generations into his composition, *The Scarlet Letter* was, as it were, the vessel that gathered up the last of the precious drops. And I say this not because the story happens to be of so-called historical cast, to be told of the early days of Massachusetts, and of people in steeple-crowned hats and sad-coloured garments. The historical colouring is rather weak than otherwise; there is little elaboration of detail, of the modern realism of research; and the author has made no great point of causing his figures to speak the English of their period. Nevertheless, the book is full of the moral presence of the race that invented Hester's penance—diluted and complicated with other things, but still perfectly recognisable. Puritanism, in a word, is there, not only objectively, as Hawthorne tried to place it there, but subjectively as well. Not, I mean, in his judgment of his characters in any harshness of prejudice, or in the obtrusion of a moral lesson; but in the very quality of his own vision, in the tone of the picture, in a certain coldness and exclusiveness of treatment.

The faults of the book are, to my sense, a want of reality and an abuse of the fanciful element—of a certain superficial symbolism. The people strike me not as characters, but as representatives, very picturesquely arranged, of a single state of mind; and the interest of the story lies, not in them, but in the situation, which is insistently kept before us, with little progression, though with a great deal, as I have said, of a certain stable variation; and to which they, out of their reality, contribute little that helps it to live and move. I was made to feel this want of reality, this over-ingenuity, of *The Scarlet Letter*, by chancing not long since upon a novel which was read fifty years ago much more than to-day, but which is still worth reading—the story of *Adam Blair*, by John Gibson Lockhart. This interesting and powerful little tale has a great deal of analogy with Hawthorne's novel—quite enough, at least, to suggest a comparison between them; and the comparison is a very interesting one to make, for it speedily leads us to larger considerations than simple resemblances and divergences of plot.

Adam Blair, like Arthur Dimmesdale, is a Calvinistic minister who becomes the lover of a married woman, is overwhelmed with remorse at his misdeed, and makes a public confession of it; then expiates it by resigning his pastoral office and becoming a humble tiller of the soil, as his father had been. The two stories are of about the same length, and each is the masterpiece (putting aside, of course, as far as Lockhart is concerned, the *Life of Scott*) of the author. They deal alike with the manners of a rigidly theological society, and even in certain details they correspond. In each of them, between the guilty pair, there is a charming little girl; though I hasten to say that Sarah Blair (who is not the daughter of the heroine, but the legitimate offspring of the hero, a widower) is far from being as brilliant and graceful an apparition as the admirable little Pearl of *The Scarlet Letter*. The main difference between the two tales is the fact that in the American story the husband plays an all-important part, and in the Scottish plays almost none at all. *Adam Blair* is the history of the passion, and *The Scarlet Letter* the history of its sequel; but nevertheless, if one has read the two books at a short interval, it is impossible to avoid confronting them. I confess that a large portion of the interest of *Adam Blair*, to my mind, when once I had perceived that it would repeat in a great measure the situation of *The Scarlet Letter*, lay in noting its difference of tone. It threw into relief the passionless quality of Hawthorne's novel, its element of cold and ingenious fantasy, its elaborate imaginative delicacy. These things do not precisely constitute a weakness in *The Scarlet Letter*; indeed, in a certain way they constitute a great strength; but the absence of a certain something warm and straightforward, a trifle more grossly human and vulgarly natural, which one finds in *Adam Blair*, will always make Hawthorne's tale less touching to a large number of even very intelligent readers, than a love-story told with the robust, synthetic pathos which served Lockhart so well. His novel is not of the first rank (I should call it an excellent second-rate one), but it borrows a charm from the fact that his vigorous, but not strongly imaginative, mind was impregnated with the reality of his subject. He did not always succeed in rendering this reality; the expression is sometimes awkward and poor. But the reader feels that his vision was clear, and his feeling about the matter very strong and rich. Hawthorne's imagination, on the other hand, plays with his theme so incessantly, leads it such a dance through the moon-lighted air of his intellect, that the thing cools off, as it were, hardens and stiffens, and, producing effects much more exquisite, leaves the reader with a sense of having handled a splendid piece of silversmith's work. Lockhart, by means much more vulgar, produces at moments a greater illusion, and satisfies our inevitable desire for something, in the people in whom it is sought to interest us, that shall be of the same pitch and the same continuity with ourselves. Above all, it is interesting to see how the same subject appears to two men of a thoroughly different cast of mind and of a different race. Lockhart was struck with the warmth of the subject that offered itself to him, and Hawthorne with its coldness; the one with its glow, its sentimental interest—the other with its shadow, its moral interest. Lockhart's story is as decent, as severely draped, as *The Scarlet Letter;* but the author has a more vivid sense than appears to have imposed itself upon Hawthorne, of some of the incidents of the situation he describes; his tempted man and tempting woman are more actual and personal; his heroine in especial, though not in the least a delicate or a subtle conception, has a sort of credible, visible, palpable property, a vulgar roundness and relief, which are lacking to the dim and chastened image of Hester Prynne. But I am going too far; I am comparing simplicity with subtlety, the usual with the refined. Each man wrote as his turn of mind impelled him, but each expressed something more than himself. Lockhart was a dense, substantial Briton, with a taste for the concrete, and Hawthorne was a thin New Englander, with a miasmatic conscience.

In *The Scarlet Letter* there is a great deal of symbolism; there is, I think, too much. It is overdone at times, and becomes mechanical; it ceases to be impressive, and grazes triviality. The idea of the mystic A which the young minister finds imprinted upon his breast and eating into his flesh, in sympathy with the embroidered badge that Hester is condemned to wear, appears to me to be a case in point. This suggestion should, I think, have been just made and dropped; to insist upon it and return to it, is to exaggerate the weak side of the subject. Hawthorne returns to it constantly, plays with it, and seems charmed by it; until at last the reader feels tempted to declare that his enjoyment of it is puerile. In the admirable scene, so superbly conceived and beautifully executed, in which Mr. Dimmesdale, in the stillness of the night, in the middle of the sleeping town, feels impelled to go and stand upon the scaffold where his mistress had formerly enacted her dreadful penance, and then, seeing Hester pass along the street, from watching at a sick-bed, with little Pearl at her side, calls them both to come and stand there beside him—in this masterly episode the effect is almost spoiled by the introduction of one of these superficial conceits. What leads up to it is very fine—so fine that I cannot do better than quote it as a specimen of one of the striking pages of the book.

. . . .

That is imaginative, impressive, poetic; but when, almost immediately afterwards, the author goes on to say that "the minister looking upward to the zenith, beheld there the appearance of an immense letter—the letter A—marked out in lines of dull red light," we feel that he goes too far, and is in danger of crossing the line that separates the sublime from its intimate neighbour. We are tempted to say that this is not moral tragedy, but physical comedy. In the same way, too much is made of the intimation that Hester's badge had a scorching property, and that if one touched it one would immediately withdraw one's hand. Hawthorne is perpetually looking for images which shall place themselves in picturesque correspondence with the spiritual facts with which he is concerned, and of course the search is of the very essence of poetry. But in such a process discretion is everything, and when the image becomes importunate it is in danger of seeming to stand for nothing more serious than itself. When Hester meets the minister by appointment in the forest, and sits talking with him while little Pearl wanders away and plays by the edge of the brook, the child is represented as at last making her way over to the other side of the woodland stream, and disporting herself there in a manner which makes her mother feel herself, "in some indistinct and tantalising manner, estranged from Pearl; as if the child, in her lonely ramble through the forest, had strayed out of the sphere in which she and her mother dwelt together, and was now vainly seeking to return to it." And Hawthorne devotes a chapter to this idea of the child's having, by putting the brook between Hester and herself, established a kind of spiritual gulf, on the verge of which her little fantastic person innocently mocks at her mother's sense of bereavement. This conception belongs, one would say, quite to the lighter order of a story-teller's devices, and the reader hardly goes with Hawthorne in the large development he gives to it. He hardly goes with him either, I think, in his extreme predilection for a small number of vague ideas which are represented by such terms as "sphere" and "sympathies." Hawthorne makes too liberal a use of these two substantives; it is the solitary defect of his style; and it counts as a defect partly because the words in question are a sort of specialty with certain writers immeasurably inferior to himself.

I had not meant, however, to expatiate upon his defects, which are of the slenderest and most venial kind. *The Scarlet Letter* has the beauty and harmony of all original and complete conceptions, and its weaker spots, whatever they are, are not of its essence; they are mere light flaws and inequalities of surface. One can often return to it; it supports familiarity, and has the inexhaustible charm and mystery of great works of art. It is admirably written. Hawthorne afterwards polished his style to a still higher degree; but in his later productions—it is almost always the case in a writer's later productions—there is a touch of mannerism. In *The Scarlet Letter* there is a high degree of polish, and at the same time a charming freshness; his phrase is less conscious of itself. His biographer very justly calls attention to the fact that his style was excellent from the beginning; that he appeared to have passed through no phase of learning how to write, but was in possession of his means, from the first, of his handling a pen. His early tales, perhaps, were not of a character to subject his faculty of expression to a very severe test; but a man who had not Hawthorne's natural sense of language would certainly have contrived to write them less well. This natural sense of language—this turn for saying things lightly and yet touchingly, picturesquely yet simply, and for infusing a gently colloquial tone into matter of the most unfamiliar import—he had evidently cultivated with great assiduity. I have spoken of the anomalous character of his Note-Books—of his going to such pains often to make a record of incidents which either were not worth remembering, or could be easily remembered without its aid. But it helps us to understand the Note-Books if we regard them as a literary exercise. They were compositions, as schoolboys say, in which the subject was only the pretext, and the main point was to write a certain amount of excellent English. Hawthorne must at least have written a great many of these things for practice, and he must often have said to himself that it was better practice to write about trifles, because it was a greater tax upon one's skill to make them interesting. And his theory was just, for he has almost always made his trifles interesting. In his novels his art of saying things well is very positively tested; for here he treats of those matters among which it is very easy for a blundering writer to go wrong—the subtleties and mysteries of life, the moral and spiritual maze. In such a passage as one I have marked for quotation from *The Scarlet Letter,* there is the stamp of the genius of style:—

> "Hester Prynne, gazing steadfastly at the clergyman, felt a dreary influence come over her, but wherefore or whence she knew not, unless that he seemed so remote from her own sphere and utterly beyond her reach. One glance of recognition she had imagined must needs pass between them. She thought of the dim forest, with its little dell of solitude, and love, and anguish, and the mossy tree-trunk, where, sitting hand in hand, they had mingled their sad and passionate talk with the melancholy murmur of the brook. How deeply had they known each other then! And was this the man? She hardly knew him now! He, moving proudly past, enveloped as it were in the rich music, with the procession of majestic and venerable fathers; he, so unattainable in his worldly position, and still more so in that far vista in his unsympathising thoughts, through which she now beheld him! Her spirit sank with the idea that all must have been a delusion, and that vividly as she had dreamed it, there could be no real bond betwixt the clergyman and herself. And thus much of woman there was in Hester, that she could scarcely forgive him—least of all now, when the heavy footstep of their approaching fate might be heard, nearer, nearer, nearer!—for being able to withdraw himself so completely from their mutual world; while she groped darkly, and stretched forth her cold hands, and found him not!"

WILLIAM DEAN HOWELLS [1837–1920], as an important novelist and as editor of *The Atlantic Monthly,* was a significant figure in establishing realism as the basis of fiction. Although he admired Hawthorne's works, his favorite was *The Blithedale Romance* because of its seemingly realistic treatment of human experience. In a review of James's *Hawthorne* in

The Atlantic Monthly (February 1880), Howells argues that Hawthorne's "provinciality" is "somewhat over-insisted upon," and he criticizes James for putting "too slight a value upon some of Hawthorne's works." Howells also claims to draw a sharper distinction between the romance and the novel than James does. Yet he finds James's book "refined and delicate in perception, generous in feeling, and a worthy study of the unique romancer. . . ."

From *Heroines of Fiction*

WILLIAM DEAN HOWELLS

. . . .

There is, of course, a choice in Hawthorne's romances, and I myself prefer "The Blithedale Romance" and "The Scarlet Letter" to "The Marble Faun" and "The House of the Seven Gables." The last, indeed, I have found as nearly tiresome as I could find anything of Hawthorne's. I do not think it is censuring it unjustly to say that it seems the expansion of a short-story motive to the dimensions of a novel; and the slight narrative in which the concept is nursed with whimsical pathos to the limp end, appears sometimes to falter, and alarms the sympathetic reader at other times with the fear of an absolute lapse. The characters all lack the vitality which the author gives the people of his other books. The notion of the hapless Clifford Pyncheon, who was natured for happiness and beauty, but was fated to such a hard and ugly doom, is perhaps too single for the realization of a complete personality; and poor old Hepzibah, his sister, is of scarcely more sufficient material. They move dim, forlorn wraiths before the fancy, and they bring only such proofs of their reality as ghosts seen by others can supply. The careful elaboration with which they are studied seems only to render them more doubtful, and there is not much in the pretty, fresh-hearted little Phœbe Pyncheon, or her lover Holgrave, with all his generous rebellion against the obsession of the present by the past, to render the central figures convincing. Hawthorne could not help giving form to his work, but as nearly as any work of his could be so "The House of the Seven Gables" is straggling. There is at any rate no great womanly presence to pull it powerfully together, and hold it in the beautiful unity characteristic of

(New York, 1901) 163–64, 173–75, 188–89.

"The Blithedale Romance" and "The Scarlet Letter." What solidarity it has is in the simple Salem circumstance of the story, where the antique Puritanic atmosphere merges with the modern air in a complexion of perennial provinciality.

. . . .

[Long excerpts from Chapter XVII of *The Scarlet Letter*: "The Pastor and His Parishioner"]

There is a greatness in this scene which is unmatched, I think, in the book, and, I was almost ready to say, out of it. At any rate, I believe we can find its parallel only in some of the profoundly impassioned pages of the Russian novelists who, casting aside all the common adjuncts of art, reveal us to ourselves in the appeal from their own naked souls. Hawthorne had another ideal than theirs, and a passing love of style, and the meaning of the music of words. For the most part, he makes us aware of himself, of his melancholy grace and sombre power; we feel his presence in every passage, however deeply, however occultly, dramatic; he overshadows us, so that we touch and see through him. But here he is almost out of it; only a few phrases of comment, so fused in feeling with the dialogue that they are like the voice of a chorus, remind us of him.

It is the most exalted instant of the tragedy, it is the final evolution of Hester Prynne's personality. In this scene she dominates by virtue of whatever is womanly and typical in her, and no less by what is personal and individual. In what follows, she falls like Dimmesdale and Chillingworth under the law of their common doom, and becomes a figure on the board where for once she seemed to direct the game.

In all fiction one could hardly find a character more boldly, more simply, more quietly imagined. She had done that which in the hands of a feeble or falser talent would have been suffered or made to qualify her out of all proportion and keeping with life. But her transgression does not qualify her, as transgression never does unless it becomes habit. She remains exterior and superior to it, a life of other potentialities, which in her narrow sphere she fulfils. What she did has become a question between her and her Maker, who apparently does not deal with it like a Puritan. The obvious lesson of the contrasted fates of Dimmesdale and herself is that to own sin is to disown it, and that it cannot otherwise be expropriated and annulled. Yet, in Hester's strong and obstinate endurance of her punishment there is publicity but not confession; and perhaps there is a lesson of no slighter meaning in the inference that ceasing to do evil is, after all, the most that can be asked of human nature. Even that seems to be a good deal, and in "The Scarlet Letter" it is a stroke of mastery to show that it is not always ours to cease to do evil, but that in extremity we need the help of the mystery "not ourselves, that makes for righteousness," and that we may call Chance or that we may call God, but that does not change in essence or puissance whatever name we give it.

. . . .

Hester Prynne in "The Scarlet Letter" is studied in the round, with an effect of life which is wanting to heroines in the flat, whatever their charm of color and drawing may be; and Zenobia and Priscilla—especially Zenobia—are still more vitalized by the same method of handling, in "The Blithedale Romance." That romance, as I have elsewhere expressed, is nearer a novel than any other fiction of the author. At times we find ourselves confronted there, in spite of the author, with a very palpitant piece of naturalism. This is not more the fact in the case of the brawny, tobacco-chewing Silas Foster, who instructs the town-bred communists at Blithedale in farming, than in the sumptuous personality of Zenobia, the woman with a mysterious past, who glows upon us in tropical splendor from the first chapters of the romance, and illumines it throughout with the rich ardor of her impassioned presence.

. . . .

[Long excerpts from Chapters XXVIII and XIX of *The Marble Faun:* "On the Edge of a Precipice" and "The Faun's Transformation"]

Now that I have obeyed a sort of imperious necessity in selecting the passage given as supremely illustrative, I have my misgiving whether I had not better chosen that scene in the Medici Gardens, where shortly after the murder Miriam and Donatello are together. Their terrible exaltation is past, that "freedom of a broken law" which was briefly theirs has already lapsed into the bondage of remorse; and she realizes that all the love of her blood-stained soul avails nothing to purge his listless spirit of its new-found sense of guilt. This is a great scene; and that again is a great scene where Miriam goes to Hilda in her dove-haunted tower, and the girl's cruel truth accuses and convicts the unhappy woman, and casts her off and disowns her. Did Hawthorne here, I wonder, mean to let us see something ugly in the angelic Hilda's effort for self-protection and her ruthless self-pity for her own involuntary privity to Miriam's guilt? That would be like his subtlety; and it is certain that the effect is to enlist the sympathy of the witness for Miriam, and to render her for the moment less abhorrent than Hilda. In fact, if I must empty the sack altogether, I cannot conceal that at the bottom of it is a dislike for that cold spirit of Hilda and a sense of something selfish in her relation to the whole affair.

Perhaps it is not a real relation. The whole action loses vitality after the parting of Hilda and Miriam; and though it is bravely and beautifully managed to the end, it *is* managed, and does not manage itself. The rest of the story is as intentional, as operated, as the second part of "Faust"; and in this "The Marble Faun" must rank below "The Scarlet Letter" and "The Blithedale Romance," which are of a vitality that carries them strongly to the close. For the same reason Miriam cannot be placed with Hester Prynne and Zenobia, who have no galvanic palingenesis, but live warmly and richly in the memory, while the Miriam of the second volume has to be recalled with a constant effort. It may be said in her defence that the author put upon her a burden to which she was not equal; he was not equal to it himself, as Goethe also was not; and, indeed, no man is. The problem of evil will not be solved.

If we reduce the question which is Hawthorne's greatest heroine to a choice between Hester Prynne and Zenobia, I must give my voice for Zenobia. Few heroines survive so far beyond their story, and remain in a sort so fully a part of experience as she; I know of no other in Anglo-Saxon fiction, and only three or four outside of it. She is not a very great or noble character. She has moments of being rather hard and jealous with Priscilla and rather "nasty" to Coverdale, who doubtless deserves it; but she is largely planned and generously built. She has, as I have owned, a touch of vulgarity, and we are allowed to suspect her of a lawless and sufficiently foolish fancy. She is a half-caste literary talent, and some of her ideals are apparently tawdry; but she is a very woman-soul; what she does and suffers is by the law of her womanhood, which in her death as in her life asserts itself in defeat so cruel as to leave the reader with a lasting pang for her.

GEORGE EDWARD WOODBERRY [1855–1930] was a poet, critic, biographer, and professor at Columbia University. He wrote biographies of Poe, Emerson, and Hawthorne, as well as literary history, *America in Literature*. In addition to his life of Hawthorne, Woodberry wrote *Nathaniel Hawthorne: How to Know Him* (1918). His criticism in the two volumes marks him as one of the most perceptive readers of Hawthorne during the first two decades of the twentieth century.

The Old Manse

GEORGE E. WOODBERRY

. . . .

Probably in no one point is Hawthorne's peculiarity so obviously marked as in the persistency with which he clings to a physical image, vividly impressing it upon the mind, like a text which gathers atmosphere and discloses significance under the special treatment of the preacher. It is said that he had, artistically, the allegorizing temperament, and he in fact did use all those forms of imagery—the fable, apologue, parable—which belong to this mode of presentation; but in his most effective work the allegory is more subtly embodied,—it exists in suggestion, and its appeal is as much emotional as didactic. The nucleus of this new mystery is the physical object that he seizes upon and in which his imagination works as if it were clay, recreating it so that it becomes more than pure symbol, as has been illustrated in "Lady Eleanore's Mantle;" and sometimes it is almost vitalized into a life of its own. This power of such an object to become the medium of thought and emotion as well as to convey merely allegorical meaning he gradually discovered; and doubtless he especially valued its function to afford by its crude definiteness a balance to the tenuous and impalpable, the vagueness, refinement, and mystery, to which it is the complement, in his art; he gains reality by its presence for what else, as a whole, might seem too insubstantial, too much a part of that shadow world in which he dreaded to dwell altogether.

Such an object is, at all events, a necessity for him in his greater work. A crude form of it is the snake, in the tale of "The Bosom Serpent," one of those "allegories of the heart" which he apparently meant to write in a series of which he never found the

Nathaniel Hawthorne. American Men of Letters. (Boston, 1902) 143–50.

key. The idea is an old one; the man with a snake in his bosom is a hypochondriac, who by centring his thoughts on himself has developed this fancy and is tortured by it. The cure is wrought when he forgets himself in returning to the love of his wife. The almost physical dismissal of the serpent into the fountain, which is neither averred nor denied, like a devil cast out as in old times, is puerile; but Hawthorne was, in other tales, not averse to a naturalistic explanation of his mysteries, as if a basis of matter of fact, however irrelevant essentially, gave more plausibility to their truth. If the snake is "egotism," if it is the torture of self in a man, if its cure is the loss of self in love, then making the snake real and physical is absurdity; medicine and morals are confounded; the scientific fact has nothing to do with the artistic meaning and is a concession to the gross senses of the reader. The story illustrates the method, rather than its successful application; for the physical horror is really greater here than the moral revulsion. In "The Minister's Black Veil" the object is more happily dealt with. It is to be noticed that Hawthorne did not invent these objects, he found them; and, in this case, he has used the tradition of an old Puritan minister of the past age. He uses the veil to typify man's concealment of himself from others, even the nearest; and while it visibly isolates the minister among his fellow-men, it finally unites him with them in a single lot; for to the mind's eye, educated by this image to a new power of seeing, all men wear this veil; humanity is clothed with it in life, and moulders away beneath it in the grave, whither its secrets are carried. The seeming exception is found to be the rule; the horror attaching to the one unseen face is now felt in all faces; the race is veiled, and the bit of crape has fallen like the blackness of night upon all life, for life has become a thing of darkness, a concealment. Here the moral idea is predominant, and in it the symbol issues into its full life.

Hawthorne's art became always, not only more vividly symbolized, but more deeply moralized. The secrecy of men's bosoms was a matter that interested him very much; the idea had a fascination for him. It is the substance of the tale of "Young Goodman Brown," who goes to the witches' Sabbath in the Essex woods and there sees those who have taught him religion, the righteous and the good, men and women, and his own wife,—sees them or their devil-brewed phantasms; he calls on heaven, and finds himself suddenly alone; but when he returns to the village, and looks again on the venerable fathers and mothers of his childhood and his own tender and loving wife, he cannot free his mind from the doubt,—were they what they seemed or had he indeed beheld them there in the woods at their orgy? It is as if for him the veil were lifted, and he alone saw, like omniscience, into the bosoms of all. Suspicion, arising from his own contact with evil, though he escaped, has imparted the look of hypocrisy to all life; this is his bedevilment. Here the place of the physical object is taken by the incident of the woods, and the moral idea is less clearly stated; the story is one of those whose significance is felt to contain mystery which Hawthorne meant to remain in its dark state.

In "The Birthmark" the physical object is again found as the initial point of the tale and the guiding clue of the imagination in working it out. The situation presents the opposition of the love of science to human love, but no conflict is described, because the first is the master passion from the beginning, and, being indulged, leads to the loss of the second in the death of the wife, who perishes in having the birthmark removed. The moral idea, as not unfrequently happens, seems to flake off from the tale, like the moral of the old fable, and is to the effect that imperfection belongs to mortal life, and if it is removed wholly mortality must go with it; and the lesson is of the acceptance of imperfection in what men love, as a permanent condition, and indeed almost as the humanizing feature, of earthly life. It is noticeable that the clergyman, the physician, and the artist are the only specific types that attracted Hawthorne; he held them all romantically, and science he conceived as alchemy. This same predisposition appears in "Rappaccini's Daughter;" she was the experiment of her father in creating a live poison-woman, a vitalized flower, the Dryad as it were of the poison-tree humanized in mortal shape; the physical object is here the flowering tree, with its heavy fragrance; and the plot lies only in the gradual transformation of the young man by continuous and unconscious inoculation until he is drawn into the circle of death to share the woman's isolation as a lover, both being shut off from their kind by the poison atmosphere that exhales from them; the catastrophe lies in the moral idea that for such poison there is no antidote but death, and the lady dies in drinking the draught that should free her. The fact that Hawthorne, when writing the story, said he did not know how it would end, is interesting as indicating that his literary habit was to let the story tell itself from within according to its impulses, and not to shape it from without by his own predetermined purpose; a pure allegorist, it may be observed, would have followed naturally the latter method. This may account for the indefiniteness and mystery of effect often felt, as well as for the inartistic didacticism in the concluding sentences, frequently to be observed, where it appears as one or more afterthoughts possibly to be drawn from the story, but not exhausting its moral significance. In this case, powerful as the tale is, the moral intention is left vague, though except as a parable the invention is meaningless.

In the last story to be instanced, "The Artist of the Beautiful," the lucidity of the parable is complete. The physical object is the butterfly; on its wings the tale moves, and perishes in its destruction. The moral idea lies in the exposition of achievement as a freeing of the artist's soul so that his work has become a thing of indifference to him, let its fortunes be what they will,—it is the dead chrysalis from which he has escaped; and the isolation of the artist's life is set forth pathetically but with no suggestion of evil in it, for though the world has rejected him he lives in his own world in the calm of victory. No tale is so delicately wrought as this; in it the symbolism, which is carried out in minute and precise detail, the moral significance, which is as clear as it is deep, and the presence of a spiritual world in life for which a visible language is found, are all present, in harmonious blending; and it has the added and rare charm of happiness without loss of truth. It is unique; and if one were to choose a single tale, best representing Hawthorne's powers, methods, and successes, technically and temperamentally as well as in imaginative reach and spiritual appeal, it is by this he should be known.

In these six tales in which Hawthorne's originality is most characteristically expressed, the idea of isolation is common to all; like the secrecy of men's bosoms, this solitude in life is a fixed idea in his imagination, an integral part of life as it was viewed by him, and he seldom freed his attention from it even temporarily. On the other hand, sin, conscience, evil, though their realm is felt to be a neighboring province, are not here directly dealt with. His probings in that sphere belong to a later time. These tales, like the others, are studies of life, not of the evil principle by itself as a thing of special interest; they view life as lying under a shadow, it is true, but this shadow is their atmosphere, not their world. The point should be defined, perhaps more explicitly: the Calvinism of New England, its interest in the perversion of man's will, his sinful state, and the mysterious modes of salvation, is not the region of Hawthorne's imagination, as here disclosed. It is enough to note this, here, as bearing on his representative character. The most surprising thing, however, is that his genius is found to be so purely objective; he himself emphasized the objectivity of his art. From the beginning, as has been said, he had no message, no inspiration welling up within him, no inward life of his own that sought expression. He was not even introspective. He was primarily a moralist, an observer of life, which he saw as a thing of the outside, and he was keen in observation, cool, interested. If there was any mystery in his tales, it was in the object, not in the author's breast; he makes no confessions either direct or indirect,— he describes the thing he sees. He maintained that his tales were perfectly intelligible, and he meant this to apply not only to style but to theme.

. . . .

PAUL ELMER MORE [1864–1937] taught at Princeton and edited *The Nation*. He wrote several important essays on Hawthorne: "The Solitude of Nathaniel Hawthorne," "The Origins of Hawthorne and Poe," and "Hawthorne: Looking Before and After." In the first he deals with a major problem in Hawthorne biography and criticism. In the other two essays he traces both the antecedents and the influence of Hawthorne's concept of human experience. Although first published in 1901, "The Solitude of Nathaniel Hawthorne" re-appeared in 1904 and became part of the extensive commentary elicited by the centennial celebration of Hawthorne's birth.

The Solitude of Nathaniel Hawthorne

PAUL ELMER MORE

. . . .

I have spoken as if the mental attitude of Hawthorne was one common to the race, however it may be exaggerated in form by his own inner vision; and to us of the western world, over whom have passed centuries of Christian brooding, and who find ourselves suddenly cut loose from the consolation of Christian faith, his voice may well seem the utterance of universal experience, and we may be even justified in assuming that his words have at last expressed what has long slumbered in human consciousness. His

Shelburne Essays, First Series (New York, 1904) 47–50.

was not the bitterness, the fierce indignation of loneliness, that devoured the heart of Swift; nor yet the terror of a soul like Cowper's, that believed itself guilty of the unpardonable sin, and therefore condemned to everlasting exile and torment; nor Byron's personal rancour and hatred of society; nor the ecstasy of Thomas à Kempis, whose spirit was rapt away out of the turmoil of existence; but rather an intensification of the solitude that invests the modern world, and by right found its deepest expression in the New England heart. Not with impunity had the human race for ages dwelt on the eternal welfare of the soul; for from such meditation the sense of personal importance had become exacerbated to an extraordinary degree. What could result from such teaching as that of Jonathan Edwards but an extravagant sense of individual existence, as if the moral governance of the world revolved about the action of each mortal soul? And when the alluring faith attendant on this form of introspection paled, as it did during the so-called transcendental movement into which Hawthorne was born, there resulted necessarily a feeling of anguish and bereavement more tragic than any previous moral stage through which the world had passed. The loneliness of the individual, which had been vaguely felt and lamented by poets and philosophers of the past, took on a poignancy altogether unexampled. It needed but an artist with the vision of Hawthorne to represent this feeling as the one tragic calamity of mortal life, as the great primeval curse of sin. What lay dormant in the teaching of Christianity became the universal protest of the human heart.

In no way can we better estimate the universality, and at the same time the modern note, of Hawthorne's solitude than by turning for a moment to the literature of the far-off Ganges. There, too, on the banks of the holy river, men used much to ponder on the life of the human soul in its restless wandering from birth to birth; and in their books we may read of a loneliness as profound as Hawthorne's, though quite distinct in character. To them, also, we are born alone, we die alone, and alone we reap the fruits of our good and evil deeds. The dearest ties of our earthly existence are as meaningless and transient as the meeting of spar with drifting spar on the ocean waves. Yet in all this it is the isolation of the soul from the source of universal life that troubles human thought; there is no cry of personal anguish here, such as arises from Christianity, for the loss of individuality is ever craved by the Hindu as the highest good. And besides this distinction between the Western and Eastern forms of what may be called secular solitude, the Hindu carried the idea into abstract realms whither no Occidental can penetrate.

> HE, in that solitude before
> The world was, looked the wide void o'er
> And nothing saw, and said, Lo, I
> Alone!—and still we echo the lone cry.
>
> Thereat He feared, and still we fear
> In solitude when naught is near:
> And, Lo, He said, myself alone!
> What cause of dread when second is not known!

But into this dim region of Oriental mysticism we have no reason to intrude. We may at least count it among the honours of our literature that it was left for a denizen of this far Western land, living in the midst of a late-born and confused civilisation, to give artistic form to a thought that, in fluctuating form, has troubled the minds of philosophers from the beginning. Other authors may be greater in so far as they touch our passions more profoundly, but to the solitude of Nathaniel Hawthorne we owe the most perfect utterance of a feeling that must seem to us now as old and as deep as life itself.

It would be easy to explain Hawthorne's peculiar temperament, after the modern fashion, by reference to heredity and environment. No doubt there was a strain of eccentricity in the family. He himself tells of a cousin who made a spittoon out of the skull of his enemy; and it is natural that a descendant of the old Puritan witch judge should portray the weird and grotesque aspects of life. Probably this native tendency was increased by the circumstances that surrounded his youth: the seclusion of his mother's life; his boyhood on Lake Sebago, where, as he says, he first got his "cursed habit of solitude;" and the long years during which he lived as a hermit in Salem. But, after all, these external matters, and even the effect of heredity so far as we can fathom it, explain little or nothing. A thousand other men might have written his books if their source lay in such antecedents. Behind it all was the dæmonic force of the man himself, the everlasting mystery of genius habiting in his brain, and choosing him to be an exemplar and interpreter of the inviolable individuality in which lie the pain and glory of our human estate.

For many years BLISS PERRY [1860–1954] edited *The Atlantic Monthly* and taught at Harvard. He wrote biographies of Whitman and Whittier, as well as more inclusive studies of American literature. His address, "The Centenary of Hawthorne," first appeared in *The Atlantic Monthly* (August 1904) and was reprinted in *Park-Street Papers*, which also includes centenary commentaries on Longfellow and Whittier. Perry's essay on Hawthorne represents one of the better appraisals of the author among the numerous tributes during the celebrations in 1904.

The Centenary of Hawthorne

BLISS PERRY

. . . .

And what a writer this provincial New Englander is! We talk glibly nowadays about painting and writing with one's eye on the object. Hawthorne could do this when he chose; but think of writing with your eye on the consciences of Arthur Dimmesdale and Hester Prynne, and never relaxing your gaze till the book is done! What concentration of vision! What exposing power! Hawthorne's vocabulary is not extraordinarily large;—nothing like Balzac's or Meredith's; but the words are chosen like David's five smooth stones out of the brook. The sentences move in perfect poise. Their ease is perhaps a little self-conscious;—pains have been taken with their dressing,—it is not the careless inevitable grace of Thackeray,—but it is a finished grace of their own. It is a style exquisitely simple, except in those passages where Hawthorne's fancy gets the better of him, and leads him into forced humor, all the worse for its air of cultivated exuberance. Yet even when he sins against simplicity, he is always transparently clear. The certainty of word and phrase, the firmness of outline are marvelous, when we consider the airy nature of much of his material; he may be building cloud-castles, but it is in so pure a sky that the white battlements and towers stand out sharp-edged as marble.

Because Hawthorne gave his work such an elaborate finish, some readers are apt to forget its underlying strength. Our own day of naturalistic impressionism and correct historical costuming has invented a hundred sensational and clever ways of tearing a passion to tatters. But it is well for us to remember that the real

Park-Street Papers (Boston, 1908) 97–103.

strength of a work of fiction is in the conception underlying it, and that the deepest currents of thought and feeling are

> Too full for sound and foam.

Strong-fibred, sane, self-controlled, as was Hawthorne, one may nevertheless detect in his style that melancholy vibration which marks the words of all—or almost all—those who have interpreted through literature the more mysterious aspects of life. This pathos is profound, though it is quiet; it is an undertone, but not the fundamental tone; "the gloom and terror may lie deep, but deeper still is this eternal beauty."

Yet the most marked quality of Hawthorne's style is neither simplicity, nor clearness, nor reserve of strength, nor undertone of pathos. It is rather its unbroken melody, its verbal richness. Its echoes linger in the ear; they wake old echoes in the brain. The touch of a few other men may be as perfect, the notes they evoke more brilliant, certainly more gay; but Hawthorne's deep-toned instrument yields harmonies inimitable and unforgettable. The critics who talk of the colorless life of New England and its colorless reflection in literature had better open their Hawthorne once more. His pages are steeped in color. They have a dusky glory like the great window in Keats's "Eve of St. Agnes":—

> . . . diamonded with panes of quaint device,
> Innumerable of stains and splendid dyes,
> As are the tiger-moth's deep-damask'd wings;
> And in the midst, 'mong thousand heraldries,
> And twilight saints, and dim emblazonings,
> A shielded scutcheon blush'd with blood of queens and kings.

This subdued splendor of Hawthorne's coloring is a part of the very texture of his style; compared with it the brushwork of his successors seems thin and washy, or else crude and hard; it is like comparing a rug woven in Bokhara with one manufactured in Connecticut. But surely our New England soil is not wholly barren if even for once it has flowered into such a consummate artist as Nathaniel Hawthorne, who, while he devoted his art to the interpretation of truth, was nevertheless dowered with such instinct for beauty that his very words glow like gems and echo like music, and grant him a place among the few masters of English style.

After all, we do not celebrate the centenary of Hawthorne's birth merely because he was a skillful, an admirable writer. Rather do we take a solemn pride in commemorating one who steadfastly asserted the claims of spiritual things. He wrote in a generation fortunate in its balance between the hard material struggles of the colonist and pioneer, and the far more dangerous materialism that comes with luxury and power. America had lived through sufficient history to give perspective to her romancers; she had not yet undergone the demoralizing strain of prosperity which has followed upon the epoch of the Civil War. Never were Americans so profoundly idealistic, so temperamentally fit to understand the spiritualized art of Hawthorne, as between 1840 and 1860. And our pride in him is touched with a subtle regret at the disappearance of a fine civilization, provincial as it was. A more splendid civilization is still to come, no doubt; but the specific conditions that blossomed into many of Hawthorne's tales are irrevocably gone. Great as he seems when we look back, he seems still greater when we look around us. It is no service to Hawthorne's memory to disparage the industrious men and women who are producing our fiction of to-day. But to glance at them, and then to think of him, is to perceive the startling difference between talent and genius.

No one would claim that that genius was faultless in all its divinations. Feeble drawing, ineffective symbolism, morbid dallying with mortuary fancies, may indeed be detected in his books. That sound critic Edwin P. Whipple, who is passing into such ill-deserved oblivion, once said of Hawthorne: "He had spiritual insight, but it did not penetrate to the sources of spiritual joy." The note of robust triumph, of unquestioning faith in individual happiness and in the sure advance of human society, is indeed too rarely heard in his writings. In repeating his paternoster, the stress falls upon "Forgive us our trespasses" rather than upon "Thy Kingdom come."

Yet he believed that the sin and sorrow of humanity, inexplicable as they are, are not to be thought of as if we were apart from God. A neighbor of Hawthorne in Concord has recently written me that once, when death entered a household there, Hawthorne picked the finest sunflower from his garden, and sent it to the mourners by Mrs. Hawthorne with this message: "Tell them that the sunflower is a symbol of the sun, and that the sun is a symbol of the glory of God." A shy, simple act of neighborhood kindness,—yet treasured in one memory for more than forty years; and how much of Hawthorne there is in it! The quaint flower from an old-fashioned garden; the delicate sympathy; the perfect phrase; the faith in the power of a symbol to turn the perplexed soul to God! Hawthorne was no natural lover of darkness, but rather one who yearned for light. The gloom which haunts many of his pages is the long shadow cast by our mortal destiny upon a sensitive soul, conscious of kinship with the erring race of men. The mystery is our mystery, perceived, and not created, by that finely endowed mind and heart. The shadow is our shadow; the gleams of insight, the soft radiance of truth and beauty, are his own.

WILLIAM CRARY BROWNELL [1851–1928] was a journalist and a commentator on literature, art, and social phenomena. Among his books are *Victorian Prose Masters* (1901), *American Prose Masters* (1909), and *The Genius of Style* (1924). In *American Prose Masters* his favorites are Cooper and Emerson. In his essay on Hawthorne Brownell concedes that the "beautiful and profound story" of *The Scarlet Letter* is "our chief prose masterpiece" and that "it is as difficult to overpraise it as it is to avoid poignantly regretting that Hawthorne failed to recognize its value and learn the lesson it might have taught him." Most of the essay condemns Hawthorne's placidity and reserve, "the evil eye of Allegory under whose baleful spell for some reason or other he early fell," "the cultivation of fancy to the neglect of imagination," Hawthorne's failure to achieve "actual reality," and the basic impoverishment of his mind.

Nathaniel Hawthorne

W. C. BROWNELL

Hawthorne's style, doubtless less original than his substance, is nevertheless indubitably his own. It is far more the general cultivated medium of writing than his works are within the general lines of romance, but it is that medium colored and modelled—or, perhaps, one should rather say, tinted and traced—by his own idiosyncrasy. This indeed is its importance. As style it has no other. Its hue and figure are of interest as their faintness and evenness mirror his personal traits. These are, however, very crisply reflected by it, and a study of it is useful as certifying the impressions made by its substance. It is, to begin with, difficult to define, and its lack of positive qualities quite exactly parallels the insubstantiality of its

American Prose Masters (New York, 1909) 123–30.

subject-matter. Only by a miracle, one reflects, could subject-matter of much vital importance be thus habited—so plainly, placidly, unpretendingly presented, though in such an exceptional instance as "The Scarlet Letter" the latent intensity of the theme is doubtless set off by the sobriety of its garb, to which also it gives a deepened tone. But the harmonious, rather than contrasting, services of such a style as Hawthorne's in general, could be useful only for the direct expression of something bordering on informing insipidity. It is above all a neat style. It wears no gewgaws of rhetoric and owes little or nothing to the figures of speech. It is saved from the conventional mainly by the author's own interest in its substance, and would be prim if it were not personal. But it is too sincere for any, even Puritan, affectation. Its neatness is a native, not a cultivated quality. It is the neatness of innocence, not of virtue. It has never been assailed by the temptations of the meretricious, and its avoidance of ornament is preference for the plain, not distaste for the rococo. It views the purple patch with the unmoved placidity of the color-blind, and the staidness of its expression corresponds to the propriety of its thought, whose wildest antics are decorous with the consciousness that it is "all pretend." Nothing shows more clearly the dilettante character of Hawthorne's exercise of his fancy than this neatness, which is never discomposed by fervor or thrown into disarray by heat.

It is in fact the antithesis of heat, and the absence of heat in Hawthorne's genius appears nowhere so markedly as in his style. His writings from beginning to end do not contain an ardent, or even a fervent passage. They are as empty of exaltation as of exhilaration. Here, for example, is a single sentence by a fellow-townsman of his descriptive of one of nature's daily phenomena: "In deep ravines, under the eastern sides of cliffs, Night forwardly plants her foot even at noonday, and, as Day retreats, she steps into his trenches, skulking from tree to tree, from fence to fence, until at last she sits in his citadel and draws out her forces into the plain." No one can read that without recognizing its almost incandescent quality, or compare it with the most glowing period to be found in Hawthorne, without distinguishing between the imaginative flame that burned in Thoreau's Walden cabin and the flicker of fancy that played over the embers of the Old Manse hearth. Or take a few phrases inspired by the little convent cemetery at Brussels, the writer of which

> came to this spot one summer evening of spring and saw among a thousand black crosses casting their shadows across

the grassy slope that particular one which marked his mother's resting-place. . . . A thousand such hillocks lay round about, the gentle daisies springing out of the grass over them, and each bearing its cross and requiescat. A nun, veiled in black, was kneeling hard by at a sleeping sister's bedside (so freshmade that the spring had scarce had time to spin a coverlid for it); beyond the cemetery walls you had glimpses of life and the world and the spires and gables of the city. A bird came down from a roof opposite, and lit first on a cross and then on the grass below it, whence it flew away presently with a leaf in its mouth: then came a sound as of chanting, from the chapel of the sisters hard by. . . . Might she sleep in peace— might she sleep in peace; and we, too, when our struggles and pains are over! But the earth is the Lord's as the heaven is; we are alike his creatures here and yonder. I took a little flower off the hillock and kissed it, and went my way, like the bird that had just lighted on the cross by me, back into the world again. Silent receptacle of death, tranquil depth of calm, out of reach of tempest and trouble! I felt as one who had been walking below the sea, and treading amid the bones of shipwrecks.[1]

To curtail this passage of perhaps the foremost master of English prose is to mutilate it, but I have transcribed enough of it to exemplify precisely the quality that Hawthorne's style most conspicuously and most characteristically lacks. It exemplifies perfectly the exaltation of an ardent imagination constrained and modulated by instinctive artistic reserve. It is as far removed from the purple splendors of rhetoric as Hawthorne at his simplest, but it is simplicity sublimated by feeling, not expressed with placid adequacy. Imagine "the rarest imagination since Shakespeare" exclaiming, "The earth is the Lord's!" He has not the authority requisite for such an utterance. He writes as the scribes, and lacks the conviction, the assurance of his vocation, the authentic literary and artistic commission for exclamation or utterance with any fire or particular fervor. It is simply extraordinary that so voluminous a writer should care so little for writing as an art of effective expression, should practise it so exclusively as an exercise—as mere record and statement. In "The Scarlet Letter," as I have intimated, the style to a certain extent reflects the greater depth and richness of the substance. But compare its most moving passage with the sentences just cited from Thackeray:

[1]*Henry Esmond*, Book I, Chapter XIII, final paragraph.

They sat down again side by side and hand clasped in hand on the mossy trunk of the fallen tree. Life had never brought them a gloomier hour; it was the point whither their pathway had so long been tending, and darkening ever as it stole along;—and yet it enclosed a charm that made them linger upon it, and claim another, and another and, after all, another moment. The forest was obscure around them and creaked with a blast that was passing through it. The boughs were tossing heavily above their heads; while one solemn old tree groaned dolefully to another, as if telling the sad story of the pair that sat beneath, or constrained to forebode evil to come.

The drop—in tone, in spirit and in rhythm—from real elevation to that "one solemn old tree" groaning "dolefully" and the perpetual symbolism, is characteristic. It is just what the instinct for style would save a writer from. And it is but a partial explanation to attribute Hawthorne's lack of this instinct to his lack of plastic sense. It is explained ultimately by his lack of real energy, to which no doubt his lack of plastic sense is itself due; though it may be said that his imagination, cool enough in his view of life, content to contemplate instead of construct, seems to lose still more heat in his expression, and his style to have even less warmth than his conceptions. Evidently, though these amuse, they do not impose upon him, and his extremely detached treatment of them is the most convincing impeachment of his "high seriousness" as a writer, however sombre, even, his philosophy of life.

And though it is only superficially strange, it is at least superficially piquant, that his style should disclose his lack of ardor by its absence of restraint as well as by poverty of feeling. Never was such copiousness associated with so little exuberance, or at any rate exuberance with so little enthusiasm. His simplicity appears thus as the expression not of contained but of uncomplicated substance. Simple as his style is it is never severe and its quietness is not the result of reserve. Just as its purity is due to the absence of sensuousness rather than to spiritual elevation, its simplicity is that of a map rather than that of a picture. The fertility of his fancy is not matched by the subtlety of its expression. He does not deal in *nuances*, but accumulates detail. No writer was ever fonder of detail. The flood of it drowns his descriptions. One cannot trace the general skeleton, the grand construction. He does not even subordinate the trivial, but chronicles everything that occurs to him with an amused and sportive assiduity. His personal taciturnity disappears as he contemplates his subject and he abandons himself, with more zest than he ever otherwise betrays, to a kind of quaintly otiose but unmistakable garrulity. In this respect not his first but his very last story—written after a lifetime of professional practice —gives a very striking impression of the amateur with a pen in his hand and endless leisure before him. Our peculiar Anglo-Saxon delusion of arguing inner intensity from outward composure can find no support in Hawthorne's style for ascribing to him any elements of energy that are indicated by restraint in their expression. What his extreme copiousness witnesses is the diffusion instead of the concentration of his interest. His interest is extraordinarily spread out over the rather narrow field that awakens it at all and perhaps could not be so inclusive if it centred around any cardinal foci to the disparagement of the apparently negligible.

Such copiousness is, naturally, inconsistent with any effective ordering of the elements of style, and Hawthorne's is as unaccented periodically as it is monotonous in color. But it has the great merit of ease, conjoined with exactness. One without the other is not uncommon, but the combination is rare. The kind of care that goes with deliberateness he undoubtedly took, though he certainly took none that demanded strenuous and scrupulous effort, or his result would have been more distinguished instead of being purely satisfactory—markedly felicitous as well as adequate and correct. But his ease, thus untinctured by either study or sloth, and marking the free movement of a style that is not only flexible but correct, was undoubtedly a natural gift. He had it in the form that is both academic and elastic. Hence his style has in some degree the classic note. As free from eccentricity or excess as from any particular pungency or color it is eminently the style of literary good-breeding and images its author's personal fastidiousness. Its vocabulary is that of cultivated English. It is as free from the crude as from the far-fetched. And though often as familiar in tone as it is simple in diction its smoothness never lacks dignity and often attains grace. Why has it not in greater degree the truly classic note? Why is it that after all—perfectly adapted as it is to the expression of its substance, to the purpose of its author—it lacks quality and physiognomy? Or at all events why is its quality not more marked, more salient? Because it *is* such an adequate medium for its content, for the expression of a nature without enthusiasm, a mind unenriched by acquisition and an imagination that is in general the prey of fancy rather than the servant of the will. Hawthorne should have taken himself more seriously at the outset—in his formative period—and less so in the maturity of powers whose development would have produced far more important results than those achieved by their leisurely exercise in tranquil neglect of their evolution.

1911 to the Present

T. S. ELIOT [1888–1965] has been designated by René Wellek as "by far the most important critic of the twentieth century in the English-speaking world." To *The Little Review*, edited by Margaret Anderson and Ezra Pound, he contributed two selections in the "Henry James Number" of August 1918. The first is called "In Memory," and the second, "The Hawthorne Aspect," reprinted below. Eliot's choice of *The House of the Seven Gables* as Hawthorne's "best novel" runs contrary to the views of many critics, including James. "The Hawthorne Aspect" is notable for the wide-ranging literary contexts in which the James-Hawthorne relationship is placed and for the delineation of a tradition in which Hawthorne is the chief predecessor to James.

The Hawthorne Aspect

T. S. ELIOT

My object is not to discuss critically even one phase or period of James, but merely to provide a note, *Beitrage*, toward any attempt to determine his antecedents, affinities, and "place". Presumed that James's relation to Balzac, to Turgenev, to any one else on the continent is known and measured—I refer to Mr. Hueffer's book and to Mr. Pound's article—and presumed that his relation to the Victorian novel is negligible, it is not concluded that James was simply a clever young man who came to Europe and improved himself, but that the soil of his origin contributed a flavour discriminible after transplantation in his latest fruit. We may even draw the instructive conclusion that this flavour was precisely improved and given its chance, not worked off, by transplantation. If there is this strong native taste, there will probably be some relation to Hawthorne; and if there is any relation to Hawthorne, it will probably help us to analyse the flavour of which I speak.

When we say that James is "American", we must mean that this "flavour" of his, and also more exactly definable qualities, are more or less diffused throughout the vast continent rather than anywhere else; but we cannot mean that this flavour and these qualities have found literary expression throughout the nation, or that they permeate the work of Mr. Frank Norris or Mr. Booth Tarkington. The point is that James is positively a continuator of the New England genius; that there is a New England genius, which has discovered itself only in a very small number of people

The Little Review, Vol. 5 (August 1918) 47–53.

in the middle of the nineteenth century—and which is *not* significantly present in the writings of Miss Sara Orne Jewett, Miss Eliza White, or the Bard of Appledore whose name I forget. I mean whatever we associate with certain purlieus of Boston, with Concord, Salem, and Cambridge, Mass.: notably Emerson, Thoreau, Hawthorne and Lowell. None of these men, with the exception of Hawthorne, is individually very important; they all can, and perhaps ought to be made to look very foolish; but there is a "something" there, a dignity, about Emerson for example, which persists after we have perceived the taint of commonness about some English contemporary, as for instance the more intelligent, better educated, more alert Matthew Arnold. Omitting such men as Bryant and Whittier as absolutely plebeian, we can still perceive this halo of dignity around the men I have named, and also Longfellow, Margaret Fuller and her crew, Bancroft and Motley, the faces of (later) Norton and Child pleasantly shaded by the Harvard elms. One distinguishing mark of this distinguished world was very certainly leisure; and importantly not in all cases a leisure given by money, but insisted upon. There seems no easy reason why Emerson or Thoreau or Hawthorne should have been men of leisure; it seems odd that the New England conscience should have allowed them leisure; yet they *would* have it, sooner or later. That is really one of the finest things about them, and sets a bold frontier between them and a world which will at any price avoid leisure, a world in which Theodore Roosevelt is a patron of the arts. An interesting document, of this latter world is the *Letters* of a nimbly dull poet of a younger generation, of Henry James's generation, Richard Watson Gilder, Civil Service Reform, Tenement House Commission, Municipal Politics.

Of course leisure in a metropolis, with a civilized society (the society of Boston was and is quite uncivilized but refined beyond the point of civilisation) with exchange of ideas and critical standards would have been better; but these men could not provide the metropolis, and were right in taking the leisure under possible conditions.

Precisely this leisure, this dignity, this literary aristocracy, this unique character of a society in which the men of letters were also of the best people, clings to Henry James. It is some consciousness of this kinship which makes him so tender and gentle in his appreciations of Emerson, Norton and the beloved Ambassador. With Hawthorne, as much the most important of these people in any question of literary art, his relation is more personal; but no more in the case of Hawthorne than with any of the other figures of the background is there any consideration of influence. James owes little, very little, to anyone; there are certain writers whom he consciously studied, of whom Hawthorne was not one; but in any case his relation to Hawthorne is on another plane from his relation to Balzac, for example. The influence of Balzac, not on the whole a good influence, is perfectly evident in some of the earlier novels; the influence of Turgenev is vaguer, but more useful. That James was, at a certain period, more moved by Balzac, that he followed him with more concentrated admiration, is clear from the tone of his criticism of that writer compared with the tone of his criticism of either Turgenev or Hawthorne. In *French Poets and Novelists*, though an early work, James's attitude toward Balzac is exactly that of having been very much attracted from his orbit, perhaps very wholesomely stimulated at an age when almost any foreign stimulus may be good, and having afterwards reacted from Balzac, though not to the point of injustice. He handles Balzac shrewdly and fairly. From the essay on Turgenev there is on the other hand very little to be got but a touching sense of appreciation; from the essay on Flaubert even less. The charming study of Hawthorne is quite different from any of these. The first conspicuous quality in it is tenderness, the tenderness of a man who had escaped too early from an environment to be warped or thwarted by it, who had escaped so effectually that he could afford the gift of affection. At the same time he places his finger, now and then, very gently, on some of Hawthorne's more serious defects as well as his limitations.

> "The best things come, as a general thing, from the talents that are members of a group; every man works better when he has companions working in the same line, and yielding the stimulus of suggestion, comparison, emulation."

Though when he says that

> "there was manifestly a strain of generous indolence in his (Hawthorne's) composition"

he is understating the fault of laziness for which Hawthorne can chiefly be blamed. But gentleness is needed in criticising Hawthorne, a necessary thing to remember about whom is precisely the difficult fact that the soil which produced him with his essential flavour is the soil which produced, just as inevitably, the environment which stunted him.

In one thing alone Hawthorne is more solid than James: he had a very acute historical sense. His erudition in the small field of American colonial history was extensive, and he made most fortunate use of it. Both men had that sense of the past which is peculiarly American, but in Hawthorne this sense exercised itself in a grip on the past itself; in James it is a sense of the sense. This, however, need not be dwelt upon here. The really vital thing, in finding any personal kinship between Hawthorne and James, is what James touches lightly when he says that

> "the fine thing in Hawthorne is that he cared for the deeper psychology, and that, in his way, he tried to become familiar with it."

There are other points of resemblance, not directly included under this, but this one is of the first importance. It is, in fact, almost enough to ally the two novelists, in comparison with whom almost all others may be accused of either superficiality or aridity. I am not saying that this "deeper psychology" is essential, or that it can always be had without loss of other qualities, or that a novel need be any the less a work of art without it. It is a definition; and it separates the two novelists at once from the English contemporaries of either. Neither Dickens nor Thackeray, certainly, had the smallest notion of the "deeper psychology"; George Eliot had a kind of heavy intellect for it (Tito) but all her genuine feeling went into the visual realism of *Amos Barton.* On the continent it is known; but the method of Stendhal or of Flaubert is quite other. A situation is for Stendhal something deliberately constructed, often an illustration. There is a bleakness about it, vitalised by force rather than feeling, and its presentation is definitely visual. Hawthorne and James have a kind of sense, a receptive medium, which is not of sight. Not that they fail to make you *see*, so far as necessary, but sight is not the essential sense. They perceive by antennae; and the "deeper psychology" is here. The deeper psychology indeed led Hawthorne to some of his absurdest and most characteristic excesses; it was for ever tailing off into the fanciful, even the allegorical, which is a lazy substitute for profundity. The fancifulness is the "strain of generous indolence", the attempt to get the artistic effect by meretricious means. On this side a critic might seize hold of *The Turn of the Screw,* a tale about which I have many doubts; but the actual working out of this is different from Hawthorne's, and we are not interested in approximation of the two men on the side of their weakness. The point is that

Hawthorne was acutely sensitive to the situation; that he did grasp character through the relation of two or more persons to each other; and this is what no one else, except James, has done. Furthermore, he does establish, as James establishes, a solid atmosphere, and he does, in his quaint way, get New England, as James gets a larger part of America, and as none of their respective contemporaries get anything above a village or two, or a jungle. Compare, with anything that any English contemporary could do, the situation which Hawthorne sets up in the relation of Dimmesdale and Chillingworth. Judge Pyncheon and Clifford, Hepzibah and Phoebe, are similarly achieved by their relation to each other; Clifford, for one, being simply the intersection of a relation to three other characters. The only dimension in which Hawthorne could expand was the past, his present being so narrowly barren. It is a great pity, with his remarkable gift of observation, that the present did not offer him more to observe. But he is the one English-writing predecessor of James whose characters are *aware* of each other, the one whose novels were in any deep sense a criticism of even a slight civilization; and here is something more definite and closer than any derivation we can trace from Richardson or Marivaux.

The fact that the sympathy with Hawthorne is most felt in the last of James's novels, *The Sense of the Past*, makes me the more certain of its genuineness. In the meantime, James has been through a much more elaborate development than poor Hawthorne ever knew. Hawthorne, with his very limited culture, was not exposed to any bewildering variety of influences. James, in his astonishing career of self-improvement, touches Hawthorne most evidently at the beginning and end of his course; at the beginning, simply as a young New Englander of letters; at the end, with almost a gesture of approach. *Roderick Hudson* is the novel of a clever and expanding young New Englander; immature, but just coming out to a self-consciousness where Hawthorne never arrived at all. Compared with *Daisy Miller* or *The Europeans* or *The American* its critical spirit is very crude. But *The Marble Faun (Transformation)*, the only European novel of Hawthorne, is of Cimmerian opacity; the mind of its author was closed to new impressions though with all its Walter Scott-Mysteries of Udolpho upholstery the old man does establish a kind of solid moral atmosphere which the young James does not get. James in *Roderick Hudson* does very little better with Rome than Hawthorne, and as he confesses in the later preface, rather fails with Northampton.

He does in the later edition tone down the absurdities of

Roderick's sculpture a little, the pathetic Thirst and the gigantic Adam; Mr. Striker remains a failure, the judgment of a young man consciously humourising, too suggestive of Martin Chuzzlewit. The generic resemblance to Hawthorne is in the occasional heavy facetiousness of the style, the tedious whimsicality how different from the exactitude of *The American Scene*, the verbalism. He too much identifies himself with Rowland, does not see through the solemnity he has created in that character, commits the cardinal sin of failing to "detect" one of his own characters. The failure to create a situation is evident: with Christina and Mary, each nicely adjusted, but never quite set in relation to each other. The interest of the book for our present purpose is what he does *not* do in the Hawthorne way, in the instinctive attempt to get at something larger, which will bring him to the same success with much besides.

The interest in the "deeper psychology", the observation, and the sense for situation, developed from book to book, culminate in *The Sense of the Past* (by no means saying that this is his best) uniting with other qualities both personal and racial. James's greatness is apparent both in his capacity for development as an artist and his capacity for keeping his mind alive to the changes in the world during twenty-five years: It is remarkable (for the mastery of a span of American history) that the man who did the Wentworth family in the '80s could do the Bradhams in the '00s. In *The Sense of the Past* the Midmores belong to the same generation as the Bradhams; Ralph belongs to the same race as the Wentworths, indeed as the Pyncheons. Compare the book with *The House of the Seven Gables* (Hawthorne's best novel after all); the situation, the "shrinkage and extinction of a family" is rather more complex, on the surface, than James's with (so far as the book was done) fewer character-relations. But James's real situation here, to which Ralph's mounting the step is the key, as Hepzibah's opening of her shop, is a situation of different states of mind. James's situation is the shrinkage and extinction of an idea. The Pyncheon tragedy is simple; the "curse" upon the family a matter of the simplest fairy mechanics. James has taken Hawthorne's ghost-sense and given it substance. At the same time making the tragedy much more etherial: the tragedy of that "Sense", the hypertrophy, in Ralph, of a partial civilization; the vulgar vitality of the Midmores in their financial decay contrasted with the decay of Ralph in his financial prosperity, when they precisely should have been the civilisation he had come to seek. All this watched over by the absent, but conscious Aurora. I do not want to insist upon the Hawthorneness of the confrontation of the portrait, the im-

portance of the opening of a door. We need surely not insist that
this book is the most important, most substantial sort of thing that
James did; perhaps there is more solid wear even in that other
unfinished *Ivory Tower*. But I consider that it was an excursion
which we could well permit him, after a lifetime in which he had
taken talents similar to Hawthorne's and made them yield far
greater returns than poor Hawthorne could harvest from his granite
soil; a permissible exercise, in which we may by a legitimately
cognate fancy seem to detect Hawthorne coming to a mediumistic
existence again, to remind a younger and incredulous generation
of what he really was, had he had the opportunity, and to attest
his satisfaction that that opportunity had been given to James.

FRED LEWIS PATTEE [1863–1950] was a professor of American literature
at Pennsylvania State College. Among his books are *The First Century of American Literature, 1770–1870; History of American Literature Since 1870; The Development of the American Short Story;* and
The Feminine Fifties. Although the selection printed below is a judicious evaluation of Hawthorne's place in the development of the short
story in America, Pattee's assessment of the romancer in *The First
Century of American Literature* (1935) emphasizes his solitude, depicts
him as suicide-haunted, and claims that in *The Scarlet Letter* Hawthorne accomplishd his ends by artificial means. Pattee's brief remarks
about Hawthorne in *The Feminine Fifties* (1940) are condemnatory—
perhaps as severe as Hawthorne's estimate of the scribbling women
discussed in Pattee's book.

Nathaniel Hawthorne

FRED LEWIS PATTEE

Despite Poe's elaborate formulation of the rules governing the
art of the *Twice-Told Tales*, it is to be doubted if Hawthorne had
any theory of the short story or any suspicion that the tale differed
from the novel save in the one attribute of length. A few of the
tales obey in full the laws of Poe, but they are so few they may
be counted as exceptions, so few, indeed, that they seem accidental

The Development of the American Short Story (New York, 1923) 107–10.

rather than intentional. Hawthorne was most at home in the sketch, the rambling essay type of reminiscent description, as in "The Old Manse" and the introduction to *The Scarlet Letter*, and in expository analyses of situations or personalities or mental states. Everything had seemed to turn him to the shorter varieties of prose—the demands of the magazines, the uncertain market for American novels, the nature of his own genius, which was more inclined to brood over moral situations than to plan elaborate structures of plot—and in his solitary chamber he wrote to please himself, using for models, if he used any at all, the older classics, the dramas of Shakespeare, and the English novel which, according to his sister's testimony, he had studied for its technique. As a result his tales, from the standpoint of form, show surprising merits and, on the other hand, equally surprising defects. Poe was the first to formulate the former, and A. P. Peabody, in a review some ten years later, the first to dwell upon the latter. "The most paltry talemaker for the magazines or the newspapers," Peabody had declared, "can easily excel him in what we might term the mechanical portion of his art. His plots are seldom well devised or skillfully developed . . . the conversations are not natural," and so on with other details. It is not hard now, in the light of modern rules, to point out Hawthorne's failures: his leisurely, expository openings; his frequent discursiveness; his characters which for the most part are as abstract and bloodless as Spenser's creations; his distance from the warm currents of actual life; his moralizing endings. But these defects, serious as some of them may be, are overbalanced by equally important excellencies, even in technique, for if we are to judge him by his work, by a dozen or more tales universally admitted now to be masterpieces, tales like "Rappaccini's Daughter," "The Birthmark," "The Great Stone Face," "The Wives of the Dead," "The Great Carbuncle," "The White Old Maid," "The Minister's Black Veil," "Ethan Brand," the four "Legends of the Province House," "The Snow Image," and a few others, we shall find that even in the matter of form Hawthorne was a pioneer, in advance of all his contemporaries save Poe.

 He conceived of his tales in terms of culminating action; there is always a dramatic moment for which everything before has been a preparation. One may most easily illustrate this from his jottings for tales in his notebook. It reveals his habit of mind:

> A sketch to be given of a modern reformer—a type of the extreme doctrines on the subject of slaves, cold water, and other such topics. He goes about the streets haranguing most

eloquently, and is on the point of making many converts, when his labors are suddenly interrupted by the appearance of the keeper of a madhouse, whence he has escaped. Much may be made of this idea.

The scene of a story or sketch to be laid within the light of a street lantern; the time, when the lamp is near going out; and the catastrophe to be simultaneous with the last flickering gleam.

Two persons, by mutual agreement, to make their wills in each other's favor, then to wait impatiently for one another's death, and both to be informed of the desired event at the same time. Both, in most joyous sorrow, hasten to be present at the funeral, meet, and find themselves both hoaxed.

Perhaps his emphasis of a single climactic moment rather than of a growing series of happenings in chronicle form came from the sermonic habit, which, like every other indigenous New-Englander, he had inherited from his Puritan ancestors. His tales came to him as texts to be illustrated and driven home. "On this theme," he observes after one of his notebook jottings, "methinks I could frame a tale with a deep moral." He wrote "Wakefield" "trusting there will be a pervading spirit and a moral, even if we should fail to find them done up neatly and condensed into the final sentence."

In the second place, Hawthorne had a keen eye for situation. Here again was he a pioneer, the first prominent writer whose tales may be defined in terms of situation. So far as I have been able to find, the first to perceive and record this fact was the English *National Review* in 1861:

All his tales embody single ideal situations, scarcely ever for a moment varied in their course.... His longer works are ideal situations expanded by minute study and trains of closely related thought into the dimensions of novels.... He prefers to assume the crisis past and to determine as fully as he can the ideal situation to which it has given rise when it is beginning to assume more of a chronic character.

No one has expressed more clearly than this what Hawthorne really added to the short story. If it be true—and no one has disputed it—then the author of the *Twice-Told Tales* rather than Poe stands as the father of the American short story. At least he was the first to direct it into its modern form.

Hawthorne was the first in America to touch the new romanticism with morals, at least the first to touch it in the department of its fiction. His situations are almost invariably moral culminations, and for presenting them he had several devices. Often he sought for a symbol that would grip and shake the reader's imagination. This from his notebooks:

> Meditations about the main gas pipe of a great city,—if the supply were to be stopped, what would happen? How many different scenes it sheds light on? It might be made emblematical of something.
>
> A snake taken into a man's stomach and nourished there from fifteen years to thirty-four, tormenting him most horribly. A type of envy or some other evil passion.

The result of the latter was "Egotism, or the Boston Serpent." Sometimes the situation is presented in order to study the psychological reactions of the victim and to probe into the depths of personality, as in "Wakefield." Most often of all, the situation is presented in order to point out a fundamental characteristic or a subtle besetting sin of humanity. In his notebook he writes this:

> A person to be in possession of something as perfect as mortal man has a right to demand; he tries to make it better, and ruins it entirely;

which is his tale, "The Birthmark," reduced to its lowest terms. If each of his tales were cut to bare single-sentence texts, as their severe unity renders it possible to do, as, for example:

> In every heart there is secret sin, and sad mysteries which we hide from our nearest and dearest, and would feign conceal from our own consciousness.—"The Minister's Black Veil";
>
> Does it not argue a superintending Providence that, while viewless and unexpected events thrust themselves continually athwart our path, there should still be regularity enough in mortal life to render foresight even partially available?—"David Swan";

In the solitude of a midnight chamber or in a desert, afar from men or in a church, while the body is kneeling, the soul may pollute itself even with those crimes which we are accustomed to deem altogether carnal.—"Fancy's Show Box";

Would all who cherish wild wishes but look around them, they would oftenest find their sphere of duty, of prosperity and happiness, within those precincts and in that station where Providence itself has cast their lot.—"The Three-Fold Destiny";—

if all his tales were so reduced and the resulting texts were gathered into a chapter, it would be a fairly complete summary of the best elements of his philosophy. His stories, the best of them, are, therefore, sermons, each with a text to which its author rigidly adheres, made vivid by a single illustration dwelt upon lingeringly, presented from new angles again and again until it becomes a haunting presence that lays its hands upon one's very soul.

Hawthorne, therefore, did four things for the short story: he turned it from its German romantic extravagances and frivolity and horrors into sane and moral channels; he made of it the study of a single intense situation; he deepened it and gave it beauty; and he made it respectable even in New England, a dignified literary form, admitted as such even by the most serious of the Transcendentalists. After *Twice-Told Tales* and *Mosses from an Old Manse* the short story had no longer to apologize for its existence and live a vagabond life in the corners of weekly papers and the pages of lady's books and annuals: it had won so secure a place that even before Hawthorne had died *The Atlantic Monthly*, the constituted mouthpiece of the Brahmins of New England, could print seventeen specimens of it in its first volume.

VERNON LOUIS PARRINGTON [1871–1929] was a professor at the University of Washington and wrote on the Connecticut wits and Sinclair Lewis. His chief work, *Main Currents in American Thought*, has had profound influence on the study of American literature and history. Parrington wrote from the perspective of the tradition of American liberalism, especially as it grew out of Thomas Jefferson's philosophy.

Parrington's admitted bias made him unsympathetic to writers like Poe and Hawthorne and led him to revive some of the old indictments of Hawthorne—his isolation, his use of allegory, and his intellectual poverty. In recent years there have been strong reactions to Parrington's approach and evaluations in *Main Currents*.

Nathaniel Hawthorne: Skeptic

VERNON LOUIS PARRINGTON

After his immersion for some months in the Utopian dreams of Brook Farm, Miles Coverdale in *The Blithedale Romance* discovered that he had drifted far from reality. "No sagacious man," he remarked, "will long retain his sagacity, if he live exclusively among reformers and progressive people, without periodically returning into the settled system of things, to correct himself by a new observation from that old standpoint."

> It was now time for me, therefore, to go and hold a little talk with the conservatives, the writers of the North American Review, the merchants, the politicians, the Cambridge men, and all those respectable blockheads who still, in this intangibility and mistiness of affairs, kept a death-grip on one or two ideas which had not come into vogue since yesterday morning.

In this suggestive pronouncement the intellectual position of Hawthorne is revealed. Cool, detached, rationalistic, curiously inquisitive, he looked out upon the ferment of the times, the clash of rival philosophies and rival interests, only to bring them into his study and turn upon them the light of his critical analysis. One after another he weighed the several faiths of New England, conservative and transcendental and radical, and ended skeptic. He was too much of a realist to change fashions in creeds. Time, experience—he is always remembering—have created men as we find them, and very likely only time and experience can make them over into something different. The conservatives would seem to have common sense on their side, for they are seeking to retain what has hitherto been won; but the reformers are not without justification as well, for impelled by an ardent faith they are seek-

The Romantic Revolution in America in *Main Currents in American Thought*. Three volumes. Vol. 2 (New York, 1927, 1930) 442–50.

ing to win new conquests. But whether that which the conservatives defend so valiantly is worth defending, or whether the goal towards which the reformers drive so furiously is worth the trouble, are questions about which the rationalist may be permitted his doubts. The universe in which he found himself was a moral universe, Hawthorne on the whole believed; and if that were true then man's chief business and urgent problem was the matter of a sufficient morality.

Radical in his intellectual processes, he could never become greatly interested in specific radicalisms. He is often thought of as a transcendentalist, and his association with the Peabodys and his venture into Brook Farm might seem to lend color to such an interpretation. Yet nothing in his intellectual sympathies marks him as of the school. The polar conceptions of transcendentalism repelled rather than attracted him. Political and metaphysical speculation left him cold, and the twin revolutionary forces of the time, French romanticism and German idealism, never deeply affected his thinking. Amid all the flux he retained much of the older Calvinist view of life and human destiny. Though nominally a Unitarian he did not share Channing's faith in the perfectibility of man. The buried voice of God that the transcendentalists professed to have discovered in instinct, he greatly distrusted. Man seemed to him quite as likely to turn out to be a child of the devil as the first-born of God. Perhaps through a long and uncertain process he may grow into something nobler than he now is, but for the present the fact remains that the human heart, if not desperately wicked, is at least on familiar terms with evil; too often it is cold, selfish, malignant, and its secret promptings need watching. Doubting the indwelling presence of the divine Over-soul, he could find no justification for the transcendental faith in the excellence of the universe, out of which came the genial optimism of the Emersonians. Too pronounced a rationalist to comprehend the mysticism that lurked in the heart of the transcendental faith, he remained cold to the revolutionary criticism that was eager to pull down the old temples to make room for nobler. Eager souls, mystics and revolutionaries, may propose to refashion the world in accordance with their dreams; but evil remains, and so long as it lurks in the secret places of the heart, Utopia is only the shadow of a dream. And so while the Concord thinkers were proclaiming man to be the indubitable child of God, Hawthorne was critically examining the question of evil as it appeared in the light of his own experience. It was the central, fascinating problem of his intellectual life, and in pursuit of a solution he probed curiously into the hidden, furtive recesses of the soul.

The isolation in which he chose to brood over the problem, seeking to take the solution by surprise in unguarded moments, was the natural consequence of his temperament and his habits. He lived singularly remote from common interests, singularly self-sufficient. Both as thinker and artist he suffered from his self-imposed isolation. The twelve years of his apprenticeship, closely immured and given over to spinning cobwebs about the old Puritan rafters, drawing the stuff of his romance out of his own bowels, may have facilitated the development of technic, but it laid narrow limitations on the matter of his art. Intellectually unlocalized in his Yankee world, he was the romancer of a dead but unforgotten past, at home only where the New England conscience brooded over sin—subduing the old nightmares to less terrifying dreams, intruding his doubts into old dogmas yet never emerging from the old shadows. Although he was a child of the liberation and had broken the web that Calvinism had woven about the mind of New England, he did not choose to quit the world from whose bondage he had freed himself. He would examine the old problem in a new light. In rejecting Calvinism as a religion, he retained it as a background for his inquisitive probing. It appealed to his imagination after his reason had rejected its dogmas; it determined his art after it had ceased to command his loyalty. In consequence, all his life Hawthorne dwelt between worlds. Though at times he tried to establish contact with Yankee reality, though he essayed to establish an intellectual *rapport* with his generation, he never quite succeeded, but remained to the last isolated, a frequenter of the twilight.

Only in a narrow and very special sense was Hawthorne a romantic. With the romance of love and adventure he was never concerned; what interested him was the romance of ethics—the distortions of the soul under the tyranny of a diseased imagination. How little he shares in common with other romantics is revealed in his detachment from his native Salem. The place was not lacking in picturesque charm, present and past. During the long years he spent in his Salem study, the city was rising to the zenith of its brisk sea life, with its ships in the China trade, its venturesome fisheries, its echoes of the whaling industry at Nantucket. Materials for romance were lying all about the Salem wharves—such a show of canvas and spars and rigging, such briny smells, such suggestions of far voyages to outlandish places, such strange figures slipping in from the ends of the earth—such romantic promptings in short as would have intoxicated the imagination of Herman Melville, and that Joseph Hergesheimer wove into the rich tapestries of *Java Head*. A romantic could scarcely have found in America a setting better calculated to awaken a sense of brave adventure than in old Salem; yet for three years Hawthorne sat in the Custom House, with such materials all about him, and then turned away to the seventeenth century to write of Hester Prynne. For a man gifted with imagination to fail to lift his eyes to the horizon beyond which the hurrying ships were seeking strange markets, and instead to turn them in upon a shadowy world of half unreal characters; to overlook the motley picturesque in the foreground of the actual, in order to brood over an old adultery and twist it into theological sin, can be explained only on the ground that Hawthorne was concerned with ethical rather than romantic values, that he was interested rather in the problem of evil than in the trappings of romance. Aloofness of time and place served to isolate the problem, stripping away the wrappings of the physical, delocalizing it, transmuting the individual act into the universal. Thus isolated, Hester's sin becomes a symbol of that ancient evil which forever waylays human life and by strange perversions brings havoc to our hopes—the greatest havoc to him whose heart, like Chillingworth's, is cold, selfish, malignant.

This temperamental aloofness from objective reality was both the strength and the weakness of Hawthorne's art. In choosing to follow the way of the inner life he was true to his Puritan breeding. The perpetual turning-in of the mind upon itself, the long introspective brooding over human motives, came naturally to one who lived in the shadow of a Puritan past. In their anxious concern over sin the Puritans had become in some measure psychologists; how else could the secret impulses of the soul be probed and its dark workings laid bare? Hawthorne was only doing what Jonathan Edwards before him had done in his psychological clinic of the Great Awakening—examining the reactions of sin on conscience and character. From this comes the simplicity of his theme and the compelling unity of his handling. To be sure it is pathological phenomena that he deals with, as the phenomena that Edwards dealt with in his *Narrative of the Surprizing Work of God*, were pathological; and like Edwards, Hawthorne is led into insubstantial and tenuous regions where he breathes with difficulty. The substantial world of Puritan reality that Samuel Sewall knew, Hawthorne seems scarcely to have been aware of; he created instead his own Puritanism, fantastic and unreal. He was forever dealing with shadows, and he knew that he was dealing with shadows, and this consciousness was a perennial source of doubt and uncertainty that bred self-distrust. In setting himself the task of dramatizing sin rather than sinners, of creating romance out of the problem of evil, he encountered difficulties that oppressed him. The wellsprings of his imagination were constantly running dry and he must wait till they filled again slowly. Hence the "development of his art is towards ever greater elaboration of scantier and scantier materials, until the joy of the whole becomes lost at last in the milder pleasures of detail."[1]

From the grave difficulties inherent in his theme came the inveterate habit of sliding into symbolism and allegory—from this and from the narrowness of his emotional life and the restrictions of his sympathies. The cold thin atmosphere of his work, one comes increasingly to feel, was due not alone or chiefly to the severity of his artistic restraint that forbade all rioting of the sensuous imagination; it was due rather to a lack of nourishment, to a poverty of ideas and sensuous imagery. His inveterate skepticism robbed him of much, but his inhibitions robbed him of more. A romantic uninterested in adventure and afraid of sex is likely to become somewhat graveled for matter. Like the Pyncheon fowls, Hawthorne's imagination had suffered from too long inbreeding; it had grown anemic, and every grain of fancy is clucked over and picked at and made much of. Once an idea comes into his head he is loath to let it go, but he must turn it about curiously and examine it from every angle. The striking chapter in *The House of the Seven Gables*, where the death of Judge Pyncheon is played upon so persistently, is only an extreme example of his habitual method. The tongues that wagged over the minister's black veil were no more inquisitive and tireless than Hawthorne's when his imagination is fired by a vivid image. He will not let it go till it is sucked as dry as last year's cider cask. It is the way of one to whom ideas are few and precious. Knowing how little is in the bottle he will linger out the flavor of every drop. Hence his fondness for symbolism, and hence his frequent lapse into allegory when imagination grows dull. Because Hawthorne was an artist he was saved from the shipwreck that such a method might seem to invite; yet perhaps it is not unreasonable to suggest that he was an artist for the reason that only through the mastery of a refined technic could his scanty stock of ideas make any show at all.

The intellectual poverty that resulted from his long immuring

[1] Amy Louise Reed, "Self-Portraiture in the Work of Nathaniel Hawthorne," *Studies in Philology*, Vol. XXIII, No. I.

himself in a void is sufficiently revealed in his *American Note-Books*. In the somewhat tedious volume covering the eighteen years between 1835 and 1853—the most vigorous years of the renaissance—there is no suggestion of interest in the creative ideas of the time, in metaphysics or politics or economics or humanitarianism. It is the occasional record of one who lived an unintellectual life, and it makes but a paltry showing when set beside the journals of Emerson for the same years. Few books are referred to; systems of thought lie beyond his ken. Compared with the thinkers and scholars of the time he is only an idler lying in wait for such casual suggestions as he may turn into stories. Almost childish is his delight in marvels. There is something of the spirit of Cotton Mather in his persistent recording of the gruesome and fantastic, in the hope that they will open a quarry for his art. In the year that Emerson wrote *Nature*, Hawthorne set down the following amongst some dozens of similar suggestions: "A snake taken into a man's stomach and nourished there from fifteen to thirty-five years, tormenting him most horribly. A type of envy or some other evil passion." The *Note-Books*, of course, are very inadequate records of his life, and yet that a mind should lie in wait for such grotesqueries, and treasure them, offers food for speculation. After his marriage they are much less frequent and his jottings become more normal—a change which the Freudians, no doubt, would be ready enough to explain.

The one great adventure of Hawthorne's life was the plunge into Brook Farm Utopianism, a plunge that only proved the waters colder and less hospitable than he had hoped. It was a curious adventure for one of his temperament to engage in, and his eventual disillusion might have been foretold. Perhaps it may be explained as reaction from his long isolation. The glowing enthusiasms of the times must often have tempted him to leave his narrow walls, and share the intellectual and emotional stimulus that others professed to discover in the work of making society over. Whatever the explanation the venture turned out to be a failure. His skepticism followed him there and came to later expression in *The Blithedale Romance*, a work as thin and unreal as anything he ever did. It is worse. There is in its pages more than a hint of ill humor that colors his interpretation of the Fourieristic stage of the experiment, and slips out in his portraiture of the major characters. Hollingsworth both fascinates and repels him. A dramatization of the intransigent spirit of reform, his single-minded zeal for righteousness, is subtly fused with an intolerant egotism that destroys Zenobia, cows Priscilla, and wrecks the venture. Perhaps Albert

Brisbane may have been in the background of Hawthorne's mind when he drew Hollingsworth, for it was Brisbane who influenced the change he seems to have resented; perhaps Garrison may have served to fill out the picture. Whoever it was, the figure of Hollingsworth is Hawthorne's reply to the summons of the social conscience of the times, done by a critic whose insistent skepticism will not shut its eyes, but discovers under a new masquerade the ancient evil of a cold imperious heart. Seventeen years before he wrote *The Blithedale Romance*, he had jotted down in his *Note-Book* the conception out of which came the later portrait:

> A sketch to be given of a modern reformer,—a type of the extreme doctrines on the subject of slaves, cold water, and other such topics. He goes about the streets haranguing most eloquently, and is on the point of making many converts, when his labors are suddenly interrupted by the appearance of the keeper of a mad-house, whence he has escaped. Much may be made of the idea. (*American Note-Books*, pp. 20–21.)

Hawthorne's interpretation of Margaret Fuller is not so easily explained. Perhaps it came out of a subconscious personal spleen. Her rich paganism may well have disturbed a nature so reticent as his, so restrained by certain Puritan inhibitions. In an early sketch he commented on the unfitness of authorship for women, on the ground that "there is a delicacy . . . that perceives, or fancies, a sort of impropriety in the display of woman's natal mind to the gaze of the world, with indications by which its inmost secrets may be searched out" (quoted by Amy Louise Reed, "Self-Portraiture in the Work of Nathaniel Hawthorne"). Margaret's frankness in displaying her natal mind to the gaze of the world, her bold discussion of prohibited subjects like prostitution, could not fail to rub across Hawthorne's deepest prejudices. She was too vigorous and outspoken, too consciously endowed with sex, too frankly feminist, not to have ruffled his instinctive squeamishness. It was not her radical feminism in the abstract that offended him, if he may be trusted; but certainly in the concrete. A sexless feminism would not greatly disturb a mind tolerantly familiar with the current radicalisms; but the frank avowal of sex touched a sensitive nerve. It offended certain latent Puritanisms in him. He was fascinated by Zenobia and yet afraid of her—or of himself; so his hero falls in love with the anemic and witless Priscilla. How characteristic of a mind long fed on symbols, to turn away from the wealth of reality and prefer a shadow!

After Brook Farm came no further experiments in the unsatisfactory business of a *rapprochement* with his generation. His marriage with Sophia Peabody brought with it the prosaic duties of providing for a family, and he had no leisure to play with social reform. Abolitionism he would have none of, nor perfectionism, nor Jacksonianism—the futility of such things became for him a fixed idea. That he once had the courage to make his plunge he seems to have rejoiced over: "Whatever else I may repent of," Miles Coverdale wrote, "let it be reckoned neither among my sins nor follies that I once had faith and force enough to form generous hopes of the world's destiny,—yes!—and to do what in me lay for their accomplishment." Yet the truer Hawthorne is to be found in the judgments set down in the *Note-Book:* "It is my opinion that a man's soul may be buried and perish under a dung-heap, or in a furrow of the field, just as well as under a pile of money." "Oh, labor is the curse of the world, and nobody can meddle with it without becoming proportionably brutified." The man who wrote that had much to learn about life and society, much that he might have learned from Thoreau. But Hawthorne never grappled with economics as Thoreau did, and he learned no more from him than from Melville, or from Emerson, or from any of the books he read by the wise of other days. Self-sufficient he remained to the last, hard-headed and practical, yet missing many a deeper truth that more receptive minds discover. He was traveling the path that leads to sterility, and the lifelong business of playing Paul Pry to the secrets of the conscience brought him at last to the comment, "Taking no root I soon weary of any soil in which I may be temporarily deposited. The same impatience I sometimes feel, or conceive of, as regards this earthly life." He was the extreme and finest expression of the refined alienation from reality that in the end palsied the creative mind of New England. Having consumed his fancies, what remained to feed on?

For many years AUSTIN WARREN [1899–] has been an acute analyst of Hawthorne. His edition of Hawthorne in the American Writers Series ranks with Randall Stewart's edition of the American notebooks as a landmark in Hawthorne scholarship of the 1930's. Warren's "Introduction" still remains one of the best relatively brief discussions of Hawthorne. In recent years Warren has written essays on Hawthorne for his books *Rage for Order* (1948) and *The New England Conscience* (1966), as well as an analysis of *The Scarlet Letter* in *The Southern Review* (January 1965). He has been most concerned with examining Hawthorne's Puritan milieu.

Introduction

AUSTIN WARREN

. . . .

For the proper comprehension of Hawthorne, one must never forget the paragraph of "The Custom House" in which the author sees himself as his ancestors would see him[139]—an idler in the world of men. "No aim, that I have ever cherished, would they recognize as laudable; no success of mine . . . would they deem otherwise than worthless, if not positively disgraceful. 'What is he?' murmurs one gray shadow of my forefathers to the other. 'A writer of story-books! What kind of business in life,—what mode of glorifying God, or being serviceable to mankind in his day and generation,—may that be? Why, the degenerate fellow might as well have been a fiddler!' "

"And yet," comments Hawthorne, "let them scorn me as they will, strong traits of their nature have intertwined themselves with mine." The judgment, like most of Hawthorne's self-interpretation, holds sound; and it was, one may be permitted to think, true in a wider sense than he doubtless intended. Not merely did he preserve much of the New England exaltation of 'character' as the one thing needful,[140] but all of that New England scrupulosity which we call 'conscience.' His inheritance passed beyond his private character and into his writing.

It has often been said, somewhat defiantly perhaps, that Hawthorne was a pure artist—or at any rate, most purely the artist of Americans in his generation or century. This would seem to forget

Nathaniel Hawthorne. Representative Selections . . . , ed. Austin Warren. American Writers Series. (New York, 1934) lxii–lxxiii.

[139]*The Scarlet Letter* in *Complete Works of Nathaniel Hawthorne*, ed. George P. Lathrop (Boston, 1883), 25. [Editor's note: wherever necessary I have provided additional data for Professor Warren's footnotes.]

[140]No word recurs more persistently in Hawthorne's writing than the adjective *moral*, used always in the sense of 'possessing substance and stability of character.'

Irving, not to say Poe. But whatever its qualifications, the judgment is, if not without truth, misleading. It is quite true that Hawthorne's writing was not motivated by the desire to enunciate and then illustrate some copybook maxim. In this restricted sense, it may fairly be cleared of what Poe called the Heresy of the Didactic.[141] And it is equally true that, though imaginatively sympathetic with the deep perceptions of Calvinism, Hawthorne was remote enough from the literal theology of his ancestors to treat the Puritans with an artist's detachment. But beyond these concessions one must be wary of going.

Hawthorne is not averse to drawing out explicitly the 'moral' of his tales and novels; and he shares to the full the liberty exercised by our literary ancestors before the Flood, the "stream of consciousness" writing of our day: he adds to the speeches and the introspections of his characters and the varied comments of the 'chorus' on the characters such generalized comments as he deems applicable to the instruction of the reader.

Above all, the simple reader, and the mature as well, cannot miss the moral earnestness of the author. His personal morality clearly belonged to what may indifferently be called the Victorian or the New England School. But that is not the point: as an author, he is never disposed to be very specific about the nature of a sin, unless it be that unpardonable pride which alienates one from his fellows. The point is Hawthorne's preoccupation with problems of character and conscience; and that preoccupation traverses the novels as well as the tales.

His "inveterate love of allegory" is a subtler aspect of his Puritan didacticism. For him, it has been charged,[142] everything means something else: that is to say, image always equates idea. Material objects serve rarely, as they persistently do with Poe, for *décor* or atmosphere; they are signs and tokens. In the face of Catholic art and architecture and the whole sacramental system, it would be rash to claim symbolism and allegory as the property of Puritanism; but the Puritan could adduce Spenser and Bunyan, both favorites with Hawthorne, as Protestant examples of story ministering, by the aid of these devices, to the profit of morality and religion. And there can be little question that these two writers, especially the author of *Pilgrim's Progress*, exerted a strong and persistent influence upon the New Englander. How could a descendant of the Puritans turn artist without utter betrayal of his

---

[141]Cf. "The Poetic Principle."

[142]W. C. Brownell, *American Prose Masters* (New York, 1909), 77.

heritage? Certainly not by celebrating the landscape or glorifying the human form. But, by the reduction of material objects to the status of tokens shadowing forth to the senses the spiritual states of men, he might effect a moralization of the natural world whereby the Beautiful became the vehicle of the True and the Good.

Hawthorne's *Twice-Told Tales* and *Mosses* offer some variety of type: the thin, descriptive sketch, flavored, after the fashion of Irving, with mild humor and equally mild pathos; familiar essay; satire; the historical tale and mythological (the classic transmuted into Gothic); the sketch assembling scantily vested abstract types; the allegorical tale and the moral—to which catalogue the accuracy of a Polonius would have to add that these types are not mutually exclusive, and that Hawthorne often effects his richest art when he fuses the historical and the symbolic, or the symbolic and the moral.

But there can be no doubt that to the literate world Hawthorne primarily (and justly) connotes the kind of tale represented by such masterpieces as "Rappaccini's Daughter," "The Artist of the Beautiful," "The Minister's Black Veil," and "The Birthmark"—the tale which originates in a moral idea, acquires a symbol as vehicle or accoutrement, is developed through introspective analysis, and terminates in the enforcement of the text with which its author began. Some of Hawthorne's best short stories (like his best novel) draw their nourishment directly from the New England of Puritan days. But with the exception of "Young Goodman Brown," his maturest reveal his heredity and environment not in the letter but in the spirit.

Hawthorne seems always to have admired the realistic sort of novel, and to have desired, in vain, to write such. In the introduction to *The Scarlet Letter* he expresses surprise and distress that the result of his years in the Salem Custom House should have been no creative interpretation of the world with which his recent experience acquainted him but instead a throwback into the Salem of the seventeenth century. "The wiser effort would have been to diffuse thought and imagination through the opaque substance of to-day, and thus to make it a bright transparency; to spiritualize the burden that began to weigh so heavily; to seek, resolutely, the true and indestructible value that lay hidden in the petty and wearisome incidents, and ordinary characters, with which I was now conversant. The fault was mine. The page of life that was spread out before me seemed dull and commonplace, only because I had not fathomed its deeper import. A better book than I shall ever write was there. . . ."[143] "It is odd enough," he wrote Fields at

[143]*Scarlet Letter*, 57.

the end of his life, "that my own individual taste is for quite another class of works than those which I myself am able to write. . . . Have you ever read the novels of Anthony Trollope? They precisely suit my taste. . . ."[144]

The commentators certainly judge correctly in supposing the almost pedantic externality of the *Note-Books* to be token of Hawthorne's intent to remove his tales and novels from their shadow-like tenuity.[145] His thin sketches, like "Little Annie's Ramble" and "The Toll-Gatherer's Day," are Irvingesque attempts at realism. "The Custom House," which, with a misjudgment uncommon to him, he thought would attract the reading public more than *The Scarlet Letter*, to which it served as incongruous overture, was a sketch of a more pungently and acridly realistic sort. For all the classification of his novels as "romances," he was eager to give them ballast; and he designed to effect that by drawing from his notebooks passages of detailed description, after the manner of "Ethan Brand," a moral tale with realistic backdrops supplied from the notebook recording his sojourn in North Adams. *The Scarlet Letter*, since it was laid in the past, proved incapable of such treatment: hence "The Custom House." But in *The House of the Seven Gables, The Blithedale Romance*, and *The Marble Faun*, laid respectively in the Salem, the Brook Farm, and the Rome of his own day, Hawthorne could appropriate 'sets' from the supply in his journals. He had intended his *English Note-Books* to serve him similarly when he came to write his projected English romance. As he confesses, with some naïveté of candor, in the preface to *Our Old Home:* "These and other sketches, with which . . . my journal was copiously filled, were intended for the side-scenes and backgrounds and exterior adornment of a work of fiction. . . ."[146] Readers (Howells and Browning among them)[147] have not been wanting to prefer the most realistic of his novels, *The Blithedale Romance*. His own favorite appears to have been *The House of the Seven Gables*, which he thought a work more characteristic of

---

[144]James T. Fields, *Yesterdays with Authors* (Boston, 1871), 63.

[145]E.g., Julian Hawthorne, "The Salem of Hawthorne," *Century Magazine*, XXVIII (May 1884), 4, and Randall Stewart, *The American Notebooks by Nathaniel Hawthorne* (New Haven, 1932), xxvii.

[146]*Our Old Home*, 15.

[147]W. D. Howells, *My Literary Passions* (New York, 1895), 186, and *English Notebooks*, II, 329.

his mind than the almost universally acclaimed *Scarlet Letter*,[148]— undoubtedly because his second novel relieved its painfully sombre theme with realistic and even mildly humorous relief in the episodes of the cent shop and in the persons of Uncle Venner and the Pyncheon hens.

Hawthorne's observation to Fields that he admired one kind of novel and wrote another is sign enough, however, of his recognition that a man must write the kind of books he can, not the kind he would. Hawthorne as a reader was one person; as a writer, he was another. His distinctive province as a writer he found not in the natural but in the supernatural.

It would be difficult for a son of Salem, or indeed, of the Puritans, to elude an interest in witches, ghosts, and psychic phenomena generally. To the Puritans, the Black Man and his attendant devils and those wicked persons who had surrendered their souls to the Evil Power were no figments of the fevered imagination but irreducible reality. The Indians were devil-worshippers, they thought; and the new continent, which they sought to reclaim for God and his "peculiar people," was in possession of the Devil, who had no intention of relinquishing his property without due resistance.[149]

Hawthorne read the Mathers' *Remarkable Providences* and *Wonders of the Invisible World*. But his appetite would appear to antedate his reading. If the altogether credible testimony of his boyhood friend, Symmes, be accepted, he was much inclined to talk of the supernatural even in his youth: interested, yet never credulous. "I have heard him many times tell ghost and haunted house stories, though never as if he believed what he was saying." The excerpts printed from his first diary include the legends of a haunted house; and the whole journal was said to contain many stories of the supernatural current in the neighborhood of Raymond.[150]

After his early and speedily suppressed novel, *Fanshawe*, his next work consisted of a set of short narratives which he vainly endeavored to publish, under the title *Seven Tales of My Native Land*. According to Fields, one or two of them were witch stories. And Miss Peabody writes of the same set that they were created

[148]Horatio Bridge, *Personal Recollections of Nathaniel Hawthorne* (New York, 1893), 126.

[149]Cf. John G. Whittier, *Supernaturalism in New England* (London, 1847), 38–39.

[150]*Hawthorne's First Diary*, ed. Samuel T. Pickard (Boston, 1897), 37–38.

after Hawthorne had made himself master of the ancient history of Salem, especially of the witchcraft era. In a mood of despair, he burnt up most of the tales, saying that they were perhaps the most powerful things he had done, but that they were "morbid."[151]

Interest in the psychic or supernatural was keenest in his youth and again in his last years, when he vainly tried to accomplish a romance on the theme of the elixir of life. But it never completely failed. Suggestions of witchcraft appear in *The Scarlet Letter*, hypnotism in *The House of the Seven Gables*, mesmerism in *The Blithedale Romance*, magic power over animals in *The Marble Faun*.

As a man, he was ever suspicious of the allegedly supernatural; and he warned his wife against mesmerism and spiritualism, concluding: "The view which I take of the matter is caused by no want of faith in mysteries, but from a deep reverence of the soul, and of the mysteries which it knows within itself, but never transmits to the earthly eye and ear."[152] The "mysteries" which ultimately interested Hawthorne, both as man and as artist, were psychological and philosophical, not psychic or legerdemain: in this he showed his superiority to Poe.

Yet while seriously concerned only with the human mysteries, Hawthorne found himself persistently attracted to the strictly supernatural as well. He did not personally credit miracles, whether performed by good or evil agents; but as an artist he appreciated the dusky richness of coloring and the haze of distance which intimations of the supernatural could give to a tale perfectly susceptible of naturalistic interpretation. He is never more characteristically and unforgettably himself than when, as in "Young Goodman Brown," perhaps his finest tale, he leaves the reader with his choice of two or three interpretations[153]—in this particular

---

[151]Fields, 65, and M.D. Conway, *Life of Nathaniel Hawthorne*, Great Writers Series (London, 1890), 81. In *A Study of the Sources of the Tales and Romances Written by Nathaniel Hawthorne before 1853*, Smith College Studies in Modern Languages, VII, No. 4 (Northampton, 1926), Elizabeth L. Chandler has plausibly conjectured that "Alice Doane," "An Old Woman's Tale," and "The Hollow of the Three Hills" are survivors from this early collection. All three tales concern witches, wizards, or ghosts.

[152]*Love Letters of Nathaniel Hawthorne, 1839-41 and 1841-63* (Privately printed in Chicago, 1907), II, 64-65.

[153]T. W. Higginson thought this characteristic use of "penumbra" perhaps borrowed from Austin's "Peter Rugg." For suggestive interpretations of the device, cf. George P. Lathrop, *A Study of Nathaniel Hawthorne* (Boston, 1876), 37, and Elizabeth Peabody, "The Genius of Hawthorne," *Atlantic Monthly*, XX (Sept. 1868), 360.

instance, either in terms of devils and witches (as the Mathers would have interpreted it) or in those of modern psychology. After this fashion, peculiarly his own, he reconciles his incredulity and his faith: his faith as a narrator; his incredulity as a man, if you like—yet that is too simple a formula. Aware of the essential mystery of life, he cannot but avail himself of any means to raise a mist of ambiguity about the circumference of his tales. Sceptical of the beliefs held for certain by his 'advanced' contemporaries, he doubtless never surrendered the last shadow of faith in the spectres of old Salem. The case was not quite closed. The resolute sunlight of Concord had perhaps not quite swept the lingering dusk out of all the recondite corners of the universe. Perhaps there were more things in heaven and earth than Emerson or Channing or Theodore Parker had dreamed of.

As Hawthorne desired to write realistically, so he desired to write blithely. Again his genius overruled his inclination. This disturbed him, both because he disliked the false impression of his private personality conveyed by the gloom of his novels, and because he always desired an audience ampler than the special nature of his genius could procure him. His fear of publishing *The Scarlet Letter* without relief in the form of lighter sketches or tales proceeded from his sense of its sombreness. He wrote Fields: "I found it impossible to relieve the shadows of the story with so much light as I would gladly have thrown in. Keeping so close to its point as the tale does, and diversified no otherwise than by turning different sides of the same dark idea to the reader's eye, it will weary many people and disgust some."[154] "Some portions of the book are powerfully written," he confesses to Bridge, "but . . . [it] lacks sunshine, etc. To tell you the truth it is . . . positively a hell-fired story, into which I found it almost impossible to throw any cheering light."[155]

The Marble Faun troubled him in the same way. He promises to Fields: "When I get home, I will try to write a more genial book; but the Devil himself always seems to get into my inkstand, and I can only exorcise him by pensful at a time." And again the attempt to compose *The Dolliver Romance* elicited the same protest to his publisher that he could not achieve that which he would. "There is something preternatural in my reluctance to begin. I linger at the threshold, and have a perception of very disagree-

[154]Fields, 51–52.

[155]Bridge, 111–12.

able phantasms to be encountered if I enter. I wish God had given me the faculty of writing a sunshiny book."[156]

These utterances exhibit Hawthorne's sense of being mastered, when he sat down at his desk, by a spirit quite other than his private personality. It is "important to remember that the man and the writer were, in Hawthorne's case, as different as a mountain from a cloud." His son, Julian, who gives this testimony, did not read the romances till after his father's death; and he read them then with bewilderment, "constantly unable to comprehend how a man such as I knew my father to be could have written such books. He did not talk in that way; his moods had not seemed to be of that color."[157]

Theodore Parker once professed to doubt that Hawthorne "understood his own genius or comprehended the philosophical meaning of many of the circumstances or characters found in his books." And Whipple, for whose criticism Hawthorne felt more respect than for any other's, wrote, acutely: "His great books appear not so much created by him as through him. They have the character of revelations,—he, the instrument, being often troubled with the burden they impose upon his mind."[158]

Almost universal agreement has it that *The Scarlet Letter* is Hawthorne's genius at its height. This book was written with more surrender to his 'genius' than any other—and more rapidly. *The House of the Seven Gables*, which Hawthorne thought a book more natural for him to write, varied its key, tactfully modulating from tragedy to comedy, and from realism to supernaturalism. But, gaining in variety, it lost in power. He felt no such flow in the composition. "I find the book requires more care and thought than 'The Scarlet Letter'; also I have to wait oftener for a mood. 'The Scarlet Letter' being all in one tone, I had only to set my pitch, and could then go on interminably."[159] Never before or afterwards, according to his own testimony, did he so completely yield to his creative emotions. Reading the last scene of *The Scarlet Letter* to his wife, just after writing it, his voice swelled and heaved. "I think I have never overcome my own adamant in any other instance."[160] *The Scarlet Letter* is truly a book created *through* Hawthorne.

[156]Fields, 89, 109.

[157]*Century Magazine*, XXVIII, 6, 28.

[158]Conway, 84–85, n., and E. P. Whipple, *Character and Characteristic Men* (Boston, 1866), 235–36.

[159]Fields, 55.

[160]*English Note-Books*, II, 119–20.

Hawthorne the man possessed the power to stand apart from his writing, once it was done, and appraise its character. He wrote what was given him; but his catholic reading and his usually keen power of self-criticism enabled him to discern the *genre* of his own work without the least inclination to deduce therefrom an absolute æsthetic. Rereading his own *Twice-Told Tales*, he can perceive as clearly as anyone their pallor and their excessive symbolism. "Instead of passion there is sentiment; and even in what purport to be pictures of actual life, we have allegory, not always so warmly dressed in its habiliments of flesh and blood as to be taken into the reader's mind without a shiver."[161]

The Prefaces to Hawthorne's later books attempt to define the Romance and its conditions and methods. He distinguishes the type he is essaying from the Novel, which he equates with realism, as aiming at "a very minute fidelity, not merely to the possible, but to the probable and ordinary course of man's experience."[162] Perhaps the term by which he chose to designate his *genre* was not the happiest. Hawthorne's novels are not romantic in any of the most current senses. They minimize picturesque background, minimize love, are deeply serious; and, as he avers, they may not "swerve aside from the truth of the human heart." By 'romance' he perhaps means what we today call "expressionism"—the effort to reveal men's souls instead of their vestures; to cut away the accidents of their dialect, and disclose their thoughts and emotions. He means, too, the freedom to see men in the light of Eternity, to see the Supernatural surrounding the Natural and now and again impinging upon it. The romantic novelist will best use the marvellous as overtone and penumbra rather than theme; "He can hardly be said, however, to commit a literary crime if he disregard this caution."

A novel—even a Romance—must have a setting; but Hawthorne desires to minimize setting, especially the kind of prosaic, day-lit scene which prompts the literal-minded reader to topographic studies. His *House of the Seven Gables*, he urges, has "a great deal more to do with the clouds overhead than with any portion of the actual soil of the County of Essex."[163] Perhaps these are New England clouds rather than the universal firmament: be that as it may—they are the clouds of Calvinism rather than of Salem.

Hawthorne lacked judgment in supposing that he could facilitate the necessary but difficult element of setting by transporting

[161]*Twice-Told Tales*, 16.
[162]*The House of the Seven Gables*, 13.
[163]*Ibid.*, 16.

his characters to Rome. *The Marble Faun* is indeed laid in a city more romantic than Salem; but Rome has its prose as well as its poetry, and Hawthorne's conscientious transcription of 'backgrounds' from his notebooks[164] gave the imaginative and the factual elements in his last novel a disjunction more marked than in his earlier work. Rome is more palpably before us than Salem or Boston.

Aristotle calls Poetry more philosophical than History.[165] By his definitions of the Novel and the Romance, Hawthorne intended to effect an analogous distinction. History treats of existence; Poetry of essence. Hawthorne is a philosophical poet in prose. And the reality he seeks is not of circumstance but of character and destiny.

F. O. MATTHIESSEN [1902–50] was a professor at Harvard and wrote books on Sarah Orne Jewett, Henry James, T. S. Eliot, and Theodore Dreiser. His *American Renaissance* has had great influence on criticism and scholarship devoted to American literature, particularly on studies which place American authors in a large artistic or ideational framework. In *American Renaissance* Matthiessen analyzes the literary theories and practices of five major writers. Like Parrington, Matthiessen is interested in social ideas; however, his assessment of Hawthorne is entirely different from Parrington's.

Hawthorne's Psychology: The Acceptance of Good and Evil

F. O. MATTHIESSEN

That there are aspects of art which can hardly be reached by the scalpels of economic and social analysis was maintained by Yeats' belief that poetry is not 'a criticism of life' but 'a revelation of a hidden life.' This belief would unquestionably have been accepted

[164]Cf. Stewart, XCII, n. 138.

[165]*Poetics*, cap. 9.

American Renaissance (London, 1941) 337–51.

by Hawthorne, who declared in one of his processional sketches—in another sentence marked by Melville—that human nature can be more truly represented in the wishes of its heart than in its actions, since such a portrayal has 'more of good and more of evil in it; more redeeming points of the bad and more errors of the virtuous; higher upsoarings, and baser degradations of the soul; in short, a more perplexing amalgamation of vice and virtue than we witness in the outward world.'

Why Hawthorne held this has been explained in part by such circumstances of his biography as we have dwelt on; and those circumstances were conditioned in turn by the centrifugal movement of American society. In like fashion, his conception of good and evil, which drove him to take the tragic view of life, might also be accounted for by his background, by his relation to a particular phase of the decay of the Puritan tradition. But unless the explaining of such things be considered an explaining away, unless all religious belief is held to be merely deluded fantasy to be dealt with only by the psychoanalyst, the value of Hawthorne's portrayal of spiritual conflict still remains to be reckoned with. This reckoning can be made only if we start from inside, so to speak—only if, instead of discounting his views as part of a world gone by, we try to experience to the full what he thought and felt about human destiny. For only then will we be in a position to test his interpretation against others, and against what we ourselves may believe to be primary forces in the universe.

Everywhere he looked he was struck by what, he conjectured, even confused Clifford might have seen, 'in the mirror of his deeper consciousness': how 'he was an example and representative of that great class of people whom an inexplicable Providence is continually putting at cross-purposes with the world: breaking what seems its own promise in their nature; withholding their proper food, and setting poison before them for a banquet: and thus—when it might so easily, as one would think, have been adjusted otherwise—making their existence a strangeness, a solitude, and torment.' It is no wonder that Holgrave went still farther in his conclusions about the perverse labyrinth of circumstances. Observing, as the ultimate reach of Pyncheon domineering, a timid spinster and a degraded and shattered gentleman, and thinking too of how his own poor family had been kept out of its only inheritance, he could see all the life that had passed within the house reduced to the reiterated pattern of 'perpetual remorse of conscience, a constantly defeated hope, strife amongst kindred, various misery, a strange form of death, dark suspicion, unspeakable disgrace.'

Such an accumulation of oppressive evil upon the roof of one family hardly falls short of the terrible imagination of Aeschylus. Speaking from the great range of his reading, More held (1904) that *The Seven Gables* was the one companion in modern literature 'to the Orestean conception of satiety begetting insolence, and insolence calling down upon a family the inherited curse of Ate.' This kinship in theme also throws into relief Hawthorne's difference from the Greeks in conceiving the operation of a curse: not in sudden violent disasters so much as in the prolonged 'disease of inner solitude.' More recognized this as a consequence of Hawthorne's particular Christian tradition: 'Not with impunity had the human race for ages dwelt on the eternal welfare of the soul; for from such meditation the sense of personal importance had become exacerbated to an extraordinary degree. What could result from such teaching as that of Jonathan Edwards but an extravagant sense of individual existence, as if the moral governance of the world revolved about the action of each mortal soul?' Continuing this development to Hawthorne's day, More held that with the loss of Edwards' intensity, with the partial waning of the old faith attendant on the introspection, there could only be left a great residue of anguish and bereavement, a loneliness of the individual of 'a poignancy altogether unexampled.' Thus the most compact examination of theological history brings us to the very point that we have already reached in noting the effect of American social forces on an individual like Hawthorne, who was not content with Emerson's new freedom of solitude.

It must be mentioned in passing that since More wrote, two other Americans have deliberately set themselves to re-create the Orestes story. O'Neill seems to have been drawn to it primarily as a means of projecting his sense of the violent decay of the New England heritage, and Eliot by his desire to relive a fundamental pattern of sin and suffering. Neither *Mourning Becomes Electra* nor *The Family Reunion* is one of the best works of its author, the one being especially clouded by half-assimilated Freud, the other presenting as its characters such a neutral and devitalized group of English gentry that most of the energy of the evil is lost. But it is not accidental that our modern writers,[1] with their sense of what has been implied for our society by Edwards' excessive conscience and by the moral preoccupation of Hawthorne and James, should,

[1] Robinson Jeffers has also retold the Greek story in 'The Tower Beyond Tragedy' and has stressed its incest theme as one of his many symbols for the violent consequences that have been produced by men's minds having been turned inward upon themselves.

whether impelled by O'Neill's feeling of chaotic disintegration or by Eliot's belief in the need for regeneration, still create characters whose inner torment makes them imagine that they are followed by the furies.

Unlike these others, Hawthorne gave no indication that he was thinking of the example of Greek tragedy. But he did envisage his romance as the end of a drama, which, according to Holgrave, has been dragging its slow length over this very ground for so long that now at last 'Destiny is arranging its fifth act for a catastrophe.' Moreover, Hawthorne went so far with this analogy as to provide his scene with a Chorus. This is composed of the two laborers who, as the harsh voice of the world, comment loudly at the outset on old maid Pyncheon's folly in having opened a cent-shop under the front gable. One of them dug up her garden once, and knows that her scowl is enough to frighten Old Nick; while the other adds that when even so good a hand as his wife tried such a shop, she lost five dollars on her outlay. To Hepzibah, cowering inside her window on the first morning of this desperate venture to which she has been driven by her determination to keep the house ready for Clifford, the blank indifference of Dixey and his friend to either her dignity or her degradation 'fell upon her half-dead hope like a clod into a grave.'

The pair turn up again on the morning after the great storm, and seeing the shop door closed, repeat their same lines, unaware of the gulf between the petty failure over which they are gloating and the real state of the house: from it the old brother and sister have fled; inside, alone, sits a corpse. To clinch for the imagination how public opinion drifts with appearances, Hawthorne gave the final speeches in the book to the same pair. Their refrain is now different as they watch the Pyncheons go away in their carriage: 'Pretty good business, pretty good business!' They can understand this change as luck, but they can't 'exactly fathom it . . . as the will of Providence'—a faint sign, at least, of Hawthorne's own dissatisfaction with his close.

Hawthorne's tragic vision is hardly attested by his adoption of a few of the devices of drama, but rather by his ability to endow such a pathetic character as Hepzibah with a measure of heroic dignity. He presents her absurd confusion of feelings as she stands behind her counter: her desire to be treated like a lady, and her recoil from expressions of sympathy; her inability to suppress a sense of superiority to her customers, and her bitter virulence against 'the idle aristocracy,' to which she had so recently been proud to belong. She had lived so long alone in the house that its dry-rot had begun to eat into her mind. 'She needed'—and we know how much Hawthorne implied in such a remark—'a walk along the noonday street to keep her sane.'

He was aware of the problem with which he had confronted himself by choosing for one of his protagonists not 'even the stately remains of beauty, storm-shattered by affliction—but a gaunt, sallow, rusty-jointed maiden, in a long-waisted silk gown, and with the strange horror of a turban on her head.' Her insignificance was not even redeemed by real ugliness, and her great life-trial 'seems to be, that, after sixty years of idleness, she finds it convenient to earn comfortable bread.' Yet Hawthorne held that if a writer looked 'through all the heroic fortunes of mankind,' he would find this same mixture of the mean and ludicrous in 'the purest pathos which life anywhere supplies to him.' This was particularly the case for anyone who wanted to represent human nature as it was in a democracy, a truth that Melville was to proclaim later in this very year, in his eloquent statement of the 'august dignity' to be found in his *dramatis personae*, the miscellaneous crew of a whaler. Hawthorne's lead to a similar discovery lay in his final remark in the chapter wherein Hepzibah opened her shop: 'What is called poetic insight is the gift of discerning, in this sphere of strangely mingled elements, the beauty and majesty which are compelled to assume a garb so sordid.' Again this discovery is significantly close to Eliot's that 'the essential advantage for a poet is not, to have a beautiful world with which to deal: it is to be able to see beneath both beauty and ugliness; to see the boredom, and the horror, and the glory.' Hawthorne's belief in the dramatic reality of the issues of conscience can also be phrased most concisely in Eliot's statement, in *After Strange Gods*, that in moments of intense 'moral and spiritual struggle . . . men and women come nearest to being real.' In no conviction are the novelist and the poet more akin.

What Hawthorne could see in Hepzibah, and what Melville checked, was 'the moral force of a deeply grounded antipathy,' the strength of conscience that enabled her to stand up against the Judge and confront him with what he really was beneath the oily layers of respectability. Yet Hawthorne's somewhat wavering effort to create the scene that builds up to Hepzibah's moment is an exact instance of Whipple's observation that he was more interested in the conflict of ideas and passions than in the individuals who embodied them, that his characters were introduced 'not as thinking, but as the illustration of thought,' that he used them in order to express 'the last results of patient moral perception.'

Yet it was primarily by virtue of that perception that he broke through the individualism of his day to a reassertion not of man's idiosyncrasies, but of his elemental traits. It is no exaggeration to say that his recognition of the general bond of sin brought him closest to universality. He believed that 'man must not disclaim his brotherhood, even with the guiltiest, since, though his hand be clean, his heart has surely been polluted by the flitting phantoms of iniquity.' That bare, somewhat conventional statement of innate depravity is from one of his early sketches, but it formulates the conviction from which he never swerved. He possessed it, not as a result of any mere observation of mankind against the background of Puritan thought, but more especially in consequence of the sense of personal guilt that sprang from his dread that such a detached observer as himself was failing to participate adequately in life. Yet even such an explanation is oversimplified, and we may better describe his essential state of mind by saying that he felt in himself the presence of both Pyncheons and Maules.

When Eliot said once that you cannot understand James' quality of horror without knowing Hawthorne, he extended both background and foreground by remarking that both Judge John Hathorne and his own first American ancestor, Andrew Eliot, had been among the witch hangers. Hawthorne's imagination had not been able to rest content with its atonement, in 'The Gentle Boy,' for his first ancestor, Major William Hathorne's cruelty to the Quakers. He also remembered that in the next generation Judge Hathorne's peculiar severity towards a woman in the witch trials had called out from her husband the prophecy that God would take revenge upon such persecutors. This clearly gave Hawthorne the hint for the curse pronounced by Maule, whose name, incidentally, he had found in Felt's *Annals of Salem*, where one Thomas Maule appears as a sympathizer with the Quakers and as the author of a tract called *Truth Held Forth*, whose career involved being flogged for saying that the Reverend Mr. Higginson 'preached lies.'

One aspect of Maule's curse in operation was the mysterious disappearance of the title to a vast estate in Waldo County, in the vain dream of recovering which many Pyncheons had wasted their lives. Such a refraction of the American dream had been intertwined with his own family's waning fortunes, in the tradition that his mother's kin had been deprived of many acres in Raymond, Maine, through the loss of a deed. This tradition may not seem to have much to do with Hawthorne's sense of sin, yet it entered into his separation from the dominant Salem world to which his ancestors had belonged. In this way he became partly identified with the dispossessed Maules, whom he describes as having been marked off from other men—'not strikingly,' but 'by an hereditary characteristic of reserve.' Moreover, as Holgrave recognizes his share in other traits of the Maules, some of them are likewise those which Hawthorne felt dangerous in himself. His cool habit of scrutinizing the characters of others, which is symbolized by his daguerreotype portraits, causes the young man to say to Phoebe that this tendency, taken together with his faculty of mesmerism, might have brought him to Gallows Hill in the old days. As far as Holgrave's own career is concerned, the novelist makes clear that his unscrupulous power of analysis, his seeming lack of reverence for anyone else, inculcated in him by his feeling that the world's hand is against him, is saved from hardening into fatal arrogance by the birth of his love for Phoebe—which was also one of Hawthorne's names for his bird-like Sophia.

Seen thus, the common denominator between Holgrave and Judge Pyncheon and even Hepzibah, as well as between Hollingsworth and Ethan Brand and a dozen others, consists in pride, the worst sin in Dante's theology as well as in Milton's and Edwards'. In his stress on this sin Hawthorne's sense of innate depravity and his sense of social isolation are united. Not sin, but its consequence for human lives is Hawthorne's major theme. Newton Arvin, whose study of him (1929) contains some of the most incisive social criticism to have been stimulated by the earlier work of Van Wyck Brooks, was the first to make the linkage between this theme and the major problem of American society, its continual dissidence and dispersion. In the most eloquent passage of his book, a declaration of our newer mutual dependence, Arvin summed up the significance of our historical drift:

> What have been our grand national types of personality? The explorer, with his face turned toward the unknown; the adventurous colonist; the Protestant sectarian, determined to worship his own God even in the wilderness; the Baptist, the Quaker, the Methodist; the freebooter and the smuggler; the colonial revolutionary; the pioneer, with his chronic defections; the sectional patriot and the secessionist; the come-outer, the claim-jumper, the Mormon, the founder of communities; the Transcendentalist, preaching the gospel of self-reliance; the philosophic anarchist in his hut in the woods; the economic individualist and the captain of industry; the go-getter, the tax-dodger, the bootlegger. The best and the worst of humanity,

not to be confounded in one gesture of repudiation, but united after all in their common distrust of centrality, their noble or their ignoble lawlessness, their domination by spiritual pride. United in their refusal to work together on any but a false basis. United, finally, in paying the penalty for disunion—in becoming partial and lopsided personalities, men and women of one dimension, august or vulgar cranks. How can we forget the Dimmesdales and Hollingsworths and Pyncheons who have divided our life among them?

That Arvin's words can rise to such a pitch of feeling is evidence of another function that has been fulfilled by Hawthorne's art. In recording the tragic implications for humane living of a whole phase of American development, the novelist has helped free us from our reckless individualism in pointing to the need for a new ethical and cultural community. By understanding him, the goals of our own society become more clear. Yet what Arvin has seemingly overlooked is that it was not primarily Hawthorne's social observation, but his initial religious conception of man's nature which gave coherence to his interpretation of life.

As Melville said in his essay, existence became real for Hawthorne only through suffering. He would have agreed with the statement of his younger contemporary Dostoevsky, in *Letters from the Underworld* (1861): 'I am sure that man will never renounce the genuine suffering that comes of ruin and chaos. Why, suffering is the one and only source of knowledge.' Although Hawthorne had had no personal experience of the terrible godless freedom that became the Russian's most obsessive theme, he shared the belief that only those who can suffer intensely are fully alive, as he said, there are 'spiritual depths which no other spell can open.' Contemplating Donatello's transformation from innocence to experience, he came closer to Dostoevsky's words by saying that the faun had 'had glimpses of strange and subtle matters in those dark caverns, into which all men must descend, if they would know anything beneath the surface and illusive pleasures of existence.'

Hawthorne reached the same insights in all his books. Scrutinizing the sham that Dimmesdale had become by hiding his relationship with Hester from the world, he concluded that 'the only truth' that continued to give the minister 'a real existence on this earth was the anguish in his inmost soul.' What made Hollingsworth's notions of sin so entirely unreal in his philanthropic scheme for reforming criminals by an appeal to their 'higher instincts' was the incapacity of his stone-blind egotism to see any imperfections in himself. Hawthorne's own perceptions were at the farthest extreme from those of the self-confident reformer. He grew so absorbed with the lasting weight of misery in *The Seven Gables* that he even questioned whether good was as real as evil. With a penetration no less deep than Dostoevsky's into the discipline of suffering, he had none of the mystical fervor. He repeatedly described society as a tangled wilderness of cross-purposes, overwhelmed by which a man like Clifford became 'a ruin, a failure, as almost everybody is.'

That would seem to imply that Hawthorne was incapable of sustaining the balance of great tragedy, that he could portray the horror of existence but not its moments of transfigured glory. That would mean also that his imagination was stirred only by the subordination of his helpless characters to an iron necessity, and not by the courage of their awakened and resolute wills, or by the possibility of their regeneration. In that case his books would have to be placed in the literature of moral despair. Yet Melville's immediate response was not only to Hawthorne's blackness, but also to his 'depth of tenderness,' his 'boundless sympathy with all forms of being,' his 'omnipresent love,' to what he called Hawthorne's balance between mind and heart. Hawthorne had himself used similar terms when he stated that the Master Genius of the Age, that unknown whom the country was looking for so anxiously, must be such a one 'as never illuminates the earth save when a great heart burns as the household fire of a grand intellect.'

These terms are fundamental in the psychology with which both Hawthorne and Melville worked, but their conception of the relation between the two was less simplified than that of the head-and-heart conflict that was dramatized by the followers of Rousseau—the frustrated romantic conflict between irony and pity. For Hawthorne, and Melville after him, was primarily concerned with envisaging the kind of harmony that might be established between thought and emotion, or, as the seventeenth century would have said, between reason and passion. Both believed disequilibrium between the two to be the chief source of tragedy, so it is necessary to pin down further Hawthorne's use of the terms. We remember that at the time of his one great emotional experience, giving himself in love to Sophia Peabody, he was already in his middle thirties, and therefore felt with exceptional acuteness the release from the prison of himself. That was what caused him to declare, with a fervency so rare for him, 'We are not endowed with real life . . . till the heart is touched. That touch creates us,—then we begin to be.' The experience was no mere interlude of romantic passion: he had glimpsed the same truth long before, and had already elucidated some of its implications in 'The Maypole of Merrymount' (1829). There the Lord and Lady of the May, their hearts opening for each other, feel suddenly something vague and insubstantial in the surrounding gaiety. When the heart is touched, one is born into life, which, even at that moment of ecstasy, is sensed by the lovers as something deeper than jubilation, as the shared burden of joy and sorrow and inevitable change.

The polar opposite from such full sharing was represented in 'Ethan Brand,' Hawthorne's most intense working out of the consequences of yielding to pride, which struck Melville by its fearful revelation of what happens when 'the cultivation of the brain eats out the heart.' That was its root idea, so integral to Hawthorne's reading of human nature that he had formulated it in his journal some years before writing the story: 'The Unpardonable Sin might consist in a want of love and reverence for the Human Soul; in consequence of which, the investigator pried into its dark depths, not with a hope or purpose of making it better, but from a cold philosophical curiosity,—content that it should be wicked in whatever kind or degree, and only desiring to study it out. Would not this, in other words, be the separation of the intellect from the heart?' Such investigation was pursued by Roger Chillingworth as well as by Ethan Brand, who finally declared in a frenzy of tortured pride that he had found within himself 'the sin of an intellect that triumphed over the sense of brotherhood with man and reverence for God, and sacrificed everything to its own mighty claims! The only sin that deserves a recompense of immortal agony!'

But in determining Hawthorne's conception of the heart, it must not be supposed, though he often dramatized the tragedy of the man of adamant in whom this organ had withered, that he put any unqualified sentimental trust in its natural virtue. His most frequent way of symbolizing it was as a dark cavern. At the same period at the Manse when he articulated his view of the Unpardonable Sin, he developed this condensed allegory of the heart, an allegory which gave expression to his then prevailing vision of life:

> At the entrance there is sunshine, and flowers growing about it. You step within, but a short distance, and begin to find yourself surrounded with a terrible gloom, and monsters of divers kinds; it seems like Hell itself. You are bewildered, and wander long without hope. At last a light strikes upon you. You peep towards it, and find yourself in a region that seems,

in some sort, to reproduce the flowers and sunny beauty of the entrance, but all perfect. These are the depths of the heart, or of human nature, bright and peaceful; the gloom and terror may lie deep; but deeper still is the eternal beauty.

But though he felt himself irradiated by that beauty, especially during the first years of his marriage, he seldom neglected to point out how difficult it was for imperfect man to sustain this vision. His chief subject-matter remained the labyrinths in which man's desires became distorted; and he often wrote as though he had set himself to answer Lear's question, 'Is there any cause in nature that makes these hard hearts?' At the close of 'Earth's Holocaust' (1843), written when the activity of the Millerites had caused him to ponder how reforming zeal might bring to destruction all the age-old abuses and encumbrances of the world, he observed that 'there's one thing that these wiseacres have forgotten to throw into the fire,' without which all their efforts for perfectibility would still remain futile: 'What but the human heart itself? . . . And, unless they hit upon some method of purifying that foul cavern, forth from it will reissue all the shapes of wrong and misery—the same old shapes or worse ones . . . The heart, the heart,—there was the little yet boundless sphere wherein existed the original wrong of which the crime and misery of this outward world were merely types.' Then he added a concluding sentence in which he revealed his understanding that the act of regeneration must involve the whole man, and in what manner his conception of the heart included also the will: 'Purify that inward sphere, and the many shapes of evil that haunt the outward, and which now seem almost our only realities, will turn to shadowy phantoms and vanish of their own accord; but if we go no deeper than the intellect, and strive, with merely that feeble instrument, to discern and rectify what is wrong, our whole accomplishment will be a dream.'

Hawthorne seldom portrayed his characters in a state of grace, since he was too thoroughly aware of how the heart as well as the head could go perversely astray. Yet with his thorough skepticism of all improvement except inner purification, and with only a limited hope of that, he habitually stopped short of what the next age in New England conceived as tragedy, short of Robinson's quiet curbing of despair as the last glimmerings of transcendentalism died away for the isolated 'man against the sky.' Hawthorne was grounded in a more coherent social order than Robinson could be, in his era of decay. Still Hawthorne could seize his saving truth only at the core of a paradox. He sometimes went as far as Holgrave in a hatred of the dead oppression of the past. Exhausted by the British Museum, he could wish that even the Elgin Marbles 'were all burnt into lime,' since 'we have not time, in our earthly existence, to appreciate what is warm with life, and immediately around us . . . I do not see how future ages are to stagger onward under all this dead weight, with the additions that will be continually made to it.' Nevertheless, picturing his home in the Manse, he had prayed for a long endurance for 'the institutions that had grown out of the heart of mankind.' It continued to be one of his fundamental tenets that if men were all intellect, as the transcendental reformers struck him as being, 'they would be continually changing, so that one age would be entirely unlike another. The great conservative is the heart.' In other passages he came near to saying that the heart is the great democrat.

His chief stricture against early New England was that its feelings were less developed than its mind. As Hester stood on the pillory, he reflected that it would not have been easy to find anywhere in the world a group of judges less capable of disentangling the mesh of good and evil in a woman's nature than these rigidly virtuous founding fathers. Indeed, Hester herself seemed conscious that 'whatever sympathy she might expect lay in the larger and warmer heart of the multitude.' And so it actually proved in her gradual adjustment to the community in which she had been sentenced to live as an outcast. The rulers were longer in acknowledging her selfless work for the sick and poor than the people were. Both started with harsh prejudices, but those of the latter were not so reinforced by 'an iron framework of reasoning' as to keep their intuitions from breaking through. To this degree then does Hawthorne put trust in common humanity, since their closeness to fundamental experience has not permitted the drying up of their affections. But he does not make the romantic simplification of saying that love is enough. Hester's tragedy came upon her in consequence of excessive yielding to her heart; and that was to be even more true in the reckless careers of Zenobia and Miriam. The balance which prevents disaster is symbolized in the union of Holgrave and Phoebe. For the daguerreotypist learns, through the action of 'the one miracle . . . without which every human existence is a blank,' that his mere prying analysis can never reach the fullness of truth that comes from the insight of feeling; and that discovery gives him wholeness as a man, and keeps him from hardening into the slave of thought that Hollingsworth is.

In his essay on the *Mosses*, Melville seized upon another such balanced individual, who appears in 'The Intelligence Office,' as an image of Hawthorne himself, and quoted the following in confirmation:

> A man now entered, in neglected attire, with the aspect of a thinker but somewhat too rough-hewn and brawny for a scholar. His face was full of sturdy vigor, with some finer and keener attribute beneath. Though harsh at first, it was tempered with the glow of a large, warm heart, which had force enough to heat his powerful intellect through and through. He advanced to the Intelligencer and looked at him with a glance of such stern sincerity that perhaps few secrets were beyond its scope. 'I seek for Truth,' said he.

It is entirely unlikely that Hawthorne had any intention of self-portraiture in drawing this figure. But one reason why Melville found it a satisfying symbol was the intimate correspondence between such a man and what he himself felt to be the major cultural aspirations of the age. Though again Hawthorne probably did not so intend it, this seeker for truth is an excellent likeness of Emerson's American Scholar. He is an embodiment of the belief in the possibility of a native culture, its thought grounded on the heartfelt acceptance of the homely facts and opportunities of our life, and therefore able to make its strength prevail.

Hawthorne's way of conceiving a rounded character thus demonstrates his own kind of response to the belief in the common man. It demonstrates likewise that the one-sided and broken figures who throng his most typical pages are seen against a human norm, that he was not so immersed in presenting distortion and defeat as to be incapable of imagining harmony. But his stature as a writer of tragedy cannot be attested even by this perception of the double nature of life, of the fact that there is no such thing as good unless there is also evil, or of evil unless there is good. For tragic power springs not from the mind's recognitions, but from the depth to which the writer's emotions have been stirred by what he has recognized, from the degree to which he has really been able to comprehend and accept what Edgar meant by saying,

> Men must endure
> Their going hence even as their coming hither:
> Ripeness is all.

The briefest description of the tragic attitude is the one Keats gave when he called it 'the love of good and ill'; and by virtue of his courageous acceptance of their inevitable mixture he also gave promise of possessing more of the Shakespearean type of imagination than any other poet of the romantic movement.

The testing of an author's possession of that attitude depends on your experience of one of his whole compositions. Its presence can be briefly scrutinized, however, in his ability to hold an undismayed control between the pressure of conflicting forces. The kind of poise that is demanded is what enabled Hawthorne to say in the opening scene of *The Scarlet Letter* that if there had been a Papist among these Puritans he might have been reminded by his first glimpse of this beautiful woman, with her baby at her breast, 'of that sacred image of sinless motherhood, whose infant was to redeem the world.' Yet he would have been quickly disabused, for here, in bitterest contrast, was 'the taint of deepest sin in the most sacred quality of human life, working such effect, that the world was only the darker for this woman's beauty, and the more lost for the infant she had borne.' Nevertheless, throughout the book Hawthorne emphasizes the self-righteousness of the Puritan leaders who pursue her with such relentless rigor. Her punishment and suffering are treated as inevitable; but you are never allowed to forget the loss involved in their sacrifice of her generosity and tenderness, by the lack of which their own lives are starved.

The purgative effect of such acceptance of tragic fate was reinforced in Greek drama by what Aristotle called the recognition scene, wherein the protagonist became aware of the inexorable course of the action and of his implication in it. Such is the scene where Iphigenia, a priestess at last in a foreign country, accepts a victim for sacrifice, and then beholds him to be her brother Orestes; such, even more terrifying, is that where Oedipus finally sees in his unwitting self the criminal who has brought destruction upon the state. These crises strike us now as affecting in proportion to their not merely being discoveries of the necessity of external events, but involving also Oedipus' kind of inner, moral recognition. And this latter strain was developed to the full by Hawthorne. For his protagonists finally face their evil and know it deserving of the sternest justice, and thus participate in the purgatorial movement, the movement towards regeneration.[2] These last phrases may seem

[2] I have received some hints for this formulation from Maxwell Anderson's essay, 'The Essence of Tragedy' (1939). Meditation on the *Poetics* had taught him a primary rule for modern dramatic construction: 'A play should lead up to and away from a central crisis, and this crisis should consist in a discovery by the leading character which has an indelible effect on his thought and emotion and completely alters his course of action. The leading character, let me say again, must make the discovery; it must affect him emotionally; and it must alter his direction in the play.'

an unwarranted transfer of the tragic catharsis from the audience to the protagonist, but though I would not presume that such a formula would fit all tragedies, what I mean by purgatorial movement can be observed most fully in Shakespeare in Lear's purification through suffering; it also forms the basis for the rising inner action of Milton's Samson. Such too is the slow, heroic course by which Hester arrives at a state of penitence; such is the crisis that at last brings the wavering minister to confess his guilt and beg for mercy; such even is the desperate recognition by Chillingworth that he, 'a mortal man, with a once human heart,' has become a fiend for Dimmesdale's 'especial torment'—though by then his will has become so depraved, so remote from divine grace that he can only feel a revulsion of horror from the 'dark necessity' that he cannot escape.

Moral recognition is equally central to the remorse of Miriam and Donatello, which we have observed to be so closely analogous to that of the protagonists in *Paradise Lost*. Another of Hawthorne's most affecting scenes is that which follows Hollingsworth's icy rejection of Zenobia, when she declares with passion to Coverdale, 'The whole universe, her own sex and yours, and Providence, or Destiny, to boot, make common cause against the woman who swerves one hair's-breadth, out of the beaten track. Yes; and add (for I may as well own it, now) that, with that one hair's-breadth, she goes all astray, and never sees the world in its true aspect afterwards.' Hawthorne does not slur over the fact that many evils are irreparable, that Clifford and Hepzibah are too warped by their experience ever to merge again with the stream of outer life, that there is no release for Zenobia save in death. Yet in such a figure, as well as in Hester and Miriam, since he was able also to convey their sexual fascination, Hawthorne was most able to affirm the warmth and strength of the heart, and so to create a sense not merely of life's inexorability and sordidness, but of its possibilities of beauty and grandeur.

A professor at Brown University and at Vanderbilt, RANDALL STEWART [1896–1964] wrote numerous articles on Hawthorne and edited the American and English notebooks. He produced a biography which was the culmination of years of study and which attempted to correct or modify some of the myths which had accumulated around Hawthorne. In his "Introduction" (1932) to the American notebooks, Stewart explored Hawthorne's methods of adapting his notebook entries to fiction, his character types, and his themes. The excerpt from the biography printed below continues the examination of Hawthorne's ideas.

The Collected Works

RANDALL STEWART

. . . .

Hawthorne was an analyst of human relations, of the nice relationship of person to person, of the adjustment of the individual to society. The most tragic persons in the world are those who are divorced from the social scheme. "I want my place!" wails a pathetic, nameless figure in "The Intelligence Office," "my own place! my true place in the world! my proper sphere! my thing to do, which nature intended me to perform when she fashioned me thus awry, and which I have vainly sought all my lifetime!" In story after story Hawthorne shows the varieties of maladjustment, of estrangement. That which unites in "holy sympathy" is good; that which divorces and estranges is evil.

It may not be farfetched to discover in Hawthorne's fiction a significant criticism of nineteenth-century individualism. Many of the romantic poets in the early part of the century emphasized the idiosyncratic, glorified the lonely, exceptional individual. They enjoyed and celebrated—Byron, for example, the most influential of them all—their differentness from the mass of humanity. To such a view Hawthorne would say that the surest basis of happiness is found not in traits which make one exceptional but in those which one possesses in common with others. As the result of an intensive "education" imposed by her father, Beatrice Rappaccini at last stood above—or at least apart from—other women. But her triumph was an empty, tragic one. She wanted to share the common lot; she "would fain have been loved, not feared." The author describes her at the end of the story as "the poor victim of man's ingenuity and of thwarted nature." Hawthorne's idea clearly extends beyond the romantic individualism of a Byron. It is applicable to those who (like Margaret Fuller, Hawthorne thought) make a religion of self-cultivation.

Emerson, the leader of the New England Transcendentalists,

Nathaniel Hawthorne: A Biography (New Haven, 1948) 252–65.

may have seemed to Hawthorne to place a dangerous emphasis upon individualism—an emphasis which might jeopardize both the mental health of the individual person and the happy functioning of a democratic society. "Trust thyself," said Emerson. "No law can be sacred to me but that of my nature." He urged that "the single man plant himself indomitably on his instincts, and there abide." If his Transcendental perception of Truth should require it, Emerson's self-reliant individual would divorce himself from "father, mother, wife, brother and friend" because he "cannot sell his liberty and power to save their sensibility." He would do this "not selfishly but humbly," Emerson said, but the humility would be suspect to Hawthorne. Would not such conduct denote pride of the most insidious kind—a pride of intellect—even though it stemmed from the Transcendental premises of innate goodness and the intuitive perception of truth? Would not true humility be more likely to stem from an entirely different premise—such a premise as St. Paul's, for example, that "all have sinned and come short of the glory of God"? Would not a humility so derived restrain the individual from the breaking of ties? Would not such a humility, indeed, be a better cement for the democratic society than the Transcendentalist doctrine?

For an idealism, however noble its aims in the abstract, is a mistaken idealism if it destroys human ties, if it rends apart the social fabric. The examples in Hawthorne's stories are legion of those who, in their quest of some imagined good, violate human relationships, depart from the broad highway of mixed and varied humanity, and discover, sometimes too late, the error of their ways. Aylmer sacrificed married happiness for a chemical formula. Wakefield, who had written on the lintels of *his* doorpost "Whim," deserted his wife to live a free, solitary life in the great city of London, and saw too late that "it is perilous to make a chasm in human affections." Hollingsworth devoted himself intensely to humanitarian reform, but in so doing he hardened his own heart and marred the lives of those closest to him. The religious and social "communities" which sprang up over the country in the nineteenth century operated, Hawthorne thought, on the wrong principle—the principle of separation. As regarded society at large, he pointed out ironically, the knot of dreamers at Blithedale—his fictional Brook Farm—"stood in a position of new hostility, rather than new brotherhood." They were "inevitably estranged from the rest of mankind." The celibacy of the Shakers was another unnatural way of life. Martha Pierson, who loves Adam Colburn (in "The Shaker Bridal") but is restrained from marriage by the laws of the sect, dies of frustration and despair: "her heart could endure the weight of its desolate agony no longer." The rule of celibacy for Catholic priests, Hawthorne likewise feared, could produce no good result. As Kenyon saw the matter in *The Marble Faun*, the priests of Rome "were placed in an unnatural relation with woman, and thereby lost the healthy, human conscience that pertains to other human beings, who own the sweet household ties connecting them with wife and daughter." Happy are those who do not sever these ties, or having severed them, can knit them firmly together again. "The limits of ordinary nature," "The boundaries of ordinary life"— how often these words or their equivalents recur in Hawthorne's stories! Of all the seekers after the Great Carbuncle, only Matthew and Hannah saw the error of the quest and repented of it. "Never again," said Matthew, "will we desire more light than all the world may share with us." Much of the evil of the world seemed to Hawthorne to issue from the attempt to appropriate something for one's exclusive use, to elevate one's self above one's fellows, to attain a fancied peculiar excellence, or in some other way to violate the human ties, to transgress the social boundaries.

Pride, in Hawthorne's analysis, is the root evil, for pride is a voluntary separation. Aristocratic family pride is a common manifestation. The inordinate family pride of the Pyncheons has been a source of evil for many generations. Hawthorne can take an almost proletarian delight in the abasement of aristocratic pretensions. They have no place in the modern democratic world. He repeatedly records with approval in *The American Notebooks* the decay of proud old families and the neglected ruins of ancestral mansions. Although sympathetic in his treatment of Hepzibah Pyncheon, he scarcely conceals his satisfaction in her reduced circumstances and the consequent necessity of her becoming a tradeswoman and opening a cent shop.

Though contemptible, aristocratic family pride is less sinister than spiritual pride. The proud woman—the female incarnation of pride—is often made to suffer retributive justice. Lady Eleanore, whose intense pride is symbolized by a richly embroidered mantle, is humbled by the loathesome smallpox. The proud cruel lady in "The White Old Maid" is shown, at the end of the story, on her knees before the gentle Edith whom she had wronged—a tableau of pride abased. Zenobia, whose exotic flower is a symbol of hauteur, drowns herself.

But pride has many less obvious and more devious manifestations and effects, which perhaps only a learned casuist could disentangle. There is the pride of the religious zealot in Endicott and in Catherine, the Quakeress. There is pride of intellect as shown in characters like Aylmer, Brand, and Dr. Rappaccini. There is the moral pride of a ruthless reformer like Hollingsworth. There is even the pride of purity. Hilda is a spotless maiden who is too intent upon preserving her snow-white innocence. Though gentle and kind she is capable of a surprising hardness in her judgment of human frailty. She is so horrified at the discovery of evil that she coldly rejects the evildoer, Miriam, formerly her close friend. Hawthorne would have agreed with Miriam when she told Hilda, "You need a sin to soften you." Pride of whatever sort is evil, Hawthorne would say, because it draws one into aloofness.

Roderick Elliston (in "Egotism; or the Bosom Serpent") willfully destroyed his domestic happiness, and after his separation from his wife he was tortured by a serpent gnawing at his breast. He became "the snake-possessed." "All persons chronically diseased," the author declares,

> are egotists, whether the disease be of the mind or body; whether it be sin, sorrow, or merely the more tolerable calamity of some endless pain, such individuals are made acutely conscious of self. . . . The snake in Roderick's bosom seemed the symbol of a monstrous egotism to which everything was referred, and which he pampered, night and day, with a continual and exclusive sacrifice of devil worship. . . . In some of his moods, strange to say, he prided and gloried himself on being marked out from the ordinary experience of mankind by the possession of a double nature and a life within a life.

Roderick was not unaware of the nature of his malady but he appeared unable to throw it off. "Could I for one instant forget myself," he declared with extraordinary insight, "the serpent might not abide within me. It is my diseased self-contemplation that has engendered and nourished him."

The theme of diseased self-contemplation runs through many stories. The Reverend Mr. Hooper (in "The Minister's Black Veil") concealed his face at all times by a piece of black crepe. The veil, he said, was the symbol of the concealment practised by everyone; no one shows his inmost heart. Hawthorne leaves undetermined the reason for the minister's strange act. But whatever the reason the wearing of the veil was an act of separation, estranging Mr. Hooper from the community at large, his parishioners, even the girl he was engaged to marry. Was it not a freak of conscience, a kind of spiritual pride, which impelled him to act thus?

Reuben Bourne (in "Roger Malvin's Burial") likewise felt himself guilty of the sin of concealment. His relationship to others suffered serious disturbance from his failure to tell his wife that after the battle with the Indians he had left her mortally wounded father to lie unburied in the wilderness. Reuben felt justified in what he had done, for Malvin was dying and Reuben, himself seriously wounded, had barely reached the settlement alive. "But concealment," the author points out, "had imparted to a justifiable act much of the secret effect of guilt. . . . His one secret thought became like a serpent gnawing into his heart; and he was transformed into a sad and downcast yet irritable man."

The classic example of the morbid mind is the Rev. Arthur Dimmesdale in *The Scarlet Letter*. Concealed guilt is again the initial cause. The minister has committed adultery with Hester Prynne, and his sense of guilt is aggravated and made almost intolerable by his hypersensitive conscience, the strict mores of Puritan Boston in the seventeenth century, and his constant hypocrisy before his congregation. He resorts to flagellation and other monkish tortures; he brands, the reader is led to suppose, the letter A on his breast. He lives in constant fear lest he betray the secret in an unguarded moment, or commit some wayward act which will reveal the evil in his life. While walking the village streets he is constantly tempted by the devil to do some overt wicked deed, which would be done "in spite of himself, yet growing out of a profounder self than that which opposed the impulse": to make a blasphemous remark respecting the communion supper to an excellent deacon, to whisper in a dear old lady's ear an argument against the soul's immortality, to teach profane language to a group of children, to suggest a carnal thought to a young virgin recently converted to the church. Truly the minister is "in a maze." "Am I mad?" he cries. "Am I given over utterly to the fiend?" Torn apart by conflict Dimmesdale is on the verge of a complete physical and nervous breakdown. He must re-establish free, unconstrained relations with others before he can enjoy peace of mind again.

In his portrayal of Elliston, Hooper, Bourne, Dimmesdale, and other cases of conscience, Hawthorne doubtless intended a criticism of the introspective habits of the New England mind. Minute self-examination was a fostered Puritan practice. The following entry in Cotton Mather's *Diary* suggests Dimmesdale himself: "Was ever man more tempted than the miserable Mather? Should I tell in how many forms the Devil has assaulted me, it would strike my friends with horror." Jonathan Edwards' *Diary* contains such entries as this: "To set apart days of meditation on particular subjects, as sometimes, to set apart a day for the consideration of the Greatness of my sins." If the Puritan examined his inner consciousness to assess his sinfulness, his proneness to sin, and so the better to guard against the assaults of the Evil One, the Transcendentalist looked inward to discover hints and intimations of the divine mind which is in all men. "A man should learn," Emerson said, "to detect and watch that gleam of light which flashes across his mind from within." "If one listens," Thoreau said, repeating and amplifying Emerson's thought, "to the faintest but constant suggestions of his genius, which are certainly true, he sees not to what extremes, or even insanity, it may lead him; and yet that way, as he grows more resolute and faithful, his road lies." While recognizing the danger Thoreau recommended introspection because the Transcendental doctrine of God within required it. He and Emerson were sufficiently active in the world about them to escape the morbid effects of the inward gaze, but Hawthorne could have pointed to the Transcendentalist Charles King Newcomb as an example of self-contemplation carried to dangerous excess. The New England mind, when Hawthorne wrote, had searched itself for more than two centuries—inexorably and often with fierce castigation in Puritan times, benignly and hopefully in the contemporary age of Transcendentalism. The practice in either case was motivated by the laudable desire for perfection, for Puritans and Transcendentalists alike took to heart the biblical text, "Be ye therefore perfect, even as your Father which is in heaven is perfect." But would not the constant inward-looker become morbid? Would not the assiduous self-improver become cold and aloof? Hawthorne's stories contain many instances of the sort.

What does Hawthorne oppose as a corrective to excessive self-examination? What therapy does he offer for morbidness? What cure for the sick soul? The answer is essentially the recognition of man's fallibility, the restoration of sympathy, the sharing of the common lot. Hawthorne's "moral" comprehends the Christian doctrine of charity, the psychological doctrine of participation, the social doctrine of the democratic way.

Hawthorne set great store by the normalizing, stabilizing power of the domestic affections. The experience of love, marriage, and children had such an effect upon his own life. "We are but shadows," he wrote to Sophia Peabody in 1840, "we are not endowed with real life, and all that seems most real about us is but the thinnest substance of a dream—till the heart be touched. That touch creates us, then we begin to be, thereby we are beings of reality and inheritors of eternity." In several pieces written during his bachelorhood (a bachelorhood abnormally prolonged, though not entirely from his own choice, one must believe) the author betrays his own sense of need. The wakeful sleeper would not have been plagued by specters of the mind (in "The Haunted Mind") if he had had a wife. "How pleasant in these night solitudes," the author observes, "would be the rise and fall of a softer breathing than your own, the slight pressure of a tenderer bosom, the quiet throb of a purer heart, imparting its peacefulness to your troubled one, as if the fond sleeper were involving you in her dream." The moral of "The Village Uncle," summed up at the end, points to a domestic and social therapy: "In chaste and warm affections, humble wishes, and honest toil for some useful end, there is health for the mind, and quiet for the heart, the prospect of a happy life, and the fairest hope of heaven." The same lesson was learned, the hard way, by the wanderer in "The Three-fold Destiny," who at last returned to his original home, married the sweetheart of his boyhood, and taught in the village school.

Roderick Elliston, the pathological individual who was tortured by a "bosom-serpent," was reconciled with his wife and their new love worked a cure. In the symbolical language of the story, Rosina's touch exorcised the serpent. Hepzibah's love for the unfortunate Clifford, and for Phoebe, was a saving grace in her life. Without these influences she would have been a completely crazed old woman. Kenyon's love for Hilda saved him from the coldness of his art. Inspired by love, Drowne, the woodcarver (in "Drowne's Wooden Image"), surpassed his usual self and created a statue worthy of Copley's praise. Even Feathertop—the "wretched simulacrum," the empty, foppish man of mode destitute of mind, heart, and soul—might have been changed from shadow to substance by the love of Polly Gookin—or he pathetically conjectured as much to Mother Rigby.

To private domestic love must be added a vital sense of one's connection with the larger world. The stories abound in illustrations. Hepzibah Pyncheon, we are told, "needed a walk along the noonday street to keep her sane." When a political procession, announced by banners and drums, marched by the house of the seven gables, Clifford Pyncheon—isolated from humanity by an overexquisite sensibility as Hepzibah was by an aristocratic pride —felt an impulse to jump from the balcony above into the passing throng. He felt, the author says, "a natural magnetism tending towards the great center of humanity," the need of "a deep, deep plunge into the ocean of human life," "a yearning to renew the broken links of brotherhood with his kind." The flight of Hepzibah and Clifford and their journey on the railroad are symbolical of an attempt to establish a connection with the world.

After prolonged, unremitting application to the writer's craft— of necessity a solitary occupation—Hawthorne himself often felt a similar social need; such application he thought was "unwholesome" in its personal effect. He enjoyed mingling in the life of a great city—in Boston, Liverpool, London. His employment in the various custom houses gave him a sense of social participation, as did his labor at Brook Farm. Coverdale spoke from the author's own experience when he said, "In the sweat of my brow I had earned bread and eaten it, and so established my claim to be on earth, and my fellowship with all the sons of labor." Repeatedly in his stories Hawthorne opposes "human sympathy" to "morbid sensibility." "I would make the wide world my cell," Kenyon declares when Donatello seems inclined to adopt the monastic life, "and good deeds to mankind my prayer."

Opening an intercourse with the world (the phrase is Hawthorne's own expression of his aim in publishing the *Twice-Told Tales*) is often difficult and seemingly impossible. Hawthorne's stories emphasize the obstacles to free, reciprocal relationships. Such an obstacle may be pride, or egoism, or solitary ambition, or secret sin. The harboring of secret sin, the practice of hypocrisy, estranges the soul from God and man. That full-blown hypocrite, Judge Pyncheon, was past redemption, past contrition and confession, but Hawthorne's prescription for salvation—had the Judge by a miracle of grace been capable of following it—is a good statement of the author's ethic: "Will he go forth a humbled and repentant man, sorrowful, gentle, seeking no profit, shrinking from worldly honor, hardly daring to love God, but bold to love his fellowman and to do him what good he may? Will he bear about with him . . . the tender sadness of a contrite heart, broken at last beneath its own weight of sin?" Judge Pyncheon was completely callous and suffered no remorse. Arthur Dimmesdale, on the other hand, was sensitive and was tortured by his conscience for seven years. When, upon the point of collapse and death, he summoned sufficient strength of will to make a public confession before the congregation and townspeople whom he had deceived, a magical change was at once made evident by his facial expression and his attitude toward Pearl: "There was a sweet and gentle smile over his face, as of a spirit sinking into deep repose; nay, now that the burden was removed, it seemed almost as if he would be sportive with the child."

Confession—whether viewed religiously or psychologically—is good for the soul. In *The Marble Faun* Hilda used the Roman confessional as a means of relieving her mind of a troublesome secret. The device proved effective, but Hilda herself had committed no sin. For sinners, Hawthorne must have regarded the public confession of the Puritans, by which the guilt was laid open before the congregation and community, as preferable to the private confessional of the Catholic Church, which did not sufficiently meet the social requirements. If sin is an estrangement, then the sinner must confess—as Dimmesdale did—before those from whom he has been estranged, for how otherwise can he be restored to free and full communion with them?

Though sin often estranges (the sin of pride, for example), it may be, paradoxically, a means of sympathy. Hawthorne often remarks on the sympathy between sinners. Goodman Brown's vision of evil admitted him to a sinful brotherhood. Elliston's "serpent" heard answering hisses (recalling a scene in *Paradise Lost*) from the bosoms of his fellow townsmen. Accomplices in murder, Miriam and Donatello were united in a bond of crime. Dimmesdale's experience of sin gave new meaning and power to his preaching. Indeed, since evil is an ever-present reality in human life, a knowledge of evil—of some sort and in some degree—would seem to be a necessary condition of sympathy.

The knowledge of evil may be good or bad, depending upon its effects. In Goodman Brown's case it led to sheer misanthropy. With Donatello and Miriam the bad effects greatly preponderated because their crime, while binding the two together, isolated them from the rest of the world. Dimmesdale's experience might have been entirely good in the end had it not been for the fatal flaw of hypocrisy. Hilda was "instructed by sorrow"; she became more tolerant, more sympathetic. But her knowledge was only vicarious and for that reason the sympathy thus acquired was comparatively shallow. In *The Marble Faun* the author speaks of "those dark caverns into which all men must descend if they would know anything beneath the surface and illusive pleasures of existence." "And when they emerge," he says, "they take truer and sadder views of life forever afterwards." Once again Hawthorne sets himself against the optimism of his age and the age's chief optimist in America, Emerson, who disarmingly declared on his fifty-eighth birthday, "I could never give much reality to evil and pain." Such an inability or lack of insight, to Hawthorne, is a mark of defective sympathy. The sympathy in any case is the important thing. A knowledge of both good and evil is essential to sympathy since the nature of man comprehends both. A knowledge of one only sets up barriers to sympathy.

The problem of evil is the greatest and most baffling of human problems. The Christian statement of the problem is: Why does God, who is all-good and all-powerful, permit evil in His world? In the tales and novels Hawthorne presented the problem in many of its protean forms. He presented it from the Puritan, which was also the Christian, standpoint (for the marks which distinguished Puritanism from the rest of Christendom were, in relation to the whole body of doctrine, few and unimportant). Toward the end of *The Marble Faun* he apparently attempted to formulate a more comprehensive and summary view of the matter than can be found in his previous works. Donatello, encouraged by Miriam, has committed murder. The deed has had a variety of important effects upon the characters in the story. To portray and evaluate these effects constitute the author's chief intention. The evil deed has humbled the proud Miriam. It has broadened and deepened the sympathies of Kenyon. It has enlightened and softened Hilda, making her less self-sufficient and more responsive to Kenyon's love. It has educated Donatello, who has lost his faunlike simplicity and innocence and has gained maturity and depth of character.

Hawthorne is particularly interested in Donatello's transformation and its implications. He presents the problem first in a dialogue between Miriam and Kenyon:

"Was the crime [Miriam asked] in which he and I were wedded—was it a blessing, in that strange disguise? Was it a means of education, bringing a simple and imperfect nature to a point of feeling and intelligence which it could have reached under no other discipline?"

"You stir up deep and perilous matter, Miriam," replied Kenyon. "I dare not follow you into the unfathomable abysses whither you are tending."

"Yet there is a pleasure in them! I delight to brood on the verge of this great mystery," returned she. "The story of the fall of man! Is it not repeated in our romance of Monte Beni? And may we follow the analogy yet further? Was that very sin,— into which Adam precipitated himself and all his race,—was it the destined means by which, over a long pathway of toil and sorrow, we are to attain a higher, brighter, and profounder happiness than our lost birthright gave? Will not this idea account for the permitted existence of sin, as no other theory can?"

In a later scene Kenyon restates Miriam's idea in a conversation with Hilda:

"Donatello perpetrated a great crime; and his remorse, gnawing into his soul, has awakened it; developing a thousand high capabilities, moral and intellectual, which we never should have dreamed of asking for, within the scanty compass of the Donatello whom we knew. . . . Sin has educated Donatello, and elevated him. Is sin, then—which we deem such a dreadful blackness in the Universe—is it, like sorrow, merely an element of human education, through which we struggle to a higher and purer state than we could otherwise have attained? Did Adam fall, that we might ultimately rise to a far loftier paradise than his?"

Although Hilda strongly dissents, the view twice stated would seem to be the author's theme.

"I first look at matters," Hawthorne once wrote to his wife, "in their darkest aspect, and having satisfied myself with that, I begin gradually to be consoled, to take into account the advantages of the case, and thus trudge on, with the light brightening around me." Readers of his stories are likely to complain of the prevalence of gloom, the comparative absence of light, and the complaint is not without some justification. And yet the light, though never garish, does brighten around a score of characters, and more, as the trials of the narrative draw to a close: around the Lord and Lady of the May, the young married pair of "The Great Carbuncle," the returned wanderer and his village sweetheart in "The Three-fold Destiny," Roderick and Rosina in "The Bosom Serpent," Holgrave and Phoebe, Kenyon and Hilda—around even Dimmesdale and Hester, though in the last instance the light only prefigures a possible happiness beyond this life. It should be observed, too, that the trials through which these and other characters have passed have enriched their lives and increased their capacities for happiness.

If, nevertheless, the emphasis of *The Collected Works*, the sum and synthesis of Hawthorne's knowledge and understanding of the world, seems to fall on the somber side, the explanation may be found in his sense of the stark realities, which he was unwilling to falsify or gloss over, and his critical reaction against an age which seemed to him to brush the human difficulties aside with too easy an optimism, and to put an extravagant and unrealistic faith both in man's abilities and in the new scientific and social machinery. From the perspective of today we can see that Hawthorne touched his times at point after point with admonitory finger, giving to his age the more earnest purpose, the deeper moral, and the closer and homelier truth which it seemed to him to require. It is an admonition and a gift which are timeless. In the light of the world today (which is the heir of the nineteenth century) no one is likely to impugn Hawthorne's central moral—the importance of understanding mankind in whole, and the need of man's sympathy with man based upon the honest recognition of the good and evil in our common nature.

RICHARD HARTER FOGLE [1911–], a professor of American literature at Tulane and the University of North Carolina, has written on Romantic poets and on Melville's shorter fiction. His book on Hawthorne represents a combination of the skills of close analysis of image patterns (frequently associated with new criticism) and a vast knowledge of romanticism. He is particularly concerned with a major and continuing problem in Hawthorne criticism—ambiguity. Despite some objection to Fogle's approach, his book and the first edition of Hyatt Waggoner's *Hawthorne: A Critical Study* (1955) are among the most important studies of Hawthorne in the 1950's.

The Light and the Dark

RICHARD HARTER FOGLE

Hawthorne is a great writer in absolute terms, and many men have written well about him. Yet modern critics, led astray by mistaken notions about realism and by fallacies about inevitable progress, are still a little condescending. Most general readers, among them Somerset Maugham, find him naïve and old-fashioned. Given their perspective, both critics and readers are honestly reporting what

Hawthorne's Fiction: The Light and the Dark (Norman: University of Oklahoma Press, copyright 1952, 1964) 3–14.

they see; but the perspective itself is out of focus. A character in Mr. Marquand's recent *Point of No Return* comments sardonically upon those people who consider *The House of the Seven Gables* a good story for children. It is a fact that generations of high-school students have been reared on the book with no very favorable results. Because of premature exposure to it, I contracted a dislike for gentle Phoebe Pyncheon which was surpassed only by my distaste for Lucie Manette in Dickens' *Tale of Two Cities*, a lady who ranks among the great emetics of English literature. Doubtless most readers remember Hawthorne from an experience like mine, which also includes memories of "A Rill from the Town Pump" (interpreted as a temperance lecture), as it appeared in my eighth-grade reader.

Hawthorne's writing is misleading in its simplicity, which is genuine enough but tempts us to overlook what lies beneath. In the end, simplicity is one of his genuine charms—combined with something else. The essence of Hawthorne is, in fact, distilled from the opposing elements of simplicity and complexity. This essence is a clear liquid, with no apparent cloudiness. Hawthorne, together with Henry James, perhaps, is the only American novelist who has been able to see life whole without, in Thackeray's words, "roaring ai, ai, as loud as Prometheus," like Melville, Wolfe, and Faulkner; droning interminably an account of its details, like Dreiser; or falling into a thin, shrill irony, the batlike twittering of souls in Hades, like all the sad young men. Hawthorne's tone is equable, "not harsh nor grating, but with ample power to chasten and subdue." He is a unique and wonderful combination of light and darkness.

The light in Hawthorne is clarity of design. He has a classic balance; his language is exquisitely lucid. He gives one the sense of an invulnerable dignity and centrality; he is impenetrably self-possessed. He holds his characters to the highest standards, for he literally brings them to judgment at the bar of eternity as immortal souls. The "dark" in Hawthorne, that blackness which Herman Melville applauded in him, is his tragic complexity. His clarity is intermingled with subtlety, his statement interfused with symbolism, his affirmation enriched with ambiguity. The whole which results is captivating. In attack he is mild but deadly. His blow is so delicately delivered that a man would have to turn his head in order to realize that he had just lost it. "The Custom House" essay, for example, which rather oddly precedes *The Scarlet Letter*, seems at first sight merely agreeable. Look closer, however, and the effect is devastating. These gently humorous character portraits are murderous, not from malice or heat, but from judgment and icy cold. Hawthorne is not indignant; he is merely certain of his grounds. And his certainty is that of one whose father was called "the sternest man who ever walked a deck."

He is so entirely unsentimental that he does not need, as we sometimes do, to avoid sentimentality. He combines sympathy with a classic aloofness, participation with cool observation. "My father," said Julian Hawthorne, "was two men, one sympathetic and intuitional, the other critical and logical; together they formed a combination which could not be thrown off its feet." Thus Hawthorne's writing has a tone of exquisite gravity, harmonized strangely with a pervasive irony and humor. In the use of irony he is a lighter, more sensitive Fielding, with depths besides which Fielding could not plumb. In the matter of irony Hawthorne's antecedents in the eighteenth-century novel might well be re-examined.

Corresponding to the clarity and the complexity of Hawthorne are his "philosophy" and the crosscurrents which modify its course. For the best understanding one should always attend to the thought of the author. But one grasps that author wholly only by observing his characters, his settings, the patterns of his diction, the trends of his imagery, the concrete mechanics of telling a story. What one has grasped is admittedly not easy to describe, however—therefore the advantage of seizing upon the writer's thought, which can be systematically abstracted.

The philosophy of Hawthorne is a broadly Christian scheme which contains heaven, earth, and hell. Whether heaven and hell are realities or only subjective states of mind is one of Hawthorne's crucial ambiguities. I do not call him a Christian humanist, as do some excellent critics, for it seems to me that heaven and hell *are* real to him and play too large a part in his fiction to be relegated to the background. In his mixed macrocosm, man is a microcosm also mixed. Man's chief temptation is to forget his limits and complexities, to think himself all good, or to think himself all bad. Either way he falls into spiritual isolation and pride. He needs a proper mixture of the earthly and the ideal—with a touch of the flame to temper it. Thus Aylmer, the scientist-hero of "The Birthmark," violates the covenant of humankind when he tries to eradicate the only blemish of his beautiful wife, a tiny mark on her cheek. He succeeds, but kills her in the process. The birthmark, which is shaped like a hand, is her grip upon earthly existence. She dies to the sound of the laughter of Aminadab, Aylmer's assistant, a kind of earth-fiend. Even the pit has its claims, which must not be slighted. The conclusion epitomizes Hawthorne's thinking: ". . . had

Aylmer reached a profounder wisdom, he need not thus have flung away the happiness which would have woven his mortal life of the selfsame texture with the celestial. The momentary circumstance was too strong for him; he failed to look beyond the shadowy scope of time, and living once for all in eternity, to find the perfect future in the present." There is a time for everything, and an eternity. Aylmer should have waited.

But the system does not make the story. The tale of "The Minister's Black Veil" will illustrate the difference between an abstract and a literary meaning. The minister dons the veil as an emblem of secret sin, of which all men are presumably guilty. Elizabeth, his betrothed, implores him to discard it. The minister has found a dreadful truth, while Elizabeth may have discovered a greater—that men are evil *and also* good. The meaning lies not in either but in both. So Hawthorne condemns his strange seekers, his Aylmers, his Ethan Brands, but he makes them noble. His reconciliation is not finally in logic, for he accepts the mystery of existence. His reconciliation is the acceptance itself, realized in balance, structure, and tone.

Hawthorne still suffers from our prejudice against allegory. This prejudice comes partly from a false theory of realism, a legacy of the late nineteenth century, and partly from a misconception of what allegory is. We assume that allegory subordinates everything to a predetermined conclusion: that allegory, in short, is a dishonest counterfeit of literary value. But the great allegories, *The Faerie Queene* and *The Pilgrim's Progress*, possess the literary virtues. And Hawthorne, whose subjects are moral and psychological problems, feels for these problems a passion which transfigures them. All we can ask of a writer is that he treat his material honestly, without unduly simplifying: that he keep faith with his own imagination. T. S. Eliot has said that good religious poetry teaches us not a doctrine but how it feels to believe it; and so it should be with allegory.

Allegory is organic to Hawthorne, an innate quality of his vision. It is his disposition to find spiritual meaning in all things natural and human. This faculty is an inheritance from the Puritans, who saw in everything God's will. To this inheritance was added a gift from nineteenth-century Romanticism, which endowed the natural world with meaning by seeing it as life. In Hawthorne allegory is inseparable from moral complexity and aesthetic design, qualities to be enjoyed in themselves. So, in his "Endicott and the Red Cross" the focus of meaning and the focus of setting are one, and the conclusion takes on an increased value from the subtlety of its preparation. The scene, the village green of seventeenth-century Salem, radiates outward from a center, to return upon it once more. The center is Endicott, the iron Puritan, in whose breastplate, significantly, the scene is mirrored. Endicott is the temporal, active power, the central ethos and intelligence of the story. The Puritan meetinghouse, the spiritual power, is "the central object in the mirrored picture."

On the church porch is nailed the head of a wolf, "a token of the perils of the wilderness." Close by is the whipping-post; at the corners of the meetinghouse stand the pillory and the stocks. Various evildoers are suffering punishment: an Episcopalian, a royalist, a Wanton Gospeller who has given unsanctioned interpretations of Holy Writ, and a woman with her tongue in a cleft stick who has spoken against the elders of the church. There is also "a young woman, with no mean share of beauty," who is condemned to wear upon her breast a scarlet A. In the background are armored men, for Endicott is drilling his trainbands.

The Reverend Roger Williams appears—as he might well have done—bearing news of the English crown's intention to send a royal governor to rule the New England colonies. Endicott, in a symbolic gesture of rebellion, rips the cross from the flag of St. George, which flies over the scene.

> With a cry of triumph the people gave their sanction to one of the boldest exploits which our history records. And forever honored be the name of Endicott! We look back through the mist of ages, and recognize in the rending of the Red Cross from New England's banner the first omen of that deliverance which our fathers consummated after the bones of the stern Puritans had lain more than a century in the dust.

The story is beautifully compact; it contains an entire era of American history in a single scene and action. The allegorical economy of its dramatis personae is merged with firmly symmetrical composition. The abstract meaning is compressed into one flashing concrete image. The "moral" or summary has considerably more than its surface value, and should be read in the light of the whole story. Before his decisive action Endicottt had addressed the crowd, asking rhetorically for what purpose the Puritans fled to the New England wilderness:

> "Was it not for liberty to worship God according to our conscience?"

> "Call you this liberty of conscience?" interrupted a voice on the steps of the meeting-house.
>
> It was the Wanton Gospeller. A sad and quiet smile flitted across the mild visage of Roger Williams.

Thus the meaning of Endicott's gesture remains, but deeper and richer for the moral complexity of its context.

Even so allegorical a figure as Chillingworth, the villain of *The Scarlet Letter*, has his complexities. Hawthorne keeps before our eyes his humanity as well as his evil. So intricate, indeed, are Hawthorne's complications that he has sometimes been accused of indecision. All profound studies of spiritual problems, however, eventually run against a blank wall. Do we know the ultimate destiny of James's Isabel Archer? It is a tribute to *The Portrait of a Lady* that the question so much as occurs to us. What do we decide about Conrad's *Lord Jim*? What is the meaning of Jim's one act of cowardice? The whole book tries to tell us, and at the end we are left with the action still unexplained. There is a point where a writer must stop for fear of saying more than his imagination has authorized. The killing of the model is the central action of *The Marble Faun;* yet Donatello kills almost involuntarily, and Miriam, who has incited to murder, is honestly unaware that she has done so. Hawthorne nevertheless holds both to strict account.

This ambiguity in Hawthorne was noticed early but was not fully understood. Contemporary reviews of *The Marble Faun* objected to its vagueness. To friendlier critics Hawthorne's ambiguity was a chiaroscuro effect which deepened the tints of his picture. John Lothrop Motley wrote, "I like those shadowy, weird, fantastic, Hawthornesque shapes flitting through the golden gloom, which is the atmosphere of the book." In his prefaces Hawthorne himself speaks chiefly of this quality of picturesqueness. He says of *The House of the Seven Gables:*

> It is a legend prolonging itself, from an epoch now gray in the distance, down into our own broad daylight, and bringing along with it some of its legendary mist, which the reader, according to his pleasure, may either disregard, or allow it to float almost imperceptibly about the characters and events for the sake of a picturesque effect.

This type of ambiguity is a way of introducing the marvelous without offending against probability. It has a deeper purpose, as well—to convey in legend or superstition a moral or psychological truth. In the story of the Pyncheons the whisper of tradition is truer than history; the legend of Maule's Curse has weighty meaning concealed in it. ". . . ancient superstitions," says Hawthorne, "after being steeped in human hearts and embodied in human breath, and passing from lip to ear in manifold repetition, through a series of generations, become imbued with an effect of homely truth."

Yvor Winters and F. O. Matthiessen have illuminated Hawthorne's ambiguity, which Winters calls "the formula of alternative possibilities," and Matthiessen "the device of multiple choice." It is not, however, a device; it is a pervasive quality of mind. It can be an evasion, and it is sometimes no more than a mannerism. But as a whole it embodies Hawthorne's deepest insights. It outlines the pure form of truth by dissolving irrelevancies; this is its positive function. Negatively, it marks the limit of eyeshot, beyond which is shadow. Thus Hawthorne's effects of light—his shadows, his mirror images, his masquerades—all examine the relationships of appearance and reality. Hawthorne's ambiguity involves both light and darkness. As light it is the means of seeing through opacities; as darkness it is the difficulty of seeing.

Hawthorne's simplest ambiguity is a playful mystification. In retelling the Greek myths in *A Wonder-Book* and *Tanglewood Tales* he uses ambiguity to introduce the Olympian gods. Mortals continually have glimpses of the supernatural. In "The Miraculous Pitcher" old Baucis and Philemon entertain Jove and Mercury, who are disguised as casual wayfarers. The old couple see miracles without being able to believe their eyes, and Hawthorne also pretends to be skeptical. Thus Mercury's caduceus is ostensibly an optical illusion:

> Two snakes, carved in the wood, were represented as twining themselves about the staff, and were so very skilfully executed that old Philemon (whose eyes, you know, were getting rather dim) almost thought them alive, and that he could see them wriggling and twisting.

(This same staff is used more seriously in "Young Goodman Brown" and *The Blithedale Romance*, in both of which it indicates the presence of evil.) This ambiguity is proper to the children's tale; as with fairy stories, what is required is not real belief, but a temporary suspension of disbelief. Yet even here there is a hint of truth before eyes too blind to see it.

The issues are more serious in such legends of New England as "The Gray Champion" and the "Legends of the Province House" in the volume of *Twice-Told Tales*. In these stories the ambiguity underlines the significance by dissolving irrelevant actuality in the mists of the past and leaving only an ideal history. Ambiguity invests the events with the rich pathos and patina of time and counterpoints unreality against truth. In "The Gray Champion" the hero's background is shadowed, the better to project his image in the foreground. In "Howe's Masquerade" disguise reveals identity; the procession of royal governors is a masquerade, but there is nothing false about its meaning. The ambiguity of the "Legends" is a vision of the Past in the light of the Present, a picture in a frame of distance.

Hawthorne uses ambiguity structurally to create suspense and retard conclusions, especially in tales where the primary emphasis would otherwise be too clear. "The Celestial Railroad," an ironic nineteenth-century *Pilgrim's Progress*, is an example of this usage. Hawthorne's railroad is scheduled to the Celestial City, but its real destination is Hell. By disguising the way to Perdition as the road to Heaven, he takes the reader into his confidence by a sustained ironic reversal of values and curbs impatience for the end by supplying attractions on the way. "The Celestial Railroad," however, is closer to abstract allegory than Hawthorne generally gets. More fundamental is the tragic ambiguity which threatens the bases of accepted values, as in "Young Goodman Brown," where the final interpretation is in genuine doubt. Hawthorne judges relentlessly, yet with sympathy, and his ambiguity always leaves room for a different verdict. He preserves the sanctity and independence of his characters by allowing them at bottom an inviolable individuality.

In their recently published *Theory of Literature*, René Wellek and Austin Warren define the symbol as "an object which refers to another object but which demands attention also in its own right, as a presentation." The symbol must be interesting in itself, not merely as it points to something else. This crucial requirement, which divides *mere* allegory from literature, Hawthorne fulfills. The minister's black veil is truly a veil, as well as an emblem of secret sin. The brook of *The Scarlet Letter* has water in it, though it symbolizes life and time. The fountain in Rappaccini's garden is an object of art in addition to being an image of eternity. Hawthorne's symbols have the clarity of allegory, with the complexity and density of life. They are rarely obscure, but they will abide the test of long use without wearing out. Since they are generally accompanied by an explanation, it is natural to pass by them quickly—too quickly.

The rosebush before the prison in Chapter I of *The Scarlet Letter* is an instance of this misleading simplicity. It stands, says

Hawthorne, "in token that the deep heart of nature can pity and forgive." The rose is pitying nature, as the prison is pitiless man. The rose is also, however, Hester Prynne, a red rose against the gray Puritan background; and therefore it is the scarlet letter, the natural passion which the prison exists to quell. Beside the fortress-like prison the rose seems pitiably frail, but it is strong with the power of natural vitality.

Hawthorne's symbols are broadly traditional, drawn from the main stream of Western thought. In his pages are the red cavern of the heart and the gray cavern of isolation; the wild forest and the winding path of error (from Spenser); the fountain and the sea of eternity, and the river of time; the Garden of Eden, with Adam and Eve and the serpent; the flames of hell, strangely mingled with the forge fire of Vulcan's smithy, and the bright blaze of the hearth; the devil's stigmata, and the sunlight of holiness. Created as they are of old materials, these symbols are yet fresh from Hawthorne's imagination. He invests them with a new vitality and suggestiveness. They have, moreover, an advantage which our later symbolists might envy: they are comprehensible in their own terms to anyone who will take reasonable pains with them.

RICHARD CHASE [1914–62] was a professor at Columbia University and wrote critical studies of Melville, Whitman, and Dickinson. In *The American Novel and Its Tradition*, he explores a genre which "in its most original and characteristic form, has worked out its destiny and defined itself by incorporating an element of romance"—the "American romance-novel." The selection below deals with *The Blithedale Romance*, which has undergone considerable and inconclusive re-evaluation in recent years.

Hawthorne and the Limits of Romance
The Blithedale Romance

RICHARD CHASE

By 1852 nearly all of Hawthorne's best work was behind him. Coming just after *The Scarlet Letter* and *The House of the Seven*

The American Novel and Its Tradition (Garden City, N.Y., 1957) 82–87.

Gables, and just before Hawthorne's life was to be markedly changed by his long sojourn in Europe, *The Blithedale Romance* is the culmination of his most concentrated attempt to write fiction of novel length. Except for *The Scarlet Letter*, Hawthorne's longer fictions never succeed perfectly, despite the many incidental successes which this author could always score. His books falter at various points and then, not knowing how to re-establish the progression, he trots out a traveling puppet show, a masquerade, a symbolic well, an old legend, a mesmerist, as if he were an entertainer on the stage who must improvise in order not to lose his audience. The shorter form of the tale fitted his genius better, and although his work gave him an important place in the history of the novel, he was, strictly speaking, finally unable to master the novel form, without imparting to it a preponderance of romance. This he appears to admit in *The Blithedale Romance*.

Technical questions aside for the moment, this book must always find a place in the affections of readers for being so genuinely original in conception. The Brook Farm experiment, in which Hawthorne himself briefly partook, offered him a various display of manners, attitudes, and odd and salient characters. And if we must suppose that he chose to report only a little of what was to be seen, we have to admit that he did well with that little. As a study of the manners of liberal intellectuals that took a comic view of their advanced ideas, *The Blithedale Romance* had no precedent in America nor, except for the satires of Swift and Peacock, in Europe either. Had any author discovered that the feelings of intellectual women who have to wash dishes and make gruel and who, being modern women, have to form at the same time *ideas about* washing dishes and making gruel was proper material for the novelist?

Zenobia, the tragicomic heroine, is the center of the piece. She is a novelist's success in her faultful and appealing humanity, and sketchy as she is by the strictest standards, Henry James was right in admiring her and in calling her "the nearest approach that Hawthorne has made to the complete creation of a person." The point about Zenobia is the waste and confusion of her inner life, which result from her always living according to this or that literary or political idea rather than according to the natural urgencies of her being. Even in committing suicide, we are told, she "was not quite simple." In actuality the details of her death are repulsive and grotesque; but she had tried to die like "drowned persons" in pictures—"in lithe and graceful attitudes."

As in *The Scarlet Letter*, the general theme is the loss or submergence of emotion. Coverdale, the narrator, is too timid and cold to live the emotional life which his intellect perceives. Hollingsworth, a spiritual cousin of Chillingworth and second-cousin of Melville's Ahab, is a monomaniac, in whom an obsessive goal has compressed and destroyed emotion. Priscilla is a pale New England blossom (like Mrs. Hawthorne), given to psychic experiences which bypass or merely symbolize an emotional life. Zenobia, like Hester Prynne a darkly beautiful and supposedly passionate woman, is a study in the emotional hazards of feminism and transcendentalist utopianism.

By exemplifying this theme in the lives of intellectuals and reformers, Hawthorne launched a small but important group of novels, all of which owe a debt to the original—among them James's *The Bostonians*, Howells's *Vacation of the Kelwyns*, Lionel Trilling's *The Middle of the Journey*, and Mary McCarthy's *The Oasis*. But there is in *The Blithedale Romance* a certain poetic beauty and charm, a finally unnamable Hawthorne magic that is beyond those who follow his lead in subject and theme.

As for the symbols of the piece, they are plain and effective, lending a charm to the story and enhancing its psychology—the veils and masquerades to suggest the falseness of motive and belief; mesmerism to suggest falseness of spirit and emotional confidence tricks; hearth-fire to suggest the genial emotional life which ironically eludes the cold ideology of the Blithedalers. There is also the pastoral setting itself, representing the innocence which these all too civilized utopians cannot recapture. And we note that in a literature rich in pastoral idyls *The Blithedale Romance* is one of the few anti-pastorals—Hawthorne is a partisan of conventional society as he finds it.

Unlike his descendants in the satirical-utopian genre Hawthorne is unable to follow through with his original conception. Blithedale and its interesting people, never very solidly established in the first place, grow dimmer and dimmer, and the story is dissipated into rather weakly related static scenes—a masquerade in the forest (rich in comic possibles of which nothing is made), a series of set speeches at "Eliot's pulpit," the suicide of Zenobia.

Part of the trouble is that as the story goes along the author becomes more and more interested in the status of Coverdale as the observer, a problem that for him has literary and moral implications. These reflections in the end lead him to concede that he must make certain fundamental moral objections to what one must think and feel in order to write a novel. In effect he admits that it is not only the poverty of materials in America that has led him, as he says in his prefaces, to write romances rather than novels, but also his puritan scruples—the romance allowing him to treat the physical passions obliquely. And whether it is a separate objection, or merely a rationalization of his scruples, he comes to think, in *The Blithedale Romance*, that the novelist commits the unpardonable sin, that he is a kind of Chillingworth whose probing intellect violates the human heart.

That Hawthorne is deliberately experimenting with the point of view in *The Blithedale Romance* is made clear by the repeated reflections of the narrator, Coverdale, on his own position as observer. Our narrator is a minor poet; he is rather selfish, fastidious, and aloof; he is also mildly ironic and cherishes his ready insight into people and things. There is something illicit about him however. He looks at life furtively; he is a bit of a *voyeur;* he blushes and is a little coy. We are not allowed to see Coverdale directly and the author, having granted him the privileged position of first-person narrator, cannot question his behavior and does not put him on the spot by involving him very deeply in the action.

Thus to his usual method of conducting us through a series of static scenes, Hawthorne adds here a series of positions in the story from which we behold the scenes. And a part of the interest is in the changes of position. We observe the characters at close range in the living room of the farmhouse; we get a more general long-distance view of them from Coverdale's pine-tree eyrie; we see them theatrically framed in the back window of a boardinghouse, as Coverdale watches them from his upstairs room in an opposite building.

We see things differently, too, according to the state of Coverdale's health or mood. When he is sick and feverish, his perceptions are heightened and somewhat morbid. He has been fascinated with the lush Zenobia but now he allows himself to call her an "enchantress" and even wonders if in Zenobia's life "the great event of a woman's existence had been consummated." Convalescing, he reflects that his sickness has been a kind of death and his recovery a rebirth. He has now been reborn to reality and will be able fearlessly and accurately to analyze the community and its inhabitants—as he is really able to do with considerable perspicacity, up to a point.

He sees things clearly if not profoundly. He attempts to look through the eyes of others, in order to compare what he sees with what they see. He rejects the leadership of Hollingsworth when he perceives that what Hollingsworth demands of his friends is precisely that they should surrender their right to see with their own eyes.

At one point Coverdale reflects that his position in the story "resembles that of the Chorus in a classic play, which seems to be set aloof from the possibility of personal concernment." His only relation to the other characters is the sympathy he feels for them as he watches their fate work itself out. Yet, as Coverdale concludes, near the end of the story, there is for the aloof observer an insoluble dilemma in the very nature of story-telling. "It was both sad and dangerous, I whispered to myself, to be in too close affinity with the passions, the errors, and the misfortunes of individuals who stood within a circle of their own, into which, if I stept at all, it must be as an intruder, and at a peril that I could not estimate."

This is sound morality but a bad state of mind for a novelist. The moral question has been interesting Hawthorne all the way through the book. And although we too are interested, we cannot help thinking that he would have written a better novel if only he could have allowed his observer to see what he could see instead of what would test the moral significance of observing. Thus in *The Blithedale Romance* Hawthorne confronts the dilemma his moral views have brought him to. As a novelist, he is more than likely guilty of the Unpardonable Sin. He must perforce pitilessly scrutinize his characters without being able to share with them their imperfect humanity, to acknowledge his kinship with their experience and destiny.

This crisis in Hawthorne's understanding of the limits of his art is retold in Zenobia's legend of "The Silvery Veil" (Chapter 13). This is the story of Theodore (Coverdale) who might have released from thralldom a mysterious Veiled Lady (Priscilla) by kissing her without looking under the veil. Being too cold and skeptical to surrender himself, he insists on raising the veil first. The Veiled Lady remains in thralldom, and Theodore is doomed to regret his cautious scruple for the rest of his life. So, Hawthorne seems to confess, have I failed to release my characters, especially the pallid feminine ones like Priscilla, into life.

It is clear, then, that although Hawthorne was a superb writer of romance and a considerable novelist from any point of view, he was aware that his romances, as he himself insisted on calling them, proceeded in part from his final failure to take a place among the great novelists.

WILLIAM VAN O'CONNOR [1915–66] taught at the University of Minnesota and at the University of California at Davis. He published numerous books, including *The Tangled Fire of William Faulkner* (1954). The essay on Hawthorne and Faulkner was first published in 1957 in *The Virginia Quarterly Review*. In *The Grotesque*, the volume in which the essay reappeared, O'Connor included "The Hawthorne Museum"—a fantasy in dialogue combining personal reminiscence and critical commentary.

Hawthorne and Faulkner: Some Common Ground

WILLIAM VAN O'CONNOR

Students of the American novel and especially the apologists for the fiction of Henry James have frequently pointed to this passage in his biographical and critical study of Hawthorne:

> There is a phrase in the preface to his novel of *Transformation [The Marble Faun]*, which must have lingered in the minds of many Americans who have tried to write novels and to lay the scene of them in the western world. "No author, without a trial, can conceive of the difficulty of writing a romance about a country where there is no shadow, no antiquity, no mystery, no picturesque and gloomy wrong, nor anything but a commonplace prosperity, in broad and simple daylight, as is happily the case with my dear native land."

But Hawthorne managed to find "gloomy wrongs" in the history of his own Salem, and he knew these "gloomy wrongs" had a way of living on into the "simple daylight" of the present. There is another passage, less frequently quoted, in James's study that puts Hawthorne's assets in the way of time and place very well:

> History, as yet, has left in the United States but so thin and impalpable a deposit that we very soon touch the hard substratum of nature; and nature itself, in the western world, has the peculiarity of seeming rather crude and immature. The very air looks new and young; the light of the sun seems fresh and

The Grotesque: An American Genre and Other Essays (Carbondale, 1962) 59–77.

innocent, as if it knew as yet but weariness of shining . . . I doubt whether English observers would discover any very striking trace of it in the ancient town of Salem. Still, with all respect to a York and a Shrewsbury, to a Toledo and a Verona, Salem has a physiognomy in which the past plays a more important part than the present. It is of course a very recent past; but one must remember that the dead of yesterday are not more alive than those of a century ago.

Nathaniel Hawthorne's family relationship with Salem was of even longer standing than a century. Major William Hathorne (Nathaniel inserted the *w*) came out to the Puritan settlement about 1630, belonging to the band of John Winthrop. Major William was apparently made of the right stuff for the occasion, doing his duty in disposing both of Indians and Quakers. William became a magistrate of the town of Salem, and he figures in the history of New England as having ordered "Anne Coleman and four of her friends" to be publicly whipped through Salem, Boston, and Dedham. Nathaniel refers to this ancestor in his Introduction to *The Scarlet Letter:*

> The figure of that first ancestor, invested by family tradition with a dim and dusky grandeur, was present to my boyish imagination as far back as I can remember. It still haunts me, and induces a sort of home-feeling with the past, which I scarcely claim in reference to the present, phase of the town. I seem to have a stronger claim to a residence here on account of this grave, bearded and sable-cloaked, and steeple-crowned progenitor—who came so early, with his Bible and his sword, and trod the unworn street with such a stately port, and made so large a figure as a man of war and peace—a stronger claim than for myself, whose name is seldom heard and my face hardly known. He was a soldier, legislator, judge; he was a ruler in the church; he had all the Puritanic traits, both good and evil. He was likewise a bitter persecutor, as witness the Quakers, who have remembered him in their histories, and relate an incident of his hard severity towards a woman of their sect which will last longer, it is to be feared, than any of his better deeds, though these were many.

William's son John, a colonel, is even more conspicuous in Salem history because of his part in the burning of witches. To the comments quoted above, Nathaniel adds that the condemning of the witches probably left such a stain "that his old dry bones in the Charter Street burial ground must still retain it, if they have not crumbled merely to dust." In the third generation the family fortunes fell off. Several generations of Hathornes lived on in Salem without contributing in any luminous way to its history. But gradually the family took to the sea, thereby retrieving something of the place in the world that had been lost. Throughout the eighteenth century the Hathornes were professional seamen. Nathaniel said of them: "From father to son, for above a hundred years, they followed the sea; a gray-headed shipmaster, in each generation, retiring from the quarter-deck to the homestead, while a boy of fourteen took the hereditary place before the mast, confronting the salt spray and the gale which had blustered against his sire and grandsire." The last of the shipmasters, Nathaniel Hathorne, died in Surinam in 1808, leaving behind him in Salem a widow, two daughters, and a son, also named Nathaniel.

In this same Introduction, Nathaniel Hawthorne wrote this about his two early ancestors:

> Either of these stern and black-browed Puritans would have thought it quite a sufficient retribution for his sins that after so long a lapse of years the old trunk of the family tree, with so much venerable moss upon it, should have borne, at its topmost bough, an idler like myself. No aim that I have ever cherished would they recognize as laudable; no success of mine, if my life, beyond its domestic scope, had ever been brightened by success, would they deem otherwise than worthless, if not positively disgraceful. "What is he?" murmurs one gray shadow of my forefathers to the other. "A writer of story-books! What kind of a business in life, what manner of glorifying God, or being serviceable to mankind in its day and generation, may that be? . . . And yet, let them scorn me as they will, strong traits of their nature have intertwined themselves with mine.

Of Salem itself, he says he has felt involved in its life as though he were touched by a spell. "It is no matter that the place is joyless for him; that he is weary of the old wooden houses, the mud and the dust, the dead level of site and sentiment, the chill east wind, and the chillest of social atmospheres,—all these and whatever faults besides he may see or imagine, are nothing to the purpose. The spell survives, and just as powerfully as if the natal spot were an earthly paradise."

William Faulkner also lived under the spell of his own family's history and the history of his own town, Oxford. In the family and the local histories were lives lived as high romance, and there were "gloomy wrongs" aplenty. Faulkner's great grandfather, William C. Falkner (William Faulkner, like Nathaniel Hawthorne, was responsible for adding a letter to his name) was probably the most fascinating figure living in North Mississippi during the pre- and post-Civil War periods. A picaresque novel could be written about his life: the journey as a young half-orphaned boy from Tennessee to Mississippi in search of an uncle, finding the uncle in jail on a murder charge, the boy studying law in his uncle's office, fighting as a first lieutenant in the Mexican War, organizing a Mississippi regiment during the Civil War and fighting as its colonel at Harper's Ferry and the first battle of Manassas, being demoted by the will of his men because of his excessive discipline, returning to Mississippi and organizing a group of rangers, serving under General Bedford Forrest, becoming the founder of the first railroad company in North Mississippi, writing successful romantic novels, marrying the girl he had first met as a little boy in search of his uncle, being involved in duels, and dying at the hands of a man who had once been his partner and whom he had recently defeated for a seat in the state legislature. There is a life-sized monument erected to him facing his railroad. . . . It is all there as a string of events for an episodic romantic novel. Faulkner has never written it out in this form, but he has used parts of it in various ways, especially in *Sartoris* and *The Unvanquished*. In *Sartoris*, William C's murder takes this form:

> It showed on John Sartoris' brow, the dark shadow of fatality and doom, that night when he sat beneath the candles in the dining room and turned the wineglass in his fingers while he talked to his son. The railroad was finished, and that day he had been elected to the state legislature after a hard and bitter fight, and doom lay on his brow and weariness.
> "And so," he said, "Redlaw will kill me tomorrow, for I shall be unarmed. I'm tired of killing men. . . . Pass the wine Bayard. . . ."
> And the next day he was dead.

There is this highly romantic passage about the family at the end of the novel: "For there is death in the sound of it (the name of Sartoris) and a glamorous fatality, like silver pennons downrushing at sunset, or a dying fall of horns along the road to Roncevaux."

The view that the family is fated to suffer glamorous fatalities is developed at length in *Sartoris*, but the family's coming down in the world (the Falkner family did come down, although not drastically) is treated with a tone of great *gloom* in other places, especially, one must feel, when they are identified, or partially identified, with the twentieth-century Compsons. It is relevant that at an early point in his career Faulkner was commonly called Count No Count by his fellow townsmen.

As a place to live, Oxford is pleasant enough. Faulkner once wrote a letter in which he said he was sorry for all those millions of New Yorkers because they could not live in Oxford. Phil Stone, a lifelong friend of Faulkner's, has described it as a spot out of the contemporary mad rush, as a place for those who enjoy the savor of things. It is not far, he says, to any local landmark that recalls legendary days. It is, of course, the legendary side that has interested Faulkner. In Oxford one could also know gloom and terror. There was the gloom that had settled over a defeated people, and there was the terror of sudden violences, most frequently violence between white and black. There was the old jail, the courthouse, and a few ante-bellum houses (scratched on a pane of glass in one of them Faulkner has read: "U. S. Grant 1862"). For Faulkner all of this has held the same sort of interest that the Charter St. Burial Ground, Gallows Hill, and the Custom House held for Nathaniel Hawthorne.

There are undoubtedly many differences between the New England Puritans and the North Mississippi Presbyterians, but as the former are represented in *The Scarlet Letter* and the latter in *Light in August* they have at least one characteristic in common: their minds and imaginations are thoroughly moralized. In each novel, human weakness and the need to sympathize with and to forgive are played off against an iron-like rigidity and lack of sympathy. Presumably Hawthorne's reading about his Puritan forebears gave him his image of their society, and presumably Faulkner felt that there is (or was) enough truth in his view of the Calvinistic part of his society to justify examining it in relation to the Negro problem.

Harry Bamford Parkes, in an essay entitled "The Puritan Heresy" (*Hound and Horn*, v—1932—173—74), says that the Puritans were plain men with little capacity for mysticism and no talent for speculation:

> The sign of election was not an inner assurance; it was a sober decision to trust in Christ and obey God's law. Those

who made this sober decision might feel reasonably confident that they had received God's grace; it was God, without human cooperation, who caused the sober decision to be made. But in actual practice this doctrine had the effect of unduly magnifying man's ability to save himself, as much as Calvin's conception had unduly minimized it; conversion was merely a choice to obey a certain code of rules, and did not imply any emotional change, any love of God, or for holiness, or any genuine religious experience; religion in other words was reduced to mere morality.

Parkes's comment gives sanction to Hawthorne's view that the Puritans were harsh and cold in their religion and their conduct. It does not account for the place, however slight, he gives to their belief in the mercy of God.

Hawthorne presents the Puritans as "iron men." At one point in the narrative he says the spiritual leaders "were fortified in themselves by an iron framework of reasoning." And in one of the most obviously symbolic scenes, when Hester goes to Governor Bellingham's house to beg him not to take Pearl away from her, the mother and child see themselves grotesquely mirrored in a steel breastplate:

> Little Pearl—who was greatly pleased with the gleaming armor as she had been with the glittering frontispiece of the house—spent some time looking into the polished mirror of the breastplate.
> "Mother," cried she, "I see you here. Look! Look!"
> Hester looked, by way of humoring the child and she saw that, owing to the peculiar effect of this convex mirror, the scarlet letter was represented in exaggerated and gigantic proportions, so as to be greatly the most prominent feature of her appearance. In truth, she seemed absolutely hidden behind it. Pearl pointed, also, at a similar picture in the headpiece; smiling at her mother, with the elfish intelligence that was so familiar an expression on her small physiognomy.

Hawthorne is implying that the treatment of Hester is itself grotesque and that the way she lives causes the elfin or unnatural ways of little Pearl.

Hawthorne also makes the point that Hester's exclusion from the society has given her a good understanding of it. From her perspective, the citizens of the colony, and especially its leaders, are far too rigid and unforgiving. She believes in the possibility of escape to Europe, for herself, for Dimmesdale, and for Pearl, and she almost communicates her hope to Dimmesdale. The following is an exchange between Hester and the minister:

> ". . . And what has thou to do with all these iron men and their opinions? They have kept thy better part in bondage too long already!"
> "It cannot be!" answered the minister, listening as if he were called upon to realize a dream. "I am powerless to go! Wretched and sinful as I am, I have no other thought than to drag out my earthly existence in the sphere where Providence hath placed me. Lost as my soul is, I would still do what I may for other human souls! I dare not quit my post, though an unfaithful sentinel, whose sure reward is death and dishonor, when his dreary watch shall come to an end."

For a moment, however, Dimmesdale is made to believe that escape is possible. But to escape, for him, means escape into sin—and on his way home from the forest meeting with Hester he sees himself as a member of the devil's party. Dimmesdale, a true Puritan, is unable until the very end of his life to believe that God could be merciful to him.

A major theme of *The Scarlet Letter* is that an excessive commitment to virtue, which was characteristic of the Puritans, gives rise to the spirit of persecution. There is a direct relationship between the rigid righteousness of the Puritans and the profound unhappiness and suffering in the lives of Hester Prynne and Arthur Dimmesdale. There was little or no place in the Puritan system for the idea of man as sinful and in need of forgiveness. On the contrary, they were obsessed with evil and with the need to suppress it.

Joe Christmas, the protagonist of *Light in August*, is also the victim of righteous zealots. Eupheus Hines, his grandfather, persecutes him out of a mad conviction that he, as God's agent, has been ordered to watch over him and to witness his destruction. Hines believes that God is preoccupied with bitchery and fornication and that the birth of Joe Christmas was His abomination. He is not unlike Roger Chillingworth in that he hovers at the edge of a human life relishing further and further signs of anguish and despair. Hines' own hatred of Negroes is insanely rationalized as a part of God's will. The terrible irony, of course, is that he persecutes in the name of Deity.

Simon McEachern, another of the zealots, unwittingly taught Joe Christmas to reject any human sympathy or impulse toward charity. A stern Presbyterian, he rejects any temptation to indulge the flesh. Even his gifts to the young Christmas are given in the form of opportunities to improve himself. When McEachern punishes him, as he did on one memorable occasion, for failure to learn his catechism, the punishment is given in a cold, implacable way. McEachern's "voice was not unkind. It was not human, personal, at all." Like Hines, he sees himself as God's agent. When he pursues Joe to a dance hall he is a "representative of a wrathful and retributive Throne." He is obsessed with the need to punish and to persecute—and always in the name of virtue.

Joanna Burden, New Englander by descent, is the daughter of Nathaniel Burden and the granddaughter of Calvin Burden. She too is incapable of sympathy. Christmas knows that her assistance to Negroes arises not out of charity or any acceptance of them as persons but out of a grim sense of duty. Her mind and imagination are fascinated by corruption, and when she fornicates with Christmas she feels herself in the very glare of "the fire of the New England biblical hell." Again, when she orders him to pray with her, she says it is God, not she, who is commanding him to pray. Even her attempt to murder him is God's doing. For her, like the others, religion offers neither solace nor forgiveness: It witnesses the filth and corruption of the human being.

Even the community, as Faulkner presents it, suffers from an inability to accept and forgive human weakness. Gail Hightower, separated like Hester from his fellow townsmen, says that their religion forbids them to forgive even themselves. Their pent up fury needs violent expression. But since they must act in the name of virtue, they will murder Christmas with a grim righteousness. "And they will do it gladly, gladly.... Since to pity him would be to admit self-doubt and to hope for and need pity themselves." (There is a moment in Hightower's life when he is a sort of Hawthorne character in that he is tempted to isolate himself from his fellows. Isolation is also one of the themes in *As I Lay Dying*.)

Both novels, *The Scarlet Letter* and *Light in August*, are concerned with the excesses of the thoroughly moralized imagination, and they are peopled, for the most part, by men and women committed to a vision of human conduct that is dark with a guilt that is not to be forgiven.

Henry James summarized what he conceived to be the intention behind *The House of the Seven Gables*: "Evidently, however, what Hawthorne designed to represent was not the struggle between an old society and a new, for in this case he would have given the old one a better chance; but simply, as I have said, the shrinkage and extinction of a family." Possibly this remark tells us that James was a little more inclined to reverence the past, even the Puritan past, than was Hawthorne. *The House of the Seven Gables* does describe the disintegration of a family, but thematically it says, over and over again, that the past lives on into the present. Maule's curse—that God give the Pyncheons blood to drink—is merely a part of the amusing paraphernalia of the novel; the real curse, which is in the blood and bone of the Pyncheons, is their desire for money, position, and "family." Clifford Pyncheon says that almost all men suffer from this obsession: "What we call real estate—the solid ground to build a house on—is the broad foundation on which nearly all the guilt of this world rests. A man will commit almost any wrong,—he will heap up an immense pile of wickedness, as hard as granite, and which will weigh as heavily upon his soul, to eternal ages,—only to build a great gloomy, dark chambered mansion, for himself to die in, and his posterity to be miserable in." Even Holgrave, the young radical, admits that this conservative impulse is in him. When he proposes marriage to Phoebe she tells him he is too unsettling for her. "You will lead me out of my own quiet path." Holgrave denies that he will: "It will be otherwise than you forbode. The world owes all its onward impulses to men ill at ease. The happy man inevitably confines himself within ancient limits. I have a presentiment that, hereafter, it will be my lot to set out trees, to make fences,—perhaps, even, in due time, to build a house for another generation,—in a word to conform myself to laws, and the peaceful practice of society. Your poise will be more powerful than any oscillating tendency of mine." In his famous preface to the novel Hawthorne spelled out his theme, saying the "moral" of his tale is that the wrongdoing of one generation lives on into succeeding generations, and, further, it is folly for one generation to tumble down "an avalanche of ill-gotten gold, or real estate on the heads of an unfortunate posterity." The point about the Pyncheon family then is that they, at least the dominant male members of it, are obsessively concerned with money and position, and that they brook no opposition.

A possible consequence of the family's sense of its position is that decay may set in, as it does in the case of Hepzibah. She is alone in the ruined old house and at the very end of her resources before she can bring herself to open a shop. When she says it is now necessary for her to give up her status as a lady, Holgrave tells her she is suffering no great loss:

> Let it go! You are the better without it. I speak frankly, my dear Miss Pyncheon! for are we not friends? I look upon this as one of the fortunate days of our life. It ends an epoch and begins one. Hitherto, the life-blood has been gradually chilling in your veins as you sat aloof, within your circle of gentility, while the rest of the world was fighting out its battle with one kind of necessity or another. Henceforth, you will at least have the sense of healthy and natural effort for a purpose, and of lending your strength—be it great or small—to the united struggle of mankind. This is success,—all the success that anybody meets with!

At one point in the novel, she is described as having spent so many years in the old house that "her very brain was impregnated with the dry-rot of its timbers." Her brother Clifford, with twenty years of prison life behind him, is also in an advanced state of decay. He is a sybarite with very few powers of self-discipline. Even the good fortune of their inheriting the estate of the villainous Judge Jaffrey Pyncheon, as they do at the novel's end, has a partially melancholy quality in that she and her brother are well advanced in years and the molds of their characters are set. Possibilities of health and vitality are suggested by the marriage of Phoebe and Holgrave. All four willingly depart from the seven gabled old house that had witnessed so much evil, so much avarice and ambition.

In Faulkner's stories it is everywhere evident that he is concerned with the way the past lives on into the present. Two of the novels that show this, *Absalom, Absalom!* and *The Sound and the Fury*, bear some comparison with *The House of the Seven Gables*. In *Absalom, Absalom!* Faulkner uses the word "iron" in the same way Hawthorne does, both of them using it to suggest the rigidity of their characters and of the mores by which they live; Hawthorne makes much of the Puritan heritage of the Pyncheons, and Faulkner makes much of the Mississippi Presbyterian heritage, which he frequently contrasts with New Orleans Catholicism. Thomas Sutpen is like the dominant male Pyncheons in his obsessive desire for a family line and for position in the community. No one could be more ruthless than he in using people, as he uses the Coldfields, and the Joneses, for his ends, and no one could be more tenacious. Sutpen leaves ruin everywhere, even on into the generations following him. But the Sutpen story has larger social implications than the story of the Pyncheons. The Pyncheon family is ingrown, but the Sutpens, in their rigid aversion to miscegenation, are guilty of spiritual incest. Quentin Compson, the narrator, knows this is more than Sutpen's story, that it is his own and his region's. If one will, he knows that slavery was a curse that is being slowly worked out and expiated. There is the passage, frequently quoted, in which Quentin answers Shreve McCaslin's question "why do you hate the South?" "I don't hate it . . . *I don't hate it* he thought, panting in the cold air, the iron New England dark; *I don't, I don't! I don't hate it! I don't hate it!*" Quentin Compson is a victim of his heritage. He knows that in having pieced together and understood Sutpen's story he has learned something very important about the ambitions and family pride that are nurtured in his own Southern heritage. Both Hawthorne and Faulkner may be said to have ambiguous feelings, of liking and repugnance, for their heritages.

There are also certain connections between *The Sound and the Fury* and *The House of the Seven Gables* in that both have characters who, unhappy at the decline of their family from its once eminent position, live in genteel decay, and both have plots which are resolved when there is a repudiation of the decay. (For our purposes here, it is beside the point that Hawthorne's story may be said to have a "happy ending" and that Faulkner's does not, although to say that it has an "unhappy ending" would require some qualification.) The Compson family is narcissistic, a fact symbolized by Quentin Compson's relation to his sister Candace, of which more in a moment. Jason Compson III is an alcoholic lawyer who sits in his office writing satiric verses about his fellow townsmen and contemplating the gradual loss of Compson's Mile, the land owned by his eminent forebears. Unlike his son Quentin, who wants to retrieve some sense of purpose and honor, Jason believes in nothing at all. Mrs. Compson is a little like Hepzibah but much more egregiously committed to her gentility. She does not, for example, understand how God can allow indignities to be heaped upon one of her family origins, she is ashamed of her idiot son and changes his name from Maury (her brother's name) to Benjamin, and, because of her rationalizing about her dignity, she allows her son Jason IV to cheat her out of money sent to her by Candace. Jason IV, incidentally, is a vicious character who totally repudiates everything the family ever stood for. Finally the family disintegrates, their pride and ambitions ridiculed, ignored or forgotten. The strength that remains is with a servant, the Negress Aunt

Dilsey. The Compson family suggest another theme common to both writers, incest.

The Marble Faun, though successful in much of its detail and in the way it evokes a sense of Rome, moves uneasily between the poles of reality and fantasy. One is never quite certain about Hawthorne's intentions. An important clue to them seems to lie in his references to the tragedy of Beatrice Cenci, the girl who assisted in the murder of her father after he had (or was said to have) committed incest with her. Hilda, the innocent young New England painter, sits before what is identified as Guido's *Beatrice Cenci* until she has thoroughly memorized the picture and is able to recreate it on her own canvas. In the chapter entitled "Beatrice" Miriam, the tragic young woman friend of Hilda, sits admiring the skill with which the picture has been transcribed, and Hilda is "startled to observe that her friend's expression had become almost exactly that of the portrait." During the same visit Miriam asks that Hilda deliver a packet for her to the Palazzo Cenci—and both of them discuss the story of Beatrice Cenci. (Subsequently we are shown the old palace of the Cenci as the "paternal abode of Beatrice.") In a later chapter, "Miriam and Hilda," there is further discussion of the copy Hilda has made, and on this occasion Hilda, seeing herself reflected in the mirror, thinks that she too has taken on the expression of Beatrice. Hawthorne assures the reader that Hilda, purely innocent, is suffering from her knowledge of Miriam's guilt: She had seen a look in Miriam's eyes—"a look of hatred, triumph, vengeance, and, as it were, joy at some unhoped for relief"—that asked Donatello to free her from her pursuer and persecutor. In the postscript or conclusion that Hawthorne added to the novel, Kenyon is asked what Miriam's last name was—and though the question goes unanswered the implication seems to be that she is a Cenci or at least related to them, and, further, that she was betrothed to a man who was himself either a Cenci or related to them. The most direct evidence for this inference is in the chapter entitled "The Peasant and the Contadina." It is in this chapter too that we are given various reasons why Miriam repudiated the marriage that had been arranged for her. Among them is this: "Moreover, the character of her destined husband would have been a sufficient and insuperable objection; for it betrayed traits so evil, so treacherous and vile, and yet so strangely subtle, as could only be accounted for by the insanity which often develops itself in old, close-kept races of men, when long unmixed with newer blood." (Possibly one may say that this theme was related in Hawthorne's mind to his condemnation of a man cutting himself off from his fellows.) This quotation would seem to suggest the point behind all these references to the Cenci family. The ingrown-ness of these old Roman families is itself a kind of incest. And by identifying Miriam with the Cenci Hawthorne was able to draw upon all the overtones of horror associated with that family. (Philip Young suggested the incest theme in relation to Hawthorne and Faulkner and also that Melville's *Pierre*—1852—suggested this use of the Cenci story in *The Marble Faun*—1860.)

Faulkner too uses incest as symbolic of ingrown-ness in two different novels, *The Sound and the Fury* and *Absalom, Absalom!* In *The Sound and the Fury* Quentin Compson is preoccupied with his sister's body, or, rather, as Faulkner put it in the appendix to *The Portable Faulkner*, he was preoccupied with the idea of incest. Most of the Compsons are sick with self-concern, their pride is empty pretentiousness, and they are unable to live vigorously. Quentin's preoccupation with incest (which Faulkner said Quentin did not actually want to commit) suggests a family that is narcissistic. The family's overinsistence upon its honor and dignity and upon no longer having its rightful eminence in the community is an extreme form of self love. Incest is the appropriate symbol for this diseased state of mind.

In *Absalom, Absalom!* Henry Sutpen's willingness to condone incest—to allow his half brother to marry his sister Judith—has a certain similarity to the incest theme in *The Sound and the Fury*. When Henry talks with his father Colonel Sutpen about Charles Bon's demand that he be allowed to marry Judith, he does not know that Charles is partly Negro, but he does know that the South is hovering on the brink of defeat, which he sees as shame and degradation. He says: "When you don't have God and honor and pride, nothing else matters except that you don't even care if it was defeat or victory." Henry condones incest as an ironic final mark of their shame and degradation. It is after he learns that Charles is colored that Henry shoots him to prevent the marriage. It was as Charles insisted, "the miscegenation, not the incest" which he could not bear. The reader then understands that the incest was not merely a bitter recognition of defeat but, further, though unwittingly on Henry's part, a symbol of a society that put its humanity above other humanity. Having set themselves above the Negroes, Henry and his kind had already committed spiritual incest.

It is clear that in all three novels, *The Marble Faun, The Sound and the Fury*, and *Absalom, Absalom!* incest is used as a symbol of inward-turning. And Hawthorne and Faulkner have related it to evils that have their origins in a diseased sort of self-centeredness.

In *The Marble Faun* Hawthorne makes a number of observations about Catholicism, and perhaps one may say that Hilda's ambiguous attitude toward it, admiring and yet resisting it out of an allegiance to her Puritan heritage, is not unlike Hawthorne's. From her knowledge of the Roman churches and especially, as Hawthorne has it, of St. Peter's she found it "was impossible to doubt that multitudes of people found their spiritual advantage in it, who would find none at all in our own formless mode of worship." Hilda sees a young man before a shrine "writhing, wringing his hands," who finally kneels to weep and pray. Hawthorne's comment is this: "If this youth had been a Protestant, he would have kept all that torture pent up in his heart, and let it burn there till it seared him into indifference." After her visit to the confessional, Hilda tells Kenyon that the more she sees of Catholicism the more she wonders "at the exuberance that adapts itself to all the demands of human infirmity." But she adds that she is put off by the fallibility of the Church's ministers.

Faulkner, in *Absalom, Absalom!*, stresses Catholicism's acceptance of fallibility and human weakness, and contrasts its capacity for compromise with the Puritan's stern inflexibility. Young Henry Sutpen is seen thus in Catholic New Orleans: "I can imagine him, with his puritan heritage—that heritage peculiarly Anglo-Saxon—of fierce proud mysticism and that ability to be ashamed of ignorance and inexperience, in that city foreign at once feminine and steel-hard—this grim humorless yokel out of a granite heritage where even the houses, let alone clothing and conduct, are built in the image of a jealous and sadistic Jehovah, put suddenly down in a place whose denizens had created their All-Powerful and the supporting hierarchy—chorus of beautiful saints and handsome angels in the image of their houses and personal ornaments and voluptuous lives." Henry Sutpen is a stern literalist, almost as inflexible as his father, Thomas Sutpen. Most of the novel's tension is in terms of Sutpen's inflexibility and Charles Bon's needing and asking for human sympathy, acceptance and understanding. It is clear that Faulkner is saying that the Sutpen attitude and the Bon attitude have a great deal to do with their respective societies and religions.

One may point to these parallels or connections between Hawthorne's novels and Faulkner's novels without implying any very direct borrowings on the latter's part. And of course the tone of each novel is generated by its own subject matter and respective treatment. One may claim, however, both some similarity of temperament, and some knowledge on Faulkner's part of Hawthorne's work. Because of these factors and especially because of the similarity between Hawthorne's New England and Faulkner's Mississippi one can understand the very considerable similarities in their work. (Faulkner's first book was entitled *The Marble Faun*. Knowing that Phil Stone, the Oxford lawyer and friend of Faulkner, put up the money to publish it, I wrote to ask him what he thought about the connections between Faulkner and Hawthorne. The following is his reply: "Bill read some Hawthorne, but I don't think he is extremely well read in anything. I think I still have two copies of *The Marble Faun* but the title had nothing to do with Hawthorne at all. I know because I am the man that put this title on it.")

Perhaps one should add to all the above the observation that Hawthorne and Faulkner are both highly stylized writers. In each of them one finds a rhetorical style, the rigid selection proper to fiction as an art form, situations that are sparely and sharply dramatic, and characters that push away from commonplace reality toward the symbolic. Each as artist is properly respectful of the principle of aesthetic distance. It is true that Hawthorne is frequently deliberately allegorical, whereas Faulkner is not, and it is equally true that the latter writes a much more involuted style. On the other hand, both have what might be called the will to rhetoric, with the consequence that there are descriptive passages in the works of each writer that stick in a reader's memory. For example, this from "My Kinsman, Major Molineux":

> He was an elderly man, of large and majestic person, and strong, square features, betokening a steady soul; but steady as it was, his enemies had found means to shake it. His face was pale as death, and far more ghastly; the broad forehead was contracted in his agony, so that his eyebrows formed one grizzled line; his eyes were red and wild, and the foam hung white upon his quivering lip. His whole frame was agitated by a quick and continual tremor, which his pride strove to quell, even in those circumstances of overwhelming humiliation.

And this from "A Rose for Emily":

> Now and then we would see her in one of the downstairs windows—she had evidently shut up the top floor of the house

—like the carven torso of an idol in a niche, looking or not looking at us, we could never tell which. Thus she passed from generation to generation—dear, inescapable, impervious, tranquil, and perverse.

Again, both writers are concerned with legendary and imaginative as much as with realistic materials, knowing that the imagined has its meanings and "tell[s] us something about the human heart." Thus Hawthorne can have the portrait of Colonel Pyncheon staring severely at generations of Pyncheons, can have a hidden panel behind the portrait, can have Alice Pyncheon mesmerized by a member of the Maule clan, and can have the very fowls in the Pyncheon garden become ingrown in spirit and rusty in movements. He is objectifying the spiritual weight of the Pyncheon heritage. And Faulkner can create idiots to suggest the decay of a family, can have a son talking to his father on an unrealistic twilight battlefield of the Civil War, or the great house that has symbolized ambition and family burn garishly to ashes in the night. Both writers respect the rights of the imagination and the rightness for fiction of the highly stylized and the dramatic. It may even be true as with *The Marble Faun* and *The Fable*, that the processes of stylization sometimes go so far that the reader finds an insufficient number of connections with the actual commonplace world.

In conclusion, one might say that of all the sections or areas of the United States, New England and the South are most "regional," both consciously possessing a heritage from their respective pasts. Perhaps a sense of the past invites not merely exploitation of legend but, at times, a sense of gloom. It is true at least that Hawthorne and Faulkner, the American writers who most exploit their own legendary pasts, are also preoccupied with "gloomy wrongs." (For another comparison see Randall Stewart, "Hawthorne and Faulkner," *College English*, xvii—1956—pp. 258–62. Our essays may be said to complement each other.)

HYATT H. WAGGONER [1913–], professor at the University of Kansas City and at Brown University, has written books on contemporary poetry and on Faulkner. His work on Hawthorne includes editions of short stories and of *The House of the Seven Gables*, a brief study of Hawthorne for the University of Minnesota Pamphlet Series, and

"Art and Belief" in *Hawthorne Centenary Essays* (1964). His major contribution is his book *Nathaniel Hawthorne: A Critical Study* (1955), revised in 1963. The most important revision is the chapter on *The Marble Faun* reprinted on pp. 243-57.

From *Nathaniel Hawthorne*

HYATT H. WAGGONER

. . . .

Since ours is an age that has found irony, ambiguity, and paradox to be central not only in literature but in life, it is not surprising that Hawthorne has seemed to us one of the most *modern* of nineteenth-century American writers. The bulk and general excellence of the great outburst of Hawthorne criticism of the past decade attest to his relevance for us. It requires no distortion of him to see him not only as foreshadowing Henry James in his concern for "the deeper psychology" but as first cousin to Faulkner and Robert Penn Warren. In all the essentials, "My Kinsman, Major Molineux" is as "modern" a story as "The Bear." Hawthorne's themes, especially, link him with the writing and sensibility of our time.

Alienation is perhaps the theme he handles with greatest power. "Insulation," he sometimes called it—which suggests not only isolation but imperviousness. It is the opposite of that "osmosis of being" that Warren has written of, that ability to respond and relate to others and the world. Its causes are many and complex, its results simple: it puts one outside the "magic circle" or the "magnetic chain" of humanity, where there is neither love nor reality. It is Hawthorne's image of damnation. Reunion, often imaged by the hearth, is his redemptive cure. Anticipating Archibald MacLeish of *J. B.*, he would have his characters "blow on the coal of the heart." Not "knowing" or "using" but "meeting" others—to borrow Martin Buber's terms—would offer a way back into the magic circle to alienated Chillingworth, Ethan Brand, or Rappaccini.

Contemporary critics have shown an even greater interest in Hawthorne's treatment of initiation. Though he wrote only a few

University of Minnesota Pamphlets on American Writers. Number 23 (Minneapolis, 1962) 15-19.

stories directly concerned with it, several of them are among his greatest and a number of others touch it tangentially. Stories as rich, yet controlled, in meaning as "My Kinsman" are rare in this or any language. Initiated into life's complexity in a dreamlike evening in a strange city, the young man of the story achieves a difficult maturity. But the protagonist of "Young Goodman Brown" is unable to understand or accept the evil revealed to him in the forest of the soul, loses faith in the reality of the good, and lives the rest of his long life in gloomy alienation. The young couple in "The Maypole of Merrymount" are granted a happier outcome, but Giovanni in "Rappaccini's Daughter" is, like Goodman Brown, unable to accept life's ambiguous mixture of good and evil and so cannot understand his Beatrice or gain the salvation her love would grant.

When such initiations as these have happy outcomes, as in "My Kinsman," we are tempted to see them primarily in psychological terms, as dramatizing the process of maturation. When the results are less happy, so that we have a sense chiefly of the cost of losing innocence, we are likely to read them as versions of the Fall, the myth of the expulsion from the Garden. The psychological and the theological readings are perhaps just different ways of looking at the same archetypal story.

Hawthorne at any rate refused to simplify guilt by reducing it either to merely subjective and irrational "guilt feeling" or to wholly objective and external "sin." He concerned himself instead with guilt feelings that have personal and social causes and cures that are objectively real, not merely subjective or irrational, and that imply the reality of moral obligation. His special way of maintaining the ambiguous connection between the psychological, the moral, and the religious is one of the principal reasons why his works seem so relevant to us.

Moral and religious concerns, in short, are almost always central in Hawthorne's work, but Hawthorne's interest in them is primarily subjective and psychological. But his subjectivism is never solipsist and his psychologism never reductive. Rather, they are signs that his concern with matters moral and religious is existential. Like the Existentialist philosophers who articulate the sensibility of our time, Hawthorne is more concerned with the experienced toothache than with orthodontic theory. Like them he explores the nature of existential guilt, relating it to alienation, reunion, and commitment. Like them too he distrusts the claim of objective reason to be able to arrive at humanly relevant truth: his "empiricists" all end unhappily.

We may call such attitudes romantic rather than existential if we wish. Existential philosophy begins with Kierkegaard, in the romantic movement; but Kierkegaard seems more relevant to many today than John Dewey. Romanticism at this depth is still with us, and perhaps always will be, now that unquestioning certainty about life's "essences" seems unlikely ever to return. Not to be existential in the sense in which Hawthorne was is either to be content with positivism or to assume as unquestionable a fixed and absolute order of truth.

But if the first thing we should notice about Hawthorne is his "modernity," his immediate relevance to us and our concerns, the second thing, if we are to avoid the distortion of seeing in him only our own image, is the way in which he is *not* one of us. It has been said that he was an eighteenth-century gentleman living in the nineteenth century, and the remark has enough truth in it to be useful to us at this point.

His style, for instance, though at its best a wonderfully effective instrument for the expression of his sensibility, is likely to strike us as not nearly so modern as Thoreau's. It was slightly old-fashioned even when he wrote it. It is very deliberate, with measured rhythms, marked by formal decorum. It is a public style and, as we might say, a "rhetorical" one—though of course all styles are rhetorical in one sense or another. It often prefers the abstract or generalized to the concrete or specific word. Compared to what the writers of handbooks, under the influence of modernist literature, have taught us to prefer—the private, informal, concrete, colloquial, imagistic—Hawthorne's style can only be called pre-modern.

But it is not only style in this narrow sense that marks Hawthorne as a nineteenth-century writer. Apart from that aspect of his writing that we may summarize under the general heading of his symbolism, his whole procedure as a fictionist is pre-modern—which is to say, pre-Flaubert and pre-James. He is one of the most regularly intrusive of intrusive authors. The basic rule of post-Jamesian fiction, reduced by handbook writers to a simple inviolable formula, has been "Don't tell, show!" Hawthorne both tells and shows—tells not simply in his characteristic final moral comment but all the way through.

Ethan Brand, for instance, seeing the absurdity of his situation, bursts into laughter. Hawthorne, having presented the image, then comments: "Laughter, when out of place, mistimed, or bursting forth from a disordered state of feeling, may be the most terrible modulation of the human voice." Hawthorne has lost something in immediacy, and gained something in meaning. Later in the story, in his summary of Brand's career, he does not "show" at all, he merely tells: "Thus Ethan Brand became a fiend. He began to be so from the moment that his moral nature had ceased to keep the pace of improvement with his intellect." "He had lost his hold of the magnetic chain of humanity."

In its insistence that the author never appear in his own pages, that the image alone do all the work, modern fiction has paralleled Imagist poetry. Hawthorne knows nothing of this. For him, fiction was a way of exploring life to find meaning. Not being post-Jamesian, he thought he had a right to bring out and underline the meanings his images revealed. The classic forms of fiction had always permitted this.

If Hawthorne had thought he needed any excuse for his intrusive comments, he might well have said what Faulkner has said of *his* writing, that he wrote "to uplift men's hearts . . . [to] say No to death." Hawthorne wants to strengthen and encourage man, to help him to live in a world in which the ways of Providence are mostly unintelligible.

. . . .

The Marble Faun

HYATT H. WAGGONER

Hawthorne's whole career had prepared him to write *The Marble Faun*, his "story of the fall of man." Loss of innocence, initiation into the complexities of experience in a world of ambiguously mingled good and evil, experiences of guilt so obscurely related to specific acts as to seem more "original" and necessary than avoidable, these had been his subjects in story after story. Eden had never been far in the background, whether he was writing of life in a decayed mansion in Salem or of the attempts of reformers to undo the fall in a utopian community. The analogy with the

Hawthorne: A Critical Study. Revised Edition (Cambridge, Mass., 1963) 209–25.

Garden of Biblical myth had supplied the basic metaphor in "Rappaccini's Daughter." When, just after his marriage, he had experienced a happiness greater than he had ever known before, he inevitably thought of Sophia and himself in the Old Manse as a new Adam and Eve in an unfallen world.

Several of his stories that we generally think of as stories of initiation are equally stories of the fall. Robin's encounter with sin becomes a fortunate fall in "My Kinsman, Major Molineux." The innocence of this self-reliant and naïve country boy proves inadequate to guide him to his destination through the mazes of the city's streets, but thanks to a kindly Providence, he finds he may rise, after his fall, without the help he sought. Young Goodman Brown's experience in the forest was a less fortunate fall. Whether the evil he found universal there was only a dream, or a mirage contrived by the Devil to destroy him, or a false conclusion based on his inability to see the significance of his being there himself, at any rate he was destroyed by it when he lost faith in the reality of the good. From being an Innocent, he became a Cynic and so was lost because he could not accept the world as it really is. He prepares us for Giovanni in "Rappaccini's Daughter," who cannot accept the ambiguous mixture of good and evil he finds in the garden. Brown's Faith wore pink ribbons until he lost it entirely; it never became mature. So Giovanni first thought Beatrice an angel, then decided she was a fiend, but never could accept her as a human being. The Adamic falls re-enacted by Brown and Giovanni led to no subsequent rise. "My Kinsman" is perhaps the only story Hawthorne ever wrote in which there is a fall that is clearly fortunate. "Roger Malvin's Burial" ends in a reunion with God and man after isolation, to be sure, but whatever "rise" there is here is a very sad one. The vision of life it implies remains tragic.

The last story reminds us of another way in which Hawthorne's career had prepared him to write *The Marble Faun*. Hawthorne had so obscured Reuben's guilt as to make it seem like a general human condition rather than the result of a specific act which he might well have avoided. All men, Hawthorne had implied, rationalize their self interest as Reuben does, and none of us tells all the truth all the time—though in the end our evasions catch up with us, as Reuben's did with him, until at last we are guilty in fact, by a kind of negative choice, as well as by virtue of our sharing the human condition. Our sin, in short, is both "original" and ever-renewed. We are like the later Pyncheons, in part victims of the house, in part perpetrators of fresh sins—until love releases us from our inheritance. Hawthorne was more interested in guilt as a necessary human condition than he was in any specific sinful act. So he treated the central action in *The Marble Faun* in such a way that it is just as impossible to decide that Donatello is really responsible for the murder he committed as it is to decide that Reuben clearly did wrong when he left Roger Malvin to die. Miriam, herself a victim of a dreadful evil, is at least as responsible as Donatello, and the murdered man both invited and deserved his fate. All Rome, all history, made the crime inevitable, and its spreading effects leave no one untouched, not even the spotless Hilda. This murder is no ordinary crime but a re-enactment of the archetypal fall.

2

If Hawthorne had told this story many times before, he had never told it quite so directly or with so conscious an effort to determine its ultimate significance. It had generally been in the background, perhaps not consciously intended at all, as in "Young Goodman Brown," or suggested in the form of enriching allusions, as in *The House of the Seven Gables*. Now it was made the explicit subject—the too explicit subject, the modern reader is likely to decide. When innocent, faun-like Donatello, who has grown up in a rural Arcadia where he has been "close to nature," encounters evil in the corrupt city and ends by committing a murder, but is apparently deepened and matured by the experience, Miriam sees the analogy with Eden and asks the question it prompts:

> "The story of the fall of man! Is it not repeated in our romance of Monte Beni? And may we follow the analogy yet further? Was that very sin,—into which Adam precipitated himself and all his race,—was it the destined means by which, over a long pathway of toil and sorrow, we are to attain a higher, brighter, and more profound happiness, than our lost birthright gave?"

Should we think of Adam's sin as a Fortunate Fall, and therefore perhaps of each man's re-enactment of the Fall as equally fortunate? Was Donatello's murder, in fact, a blessing in disguise? "Was it a means of education, bringing a simple and imperfect nature to a point of feeling and intelligence which it could have reached under no other discipline?" If sin is not educational, how else account for the fact that God permits it?

Kenyon, to whom Miriam addresses these questions, replies

that he finds this line of speculation "too dangerous." He will not follow her into such "unfathomable abysses." Yet a little later, contemplating the significance of the fact that Donatello since his crime has perceptibly changed for the better, he *does* follow her:

> "Here comes my perplexity," continued Kenyon. "Sin has educated Donatello, and elevated him. Is sin, then,—which we deem such a dreadful blackness in the universe,—is it, like sorrow, merely an element of human education, through which we struggle to a higher and purer state than we could otherwise have attained? Did Adam fall, that we might ultimately rise to a far loftier paradise than his?"

When Hilda demonstrates "the white shining purity" of her nature and the orthodoxy of her religious faith by responding to the sculptor's questions with horror, declaring herself shocked beyond words, he quickly retracts, asks her forgiveness, and declares he never did really believe it. He is in love with Hilda and has no answer ready to give to the question she asks him. "Do not you perceive what a mockery your creed makes, not only of all religious sentiments, but of moral law? and how it annuls and obliterates whatever precepts of Heaven are written deepest within us?"

For once, in this reply to Kenyon, Hilda may seem to the modern reader to demonstrate that moral sensitivity and insight that Hawthorne so emphatically, and to us for the most part so unaccountably, attributes to her. For she seems to have realized that one of the implications of the version of the old idea of the Fortunate Fall that both Miriam and Kenyon have put forth is that, since sin is educational, we *ought* to violate our consciences in order to attain the improvement in us that will result. In effect, whether she knows it or not, she sees that her friends are confusing history and myth. The myth describes the constant human condition: sin is "original" in man's nature, shared by all alike, present even in those not clearly guilty of any specific sin. It has nothing to say about what man ought to do about this fact. Only when it is taken as history does the question arise, Ought we then to imitate Adam and sin deliberately, so that Christ, the Second Adam, may come to redeem us? The idea of the Fortunate Fall arose when devout men contemplated the story of the old and new covenants as interpreted by Christians and felt a need to express their gratitude to God for the way He had brought good out of evil. Man had fallen but God had raised him again. Calamity had turned out, then, because "God so loved the world," to have unforeseeable, fortunate consequences: God sent His only son to die on the cross for our sins. Fortunately, the Atonement does for us what we cannot do for ourselves. The idea of the Fortunate Fall has immense theological implications, but no moral ones at all, or else the wrong ones, just as Hilda says.

The question as posed by Miriam and Kenyon is never resolved in the novel. It could not be without violating both Hawthorne's sense of the truth of life as he understood it and his sense of the limitations of words and rational thought in such areas, his sense of the mystery in which man finds himself. True, Miriam, who implies that she believes the fall *is* fortunate, is a sympathetic character and often speaks for the darker side of Hawthorne's mind, but she cannot be taken as always Hawthorne's spokesman. Hawthorne presents her as warped by her tragic experience even while he gives her his full sympathy. If her view of life is closer to Hawthorne's own than is Hilda's, Hawthorne admired Hilda more and wished he might more fully share her unquestioning faith. Miriam raised a question which Hawthorne too had pondered, and decided, apparently, he could not answer, at least not with a *yes* or a *no*.

Kenyon is much more a spokesman for Hawthorne than is Miriam, and Kenyon too rejects the implication of his own and Miriam's question. A good deal of the time in the novel there is very little distance between Kenyon and Hawthorne. Essentially, Kenyon and Hilda are Nathaniel and Sophia. When Hilda rebukes him for his speculation and he explains that he never really believed it, Kenyon goes on to explain his vagary:

> "But the mind wanders wild and wide; and, so lonely as I live and work, I have neither polestar above nor light of cottage windows here below, to bring me home. Were you my guide, my counsellor, my inmost friend, with that white wisdom which clothes you as a celestial garment, all would go well. O Hilda, guide me home!"

The parallel between this and many of Hawthorne's love letters to Sophia is very close. One of the things Hawthorne must have meant when he declared himself "saved" by his marriage was that he had found Sophia's buoyant faith a needed counterbalance to his own dark questionings. So Kenyon might be wiser in the ways of the world but Hilda, as we are often reminded, was wiser in religious truth. Kenyon might well ask her to guide him home, in

Hawthorne's view of the matter. His refusal to carry on his line of speculation had Hawthorne's approval.

Depending on which aspect of it we look at, the plot either supports or does not support the rejection by Hilda and Kenyon of the idea of the Fortunate Fall. Though Donatello has been matured and humanized by his suffering, he must go to prison. Though Miriam has been ennobled by love, she ends in sad penitence, without hope of happiness with Donatello. Kenyon and Hilda decide to leave Rome, thus in effect putting the problem behind them. The plot gives no clear answer to the largest question explicitly posed by the novel.

3

But perhaps the question itself is illegitimate, impossible to answer. Hawthorne has Kenyon say, after he has looked from Donatello's tower at the landscape mottled with patches of sunlight and shadow and seen it as a symbol of life, "It is a great mistake to try to put our best thoughts into human language. When we ascend into the higher regions of emotion and spiritual enjoyment, they are only expressible by such grand hieroglyphics as these around us." By symbols, in short, and myths. Speaking in his own person as narrator, Hawthorne has already noted the loss now that man has grown beyond the archaic expressiveness of gestures, and "words have been feebly substituted in the place of signs and symbols." What words cannot do, the visual arts sometimes can. Speaking again in his own person, in one of the passages lifted from the Notebooks, Hawthorne says of Sodoma's Christ bound to a pillar that it shows what "pictorial art, devoutly exercised, might effect in behalf of religious truth; involving, as it does, deeper mysteries of revelation, and bringing them closer to man's heart, and making him tenderer to be impressed by them, than the most eloquent words of preacher or prophet." In his first chapter, describing the Faun, who was "neither man nor animal, and yet no monster," Hawthorne has despaired of putting his basic idea into abstract language: "The idea grows coarse as we handle it, and hardens in our grasp." The idea of the Faun, he decides, "may have been no dream, but rather a poet's reminiscence of a period when man's affinity with nature was more strict, and his fellowship with every living thing more intimate and dear." To discover what the novel finally, at its deepest level, means, then, we should turn from a consideration of the questions framed by Miriam and Kenyon to the myths which Hawthorne uses to shape his story.

Almost exactly in the center of his book Hawthorne has placed a chapter he calls simply "Myths." In it he gives us what Miriam, on another occasion, demands of Donatello, "the latest news from Arcady," which is, in effect, that nature has no cure for what ails us. However beautiful the old Arcadian myths are, however sad it is that we have lost our innocence, they are not true any longer in a fallen world. (In Hawthorne's terminology, the old pagan legends are "myths," the Biblical story in Genesis a symbolic truth, perhaps not literally true historically but true as a type of the human condition. He never refers to the Genesis story as a "myth.") Donatello, now that he has known sin, cannot re-enter Arcadia.

The chief substance of the chapter is the legend of Donatello's spring, which one of his ancestors found to be animated by a beautiful maiden, the spirit of the water, with whom he fell in love. On summer days she would cool his brow with her touch or make rainbows around him. Kenyon interrupts the story at this point with a skeptical comment:

> "It is a delightful story for the hot noon of your Tuscan summer . . . But the deportment of the watery lady must have had a most chilling influence in midwinter."

If this criticism seems the product only of the skeptical mind, another is implicit in the story itself. Eventually the dryad refused to appear to her lover, and Donatello explains that her refusal was caused by the effort of his ancestor to wash off a bloodstain in the water. While summer and innocence last, in short, being "close to nature" is perhaps enough; at least, Hawthorne says elsewhere, it is a very beautiful idea. But winter and guilt come, death and sin are in the world, and Arcadianism does not know how to deal with them. Attempting to communicate with the wild creatures as he once had, Donatello calls to them in the "voice and utterance of the natural man," but he is frustrated when a brown lizard "of the tarantula species" makes its appearance. "To all present appearance, this venomous reptile was the only creature that had responded to the young Count's efforts to renew his intercourse with the lower orders of nature." Donatello falls to the ground and Kenyon, alarmed, asks what has happened to him. " 'Death, death!' sobbed Donatello."

Kenyon himself supplies sufficient comment on the legend of the spring: "He understood it as an apologue, typifying the soothing and genial effects of an habitual intercourse with nature, in all ordinary cares and griefs; while, on the other hand, her mild influences fall short in their effect upon the ruder passions, and are altogether powerless in the dread fever-fit or deadly chill of guilt." After a little more talk, the two friends part, Donatello to climb up in his tower once more, Kenyon to go inside to read "an antique edition of Dante." We have met the venomous reptile and heard Donatello's answer to Kenyon before, in Rappaccini's garden, where Hawthorne also alluded to Dante to help us to get our metaphorical bearings. Sin and death have entered the world, to spoil the Arcadian dream. Whether the fall is "fortunate" or not may be impossible to answer, but at least the world we know is no unfallen earthly paradise. Evil is in it, and nature itself offers no satisfactory cure.

The cure, insofar as there is any, lies partly in repentance and love in this world, and partly in the hope of another life. These meanings emerge from the plot considered as symbolic action or myth and from the implications of the leading images with which Hawthorne supports his myth. The plot gives us three of the characters at least, and perhaps by intention four, growing in moral and spiritual stature as they experience sin and suffering. Miriam ceases to suffer in isolation and think only of herself, falls in love with Donatello, and dedicates her life to penitance and to the service of the one she has wronged. Donatello gains in wisdom and understanding, becomes in fact human. Hilda comes down from the tower of her perfect rectitude, repents having turned away Miriam in her need, and becomes human enough to marry Kenyon. All, in fact, come down from the isolation of their towers; all fall in love. That there is no cure for suffering is clear from the careers of Miriam and Donatello, but that suffering and acknowledgment of mutual complicity in guilt are necessary preludes to any redemption possible to man is clear from the careers of all of them.

The "higher hopes" of another life that will rectify the wrongs of this one are implied in Kenyon's deference to Hilda, in his plea that she lead him home, and in Hawthorne's own too often expressed admiration of her. Hilda is "the religious girl" as well as the girl of a shining purity of character, Kenyon the "thinker," potentially the skeptic. Not just Kenyon but the whole novel stands in awe of Hilda, whose precise function is to keep the lamp of religious faith, with its higher hopes, burning. (She can let the flame of the old Catholic lamp go out at the end because she herself in her own person emanates a better and purer light.)

Hilda is supported in her task of guarding religious faith and hope by much of the imagery, sometimes with images that Hawthorne makes very emphatic, sometimes with what seem mere reflexes of his habitual style. I shall give just two examples. At the end of the chapter called "The Owl Tower," in which Kenyon and Donatello have climbed to the top of Donatello's tower and Kenyon has had his vision of the symbolic landscape, Kenyon finds, growing out of the masonry of the tower, seemingly out of the very stone itself, "a little shrub, with green and glossy leaves." Donatello thinks, "If the wide valley has a great meaning, the plant ought to have at least a little one." Kenyon asks Donatello if he sees any meaning here and Donatello says he sees none, but, looking at the plant, he adds, "But here was a worm that would have killed it; an ugly creature, which I will fling over the battlements."

Kenyon does not voice the meaning he sees, and Hawthorne makes no comment. But the context makes reasonably clear what Donatello missed. We are reminded of Melville's "Bartleby the Scrivener," in which, in the Tombs, green grass could be seen by Bartleby if he would only turn his face from the wall. Kenyon's view of the valley has increased his "reliance on His providence" (whereas Donatello has seen only "sunshine on one spot, and cloud in another, and no reason for it in either case"), and he has just explained to Donatello that he "cannot preach": words will not express his "best" thoughts, that is, his religious thoughts. He has seen, as he looked at the earth spread below them, something of the way of "His dealings with mankind." Now, in the rarefied "upper atmosphere" of the tower, he finds a green shrub, the meaning of which he does not even attempt to state for his companion. Green is the traditional color of hope, and the plant is growing in a very unlikely place: "Heaven knows how its seeds had ever been planted . . ." But not only Heaven knew: Hawthorne knew how the seeds of such hope as he cherished had been planted. The chapter ends with Donatello's destruction of the "worm" that would destroy the plant.

My second example comes at the end of chapter three, "Subterranean Reminiscences," in which the four friends have been exploring one of the catacombs, where they "wandered by torchlight through a sort of dream." Hilda and Donatello, both Innocents, find the darkness especially repellent: their experience of life has in no way prepared them for it. Miriam thinks that "the most awful idea connected with the catacombs is their interminable extent, and the possibility of going astray in this labyrinth of darkness . . ." When Kenyon wonders whether in fact anyone has ever been lost in the place, he is told of "a pagan of old Rome, who hid himself in order to spy out the blessed saints, who then dwelt and worshipped in these dismal places." The pagan has been "groping in the darkness" ever since, unable to find his way out.

At this point the party reaches a chapel carved out of the walls and stops to look at it; "and while their collected torches illuminated this one small, consecrated spot, the great darkness spread all round it, like that immenser mystery which envelops our little life, and into which friends vanish from us, one by one." Miriam, it turns out, has "vanished into the great darkness, even while they were shuddering at the remote possibility of such a misfortune." Miriam shares Hilda's strict orthodoxy even less than Kenyon, who at least longs for and admires what is not as much his as he would like it to be. She has something in common with the pagan of old Rome; she is not held by the brightly illuminated consecrated spot. (At it turns out, though, she is more a victim of persecution than an unbeliever.)

We are reminded of the brightly lighted chamber in "Night Sketches," with the cold darkness all around, or of the darkness that seemed to press in on the little company at Blithedale. In the latter case, though, the hope suggested by the warmth and light was a secular one. Here everything about the context unites to suggest a purely "religious" hope—in the sense of a hope for immortality. The darkness into which our friends vanish is the darkness of death. Later, Kenyon will protest the presence of a skull in Donatello's bedroom: "It is absurdly monstrous, my dear friend, thus to fling the dead-weight of our mortality upon our immortal hopes. While we live on earth, 'tis true, we must needs carry our skeletons about with us; but, for Heaven's sake, do not let us burden our spirits with them, in our feeble efforts to soar upward." (Kenyon's higher hopes may have seemed to him feeble, but Hawthorne characterizes him elsewhere as he would have characterized himself, "a devout man in his way.") Those who know the extent of "the blackness that lies beneath us everywhere," who know that we are "dreaming on the edge of a precipice," who know that sinking into nature is equivalent to sinking into the grave and have explored the "dark caverns" of experience, will not need to keep a skull in the bedroom to remind them of man's mortality.

They will be likely to agree with the point of Hawthorne's moral and theological criticism of Sodoma's Siena fresco of Christ bound to a pillar. Hawthorne felt sure the picture sprang from sincere religious feeling: a shallow or worldly man could not have painted it. The picture is "inexpressibly touching" in its portrayal of the weariness and loneliness of the Savior:

You behold Christ deserted both in heaven and earth; that despair is in him which wrung forth the saddest utterance man ever made, "Why hast Thou forsaken me?" Even in this extremity, however, he is still divine . . . He is as much, and as visibly, our Redeemer, there bound, there fainting, and bleeding from the scourge, with the cross in view, as if he sat on his throne of glory in the heavens! Sodoma, in this matchless picture, has done more towards reconciling the incongruity of Divine Omnipotence and outraged, suffering Humanity, combined in one person, than the theologians ever did.

4

The Marble Faun ought to have been Hawthorne's finest novel. His career had pointed toward it from the beginning. In it the heart imagery that is implicit in "The Hollow of the Three Hills" has become the underground world of Rome, the catacombs, the tomb or dungeon of the heart and of dreams. In it Robin's initiation has become consciously archetypal, to be seen in the dimensions of its largest significance. In it the implications of "Earth's Holocaust" and "The Celestial Railroad" have been combined within the framework of man's basic myth. The most persistent preoccupations and the recurrent images of a lifetime of writing have been brought together in what ought to have been a definitive recapitulation.

Instead, the novel is clearly inferior to *The Scarlet Letter* and even, it seems to me, to *The House of the Seven Gables*. Richer in many respects than *Blithedale*, it is less consistently interesting: there are frequent stretches of it one wants to skip. There is a very large gap in it between intended and achieved meaning. Hawthorne failed with Rome, and he failed with Hilda, and both were essential to the achievement of his intention.

Hilda is at once a nineteenth century stereotype and Hawthorne's tribute to Sophia. The only way of interpreting her that will "save" Hawthorne and his novel is to take the portrait ironically, but this will not do if we consider all the evidence. True, Miriam points out that Hilda's innocence is like "a sharp steel sword"; so white a purity makes for judgments that are "terribly severe." And Miriam often speaks for Hawthorne. Here we should probably assume that he thought so too. But this is only a minor qualification of what, for Hawthorne, is Hilda's awe-inspiring virtue and compelling attractiveness. Once again, as in the case of Miriam's implied assent to the idea of the Fortunate Fall, we may not assume that Hawthorne is completely committed to Miriam as his spokesman. In his own person, as narrator, he pays Hilda lavish, and tiresomely repetitious, tribute, and as Kenyon he marries her and asks her to guide him home.

Yet to the modern reader Hilda is either ridiculous or, if we can take her seriously, self-righteous and uncharitable. She is not only a far less impressive character, as a literary character, than Miriam, she is far less attractive, and even less "good," as a person. Throughout most of the course of the novel her chief concern is to protect the spotlessness of the innocence assumed by her and asserted by Hawthorne. She finds everyone else's faith and everyone else's conduct corrupt. When called upon for help, she turns her friend away lest she be stained by the contact. Though the idea would have shocked Hawthorne immeasurably, it is impossible not to see her as a feminine version of the man of adamant—at least until the very end, when the rigor of her moralism is softened somewhat.

There is no consistent or effective irony in the portrait. Though this "daughter of the Puritans," as Hawthorne repeatedly calls her, comes down from her tower to marry Kenyon, the change is not so much one from spiritual pride to humility as from priestess to goddess: "Another hand must henceforth trim the lamp before the Virgin's shrine; for Hilda was coming down from her old tower, to be herself enshrined and worshipped as a household saint, in the light of her husband's fireside." It is true that Hilda thought right and wrong completely distinct, never in any degree mingled or ambiguous—the error of judgment that Hawthorne's innocent young men have to grow out of, the idea they have to unlearn by painful experience. But Hawthorne thought such an error—if indeed error it was, as he would have said—charming and admirable in innocent young girls. Hilda is like young Robin before his "evening of ambiguity and weariness"; the difference between them is that Hawthorne does not require that young girls should grow in knowledge of the world.

His century placed women on a pedestal just *because*, in their role of guardian of values that were being threatened, they knew nothing of the world. If their innocence rendered them helpless to deal with reality, it was nevertheless to be both protected and admired, for reality was very nasty. If they did not truly partake of the human condition, it was a good thing they didn't. A comment Hawthorne makes in the novel on a work of art, without suggesting any connection with his portrait of Hilda, suggests the chief reason for his failure with his heroine: "It was one of the few works of antique sculpture in which we recognize womanhood, and that, moreover, without prejudice to its divinity." Womanhood's "divinity"? Since Hilda was more than normally pretty and good, no wonder her destiny was to be "enshrined and worshipped" at the fireside.

As he depended greatly on Hilda to give his novel an affirmative meaning, so Hawthorne depended chiefly on Rome and its art treasures to give it thematic density. Here too he failed, though for quite different reasons. Again, recent efforts to "save" the novel do not really work. To be sure, Hawthorne anticipates James in developing the Europe versus America theme: Rome is the past, experience, culture, and corruption, in contrast with America's present, ideals, morality, and innocence: Miriam versus Hilda. This is fine, theoretically. But Hawthorne too often simply lifts long passages of description from the Notebooks, and the passages remain inert in the novel. There is too *much* of Rome, and too much about art. They are a burden the story is simply incapable of carrying.

Examples could easily be given of passages in which Hawthorne succeeds in making his comments on art and descriptions of Rome work for his story. Perhaps the best one is Miriam's comment on Guido's "dapper" Archangel, whose feathers are unruffled in his struggle with Satan: "Is it thus that virtue looks the moment after its death-struggle with evil? . . . A full third of the Archangel's feathers should have been torn from his wings . . ." But for page after page there is nothing like this, nothing in fact that is not very tedious. And Hawthorne seems to know it. At least he keeps apologizing for his descriptions while the story halts, sometimes for a chapter at a time, to accommodate them. This is simply awkward novel writing and no amount of demonstration that, where there are symbolic implications in the Notebook material they are consistent with the general theme, will really save the romance as a work of art. Thematic considerations alone cannot save any novel.

The effect on the reader of all this inert material is to suggest that Hawthorne was not sufficiently interested in his *story*—an effect reinforced by his embarrassed and coy protestations at the end, in the added conclusion, when he refused to make more than a slight gesture toward clearing up the mysteries of his plot. What he is really saying in his "Conclusion" is that he doesn't *care* whether Donatello had furry ears or not or who detained Hilda, and we the readers shouldn't either. But he had cared about Hester, and Hepzibah, and Zenobia, cared about them as people and not merely as allegoric or mystic symbols. Despite the elaborate density of its background, it might well be argued that *The Marble Faun* is more allegorical than any of the three preceding romances.

5

Still, if it is true that the work has been generally underestimated, as I think it has, the reason is not hard to find. Its weaknesses are very obvious, impossible I should think to overlook, while its strength is subtle and delicate. It is easy to read this work in which "Adam falls anew, and Paradise . . . is lost again" without responding to a good deal of its multiple suggestiveness. There is nothing in its period quite like the way it plays theological, philosophical, and psychological perspectives against each other in the image of the catacombs. Here the characters wandered in "a sort of dream," a dark labyrinth of guilt, an "ugly dream" indeed: "For, in dreams, the conscience sleeps, and we often stain ourselves with guilt of which we should be incapable in our waking moments." The "dark caverns" of experience in Hawthorne's novel are so richly meaningful that we should have to read the work for this if there were nothing else to draw us.

There is of course much else. The scene at the precipice (we are all, in some sense, "dreaming on the edge of a precipice"), the whole series of chapters laid in Donatello's country, where the serpent is discovered in nature's garden, the descriptions of the several studios (Miriam's is said to be "the outward type of a poet's haunted imagination," and the description justifies the comment)—all these parts of the work, and more, make it more worth reading than most American novels of the nineteenth century, even if we are not already committed to Hawthorne before we start it.

If we are, we shall find it an even more rewarding failure. For on the thematic level it is, for the most part, such *good* Hawthorne. It is not just Donatello but all of us who "travel in a circle, as all things heavenly and earthly do." The loss of innocence is very sad, but it is at least naïve and may be disastrous to suppose that we haven't lost it. Guilt is original, a necessary aspect of the human condition, not something that sets conspicuous sinners apart from the rest of us. And it is mutual, so that in our inevitable complicity we may not relieve ourselves of its burden by pointing the finger, casting the stone. Still, we need not despair if only we will acknowledge our complicity and enter the human circle.

"Outraged, suffering humanity" must learn to live with "the blackness that lies beneath us, everywhere," but Kenyon, taking the long view from the height of Donatello's tower, saw, above the stormy valley, "within the domain of chaos, as it were,—hill-tops ... brightening in the sunshine; they looked like fragments of the world, broken adrift and based on nothingness, or like portions of a sphere destined to exist, but not yet finally compacted." Kenyon's images give us Hawthorne's answer to the question whether the fall was fortunate or not, an answer that springs from his "best thought" and that was otherwise inexpressible.

HUBERT H. HOELTJE [1894–1968] taught at the University of Oregon and wrote *The Sheltering Tree* and *Inward Sky: The Mind and Heart of Nathaniel Hawthorne*, a biography published in 1962. In the final chapter of *Inward Sky*. Hoeltje writes, "In a review of Hawthorne's life and writings nothing is more prominent than a quiet, deeply joyful affirmation." In Hoeltje's essay reprinted below, he evaluates the essays of Melville and Tuckerman (see pp. 28–41 and 54–63) and refutes the emphasis among critics on "the power of blackness" in Hawthorne's vision of human experience.

Hawthorne, Melville, and "Blackness"

HUBERT H. HOELTJE

The growth of the reputation of Herman Melville as a writer of fiction, once so astonishing, has become a commonplace in contemporary commentary on American literature. The interest in Melville as a critic, and more specifically as a critic of Hawthorne, is, however, a fairly recent and, to some of us, a startling phenomenon. For instance, thirteen years after the appearance of R. M. Weaver's pioneering *Herman Melville, Mariner and Mystic* in 1921, a scholarly selection of Hawthorne's writings, with introduction, bibliography, and notes, and having a wide currency among our colleges and universities, made no reference whatever, either in the introduction or in the bibliography, to Melville's "Hawthorne and His Mosses."[1]

Today the picture is different. Now we have been assured that

American Literature, Vol. 37 (March 1965) 41–51.

[1]Austin Warren, ed., *Nathaniel Hawthorne: Representative Selections, with Introduction, Bibliography, and Notes* (New York, 1934).

the so-called "blackness" which Melville thought he found in Hawthorne's fiction has emerged as "Hawthorne's trademark," so impressed by the significance of Melville's criticism has one of our contemporaries become. Indeed, so impressed has this critic been by Melville's comment that he apparently finds this "blackness" even more characteristic of Hawthorne than of Melville himself.[2] Perhaps a veteran reader of Hawthorne might be inclined to dismiss such judgments as evidence of an unrestrained enthusiasm did these views not seem to be supported by the remark of a distinguished Hawthorne scholar that " 'Hawthorne and His Mosses' is one of the great critical essays of the nineteenth century. . . ."[3] Melville, it appears, has now been adjudged a great critic as well as a great novelist—or, at least, a great critic of Hawthorne.

Before this seeming tide of opinion quite oversweeps discretion, it might be well to do what appears not yet to have been done—namely, to examine Melville's essay on Hawthorne's *Mosses* in some detail and to determine whether it represents a sound criticism supported by irrefutable evidence or whether it reveals a mistaken view which, in our day, has turned much of the comment on Hawthorne into a quagmire of erroneous interpretation.

One need not quarrel with Melville's ardor for the prospects for American literature, especially since one can now be confident that our literature has established itself among the literatures of the world. Nor need one quarrel in its general nature with Melville's high regard for the fiction of Hawthorne, since that fiction withstood the debunkers of several decades and has maintained its standing through the re-evaluations of recent years. As mature criticism, however, Melville's essay may seem to lose some of its force when one becomes aware that the young man who rather cavalierly takes to task the "endless commentators and critics" of Shakespeare[4] had himself discovered Shakespeare only a little more than a year before,[5] and could therefore hardly have read very widely in the critics. And what can one say of Melville's assertion that " 'The Mosses from an Old Manse' will be ultimately ac-

[2]Harry Levin, *The Power of Blackness: Hawthorne, Poe, Melville* (New York, 1958), p. 26.

[3]Randall Stewart, review of *Inward Sky, the Mind and Heart of Nathaniel Hawthorne*, by Hubert H. Hoeltje, Durham, N.C., 1962, *American Literature*, XXXIV, 577-578 (Jan., 1963).

[4]Willard Thorp, ed., *Herman Melville: Representative Selections, with Introduction, Bibliography, and Notes* (New York, 1938), p. 334.

[5]*Ibid.*, p. 370.

counted [Hawthorne's] masterpiece,"⁶ except to reply that apparently the prophecy after one hundred years has not yet been fulfilled? Even more disturbing, what scholarly charity can accept such a judgment when the prophet has apparently only a very slight acquaintance with any other book by Hawthorne, and so bases his prophecy and makes all his allegations regarding "blackness" as a dominating trait in Hawthorne after reading only one book?⁷ Surely even the most gentle reader who judges Melville's commentary with his eyes open must have some doubts regarding the validity of the essay as a whole.

I

Before examining Melville's major theme, that is, the "blackness" which he is assured he has personally discovered in Hawthorne's writing, it may not be amiss briefly to scan Melville's approach to his concluding thought. It is a gradual approach, skilfully made, leading the reader from commonly accepted views to the view which Melville offers climactically as deeper and truer than any ever offered before. Early in his essay he speaks of the "noon-day repose of Hawthorne's spell," and then, presently, of the melancholy which rests like an Indian summer all over Hawthorne. But these qualities, he says, are only the least part of the genius of Hawthorne which has attracted admiration. In spite of "the Indian-summer sunlight on the hither side of Hawthorne's soul," the other side, he now asserts, "is shrouded in blackness, ten times black." Whether this blackness is only an artistic device or evidence of a Puritanic gloom in Hawthorne himself, Melville at this point is not ready to say, though within the limits of the same paragraph he is ready to say that "the world is mistaken in this Nathaniel Hawthorne." Then, with an apparently cautious reserve, he approaches the heart of his argument: "Perhaps he does not give us a ray of his light for every shade of his dark." Having made this advance, he at once qualifies and reasserts his position by saying that the reader need not fix upon the blackness in Hawthorne, nor will all readers discern it, though it will be evident to those best qualified to understand it—a remark surely calculated to encourage the reader to wish to be among the discerning ones.

Now, too, Melville dissolves the doubt whether Hawthorne

⁶*Ibid.*, p. 345.

⁷*Ibid.*, p. 385. In a letter to Duyckinck, Melville, now having read *Twice-Told Tales*, says that they "far exceed the Mosses"!

treats his subject matter as mere material for art, or whether it represents the man himself, for, like "all true, candid men," Hawthorne, in Melville's eyes, is "a seeker, not a finder yet." Furthermore, in the second part of his essay, after the lapse of the twenty-four hours during which he has read more of the tales in *Mosses*, and during which he has discovered "Young Goodman Brown," Melville seemingly throws all qualification to the winds by offering that celebrated story as a "strong positive illustration of that blackness in Hawthorne, which I had assumed from the mere occasional shadows of it, as revealed in several other sketches."

In short, when the essay comes to an end, "blackness," which has earlier been offered as "the very axis of reality," has become, so Melville is convinced, the basic quality in Hawthorne's writing, a quality inherent in the constitution of the man Hawthorne, and not a mere device of artistry. And if any doubt may hover in the mind of the reader regarding the meaning of "blackness" as the word is used by Melville, that doubt is dispelled by Melville's letter written to Hawthorne subsequent to his reading of *The House of the Seven Gables*, a letter appearing less than a year after the essay: "There is the grand truth about Nathaniel Hawthorne. He says NO! in thunder; but the devil himself cannot make him say *yes*. For all men who say *yes*, lie . . . ."[8] The remark is obviously a caustic reference to Carlyle's exulting "Everlasting Yea" in *Sartor Resartus*, and, though more literary in flavor, is no less to the point than a later blunt pronouncement by Mark Twain—namely, "the man who *isn't* a pessimist is a d——d fool."[9]

If, then, Melville stamps the brand of pessimism on Hawthorne, it will be interesting to examine the major tales and sketches in the one book which Melville has read and to which he alludes. He has, for instance, read the introductory essay, "The Old Manse," as well as "Buds and Bird Voices," in which he finds the "noon-day repose" of Hawthorne's spell, and the delicious apples of the "thoughts and fancies of this sweet man of Mosses," remarks sufficiently appreciative. But since these qualities, though granted and shortly to be spoken of as "the least part" of Hawthorne's genius, presumably discernible even to the "superficial

---

[8]Julian Hawthorne, *Nathaniel Hawthorne and His Wife* (Boston, 1885), I, 388. Leslie A. Fiedler, in *No! in Thunder* (Boston, 1960), p. 6, quotes Melville's comment on Hawthorne's *The House of the Seven Gables* as the most explicit of all expressions of the "Modern Muse," which Fiedler characterizes as "demonic, terrible and negative."

[9]Albert B. Paine, *Mark Twain, a Biography* (New York, 1912), III, 1508.

skimmer of pages," it may be well to point out in particular some aspects of these essays to which Melville makes no specific reference but which may have more bearing upon Hawthorne's ultimate thought than Melville has seen or admitted. For instance, in "The Old Manse," is it truly only the least part of his genius that is to be found in Hawthorne's remark, after a wild day on the Concord with Ellery Channing, "how sweet was it to return within the system of human society"? Is Hawthorne not truly serious when he returns to the Old Manse and home with the prayer "that the upper influences might long protect the institutions that had grown out of the human heart"? Is he expressing only a soothing pleasantry, and not a deep conviction near "the very axis of reality," when, reclining on the withered autumn grass, he whispers to himself, "O perfect day! O beautiful world! O beneficent God!" Is he writing only for the "superficial skimmer of pages" when he says, in "Buds and Bird Voices," "But who can estimate the power of gentle influences"? Or, "There is no decay. Each human soul is the first created inhabitant in its own Eden"?

One may feel sympathetic with Melville's finding, in "The Old Apple Dealer," "the subtlest spirit of sadness," but the use of this sketch as an example of the "melancholy" which rests all over Hawthorne—the melancholy which Melville employs as a transition to the "blackness" which he is about to introduce—needs the careful examination for which Melville himself has pleaded. If there is melancholy in this sketch, it is not the melancholy of despair. The climactic sentences in the character sketch of the old apple dealer Melville seems not to have observed: "the soundless depths of the human soul and of eternity have an opening through your breast. . . . There is a spiritual essence in this gray old shape that shall flit upward too." Shall one say that this Christian hope of immortality is not honestly expressed, or that it is the least part of Hawthorne's genius? This sketch, if it is representative of Hawthorne, is representative, not of a melancholy tinged with "blackness," but of his idealism and his high hopes for even the humblest of men.

It is, however, when Melville enters the body of his essay that he becomes most convinced that he has found the true Hawthorne who is pervaded by blackness "through and through." "How profound, nay appalling, is the moral evolved by 'Earth's Holocaust'. . . ." What is so appalling, one might ask. The poor deceived girl, who would throw herself into the conflagration, is advised by the good man: "Be patient, and abide Heaven's will. So long as you possess a living soul, all may be restored to its first freshness. These things of matter and creations of human fantasy are fit for nothing but to be burned when once they have had their day; but your day is eternity." Is it so appalling to be assured that "Our faith can well afford to lose all the drapery that even the holiest men have thrown around it, and be only the more sublime in its simplicity," or that "Not a truth is destroyed nor buried so deep among the ashes but it will be raked up at last"?

Of course it is the last paragraph of "Earth's Holocaust" that Melville finds most appalling: "The heart, the heart. . . . Purify that inward sphere, and the many shapes of evil that haunt the outward, and which now seem almost our only realities, will turn to shadowy phantoms and vanish of their own accord; but if we go no deeper than the intellect, and strive, with merely that feeble instrument, to discern and rectify what is wrong, our whole accomplishment will be but a dream. . . ." Are these sentiments so very different from those of one of Hawthorne's contemporaries?

> The problem of restoring to the world original and eternal beauty is solved by the redemption of the soul. . . . Love is as much its demand as perception . . . when a faithful thinker, resolute to detach every object from personal relations and see it in the light of thought, shall, at the same time, kindle science with the fire of holiest affections, then will God go forth anew into the creation. . . . Build therefore your own world. As fast as you conform your life to the pure idea in your mind, that will unfold its great proportions. A correspondent revolution in things will attend the influx of spirit . . . until evil is no more seen.

Do not both passages emphasize love or the heart and the need for the redemption of the soul, and the weakness of the intellect as the sole instrument of that redemption, a redemption following which the many shapes of evil which haunt us shall vanish? Are we to say, therefore, that Emerson's *Nature*, too, ends in an appalling moral?

If the nature of the human heart seemed appalling to Melville, it did not seem so to Hawthorne. In the very period at the Old Manse when he was planning "Earth's Holocaust," Hawthorne was contemplating another sketch, the plans for which show how completely Melville misunderstood him:

> The human heart to be allegorized as a cavern; at the entrance there is sunshine, and flowers growing about it. You step within, but a short distance, and begin to find yourself

surrounded with a terrible gloom, and monsters of divers kinds; it seems like Hell itself. You are bewildered, and wander long without hope. At last a light strikes upon you. You peep towards it and find yourself in a region that seems, in some sort, to reproduce the flowers and sunny beauty of the entrance, but all perfect. These are the depths of the heart, or of human nature, bright and peaceful; the gloom and terror may lie deep; but deeper still is the eternal beauty.[10]

It is in reference to "The Christmas Banquet" and "The Bosom Serpent" that Melville finds the "other side" of Hawthorne's soul "shrouded in blackness, ten times black." Why so? The former is patently an indirect plea for the preciousness of the human affections, a recurring theme in Hawthorne's writing; and as for the latter, could Melville have read its conclusion? "Rosina had emerged from the arbor and was bending over [Roderick Elliston] with the shadow of his anguish reflected in her countenance, yet so mingled with hope and unselfish love that all anguish seemed but an earthly shadow and a dream." And when the question is asked, "Can a breast where jealousy has dwelt so long, be purified?" Rosina replies, "O yes. . . . The serpent was but a dark fantasy, and what it typified was as shadowy as itself. The past, dismal as it seems, shall fling no gloom upon the future. To give it its due importance we must think of it but as an anecdote in our Eternity." Hope, love, forgiveness, Eternity. Do the ideas encompassed in these words suggest "blackness"? Melville's inversion of meanings is here surely beyond the bounds of rational thought.

It is in "Young Goodman Brown," however, that Melville sees "such a strong positive illustration" of blackness in Hawthorne—presumably because he sees in it "that Calvinistic sense of Innate Depravity and Original Sin" to which he had earlier attributed the "Puritanic gloom" in Hawthorne. That Hawthorne was dramatizing the repulsive elements of Puritanism is a thought that seems not to have occurred to Melville in his hasty two-day reading.

II

If these remarks seem unfair to Melville, perhaps the reactions of Hawthorne himself and those of his wife Sophia,[11] may throw

---

[10]Randall Stewart, ed., *The American Notebooks by Nathaniel Hawthorne* (New Haven, 1932), p. 98.

[11]Both letters are quoted in Thorp, p. 423.

some light on the accuracy of Melville's interpretations, for both read Melville's reviews when neither as yet knew who was their author. That Hawthorne was pleased by Melville's generous appreciation of his book is clear enough from his letter to Evert Duyckinck, though he protests that with his wife's admiration he should do very well without any other. What may not be apparent at first reading is the fact that Hawthorne limits his remarks to Melville's praise (not all of which he necessarily accepts), and that he says not one word about Melville's interpretation of his tales and sketches. Sophia in her letter to Duyckinck is of course happy over such an enthusiastic review of her husband's writings, as she is in her letter on the same subject to her mother. In the latter, however, Sophia indicates clearly enough that Melville has misinterpreted her husband's thought: "But it is funny to see how he [the anonymous writer, Melville] does not know how this heart and this intellect are enshrined."[12] Like her husband, she had said nothing, in her letter to Duyckinck, to approve of Melville's interpretation. In her letter to her mother she had not hesitated to qualify her pleasure in Melville's review.

What Hawthorne thought of Melville's interpretation of his writing after he probably knew that Melville was the author, may be clearly indicated by his remarks on a general review of all his writings by Henry T. Tuckerman in the *Southern Literary Messenger* following the publication of *The House of the Seven Gables*. When Tuckerman's essay was republished in *Littell's Living Age* on June 11, 1864, shortly after Hawthorne's death, it was preceded by a letter to Tuckerman from Hawthorne written at Lenox, Massachusetts, and dated June 20, 1851, a letter which, with the accompanying essay by Tuckerman, will place Melville's review in proper perspective.

> I have received the *Southern Literary Messenger*, and have read your beautiful article on my, I fear, unworthy self. It gave me, I must confess, the pleasantest sensation I have ever experienced, from any cause connected with literature; not so much for the praise as because I felt that you saw into my books and understood what I meant. I cannot thank you enough for it.

It is obvious that this letter is quite different from the one that Hawthorne wrote to Duyckinck. In his comment on Melville's

---

[12]Rose Hawthorne Lathrop, *Memories of Hawthorne* (Boston, 1897), p. 173.

review, Hawthorne had spoken of his pleasure in Melville's praise, not of Melville's understanding of his writing. In his letter to Tuckerman he minimizes the praise and emphasizes Tuckerman's understanding. That Hawthorne valued Tuckerman's comment much more than he did Melville's is clearly implied. Hence, though Tuckerman's excellent essay is too long even to be outlined here, some of its more salient aspects are offered as pertinent to a criticism of Melville's enthusiastic but faulty commentary.

In the first place, Tuckerman had done what Melville should have done before he undertook to make such broad and sweeping generalizations—that is, Tuckerman had read thoroughly all of Hawthorne's writing, and hence did not superficially base his judgment on one solitary volume. Consequently, Tuckerman's review possesses, among other things, a balance quite lacking in what Melville had to say. It is apparent, too, that Tuckerman had a width of experience in reading, and certainly in reviewing, unknown to Melville. He was aware that the first duty of a good critic is to see what an author has to say, and not merely to express the reviewer's predilections. Melville's essay, however revelatory of Melville, is much less satisfactory than Tuckerman's for the simple reason that Melville ignored this first principle of criticism.

More specifically, the balance present in Tuckerman's review and absent from Melville's is indicated by Tuckerman's awareness of the variety in Hawthorne's writing. Instead of reducing all to melancholy and "blackness," Tuckerman sees not only the variety of subject matter, but also the variety of tone. The tragic element and the comic element, the cheerfulness and the solemnity, the tactful humor and the grave undertone, the "alternating melancholy and brightness which is born of a genuine moral life," all receive due recognition; hence there emerges not the emaciated author whom Melville's imperfect vision had imagined, but the healthy and affirmative man and author that Hawthorne really was. Furthermore, though Tuckerman gives but a nod of recognition to "Young Goodman Brown," which to Melville seems to have been such a positive illustration of the Puritanic gloom in Hawthorne, he fully disposes of the question of such gloom in his comment on *The Scarlet Letter*, which Melville had not read when he rushed into his broad generalizations. Beneath "the picturesque details and intense characterization" of *The Scarlet Letter*, said Tuckerman, "there lurks a profound satire. The want of soul, the predominance of judgment over mercy, the tyranny of public opinion, the look [lack?] of genuine charity, the asceticism of the Puritan theology, the absence of all recognition of natural laws, and the fanatic substitution of the letter for the spirit, which darken and harden the spirit of the pilgrims to the soul of a poet are shadowed forth with keen, stern, and eloquent, yet indirect emphasis that haunts us like 'the cry of the human.'" The profound satire and the indirectness which Tuckerman correctly perceived in *The Scarlet Letter*, and which are present with equal subtlety in "Young Goodman Brown," have, of course, escaped the observation of many a "superficial skimmer of pages."

But it is among his concluding remarks on *The House of the Seven Gables* that Tuckerman focuses the final and true aim and accomplishment of Hawthorne as man and author. In reading this statement, one should remember that it had Hawthorne's own approbation as what he meant to do in his writing, though that writing itself, to the careful reader, is ample evidence of Tuckerman's judgment.

> Thus narrowly, yet with reverence, does Hawthorne analyze the delicate traits of human sentiment and character; and opens vistas into that beautiful and unexplored world of love and thought that exists in every human being, though overshadowed by material circumstance and technical duty. This . . . is his great service.[13]

"Reverence . . . human sentiment and character . . . love and thought. . . ." In the recognition of these ultimates, what must one think of the "blackness ten times black" which Melville, in holding a mirror up to himself, saw pervading Hawthorne "through and through"? What now of the hectic assertion, "There is the grand truth about Nathaniel Hawthorne. He says NO! in thunder; but the devil himself cannot make him say *yes*. For all men who say *yes*, lie. . . ." Coolly appraised, these remarks of Melville are sophomoric distortions. Sympathetically viewed, they are the words of an unhappy, lonely man who longs for the understanding of a kindred pessimistic spirit—one whom he quite mistakenly supposes he has found in Hawthorne.[14]

As for our contemporary who has convinced himself that "blackness" is "a virtual obsession with Hawthorne," and that "it

[13] Tuckerman's essay deserves to be reprinted because it won such high approval from Hawthorne and because of its inherent excellence.

[14] The story of the friendship of Hawthorne and Melville I have told in some detail in *Inward Sky*, mentioned earlier in these notes. It was a true friendship in spite of limitations, respected and valued by both men.

became Hawthorne's trademark after Melville had pointed it out" —well, one should perhaps be willing to forgive what may only be a tender susceptibility to the maladies current in our present-day critical climate. That Melville's "Hawthorne and His Mosses" is an interesting essay as revealing somewhat of the literary hope of the time, and much more interesting as disclosing the mind of Herman Melville ("a seeker, not a finder yet"), may readily be granted; but as an interpretation of Nathaniel Hawthorne it is certainly not "one of the great critical essays of the nineteenth century" for the one overpowering reason that it lacks a necessary ingredient of greatness —namely, Truth.

MARTIN GREEN [1927–] is the author of four books. In *Re-Appraisals* Martin condemns a large body of American criticism because of misinterpretation of authors of the past in order to make them fit the theories of contemporary alienation—"the power of blackness in the American imagination." In response to such criticism he offers a series of "pamphlet-essays" designed to excite his readers. In the process Hawthorne, Melville, James, and Faulkner are severely condemned; and Emerson, "the rejected leader," is restored to prominence. Green's assessment of Hawthorne, a version of which was first published in 1963, should be read in conjunction with Lionel Trilling's "Our Hawthorne," which appeared in *Hawthorne Centenary Essays* (1964). The two works constitute the most recent expression of the case against Hawthorne.

The Hawthorne Myth: A Protest

MARTIN GREEN

Hawthorne's reputation remains very high in America. In the last ten years at least seven book-length studies have appeared (by authors as well known as Marius Bewley and Harry Levin) which all present him as a moulder and hero of the modern sensibility. They differ in details of their interpretation, but there is on the whole a remarkable critical unanimity about his work; as an

Re-Appraisals: Some Commonsense Readings in American Literature (New York, 1965) 61–85.

allegorical articulation of the deepest and darkest experience of the American psyche. It is still, however, possible to take a different view, and to feel that the critics are inventing meanings for their texts; that Hawthorne's own account of his work is shrewder than theirs.

Hawthorne called his longer works of fiction romances, and his shorter ones tales or sketches, and he defined his sense of those terms.

> 'The sketches are not, it is hardly necessary to say, profound . . . They never need translation . . . They are not the talk of a secluded man with his own mind and heart (had it been so, they could hardly have failed to be more deeply and permanently valuable) but his attempts, and very imperfectly successful ones, to open an intercourse with the world.'

This comes from Hawthorne's preface to the third edition of *Twice-Told Tales*; a collection which includes 'Young Goodman Brown'. None of Hawthorne's critics has failed to praise his judgement of his own work; but they have all assumed such remarks to be not the modifications of modesty, but a flat contradiction of the truth. They have insisted that the sketches fall into a quite opposite category; that they are 'profound', that they always need translation, that they *are* a dialogue with his own mind and heart, and *not* a performance as clubman-author.

The Preface to *The House of the Seven Gables* begins,

> 'When a writer calls his work a Romance, it need hardly be observed that he wishes to claim a certain latitude, both as to its fashion and material, which he would not have felt himself entitled to assume, had he professed to be writing a Novel.'

This latitude is a freedom from the rigorous discipline of realism, and a freedom in the management of 'his atmospherical medium'; a freedom to 'bring out or mellow the lights, and deepen and enrich the shadows, of the picture'. The device he has most in mind, it appears, is 'the Marvellous'; ghosts, curses, legends, superstitions, omens, etc. The romance writer will not ask his reader to believe in these things; he will be wise, no doubt, 'to mingle the Marvellous rather as a slight, delicate, and evanescent flavor . . .' He will describe the superstition, that is, dismiss it laughingly, and then give a hint that perhaps something uncanny really did happen; and isn't it anyway rather nice to think it did. He will not ask us to believe in anything supernatural, or make it 'any portion of the actual substance of the dish offered to the public'. In all this, as he himself observes, Hawthorne is describing a genre with which the readers of 1851 were very familiar. In calling his book a romance and not a novel, he is promising them something in the manner of Mrs Radcliffe and her successors. That, moreover, is what he gave them. *The House of the Seven Gables, The Scarlet Letter, The Marble Faun, The Blithedale Romance,* are romances in that sense. They differ from novels just in the thinness of their psychological and sociological detail, in their fascination with the supernatural, in the liberties they take with their own verisimilitude; their essential meaning lies in the author's persona, in his comments as he conjures up before us, and then dispels, various quaint, gloomy, or charming scenes.

The critics, however, insist that Hawthorne had his own conception of the romance, quite different from Mrs Radcliffe's; that for him it was a form in which the psychological aspects of spiritual experience could be symbolically rendered. First of all, it is unlikely that *any* writer could do that without being conscious of it; without in fact saying something about it, in notebook or journal if not in conversation. This is a complex aesthetic strategy; not the sort of thing that gets done unconsciously. Hawthorne made copious notes for and about his own writing; but they contain no proof that he thought of writing anything but the tales and romances he defined in his prefaces. Secondly, Hawthorne in particular was not an intellectual writer in any sense. James remarks several times on how empty of ideas the Journals are, and there is every evidence that Hawthorne never took part in a conversation about ideas or forms in his life. He spent a lot of time in solitary meditation, but he described this as musing or dreaming, and the evidence supports him. When irritated by the intellectual enthusiasm of his Concord neighbours, Hawthorne's recourse was not to a profounder understanding of the American experience, but to the great established truths of the popular heart, Christianity, marriage, democracy.

No one, of course, can read Hawthorne without realising that there is something very different and very deep below the surface. As he makes his comments, and invokes his pieties, his voice moves into and out of disturbing echoes produced by a hollow cavity below, quite thinly iced over. But one can feel that Hawthorne gave those depths no voice of their own; that they remained only a distorting and ominous echo. In fact, though they constitute the prime interest of his work for us now, they probably spoiled it for him and his readers then; they probably prevented him from doing well the kind of writing he was aiming at.

To explain this reading of Hawthorne, it is simplest to refer directly to the facts of his life. His father died while he was a child, his mother withdrew from the world, and his sisters treated him as the most important member of the family. A very handsome, sensitive boy, much petted by them and by his aunts and uncles, and invited into solitude both by the decline of the family fortunes and by his own illness, he seems to have drifted away from normal contacts into a dreamland of stories, totally unchallenged, unaroused, knowing no equals.

At Bowdoin he cultivated the less perceptive, less challenging companions. 'He would sit for a whole evening with head gently inclined to one side, hearing every word, seeing every gesture, and yet scarcely a word would pass his lips. . . . He lives in a mysterious world of thought and imagination which he never permits me to enter.' Cilley assumed that since his friend did not live fully in the normal world of people and things, then he must live in the world of thought and imagination. But Hawthorne tells us over and over that a man may live in neither, may refuse fruitful reciprocation with any aspect of reality. And all the details of Cilley's account confirm Hawthorne's diagnosis; the silence, the watchfulness, the head on one side, the physical clumsiness, the hours of dreaming, the shyness and the lethargy.

Then came twelve appalling years at Salem. Mark van Doren may think them a period of hard work, relieved by diversions and friendships, punctuated by the excitements of artistic accomplishment. Hawthorne was appalled by them. He sat alone in his room all day and night for twelve years; he even sent his sister to the library for him, and only went out himself after dark; he read without studying, mused without thinking, and wrote fanciful, unreal, little sketches. He watched people in the street and made up stories about them, but refused to meet them socially. Such behaviour could seem, in the 1830s, typical of a writer, and even distinguished, though eccentric. But when he found that his stories were malicious, that they invaded the other person's most sacred privacy, that they were not at all as warm and kindly as, for instance, Dickens's stories, then he felt guilty and frightened. He made great efforts to come out into the world and 'open an intercourse' with people. But part of his nature resisted. Playing with imaginary characters was much easier for him than responding to real ones. All his life he spoke of 'the heart' as something that needed constant attention and encouragement, needed will-power and work behind it, not to wither and dwindle away. He was, it appears, strongly tempted to dissipate reality, and especially the reality of other people and their demands on him, by absorbing himself in stories which he did not really believe; to divert all his energy to the creation of an imaginary universe which he could dismiss at will, and which could never, therefore, achieve independent reality. He found a temporary safety from this temptation in marriage; but it seems from the history of the years after his return from Europe that it renewed its attack on him and finally triumphed.

This is the picture that emerges from Newton Arvin's account of Hawthorne's life. It is of course somewhat simplified, and relies heavily on Hawthorne's own testimony; perhaps it overlooks the mitigating features. But it is much more convincing than any interpretation based on those mitigating features alone, as Mark van Doren's and Randall Stewart's seem to be.

The Notebooks are full of evidence that this temptation was in fact the problem that interested Hawthorne most, and most personally; that this was the experience that demanded expression in him, which he approached, backwards, so often, and which gave that disturbing echo to his cheerfully pitched voice, in, for instance, 'Wakefield'. In 1837 he wrote:

> 'Insincerity in a man's own heart must make all his enjoyments, all that concerns him, unreal; so that his whole life must seem like a merely dramatic representation. And this would be the case even though he were surrounded by true-hearted relatives and friends.'

The precision and sombreness of his observations on this theme are far superior to anything else in the Notebooks. In 1838:

> 'Character of a man who, in himself and his external circumstances, shall be equally and totally false; his fortune resting on baseless credit—his patriotism assumed—his domestic affections, his honor and honesty, all a sham. His own misery in the midst of it—it making the whole universe, heaven and earth alike, an unsubstantial mockery to him.'

Let us note that the insincerity and the falsity are not only in the man's relations with the outside world, but also in himself; so that everything is *unreal* to him. These are the thoughts, the experience, we must recall when he described those years in such terms as 'dreamy', 'dreary', 'idle musings', 'the Dreamland of my youth', and 'an attempt to open an intercourse with the world'. In his letters to his wife he was always quite explicit about the unreality, the unsubstantiality, of his life before he met her. And if we remember the mid-Victorian standard of sensibility, sympathy, warm-heartedness; a standard his wife lived up to, and Hawthorne acted up to in his public persona—all the 'sweet young girls' and 'dainty little children' he invoked; then we need not wonder that this kind of guilt should have been so appalling, so unspeakable.

In his fiction, his tales and romances, this disease shows its effects most obviously in his delight in unreality. He plays on the doubtful distinction between appearance and reality, especially in the matter of the supernatural, more than any other writer. He is always pretending that something frightening or abnormal has happened (that Mistress Hibbins is literally a witch) without letting go of a safe contrasting ordinariness underneath. It appears also in his descriptions. His finest pieces of this kind, for instance that of Peterborough Close, or the gardens of the Villa Borghese, have an extraordinarily suspended, timeless, unreal quality; the exact opposite of the quality D. H. Lawrence caught in his descriptions. And in his last piece of fiction, *Septimius Felton*, we find the same painful chord being struck as in the early years.

> 'Septimius went into his house, and sat in his study for some hours, in that unpleasant state of feeling which a man of brooding thought is apt to experience when the world around him is in a state of intense action, which he finds it impossible to sympathise with. There seemed to be a stream rushing past him, by which, even if he plunged into the midst of it, he could not be wet. He felt himself strangely ajar with the human race, and would have given much either to be in full accord with it, or to be separated from it forever.'

The simplicity and vividness of the metaphor in the second sentence, and the recklessness of the last, are a guarantee that Hawthorne's imagination was excited personally by this theme.

> 'I am dissevered from . . . the human race . . . It is my doom to be only a spectator of life; to look on as one apart from it . . . How cold I am now, while this whirlpool of public feeling is eddying around me! It is as if I had not been born of woman.'

So far, however, this reading of Hawthorne does not differ importantly from that of many critics who include him in the highest pantheon. Newton Arvin, for instance, thinks him a sick man but a great writer.

Hawthorne himself aimed at being a *good* writer, in the Victorian sense, with a charming, cheerful, humorous style, tolerant, bourgeois, warm-hearted, full of honest sentiment and stout common sense. He hoped his tales would pass an hour pleasantly, cause an agreeable shudder, even dampen the eye of an especially soft-hearted maiden; greatness he did not aim at.

This moreover is the Hawthorne Henry James admired. In James's comments on the Notebooks and on Hawthorne's style in general, it is the word charming that recurs more than any other. But modern readers find Hawthorne unsuccessful in this genre. All his children are little personages, all his girls snowy virgins, who trip instead of walking, all his boys honest youths, all unmarried women ancient or withered or decayed maidens. Reading Hawthorne, you never touch reality, but a thick layer of literary quilting.

> 'In short, to bring the matter at once to a point, it was incontrovertibly evident that somebody had taken the shop and fixtures of the long-retired and forgotten Mr Pyncheon and was about to renew the enterprise of that long-departed worthy, with a different set of customers.'

A thick wadding of words interposes between the reader and the object; and those words have in them no freshness or tension; they come from the stock-pile of literary language.

The emotion, moreover, often strikes us as false and even ungenerous; unless we suppose his control of language so very clumsy as to absolve him of all responsibility. The whole treatment of Hepzibah Pyncheon is an example of this. She

> 'began what it would be mockery to term the adornment of her person. Far from us be the indecorum of assisting, even in imagination, at a maiden lady's toilet! Our story must therefore await Miss Hepzibah at the threshold of her chamber; only presuming, meanwhile, to note some of the heavy sighs that laboured from her bosom, with little restraint as to their lugubrious depth and volume . . . We suspect Miss Hepzibah, moreover, of taking a step upward into a chair, in order to give heedful regard to her appearance on all sides, and full

> length, in the oval, dingy-framed, toilet glass, that hangs above her table. Truly! well indeed! who would have thought it! Is all this precious time to be lavished on the matutinal repair and beautifying of an elderly person . . .'

This is obviously intended to be charming, as well as graceful. In between his exclamatory titterings, he describes her prayers and her kissing her brother's picture quite solemnly. But no one who reads it honestly can find it anything but offensive.

> 'And therefore, since we have been unfortunate enough to introduce our heroine at so inauspicious a juncture, we would entreat for a mood of due solemnity in the spectators of her fate.'

Here again Hawthorne has miscalculated the reader's reactions with a completeness that compromises his claims to be a writer at all.

> 'It was overpoweringly ridiculous,—we must honestly confess it—the deportment of the maiden lady while setting her shop in order for the public eye . . . Our miserable old Hepzibah! It is a heavy annoyance to a writer, who endeavours to represent nature, its various attitudes and circumstances, in a reasonably correct outline and true colouring, that so much of the mean and ludicrous should be so hopelessly mixed up with the purest pathos which life anywhere supplies to him.'

One is tempted to accuse him of hypocrisy as well as spite, since he has gone to such lengths to make her ridiculous. But the point at issue is merely that this is bad writing, so bad as to destroy, almost by itself, all claims for Hawthorne in the genre he himself most prized.

Above all, however, it is the accents of intelligence we miss in Hawthorne's editorial voice; the companionship he offers us fails worst in its vulgarity of thought. When the stories deal with science, inventions, or magic, for instance, we find a mismating of intellectual categories which seems to imply a startling lack of understanding. Take for instance 'The Artist of the Beautiful'. Owen Warland, the Artist, is a watchmaker; but he is obsessed with the Idea of the Beautiful; so he makes a mechanical butterfly; this machine responds to thought-waves; but also to spiritual quality in a person; and its design is the result of a deep study of butterflies. This is just the kind of grotesque muddle which, in science fiction, alienates the literate reader's confidence. In the Notebooks we find 'low', 'vulgar', 'crude', 'ungentlemanly', employed as flatly and uncritically as in the worst use of the times. Key concepts like Christian and poetic are defined very genteelly. 'Today I heard a dirty mother laughing and priding herself on the pretty ways of her dirty infant—just as a Christian mother might in a nursery or drawing-room.' There can be few good writers among those who equate Christianity with cleanliness, or at least among those who could write down and preserve such a sentence. Poetry he equated with unworldliness and other-worldliness. He declared that the English could not be poetic or even intellectual because they were so rosy and thick-set. 'Our pale, thin, Yankee aspect is the fitter garniture for poets.' The use of the word garniture alone hinders our listening to him with attention.

The most crucial instances of this imprecision in Hawthorne's mind, and also of that coldness of temperament which spoiled his geniality, occur when he treats the theme of the Unpardonable Sin. This sin Hawthorne most often specifies as Pride, and the critics have agreed with him, but here for once they have paid him too respectful attention. Ethan Brand is not proud. His wincing away from the vulgar crowd, his self-isolation in private thoughts, his self-dramatisation, are evidences rather of a lack of that normal pride that keeps one robustly indifferent to the world. The two characteristics common to all Hawthorne's 'proud' heroes is that they feel themselves to be cold and indifferent to other people, and that they feel they have violated the privacy of other souls by 'using' them for their own satisfaction. In other words, the emotional paralysis and the narcotic dissipation of reality which Hawthorne felt himself helplessly guilty of. The word 'Pride', like the idea of an Unpardonable Sin, and the stories of 'scientific' experiments, merely confuses the issue.

What Hawthorne in fact meant can be exemplified from his writing a hundredfold. Here, for instance, is a passage on John Brown.

'Nobody was ever more justly hanged. He won his martyrdom fairly, and took it fairly. He himself, I am persuaded (such was his natural integrity), would have acknowledged that Virginia had a right to take the life which he had staked and lost; although it would have been better for her, in the hour that is fast coming, if she could generously have forgotten the criminality of his attempt in its enormous folly. On the other hand, any common-sensible man, looking at the matter unsentimentally, must have felt a certain intellectual satisfaction in seeing him hanged, if it were only in requital of his preposterous miscalculation of possibilities.'

There is some spite against John Brown discernible there. But the real force of that last sentence is that it is unemotional; the writer *is* in fact taking intellectual satisfaction in seeing John Brown hanged because he miscalculated the possibilities. Put this beside the contemporary official feeling for the sacredness of a man's life, which Hawthorne endorsed in a thousand places, and the remark becomes deeply shocking. This kind of sentence often escaped Hawthorne's private censorship; about the Civil War he wrote, 'I wish they would push on the war a little more briskly. The excitement had an invigorating effect on me for a time, but it begins to lose its influence.' The sentences that did not escape his censorship, those that nobody heard but himself, presumably constituted the Unpardonable Sin.

His famous remark about English women would not have been written by a Victorianly warm, or even a normal, sensibility. 'The grim, red-faced monsters! Surely a man would be justified in murdering them—in taking a sharp knife and cutting away their mountainous flesh until he had brought them into reasonable shape.' Or this, in a letter to his wife, 'We hold the fate of England in our hands, and it is time we crushed her—blind, ridiculous, old lump of beef, sodden in strong beer, that she is; not but what she has still vitality enough to do us a good deal of mischief, before we quite annihilate her.' Or this, about the British nation as a whole. 'They feel nothing, and bring themselves no nearer to God when they pray than when they play at cards.' This is the paralysis of the heart Hawthorne spoke of, and the violation of other people's privacy. This is what made his performance as the genial author implausible, and this is the experience he was always obliquely referring to. There was no pride in this.

But if Hawthorne was not a good writer, perhaps he was a great one. Perhaps, on his own obsessive themes, he transcended his own intentions, and delivered a profound, tragic truth. This is much more what modern critics claim for him, and it is indeed obvious that Hawthorne had some of the qualifications for writing a very remarkable book. Let us take two examples of his most celebrated tales, and try to justify our resistance to the claims made for them.

'Young Goodman Brown' is said to be a Pilgrim's Progress in reverse, an anti-Puritan allegory. But the prose is not at all evocative of such meanings; it offers no evidence that the writer knew anything about faith or morality. 'Martha Carrier, who had received the devil's promise to be queen of hell. A rampant hag was she.' Hawthorne's language refers us immediately to the world of inferior literature. Bunyan's referred us to the world of common objects, and to a system of theology and morals fervently believed in. 'On he flew among the black pines, brandishing his staff with frenzied gestures, now giving vent to an inspiration of horrid blasphemy, and now shouting forth such laughter as set all the echoes of the forest laughing like demons around him.' Nothing there evokes the experience of blasphemy. Everything evokes memories of fanciful fiction. 'Another verse of the hymn arose, a slow and mournful strain, such as the pious love, but joined to words which expressed all that our natures can conceive of sin, and darkly hinted at far more.' This is the language of empty exaggeration; after all that our natures can conceive comes 'far more'. 'Young Goodman Brown' is not an allegory because it allegorises nothing. There is no experience embodied in its language, and consequently no reason to construct elaborate meanings for its oddities. The critics' profound interpretations express their own reflections on religion and morality and doubt. Hawthorne's prose sufficiently indicates the intensity of imagination *he* put into the story.

'Ethan Brand' begins with a roar of laughter far off 'like wind shaking the boughs of a forest'. We hear the voice of children's ghost stories crudely superimposed on that of the clubman author. But it is the handling of the Unpardonable Sin, and the IDEA, which most chills our responsiveness. It seems to indicate that Hawthorne does not know the experience he is discussing firsthand, that he thinks about it as well as writing about it, all in capital letters. 'That portentous night when the IDEA was first developed' tells the reader that the author does not know what it is like to have such an idea. He seems to confuse a fascination with the moral problem of sin with philosophical inquiry in general, and that again with a practical experimentation in something like hypnotism or animal magnetism. Ethan Brand had been

> 'a simple and loving man, watching his fire in the years gone by, and ever musing as it burned . . . Then ensued that vast intellectual development, which, in its progress, disturbed the counter-poise between his mind and heart. The Idea that

possessed his life had operated as a means of education; it had gone on cultivating his powers to the highest point of which they were susceptible; it had raised him from the level of an unlettered laborer to stand on a star-lit eminence, whither the philosophers of the earth, laden with lore of universities, might vainly strive to clamber after him. So much for the intellect! But where was the heart? That, indeed, had withered,—had contracted—had hardened—had perished! . . . he was now a cold observer, looking on mankind as the subject of his experiment, and at length, converting man and woman to be his puppets, and pulling the wires that moved them to such degrees of crime as were demanded for his study.'

It is not necessary to point out again the essential identity between the character's experience and the author's, or the incongruity of this with the story of practical experiments, and degrees of crime, and vast intellectual development. Quite apart from that, one cannot respond to the passage in the way the critics suggest because its ideas are handled ignorantly. One cannot even assent, however passively; one must contradict. There *is* no counterpoise between the head and the heart. Preoccupation with a moral problem does *not* give one the kind of intellectual distinction described. The development of the intellect does *not* mean the withering of the heart. Neither moral nor intellectual inquiry into the nature of sin leads one into practical experiment in crime. This is all summed up in that phrase 'vast intellectual development'; as an evocation of intellectual experience it is like 'twenty million million diamonds' as an evocation of wealth.

The same kind of objections apply to the other stories. 'The Birthmark' and 'Egotism; or the Bosom-Serpent', for instance, suffer from the same emptiness as 'Young Goodman Brown'. The moral experience behind them is unsuccessfully integrated into their symbolism. The Notebooks are full of entries which note, for instance, a legend about a bloody footprint, and which end, 'This could be symbolical of something'. That is the epitaph of all Hawthorne's symbolism. 'Wakefield', on the other hand, could have made a wonderful book. It was exactly Hawthorne's subject. But he didn't write it. He wrote about it instead. He turned away from the too-direct challenge. He had to disguise and muffle his guilt in the vague rhetoric of 'Ethan Brand'. 'O mankind, whose brotherhood I have cast off, and trampled thy great heart beneath my feet.'

The critics' essential claim, however, is that in a few cases, above all in *The Scarlet Letter*, Hawthorne's art, working perhaps against his own intentions, delivered a profound and tragic meaning. We cannot counter those claims point by point; partly because they are so numerous and so fully developed; but mostly because we deny their starting point. All we can do is offer some justification for that denial, for our refusal to begin to respond to the evocations of the story.

First of all, the book's claims to be historical are so insistent and so unacceptable. Hawthorne presents his seventeenth-century people as dramatically and radically unlike his readers, because of their distance in time.

> 'Morally, as well as materially, there was a coarser fibre in those wives and maidens of old English birth and breeding than in their fair descendants, separated from them by a series of six or seven generations; for throughout that chain of ancestry, every successive mother has transmitted to her child a fainter bloom, a more delicate and briefer beauty, and a slighter physical frame, if not a character of less force and solidity, than her own.'

This is a very crude and unhistorical version of historicity (by such a system medieval man becomes neolithic) and it has the additional disadvantage of prescribing, or legitimising, a quite barbarous use of language for these people. Thus the children of Boston are represented as saying to each other, 'Behold, verily, there is the woman of the scarlet letter: and of a truth, moreover, there is the likeness of the scarlet letter running along by her side! Come, therefore, and let us fling mud at them.'

But when Hawthorne turns to his main characters he makes no attempt to make them 'seventeenth-century' or historically true in any sense. T. S. Eliot has said that Hawthorne's is a true criticism of the Puritan morality, true because it has the fidelity of the artist and not a mere conviction of the man, but there is very little that is Puritan in *The Scarlet Letter*. The thoughts and emotions expressed all belong to the nineteenth century. The only one of the main characters who is even said to hold Puritan beliefs is Dimmesdale, and he is a perfectly Rousseauistic hero. He is the man of sensibility. His preaching syle, his physical frailty, his pallor, his eloquent, tremulous voice, his lofty brow and hollow cheek and burning eye, all these announce the romantic hero, quite incongruously translated into seventeenth-century Boston. He is no more a study in Puritanism than is Edgar Linton in *Wuthering Heights*, and the affront to our historical sense (so insistently aroused by the writer) is one of the minor sources for our distrust of the book.

More importantly, the book is full of inconsistencies. When Dimmesdale saw the scarlet letter in the sky, Hawthorne tells us that though a nation's destiny might worthily be thought to be revealed in an astronomical portent, this could not be true for an individual. He could only think he read his own fate there if he

> 'rendered morbidly self-contemplative by long, intense, and secret pain, had extended his egotism over the whole expanse of nature ... We impute it, therefore, solely to the disease in his own eye and heart, that the minister, looking upward to the zenith, beheld there the appearance of an immense letter —the letter A—marked out in lines of dull red light.'

Quite clearly, therefore, there was no such phenomenon. But next morning the sexton says, 'But did your reverence hear of the portent that was seen last night—a great letter in the sky—the letter A?' So there was such a phenomenon, visible to others. These inconsistencies are usually explained as examples of Hawthorne's irony. That point must be answered later. For the moment let us offer only the alternative explanation that Hawthorne had not noticed his mistake.

But most important of all, since the book is said to be a study of the psychology of sin, we do not believe in Hawthorne's understanding of complex characters or emotions. Let us take Chillingworth as an example, and claim that his character does not develop during the book. We are told that he changed greatly, but we are shown nothing of it; in fact we are given evidence that he did not. A novelist who makes this kind of muddle does not have much to tell us about spiritual psychology, and we do not listen patiently to critics who attribute to him such subtle and striking intentions in, say, the scene in the forest.

We are told that when Chillingworth arrived in Boston, the day the book opens, he was calm, just, scholarly, severe, upright in all his dealings with the world, cold but kindly. Yet his first action, when Hester sees him in the crowd, was that a writhing horror twisted itself across his face, and he signed to her not to recognise him. Neither reaction is congruous with the character he is given. Such a man, cold, selfish, just, had nothing to lose by coming forward. Such a man, with no sexual passion for his wife, had no reason for a writhing horror. One can imagine, indeed, a selfish anger with Hester, for disgracing him and disappointing him of the conjugal comforts he had hoped for; one can imagine the gradual development, within that anger, of primitive passions hitherto unawakened in him; but that is not what Hawthorne describes. What is described is of the same kind of melodramatic diabolism as his behaviour at the end of the book. We are shown no development.

We are given no reason for Chillingworth's being in the Puritan settlement at all. There is no hint of religious feeling in him, in the present or the past. A scholar, remote from all emotional or practical problems, he was surely the last type of man to leave Europe for the New World. Moreover, given his view of Hester as a beautiful object and a cheering influence, it is equally difficult to understand his sending her ahead, alone, to wait two years for him in such extraordinary circumstances. Surely the most satisfactory explanation of these oddities is that Hawthorne did not think of them; because he was not dealing in human realities but in stage properties. But even if you think he was dealing in truths of the heart, and that these truths of contingency were not immediately relevant, the fact remains that an author who offers crude implausibilities of this kind forfeits our confidence.

In the scene in prison Chillingworth is shown as (implausibly) dispassionate with Hester, but implacably bent on destroying the seducer.

> ' "But, Hester, the man lives who has wronged us both" . . . with a smile of dark and self-relying intelligence . . . "I shall seek this man, as I have sought truth in books; as I have sought gold in alchemy . . . Sooner or later he must needs be mine!" The eyes of the wrinkled scholar glowed so intensely upon her . . . "Thine acts are like mercy," said Hester, bewildered and appalled, "but thy words interpret thee as a terror . . . Why dost thou smile at me so?" inquired Hester, troubled at the expression of his eyes. "Art thou like the Black Man that haunts the forest round us? Hast thou enticed me into a bond that will prove the ruin of my soul?" "Not thy soul," he answered, with another smile, "no, not thine." '

This is the first day of the action of the book, and Chillingworth is as diabolical as he ever becomes. He is already on the track, dark, stealthy, furious. He is already identified with the devil, with a snake, with the Black Man. He accepts that identification himself, in his last remark. Yet in chapter 10 Hawthorne says,

> 'He had begun an investigation, as he imagined, with the severe and equal integrity of a judge, desirous only of truth, even as if the question involved no more than the air-drawn lines and figures of a geometrical problem, instead of human passions, and wrongs inflicted on himself.'

This is as flat a contradiction as one could find in fiction.

The next time we see Chillingworth is at the Governor's Hall, a third of the way through the book, when he is 'much uglier—how his dark complexion seemed to have grown duskier, and his figure more misshapen'. (This is repeated every so often throughout the book; but one hardly calls this development.) He is walking very close beside Dimmesdale, always whispering in his ear, and directing significant remarks at him. 'Would it be beyond a philosopher's research, think ye gentlemen, to analyse that child's nature, and, from its make and mould, to give a shrewd guess at the father?' By all the devices of fiction, that is, we are given to understand that he knows Dimmesdale to be Hester's seducer; or at least he suspects him and is probing his conscience. But we have not, let us note, been shown, or even told about, the birth of this suspicion. In a study of this kind, surely such a moment cries out for some kind of treatment. Hawthorne merely omits it. Nor does he, in this scene, tell us anything about the form or function of the suspicion. He parades the two men before our eyes, gives them a couple of perfunctory gestures, and whisks them away again.

His account of Chillingworth's probing, when it does come, is purely rhetorical.

> 'So Roger Chillingworth—the man of skill, the kind and friendly physician—strove to go deep into his patient's bosom, delving among his principles, prying into his recollections, and probing everything with a cautious touch, like a treasure-seeker in a dark cavern.'

This is a picture of the idea of the thing; a reader might talk like that, describing Porfiry Petrovitch's conversations with Raskolnikov. Dostoevsky, however, did not talk like that; he gave us the reality.

Then, at this point in the book, it is insinuated—as a device of fiction it amounts to an assertion—that Chillingworth had been mixed up in the Overbury murder case, a friend of Dr Forman's, and that he had joined in evil Indian rituals. If this is true, it makes nonsense of the purity, justice, and uprightness he was credited with on arrival. If it is not true, what is it there for?

Then comes the crucial scene in which he uncovers Arthur's chest, and sees whatever he sees there, and throws his arms up and stamps on the floor and exults like the devil. We gather that he discovered something important then.

> 'After the incident last described, the intercourse between the clergyman and the physician, though externally the same, was really of another character than it had previously been. The intellect of Roger Chillingworth had now a sufficiently plain path before it. . . . Calm, gentle, passionless as he appeared, there was yet, we fear, a quiet depth of malice, hitherto latent, but active now, in this unfortunate old man.'

In what sense the malice had been latent before is difficult to discover. As far as the reader is concerned (and the author is presumably addressing the reader) he has never appeared calm, gentle, or passionless; and other characters, we have been told, instinctively felt him to be diabolical.

> 'A revelation, he could almost say, had been granted to him. It mattered little, for his object, whether celestial, or from what other region. By its aid, in all the subsequent relations betwixt him and Mr Dimmesdale, not merely the external presence, but the very inmost soul, of the latter, seemed to be brought out before his eyes, so that he could see and comprehend its every movement . . . He could play upon him as he chose.'

But what had been discovered? That Arthur had been Hester's lover? He knew that before. That Arthur was suffering? He knew that. That there was a red A on Arthur's chest? This, as something extra to its meanings, which he was already sure of, could not *tell* him very much. Of course, it would be a gratification; one understands the dance of joy; but what information was conveyed, what clue given, what path was *now* opened before Chillingworth's intellect?

There is no development in the book. We are told, many times, that Chillingworth came to Boston calm and studious, and became dark and devilish. But we are not shown how this happened. We get no insight into the process. We are told that he long suspected and finally discovered that Dimmesdale was Hester's seducer; but we get no insight into the process of suspicion. We are told that he tortured his victim; but we do not see this happen. What we do see is a fundamental confusion in Hawthorne's mind about the characters and incidents of his fable. We have therefore no readiness to respond to any of the book's dramatic moments, no readiness to believe the critics when they construct large interpretations of them.

Hawthorne himself rated *The Scarlet Letter* below *The House of the Seven Gables*; just as he 'could not remember' what his 'blasted allegories' were about. For him *The Scarlet Letter* was a 'gloomy' book, and he preferred his sunnier work. A plain reading must surely lead us to agree with him. However, there is no hope of convincing, with one short chapter, those who have invested thought and emotion in an opposite valuation, or of answering all the multifold objections that must spring to their lips. But one point must be tackled. Hawthorne's most complete inconsistencies are usually dismissed by claiming that they are examples of his irony; that he meant to keep us in doubt, for instance, about whether there was a scarlet letter in the sky. Hawthorne is taken to be the most ironical writer of the nineteenth century; the only member of the New England Renaissance too subtle to be satisfied with Emerson's facile optimism.

It is indeed obvious that it was Hawthorne's general policy to avoid committing himself on every issue, and to take up more than one attitude to it. But whether, in any particular case, this deserves the name of irony, must depend on whether there is any point made by the equivocation, and any evidence the writer took responsibility finally for one of the alternatives. If not, it remains an equivocation, and, in instances like this of the letter in the sky, a mistake. For Hawthorne certainly was not asking us to believe that an astronomical portent actually occurred. That would be against his insistent practice of providing a possible natural explanation for every supernatural appearance. This time he forgot his escape route.

It is our case that there is no *a priori* reason to accept *any* ambiguity in Hawthorne as meaningful irony; that it is usually a device of caution or a carelessness. In support of that, we can point to ample evidence, in the prose, the characterisation, the narrative, that Hawthorne did occasionally make mistakes, and did habitually equivocate. We can also point to evidence of habitual naïveté.

> 'When an uninstructed multitude attempts to see with its eyes, it is exceedingly apt to be deceived. When, however, it forms its judgements, as it usually does, on the intuitions of its great

and warm heart, the conclusions thus attained are often so profound and so unerring, as to possess the character of truths supernaturally revealed.'

If a man were capable of useful irony, the sort that is a finer wisdom than Emerson's, it would prevent his saying that. When Hawthorne compares Hester on the scaffold to a Madonna and child, he continues, 'Here there was the taint of deepest sin in the most sacred quality of human woman's beauty, and the more lost for the infant that she had borne'. This is explicit and extreme. At other times, however, he takes the opposite attitude; 'what we did had a consecration of its own'. If this inconsistency is ironical, what is the point of the irony? And which was Hawthorne's final position? The questions are unanswerable. These are in fact recognisably the two halves of the stock Victorian fiction attitude to the fallen woman; public condemnation and private reverence; the incompatibility of the two in Hawthorne is due to greater naïveté, not greater sophistication.

Hawthorne's hypertrophied reputation and interpretation in modern times is no accident. It is due partly to his habit of equivocation, which made him available both for the defence of irony, and for semi-creative explanations by critics. Partly to his rejection of realism; which seemed an anticipation of the modern quest for a bolder fictional poetry, though it was in fact a retreat from the highest standards of his own day. Most of all, it is due to his quite petty and carping (because miserable) pessimism. For the last thirty years or more, all the brightest minds in American literature have been guided by an aversion from the self-consciously noble and expansive in art, the uplifting, simplifying, energising; and a corresponding enthusiasm for irony and obscurity in the method, and tragedy, pessimism, a sense of evil, in the material. We have had nearly half a century of anti-Emersonianism, and Hawthorne's reputation is one of the major forms it has taken.

TERENCE MARTIN [1925–], professor at Indiana University, wrote *Instructed Vision: Scottish Common Sense Philosophy and the Origins of American Fiction* and *Hawthorne* for the Twayne United States Authors Series. To *Hawthorne Centenary Essays* he contributed "The

Method of Hawthorne's Tales." The last chapter of the Twayne *Hawthorne*, reprinted below, should be read in the context of some of the extreme, though important, assessments also represented in this anthology.

A Significant Legacy

TERENCE MARTIN

Hawthorne's career, like that of many writers, ended on a note of frustration. Success was something he looked back on, failure something he lived with from day to day. Themes of recovering a "lost estate" and of discovering an "elixir of life" thwarted an imagination intent on securing the future by reduplicating the past.

But Hawthorne had already secured a larger future than he knew and in large part by his way of possessing the past. At a time when the American writer struggled to compensate for the lack of a national history, Hawthorne explored the meaning of an ancestral past. At a time when the absence of antiquity, legend, and myths of origin threw the writer onto the personal resources of his imagination, Hawthorne responded by investigating the origins of that imagination. His feat was to believe in the reality of what he explored and thereby to work with a sense of the past and a concomitant sense of community.

Hawthorne's best work demonstrates, even as it depends on, his sense both of past and of community. In "The Custom-House" sketch, the Custom House embodies memory gone blank; an enervated present nods over a forgotten past, which (as symbolized by the scarlet letter) has failed to clear customs. In "The Custom-House," Hawthorne re-opens commerce with the past. He bandies imaginary remarks with his inflexible ancestors; he "discovers" the letter itself, and thereby allows the vitality and suppressed emotion of the past to find release in the present. *The Scarlet Letter* takes its fictional life from a vital sense of community, dramatic evidence of Hawthorne's triumph in possessing the Puritan past for the purposes of his imagination.

In its widest implications, Hawthorne's sense of community involves mankind. His isolated individuals stand apart from humanity, obsessed by their guilt, their pride, their need for revenge or for perfection. Separated from the community, whose bond is of

Nathaniel Hawthorne. Twayne United States Authors Series (New York, 1965) 177–80.

the heart, such characters involve themselves in futile efforts to cultivate the icy ranges of abstraction. Even the artist, who ought to bear a special reverence for the heart, can draw (or be forced) apart from mankind and adopt the role of spectator.

Hawthorne's interest in the past, his concern over the danger of abstraction, and his treatment of the artist and society have constituted a significant legacy for American fiction. The effect of any such legacy is difficult to formulate precisely. But we have learned that ideas can pervade a culture in protean forms; we have validated the idea of influence in a broad, inclusive sense. It is thus possible to suggest, albeit briefly here, the kind of tradition in which Hawthorne was an early worker.

American fiction has inherited Hawthorne's interests and concerns. The work of such writers as Henry James, William Faulkner, and Robert Penn Warren explores the meaning of the human condition in a manner familiar to readers of Hawthorne. In Warren's fiction, as I remarked earlier, the man of idea stands revealed once again in his essential inhumanity. Adam Stanton in *All the King's Men* explodes into violence when confronted with the fact that all men have fallen. Percy Munn in *Night Rider* gets caught up in a noble cause that can achieve its goal only by means of threat, arson, and murder. Repeatedly, in Warren's work, the means defile the end; when the end becomes abstract, the means become inhuman. Warren shows, too, that a man can know himself only by accepting the past which has made him what he is. The burden of the past involves guilt, which is both difficult and necessary to bear. A man who repudiates the past is consequently a man without identity; only in and through history is identity achieved; only by means of history can the present acknowledge its responsibility to the future.

Faulkner's use of a Southern past suggests a number of comparisons with Hawthorne's use of a Puritan past. In Faulkner's work, history yields myth, which, in turn, explores the meaning of history. Yoknapatawpha County, like Hawthorne's neutral ground, is a fiction for creating fiction. In that County there is "strife amongst kindred" (to use Holgrave's remark about the Pyncheon family), pride fed only by futile hope and embellished memory, ancient wrong which continues to haunt the present. There is also a strong sense of community, which allows Faulkner to range freely in time, to chronicle the depredations of the Snopes clan in one era, to depict the ravages of high ambition in another. And there is always guilt, the burden of something gone wrong, perhaps the repudiation of a tainted heritage—as in "The Bear," a story which rehearses some of the most persistent themes in American literature.

A good deal of profitable study has been devoted to the subject of James and Hawthorne. In *The Complex Fate*, Marius Bewley investigates the relationship of the two writers to the tradition of the American novel and points out similarities between *The Blithedale Romance* and *The Bostonians* and between *The Marble Faun* and *The Wings of the Dove*. T. S. Eliot asks us to consider *Roderick Hudson* in relation to *The Marble Faun* and James's late *The Sense of the Past* in relation to *The House of the Seven Gables* as a way of seeing the "Hawthorne aspect" of James's imagination.

In James's work, one finds a deep and implied sense of community, which sustains the various judgments he makes on his Americans who confront European experience. Christopher Newman in *The American* may go to Europe because of moral repugnance toward the society which has made him rich; but he is, as he comes to understand, essentially a part of that society. In the novel, James gives us not Newman's society but rather a sense of his community (sprawling, inchoate, yet vibrant). Lambert Strether in *The Ambassadors* perceives what he has missed in life only in terms of what Woollett, Massachusetts, has made him. Although Mrs. Newsome and Woollett are not *in* the novel, no one would argue their importance *for* the novel.

In *Portrait of a Lady*, Isabel Archer's refusal of the best offers of marriage that two continents and two cultures can make is possible only on the grounds of her being an American girl. Americans estranged from a sense of community abound in *Portrait of a Lady*, and they prove to be pitiful or villainous. Ned Rosier is as futile as he is precious; the mask of the cosmopolite hides Madame Merle's helplessness; and Gilbert Osmond is a consummate egotist, whose self-devotion is worthy of any Hawthorne villain. These characters, unlike Casper Goodwood who brings increasing force and virility into the novel, are cut off from the provincial and no doubt vulgar resources of their community. At best, they could but echo Mrs. Touchett when she objects that her point of view is not American: "that's shockingly narrow," she exclaims; "thank God, my view is personal."

James also shares Hawthorne's interest in the relation of the artist to society. The problems of his artists are not precisely those of Hawthorne's. But a theme in James's work second in importance only to that of American innocence confronting European experience concerns the artist, his work, and his audience. It is a theme to which American writers have been perennially attracted. The role of the artist seems to have remained a troubled and tentative one throughout the development of American letters.

James's American characters, like those of Hawthorne, are equipped with Puritan consciences, which have become portable, more refined, but not attenuated with the passage of time. When Madame de Mauves (which is what marriage has made of an American *jeune fille*) says to Longmore that she has "only a clinging, inexpugnable conscience" to sustain her, she speaks for any James character who has not surrendered his birthright. James gives us European society, carefully portrayed; he gives us an American sense of community, deeply implied.

Hawthorne's achievement with symbolic technique has contributed to a vital aspect of the heritage of American fiction. His work in the tale and in the romance, forms which fostered an enlargement rather than a close delineation of life and character, has an analogue in the Naturalistic novel, which Frank Norris has defined as the "romance of the gutter." The Naturalistic novel, like Hawthorne's romance, attempts to refract and enlarge reality rather than to picture or copy it. The angle of refraction differs radically, of course—the purport is obviously distinct. But the analogy, as Richard Chase maintains in *The American Novel and Its Tradition*, suggests that the romance has different guises, under one of which it has continued to affect the writing of American fiction.

One need not protest Hawthorne's importance too much; it is profound and demonstrable in many ways. But one must see it in some context. Cooper, Poe, and Melville, among Hawthorne's contemporaries, did much to shape the course of American fiction. The work of Henry James and Mark Twain has been crucial for modern writers. Hawthorne, one should add, was not concerned to assault language for the purposes of story. Melville did so in *Moby Dick* and extended his language into something astonishing and original. Mark Twain did so in *Huckleberry Finn* and created an idiom with such resources that we are still glorying in the discovery. But Hawthorne worked with an established prose style which served him so well that he left it pretty much where he found it.

A revolution in novelistic technique has occurred since Hawthorne's time, in the light of which his longer work appears somewhat more ponderous than it must have appeared before. But the economy and brilliance of *The Scarlet Letter* and of the best of his tales have come undisturbed through the revolution to command the respect given only to triumphs in form. We recognize that Hawthorne came early and did much. That significant later writers have found it important and even necessary to do similar things is the fullest tribute to the enduring quality of his achievement.

FREDERICK C. CREWS [1933–] teaches at the University of California at Berkeley. He has written books on Henry James and E. M. Forster. In 1963 he published *The Pooh Perplex*, a collection of parodies of approaches to literary criticism. *The Sins of the Fathers* attempts to correct two erroneous developments in the study of Hawthorne: the biographers' insistence on Hawthorne's adjustment to society and their dismissal of the "phantom" quality in Hawthorne; and the literary critics' depiction of Hawthorne as "a great allegorical poet." Crews's Freudian approach confronts the seemingly baffling disparity between Hawthorne the man and Hawthorne the writer. *The Sins of the Fathers* has already stirred up considerable controversy.

Hawthorne, Freud, and Literary Value

FREDERICK C. CREWS

"It has to do with drawing a reality out of the unconscious in such a way as to make it enter into the realm of the intellect, while trying to preserve its life, not to garble it, to subject it to the least possible shrinkage . . ."
—MARCEL PROUST on the writing of an introspective novel.

The psychological emphasis of this book, and the untraditional account of Hawthorne's career that results from such an emphasis, must pose some questions about our aesthetic criteria. If some of our early chapters create an impression that Hawthorne is good insofar as he is Freudian, some later ones may support the opposite fallacy: Hawthorne is obsessed and therefore artistically handicapped. I would be as sorry to leave the reader with one of these crude formulas as the other. Plainly, I am convinced that some correlation exists between Hawthorne's psychological themes and the enduring appeal of his works; the question is whether that

The Sins of the Fathers: Hawthorne's Psychological Themes (New York, 1966) 258–71.

correlation is simple and direct. In this final chapter I propose to review the evidence that justifies our calling Hawthorne Freudian; to measure, as best I can, the part played by psychological insight in the effect of his plots; and finally to define the limitations of the Freudian aesthetic on which so much of Hawthorne's claim to greatness must rest.

I hope, after all that has gone before, that I need not insist at length on the propriety of using psychoanalytic terms to describe authors and works that antedate Freud. Revolutionary as his influence has been, Freud did not alter human nature; either we are entitled to use Freudianism retroactively or we must say that it is false. The point seems obvious enough, yet in the academic world —and conspicuously in Hawthorne studies—there persists a quixotic attempt to say that an author's psychological portraiture can be nothing other than a conscious illustration of the theories current in his day. Thus in Hawthorne's instance we have not only the venerable claim that his deliberate antitheses of head and heart adequately account for his characters' behavior, but a more recent and bolder effort to bind him to the "mental philosophy" of his college professor, Thomas Upham. Hawthorne, it seems, loyally followed Upham's schematization of the mind into intellect, sensibilities, and will, and used his fictional characters as personifications of one or another of these functions.[1]

Such a proposal seems scarcely worth pausing over. Though Upham was the best-known psychological theorist of his day,[2] Hawthorne never mentions his teachings and is not known to have read his books. The mixed motives, hidden scruples, and maniacal projects of Hawthorne's heroes would have appalled Upham, whose system was frankly designed as a justification for Christian

---

[1] For the head-heart dualism see Austin Warren, *Nathaniel Hawthorne: Representative Selections*, pp. xlv–xlvi; F. O. Matthiessen, *American Renaissance*, pp. 337–51; and Donald A. Ringe, "Hawthorne's Psychology of the Head and Heart," *PMLA*, LXV (March 1950), 120–32. The Uphamite position is defended by Leon Howard, "Hawthorne's Fiction," *Nineteenth-Century Fiction*, VII (March 1953), 237–50; Marvin Laser, "'Head,' 'Heart,' and 'Will' in Hawthorne's Psychology," *Nineteenth-Century Fiction*, X (September 1955), 130–40; and John T. McKiernan, "The Psychology of Nathaniel Hawthorne," *Dissertation Abstracts*, XVII (1957), 3019.

[2] See Jay Wharton Fay, *American Psychology Before William James* (New Brunswick, 1939), passim. Upham's chief works were *Elements of Intellectual Philosophy* (1827); *A Philosophical and Practical Treatise on the Will* (1834); *Outlines of Imperfect and Disordered Mental Action* (1840); and most influentially, *Elements of Mental Philosophy* (1831; 2-volume edition, 1840 et seq.).

moral imperatives. The verdict of consciousness, says Upham, "is in the highest degree authoritative and decisive," and "No man has it in his power to refuse obedience to the decisions of reasoning . . ."[3] He ridicules the very possibility—on which most of Hawthorne's plots are based—that a man's mind might be subject to hidden forces; he even argues tautologically that muscular habits must be perfectly voluntary, for otherwise men would be "machines, mere automatons."[4] As for sexuality, without which a description of motives among Hawthorne's characters is rather incomplete, Upham refuses to discuss it. Sex has no place in his exhaustive list of human desires, instincts, appetites, and propensities.[5] To confine Hawthorne's terrible insights within Upham's tediously subdivided and inert categories is too high a price to pay for the illusion of fidelity to the history of ideas.

We are left, then, with Hawthorne the self-examining neurotic —a role highly comparable to that of Freud himself at the start of his career. Given the mechanistic science of his time, Freud's discovery of psychoanalytic principles appears almost as "anachronistic" as Hawthorne's; in both cases we are dealing not with the orderly transmission and refinement of knowledge but with a struggle to universalize the results of introspection. Not surprisingly, it is impossible to draw a clear line between Hawthorne's rational statements anticipating Freud and his inadvertent illustration of Freudian principles in his losing war against obsession. If we may suppose that his "psychoanalytic" generalizations represent efforts at self-understanding, we may appreciate why the dwindling frequency of such generalizations is paralleled by a heightening of the signs of obsession. In every phase, whether through a power of reasoning or through unwitting self-revelation, Hawthorne provides an intricate chart of the ways of the unconscious. And this fact must inevitably have some bearing on our estimation of his achievement.

Thus, to begin with concrete examples, Hawthorne appears less arbitrary, more "true to life," in some of his fantastic plots if we happen to be familiar with modern case-histories. Reuben Bourne, who murders his son out of a sense of his own prior guilt,

---

[3]*Elements of Mental Philosophy* (New York, 2 vols., 1840), I, 42, 47.

[4]*Ibid.*, I, 158.

[5]Only once in Upham's voluminous works is sex mentioned—it is reluctantly included in a quotation from Dugald Stewart—and even there Upham hastens to assure us that "on this subject, as this Treatise is designed for general reading, we do not propose to dwell." (*Outlines of Imperfect and Disordered Mental Action* [New York, 1840], p. 287.)

may outrage our sense of justice but he cannot really surprise us; "criminals from a sense of guilt"[6] are a well-defined and common type. Reuben's guilt for a crime he never committed, his ability to find a path he had consciously forgotten, even his killing of Cyrus on the exact anniversary of his deserting Roger Malvin, all are the stuff of commonplace realism in case-histories.[7] Again, Arthur Dimmesdale's impulse to blaspheme after leaving the forest—an impulse which strikes some readers as out of character and others as displaying a state of moral error—is in fact brilliantly appropriate to Dimmesdale's rigidly pious nature once repression has been suddenly relaxed. Dimmesdale's whole psychology of self-punishment and renewed indulgence in forbidden thoughts—or, to be exact, of self-punishment which *makes possible* continued indulgence—is offensive to moral logic but perfectly observes the logic of psychoanalysis.[8] And we can say that Hawthorne's ascetics generally are viewed in a Freudian light. That is, Hawthorne never rests content with the avowed spiritual motive for asceticism, but rather provides us with clues to obsessive flight from sexuality. In donning a veil which effectively shields him from an impending marriage, the Reverend Hooper illustrates a classic pattern of phobia,[9] and in retreating to a cave which turns out to be a refuge from the same threat, Richard Digby in "The Man of Adamant" likewise reveals a sub-religious motive that psychoanalysis assumes to underlie gestures of aggressive saintliness.[10] In no case does Hawthorne absolutely compel us to accept the lower and less conscious motive, and it is doubtful whether he himself would have explained his plots as we do. What matters, however, is that his insistent distinction between surface appearances and buried reality encourages us to reconstruct the causes of sublimation and monomania, and that these causes are nearly always apparent when we look for them.

This, I think, is Hawthorne's distinction as a psychologist—not simply that his characters' seemingly freakish behavior can be matched by real-life examples, but that the total fabric of his plots

---

[6]Freud, *Collected Papers*, IV, 342.

[7]On the question of anniversaries see Karl Menninger, *Man Against Himself* (New York, 1938), p. 59n.

[8]*Ibid.*, p. 238: "The punishment actually permits the continuance of guilty indulgences and in this way becomes in itself a kind of indulgence."

[9]See, for example, the parallel case of a woman who wore a veil and goggles in order to make herself sexually forbidding to her husband. Karl Abraham, *Selected Papers* (London, 1954), p. 205.

[10]See Menninger, *Man Against Himself*, pp. 111–43.

manages to display fundamental yet elusive processes of the mind. Most importantly, those plots depict with incredible fidelity the results of unresolved Oedipal conflict. After establishing, as I trust we have established, that this conflict is re-enacted everywhere in Hawthorne's fiction, we can appreciate the intense malice behind his treatment of literal and symbolic fathers—a malice which often meets with no justification on moral grounds. We can likewise appreciate why his handling of women invariably leads either to sexless idealization or to innuendoes of uncleanness, and we can grasp the adolescent dilemma of a Giovanni Guasconti or a Young Goodman Brown. All these considerations have the effect of rescuing Hawthorne's works from the charge of resting on frivolous fantasy; they do rest on fantasy, but on the shared fantasy of mankind, and this makes for a more penetrating fiction than would any illusionistic slice of life.

What shall we say, asks Hawthorne with mock concern, when a man like Arthur Dimmesdale finds divine revelations addressed to himself alone? "In such a case, it could only be the symptom of a highly disordered mental state, when a man, rendered morbidly self-contemplative by long, intense, and secret pain, had extended his egotism over the whole expanse of nature, until the firmament itself should appear no more than a fitting page for his soul's history and fate" (*C*, I, 155).* Morbid or not, this is the operative principle of some of Hawthorne's greatest plots. The ambiguity between literal outward fact and an "extension of egotism over the whole expanse of nature" not only applies to such individual protagonists as Dimmesdale, Brown, Hooper, and Brand; it is practised by Hawthorne himself when he makes psychological metaphors out of history and ancestry, God and Satan. What appears at first to be religious meaning in such works as "The Gentle Boy" and "Rappaccini's Daughter," and what appears at first as an objective theory of history in the Puritan and Revolutionary tales and in *The House of the Seven Gables,* can be shown to be Oedipal dramatization on a magnified scale. And this psychological aptness, in my judgment, is precisely what saves Hawthorne from antiquarian pedantry and affable pietism. "The fiend in his own shape," as we learn in "Young Goodman Brown," "is less hideous than when he rages in the breast of man" (II, 100). Less hideous, and less compelling for the reader.

*[Editor's note: References to Hawthorne's works are to *The Complete Works of Nathaniel Hawthorne,* ed. George Parsons Lathrop (Boston, 1882–83). Those references designated by *C* are to the emerging volumes of the *Centenary Edition,* ed. William Charvat et al. being published by the Ohio State University Press.]

Hawthorne's art acquires much of its power from the displacement of logic and fact by autonomous fantasy. His plots typically record some clash between fantasy and fact, and their customary outcome is a rash deed resulting from a confusion of the two. Thus Aylmer, Giovanni, Digby, and Brown become cruel after mistaking the impurity of their thoughts about womanhood for impurity in the women who love them, and thus Reuben Bourne exacts punishment for a murder which took place only in his imagination. In certain rare cases, such as "The Prophetic Pictures" and *The Blithedale Romance*, Hawthorne even toys with the possibility that his heroes may acquire a measure of fantasy-power over other lives.

If Hawthorne's compulsive egotists are determined to test the omnipotence of wishes, the usual pattern of his plots is to block, to distort, and finally to allow perverse and partial expression to those wishes. The sick "luxuriance" of imagery surrounding the unspoken thoughts is a sign of their isolation from consciousness.[11] The "lurid intermixture" of emotions that colors Hawthorne's most intense fiction comes not from a blending of wish and reality but from a regressive withdrawal of feeling from normal objects, a surrender to fantasies of sexual accusation and terror. Hence the curious development of a Goodman Brown, who flees from his nuptial bed to a satanic rendezvous with Gothic sexuality; and hence the sadism of the "investigators" Brand and Aylmer. Such characters can perform loathsomely aggressive acts without ever holding themselves to moral account, for the acts are aimed against fantasy-enemies and are made possible by emancipation from the surface world to which moral standards might apply. The "morals" frequently tacked onto such actions either by Hawthorne or by his critics thus have an air of irrelevance; indeed, one might almost say that the emotional sense emanating from a deed like Aylmer's is one of satanic triumph, of momentary victory over inhibition. The truth is out at last, and it is murderous.

[11] Freud himself describes this phenomenon in Hawthornian language. Instinct-presentation, he says, "develops in a more unchecked and luxuriant fashion if it is withdrawn by repression from conscious influence. It ramifies like a fungus, so to speak, in the dark and takes on extreme forms of expression . . ." (*Collected Papers*, IV, 87). A comparable image of Karl Menninger's, characterizing the effects of a smothering narcissism, is even more strikingly Hawthornian: "It is as if the personality were like a growing tree . . . But were such a tree to be so injured near the base that the sap flowed out in large quantities to promote the healing and the protection of this stem injury, an insufficient supply would be left for the development of the foliage of the branches. These, then, would remain bare, stark, aggressive—and dying, while the sap fed and overfed the basal wound." (*Man Against Himself*, p. 436.) See pages 93f. above for a closely related image with an identical psychological meaning.

Yet Hawthorne *can* be said, at least occasionally, to have a moral ideal—or rather an ideal of normality. It is simply the psychoanalytic ideal of being free from feelings of guilt. In *The House of the Seven Gables*, for example, the general task is not to exact justice or to act charitably, but to lift the oppressive weight of the past as it is applied by the figure of Judge Pyncheon.[12] The Judge's removal produces not moral insight but a vengeful euphoria—one which itself must be checked by reactionary behavior. Mental peace, in other words, consists in weakening or pacifying the superego whose symbolic agent may be a real father but is more likely to be a surrogate figure like Jaffrey, a watchful Deity, a line of stern ancestors, or even the collective past itself. It was Freud who defined neurosis as "abnormal attachment to the past" and who urged what Philip Rieff calls an "ideal contemporaneity" as the measure of health,[13] but it was Hawthorne who complained that Aylmer had "failed to look beyond the shadowy scope of time, and, living once for all in eternity, to find the perfect future in the present" (II, 69). Allowing for a difference in rhetoric, I see no difference in meaning between the two goals. And in the same light we may understand the contradiction in Hawthorne's treatment of "earthly" and "spiritual" values, of the ideal and the material. He cannot unambiguously recommend either extreme because he senses that the separation of the two is itself a sign of neurosis; his healthiest characters are invariably those to whom antitheses of body and soul never occur at all. Here again we might remind ourselves of Freud's statement that the very act of calling into question the meaning of life is a sign of sickness. The reader may find this an intellectually cramping idea, but he can hardly deny that Hawthorne's monomaniac heroes illustrate it.

Where Hawthorne truly and significantly differs from Freud is in the therapeutic application of the non-repressive ideal. The Freudian process of normal development might be called a series of adaptations to inevitable traumas. In the case of Robin Molineux one could find a similar idea; Robin appears ready for adulthood only when he has resolved, or seen symbolically resolved, his mixed feelings of awe and contempt of parental authority. More usually, however, the Hawthornian hero is doomed to abnormality from the moment he entertains any rebellious thoughts. He is rarely

---

[12] One of Abraham's patients, incidentally, had an obsessive fear of bright sunlight (Jaffrey Pyncheon's chief symbolic attribute) and "complained about his failure in life, and said that his father literally weighed him down" (Abraham, *Selected Papers*, pp. 174f.).

[13] See *Freud: The Mind of the Moralist* (New York, 1959), pp. 44, 38.

"cured" after obsession has taken hold of him, and when a cure is offered it is an obvious nostrum, the aspirin of submission to a Phoebe or a Hilda. Hawthorne grasps the causes of neurosis but cannot face its remedy; his normality is merely the negative ideal of escape. This is only to say, after all, that Hawthorne sees neurosis from the perspective of a neurotic, not a physician. In a negative way, by remaining obsessed despite all efforts to dismiss obsession from view, he illustrates Freud's hard edict: "whoever is to be really free and happy in love must have overcome his deference for women and come to terms with the idea of incest with mother or sister."[14] Hawthorne is finally a prisoner of the repression whose devastating effects he so faithfully portrays.

At the end of his life this imprisonment is clearly artistic as well as emotional; no one has yet put forward the thesis that the unfinished romances are Hawthorne's major phase. Yet at what point can we say that Hawthorne went wrong as an artist? The incest obsession which riddles the last works was present from the beginning. If, however, we turn to the fiction that is generally agreed to be his best, we invariably find a dramatic tension that is lacking not only in his slight sketches and works of popular sentiment, but also in the tales and romances where obsession has become *too* intense. Tales like "Young Goodman Brown" and "My Kinsman, Major Molineux" sustain a highly energized struggle between inadmissible fantasies and the punishment and denial of those fantasies; they reach a point of catharsis after giving simultaneous and balanced voice to outrage and confession. In the serious works that are generally thought to fail, inhibition dominates the surface effect.

Thus it seems possible to correlate Hawthorne's decline, not with the presence or absence of his obsessive theme, but with the degree of deviousness he finds necessary to avoid bringing that theme into consciousness. In *The Scarlet Letter* obsession is an overt and steady subject; in *The House of the Seven Gables* it begins to be abstracted into a whimsical theory of history and a toying with magical causality; in *The Blithedale Romance* it remains cryptically hidden in the narrator's attitude toward the story he is telling; and in *The Marble Faun* Hawthorne's inconsistent characters no longer have any conception of why they still feel a vague sense of trouble. By this point, if we have not given up the pursuit of his intention, we find ourselves decoding it from images whose meaning almost certainly remained unknown to Hawthorne himself. Forfeiting our interest in literal characteri-

[14]*Collected Papers*, IV, 211.

zation, he calls upon an astonishing but ultimately fatiguing knack for devising innuendoes—and the innuendoes are aimed against his own fervent, and by now desperate, wish to take a sunny view of things. Ambiguity and surface hypocrisy become total as Hawthorne's warring feelings increasingly elude his once-powerful will to put on view the essential truth of the heart.

Without pretending to offer a simple psychological yardstick of value, perhaps we may suggest that fiction profits both from contact with unconscious material and from the participation of consciousness in that contact. Hawthorne is truly himself only within a certain range of half-perception in which curiosity and anxiety can strike an equilibrium. And though the components may be antithetical, the effect produced must be unitary. Here, perhaps, is where a psychological aesthetic may join hands with an aesthetic of plausibility. All readers can agree that Hawthorne fails when, for whatever reason, he is forced into inconsistent characterization, embarrassed apology and digression, and incomplete plotting. What happens to his fiction after 1850 is, in the simplest terms, a lapse of illusion. In our view the immediate cause of this lapse is a dissociation of unconscious conflict from its never sturdy tie to outward reality. When heightened obsession calls forth heightened efforts at repression, no room remains for created characters to exist freely. In the words of the storyteller Zenobia, "Our own features, and our own figures and airs, show a little too intrusively through all the characters we assume" (C, III, 107).

In this light I find it significant that Hawthorne's acknowledged masterpiece, *The Scarlet Letter*, not only treats unconscious compulsion more directly than his other romances, but also keeps his specific filial obsession better concealed from view. How many readers have been aware of the allusions to incest which Leslie Fiedler has made so prominent in his reading?[15] The same theme is (or ought to be) inescapable in any reading of Hawthorne's subsequent works. Who has noticed, as well, that for both Pearl and Dimmesdale the plot eventually fulfills a need for the benevolent father who remains absent until Dimmesdale's confession—and that Dimmesdale earns his mental peace by eradicating the part of his nature that would be offensive to the parent-rival?[16] To put discussion of *The Scarlet Letter* on this level seems an impertinence; the hell-fired story is perfectly dramatic

---

[15]See *Love and Death in the American Novel*, pp. 497–500.

[16]"This man," as Chillingworth thinks to himself, "hath inherited a strong animal nature from his father or his mother" (*C*, I, 130). Only when this animal nature is wholly renounced can Dimmesdale make peace with his heavenly Father and himself become a worthy father to Pearl.

and coherent in its overt terms, as all Hawthorne's subsequent fiction is not.

And yet I think we are finally obliged to take a broader aesthetic view than one that places *The Scarlet Letter* at the summit of fictional greatness. Brilliant as he is within his province, Hawthorne must be recognized as a peculiarly narrow writer—narrow not only in the underlying sameness of his themes from work to work, but in the more obvious sense of a paucity of represented life. The traditional complaints that his lights and shades are too monotonous, his characters too alike, his dialogues too formal, his manner too uniformly distant, seem to me justified. The danger in our own age, once the extent of Hawthorne's anticipation of psychoanalysis is understood, is not that he will be neglected but that he will be overrated. For we place a high value on the dramatization of psychic strife, even to the extent of feeling impatient with literalism; as Lionel Trilling has said, "in the degree that the world can be thought of as thinly composed, the autonomy of spirit is the more easily imagined."[17] Trilling himself goes so far as to regret the degree to which "for Hawthorne the [outer] world is always and ineluctably *there*. . . ,"[18] undermining and ridiculing the truth of fantasy. Yet surely this is not Hawthorne's true limitation. The problem is not that literal reality interrupts Hawthorne's psychological drama, but that it has been too wholly assimilated to that drama. "Reality" for Hawthorne merely plays the role of censor in an unconscious dialogue between rebellion and repentance; the thread of a single obsession is too easily traced through all his efforts at rendering things as they are.

This latter point may remind us how risky it is to use our descriptive terms evaluatively. Some of Hawthorne's least satisfying works—"Alice Doane's Appeal" and the unfinished romances—lend themselves most readily to the archaeology of motives we have been practicing. Where Hawthorne's "case" is most apparent his fictional world seems least whole, his moral vision most captive to emotions of aggression and fear that lack public content. Without some degree of self-revelation, I suppose, art loses its urgency; but when self-revelation usurps every other aspect of meaning the work dwindles to a recital of symptoms. And Hawthorne at his best remains incapable of venturing much beyond the gates of his neurosis. In a unique burst of fervor he can extend ambiguous

---

[17]"Our Hawthorne," *Hawthorne Centenary Essays*, p. 448.
[18]*Ibid.*, p. 449.

sympathy to a Hester Prynne, yet Hester's very existence as a figure of sexual reproach seems in retrospect to have been too inevitable. All Hawthorne's serious fiction amounts to versions of the same unconscious challenge; not one of his characters stands apart from the endless and finally suffocating debate about the gratification of forbidden wishes.

Ultimately, however, we cannot wish away Hawthorne's narrowness without also losing his peculiar value. Good Romantic that he was, he located reality squarely in the buried life of the mind. Before the sadly gifted eye of the seer, we recall, the whole structure of an outward character like Jaffrey Pyncheon's "melts into thin air, leaving only the hidden nook, the bolted closet, . . . or the deadly hole under the pavement, and the decaying corpse within" (III, 274). Without such radical simplifications Hawthorne would not be Hawthorne. Like Sade, Baudelaire, and Swinburne; like Melville and Poe; and like the "Romantic conservative"[19] Freud, Hawthorne rested his whole achievement on the premise that the only important truth is that which has been repressed. We may doubt the premise and yet recognize that the achievement is something formidable.

Our Hawthorne, of course, ends by seeming more pathetic than the Christ-like figure depicted in recent monographs. At his best, it appears, he clung to everyday banalities as to a life raft, and at his nadir he surrendered to a neurotic despair whose origins he did not quite dare to understand. The exemplary nature of his outward life—his conspicuous dutifulness as a father, a public official, a friend—does not erase this sense of melancholy isolation, any more than his professed love of Dutch painting, of Trollope, of factual journalism can erase the fact that his own art was based on fantasy. Only an indifference to mental suffering can make us grateful for the emotional starvation that perversely nourished Hawthorne's art; we must admire the art and separately regret the life. And yet it is a fact that the two are inextricable. As Freud himself remarked in a moment of self-dramatization—and here Freud becomes one with Ethan Brand, with Aylmer, and with the Hawthorne we have met in this study: "No one who, like me, conjures up the most evil of those half-tamed demons that inhabit the human breast, can expect to come through the struggle unscathed."[20] Let that be our epitaph for a writer whose anguished brooding has given us an urgent, a subtle, and an emotionally profound fiction.

[19]Rieff, *Freud: The Mind of the Moralist*, p. 217.
[20]*Collected Papers*, III, 131f.

www.ingramcontent.com/pod-product-compliance
Lightning Source LLC
Chambersburg PA
CBHW021136230426
43667CB00005B/134